Ernest R. May was born in Fort Worth, Texas, and studied at the University of California, Los Angeles. He is the author of *Imperial Democracy* and editor of *The Ultimate Decision* and *American Foreign Policy*. He is at present Professor of History at Harvard University.

The World War and American Isolation

1914-1917

Ernest R. May

Q

QUADRANGLE PAPERBACKS

Quadrangle Books / *Chicago*

TO MY FATHER

Preface

American and European history are usually treated as separate subjects. So are diplomatic history and political history. But these barriers become increasingly artificial after 1914. American questions rise as major issues in Europe, and European questions in the United States.

Seldom have the lines been less distinct than immediately after 1914. America and Britain had previously grown increasingly friendly. With the outbreak of World War I, it became vital to both that this relationship should survive. When America and Germany quarreled over the submarine, this issue, too, became central in the politics of both countries. Indeed, scarcely any event in one of the three states failed to affect the other two.

In Britain and Germany questions of American policy became key issues in domestic struggles for power. Rational discussion dissolved in partisan passion. In England the outcome was not tragic. In Germany it was. Chancellor Bethmann Hollweg fought long and hard against reckless opponents, only in the end to fail.

On the American side the drama was less a factional struggle than a contest within one man's conscience. A near-pacifist President found himself marching step by step toward war. He faced the awful necessity of defending what Gladstone had termed "that miserable and dastardly creature called prestige." In the end he had to choose war because he dreamed of peace. Despite the paradoxes, close analysis cannot find the point at which he might have turned back or taken another road. In Wilson's dilemmas, as in the contests in London and Berlin, there were elements of high tragedy. I hope these pages convey some sense of them.

*   *   *

I need to thank a number of institutions and individuals. In the former category my heaviest debts are to the National Archives, the Library of Congress, the Yale University Library, the Hoover Institution for the Study of War and Peace, the libraries of the University of California, and above all the Harvard University Library. This brief list hides scores of debts to people, especially in the Foreign Affairs and Captured Documents Divisions of the National Archives, the Manuscripts Division of the Library of Congress, and the Acquisitions Department of the Harvard University Library. I am also obligated to Mrs. Woodrow Wilson for permission to use the Woodrow Wilson manuscripts and to Professor Charles Seymour for permission to use the papers of E. M. House.

Certain individuals have been kind enough to read all or parts of the book in manuscript. To Professor William L. Langer I am grateful not only for the time he gave to that chore but also for additional information, assistance, and encouragement. Professor Arthur S. Link has given me more than he should from his comprehensive knowledge of Wilson's life and time. Professor Klaus Epstein has been similarly generous in sharing his understanding of Wilhelmine Germany. Others who have lent insights or lifted out errors are Professors Frank Freidel, Malbone W. Graham, and Frederick Merk, Mr. Ernest H. Giusti, and Mrs. Carl A. Pitha.

My heaviest obligations are to my wife, Nancy, partly for service as typist, watchguard, and editor, and to Professor and Mrs. John W. Caughey, for all manner of things, including keen criticism, human kindness, an example of real courage, and the wife already cited.

Ernest R. May

Lexington, Massachusetts

Contents

PART I

The Preservation of
Anglo-American Friendship

I

Sir Edward Grey and America

In 1914 the Great Powers tumbled into the violence of the first World War. Only one remained outwardly unshaken. The United States, with a population of one hundred million, an industrial plant rivaling all Europe's, the third navy of the world, and a total defense budget fourth among powers, joined neither of the rival alliances. The American government proclaimed and professed neutrality. The American people, with few exceptions, took it for granted that they would have no part in the war. Most Europeans agreed.

This expectation proved wrong. As the combatants tried to stop their enemies' supplies, American traders suffered. When the government tried to help, it found itself protesting interference and demanding respect for citizens' rights. When persuasion failed, it faced the choice of submitting to bullying or backing its demands with implicit threats of intervention. Nearly all neutrals were caught in the same predicament. What made America's situation exceptional was the country's geographical remoteness, pacifist and isolationist traditions, and enormous latent power.

For the belligerents, these same distinguishing facts made the American problem one of unusual difficulty, delicacy, and danger. Never before had they faced a neutral so invulnerable, so awesomely powerful in potential, and so self-consciously detached from European politics. A reflective French scholar may say in retrospect that Germany, Britain, and the United States were the true great powers before the war, France being only first among second-class states, but few diplomatists had actually reckoned with America.[1] No one could say for certain how much of her apparent power was real. It was arguable that her remoteness, pacifist traditions, and mixed races and nationalities condemned her to impotence. If so, a belligerent could disregard her interests. Although no sane diplomatist could be cocksure of such a judgment, neither could he guarantee that America's strength should be taken at face value. The extreme alternatives were to assume that the United States could be decisive in the war or that she could have no effect upon it. Policy-makers in London and Berlin had to select some premise between these two poles.

The issues to be faced by Americans were created by the belligerents. As the naval leaders of their alliances, Britain and Germany decided how American ships and goods were to be dealt with. It was up to the British Cabinet whether copper and cotton should be permitted to reach the Central Powers. Exemption from capture meant additions to enemy stores of cartridges and explosives, while capture meant injury to American exporters and trespass on rights asserted by American lawyers. The Cabinet could either elect to avoid dispute or act, leaving the United States to choose submission or defiance. Since submarine warfare involved similar alternatives, Germany came to be in a comparable position. The hard decisions that eventually had to be taken in Washington were nearly all results of decisions taken earlier in London and Berlin.

In all three capitals the men who dealt with these problems were earnestly desirous that America should stay at peace. Even though Englishmen came to hope for American aid, it was never a deliberate policy to bring on intervention. The problem, as British diplomats saw it, was to wage economic war without making the United States an enemy. In Berlin the dilemma was to conduct a submarine campaign without causing war. It was not the goal of any German leader to force American intervention. Nor was there a responsible man in Washington who wanted war for its own sake. But statesmen in all three capitals found themselves continually in

[1] Elie Halévy, *A History of the English People: Epilogue* (2 vols.; London, 1934), II, 132.

situations where the object of keeping peace was counterbalanced by interests of equal or greater importance. [The struggle for America's peace was waged within the three nations rather than between them, and the first theater of contest was the British Cabinet.]

Britain was the only power that had troubled to define an American policy before the war. The preservation of Anglo-American friendship had become a deliberate goal of diplomacy during the 1890's. The worsening of Anglo-German relations strengthened this policy, and differences over Guiana, Panama, and Alaska were compromised. Possible disputes were studiously suppressed, while statesmen used every occasion to preach economic and cultural solidarity, even to the extent of joining in celebrations of the Fourth of July. Although only romantics contemplated an alliance, British diplomacy had consistently sought an informal entente.[2]

The war called this policy into question. Despite the effort that had been put into building cordial relations, it was impossible to forget America's large German and Irish population or the American politician's delight in twisting the lion's tail or the business rivalry between the two countries. The First Lord of the Admiralty, Winston Churchill, himself the son of an American mother, suspected the United States government of being anti-British.[3] It was evident, in any case, that American and English interests were, or soon would be, in conflict.

[Although the preservation of American friendship might continue to be an aim of British policy, war created other objects which had to be pursued with at least equal diligence.] One was to maintain the great alliance with France and Russia. Since Britain could put but a small army into the field, her contribution had to be largely financial and naval, and an important part of it would be to cut off

[2] The best study of these developments is Charles S. Campbell, Jr., *Anglo-American Understanding, 1898–1903* (Baltimore, Md., 1957). See also Lionel Gelber, *The Rise of Anglo-American Friendship, 1895–1906* (Toronto, 1938), Richard H. Heindel, *The American Impact on Great Britain* (Philadelphia, 1940), and H. C. Allen, *Great Britain and the United States* (London, 1955).

[3] Churchill to Grey, Aug. 19, 1914, in Churchill, *The World Crisis, 1911–1918* (4 vols.; New York, 1923), I, 575.

enemy supplies. [Yet two of Germany's major imports were cotton and copper, both of which came principally from the United States.] If Britain failed to halt them, she would injure her allies. To stop cotton and copper, on the other hand, would outrage the southern and Rocky Mountain states of America and perhaps stir retaliation by the United States government.

A second necessary object was to maintain domestic unity, and this aim, too, conflicted with that of preserving American friendship. Neither the far left nor the far right had shown enthusiasm for the prewar policy of conciliating the United States.[4] Yet their wartime support was almost indispensable to the government. Socialists and radicals, who looked upon America as a dangerous oligarchy, had joined in the war only reluctantly, and they might at any time raise a cry against its continuance. Even more threatening were the Tories, as rightist Conservatives and Unionists may be called, who believed by tradition that concern for the sensibilities of other nations was unmanly and un-British. Although the Tory rank and file might be barely articulate, the faction had an able and ambitious young leadership, which included such brightening lights as Sir Edward Carson, the most celebrated barrister in England, F. E. Smith (later Lord Birkenhead), and Lord Robert Cecil, a younger son of Lord Salisbury. The Tories also possessed a disproportionate voice in the press. Of England's thirty leading newspapers and periodicals, they controlled more than a quarter, even though holding less than an eighth of the House of Commons.[5] In order to preserve support from the right as well as from the left, the government had to be cautious in making sacrifices to the end of preserving America's friendship.

Another aim was at least partly inconsistent. Although most of Europe had gone to war by the end of August, 1914, a number of states remained uncommitted. Among them were Italy, the Scandi-

---

[4] Heindel, *American Impact on Great Britain*, 138-170; Henry Pelling, *America and the British Left: From Bright to Bevan* (New York, 1957).

[5] See the chart published as an appendix in Armin Rappaport, *The British Press and Wilsonian Neutrality, 1914-1917* (Stanford, 1951), 150-155, and the discussion of press affiliations in Oron J. Hale, *Publicity and Diplomacy, with Special Reference to England and Germany, 1890-1914* (New York, 1940), 13-41.

navian nations, and, even more importantly, the Balkan group. It was an indispensable goal of British diplomacy to bring these neutrals onto the Allied side cr, at least, to prevent their joining the Germans. Since these governments were opportunistic and often venal, it was possible to offer them territorial and monetary induce-ments. But one of the choice lures in the English bait-box was the ability to promise reduced or enlarged seaborne trade, and it was an American tradition to insist upon fixed rules of neutral commerce or, at any rate, upon most-favored-nation treatment for American shippers. If the British government were to appease the Americans on this score, it would be handicapped, to say the least, in dealing with states like Greece and Italy.

Yet another goal of British policy was, of course, to achieve as early a victory as possible. One obvious measure to cripple the enemy was to make as energetic use as possible of the commerce patrols. To halt Germany's imports of strategic materials was a desirable end in itself, even if these imports included American cotton and copper. There was thus not only a conflict between the goal of perserving American friendship and the alternatives of upholding the great allies, maintaining domestic unity, and manipulating the European neutrals, there was also a clash between that goal and the necessary object of securing victory. Despite the carefully nourished tradition of Anglo-American friendship, the British government faced some very hard choices indeed when defining its wartime policies toward the United States.

The earliest policies were defined within the Cabinet. It was only later that the Cabinet became unable to hold its own against oppos-ing factions in the House of Commons and only after months of grueling and frustrating stalemate on the western front that it came to tremble before blasts from radical and Tory newspapers. The decisions of the first half-year emerged almost entirely from the twenty-three men dressed in black frock coats who gathered peri-odically around the long Cabinet table at Number Ten Downing Street. In the rush and tumble of events, most decisions were made in fact by much smaller groups, and those affecting the United

States were nearly all taken among the five ruddy-faced individuals who held respectively the offices of Foreign Secretary, Prime Minister, Secretary of State for War, First Lord of the Admiralty, and Chancellor of the Exchequer.

✓ Among these five it was the Foreign Secretary, Sir Edward Grey, who placed greatest store upon the friendship of the United States. In 1905, just before taking office as Foreign Secretary, he had declared: "There are three cardinal features . . . of British policy, not one of which does the Liberal Party wish to see changed. The first is the growing friendship and good feeling between ourselves and the United States, a matter of common ground and common congratulation to all parties in this country." [6] In the Foreign Office he had upheld this policy, even at some risk to British strength and prestige. When the United States refused to recognize Victoriano Huerta's revolutionary regime in Mexico, for example, and the ensuing anarchy not only hurt British investors but also imperiled oil supplies upon which the Royal Navy was partly dependent, Grey acknowledged America's paramount interest and even sent his private secretary to Washington with a promise of cooperation in unseating the offending dictator. [7] His biographer states that he always regarded "the friendship of America . . . as England's most vital interest of all." [8]

During the early months of the war, Grey was able to insist that his own evaluation of American friendship should be reflected in British policy. Not that he dominated his fellow ministers, for many of them recognized his comparative lack of energy and imagination. A tall, quiet, angular Northumbrian squire, he greatly preferred his estate on the Scottish border to his drafty, ornate offices in Whitehall. Although he worked conscientiously at diplomacy, his enthusiasm was reserved for week-end nature study, a pursuit from which only the gravest crisis could distract him. His colleagues were aware that he took less interest in memoranda and dispatches than in fish and

[6] George M. Trevelyan, *Grey of Fallodon* (London, 1937), 102.
[7] Arthur S. Link, *Woodrow Wilson: The New Freedom* (Princeton, 1956), 369–377; Churchill, *World Crisis,* I, 134–137, 179–181.
[8] Trevelyan, *Grey of Fallodon,* 123.

birds, yet he exercised an extraordinary control over their decisions. His hold was partly due to force of character.[9] Though he did not lack subtlety, his most pronounced traits were straightforwardness, uprightness, and candor. While, contrary to superstition, it is not uncustomary for diplomatists to tell the truth, it is rare for one to disclose his thoughts so completely as Grey was in the habit of doing. To foreign representatives he was apt to state openly and frankly all the considerations that had been raised in secret memoranda by the Foreign Office staff. Parallel records of conversations with representatives of different nations show Grey, more often than not, saying the same things to each one, stressing the same points, and baring his mind to friend and rival alike. Although he had opponents, within his own party as well as outside, he enjoyed uncommon prestige because of his apparent virtuous simplicity. A hostile newspaper once described him as "a minister whose personality exercises a magnetism amounting almost to fascination over the House of Commons," and a German diplomat reported in 1909, "In questions of foreign policy no one exercises such great influence over his fellow countrymen as Sir Edward Grey. His word is its own guarantee." [10]

His command over Cabinet policy owed a good deal to circumstance as well as to character. The Prime Minister, Herbert Henry Asquith, maintained something less than firm control over the

---

[9] Trevelyan, *Grey of Fallodon,* stresses this familiar point. It is also made in Gilbert Murray, *The Foreign Policy of Sir Edward Grey, 1906–1915* (London, 1915), in Margret Boveri, *Sir Edward Grey und das Foreign Office* (Berlin, 1933), especially pp. 174–194, and in Politicus, *Viscount Grey of Fallodon* (London, 1934). There was once a German school that took a darkly romantic view of Grey's cunning not unlike the Anglo-American view of Holstein. One of the better examples is Hermann Lutz, *Lord Grey and the World War* (New York, 1928), especially pp. 191–194, which contends that Grey was only subconsciously Machiavellian. But even the least favorable comments by his own associates stress the force of principle in his policy and make-up. See *The War Memoirs of David Lloyd George* (6 vols.; London, 1933–1936), I, 81–89, and Hamilton Fyfe, *The Making of an Optimist* (London, 1921), 40.

[10] London *Daily News,* Sept. 2, 1907, quoted in Halévy, *History of the English People: Epilogue,* I, 124, note 2; Metternich to Bülow, March 23, 1909, *Die grosse Politik der europäischen Kabinette, 1871–1914* (40 vols.; Berlin, 1923–1927), XXVIII, 126.

Cabinet. Austen Chamberlain has described him at the Cabinet table, writing letters, breaking in occasionally to say, "Now that this has been decided we had better pass on to . . . ," and being rebuffed by a general cry, "But *what* has been decided!" [11] Though a man of grave and dignified appearance, he was reputed among his enemies to be seldom sober. Lord Milner and Field Marshal Sir Henry Wilson habitually referred to him as "Squiff." [12] His speeches in the House of Commons, it is true, were not only lucid but often clever, and he was a skillful parliamentarian. So detached an observer as Lord Balfour remarked that "Asquith expressed himself perfectly. He never used the word which is worth ten words, but he frequently used the word which was worth one and a half." [13] Even if accounts of his dilatory behavior as premier are prejudiced, still it is clear that he gave his Foreign Secretary free rein. He and Grey had been comrades in the imperialist faction of the Liberal party and they had risen together. When Grey advanced a policy in the Cabinet, the Prime Minister supported him without question.

The one among the five who rivaled Grey in popular prestige was the new Secretary of State for War, Field Marshal Lord Kitchener. Already a public idol as the hero of Khartoum, he quickly became an object of near worship.[14] Within the Cabinet, however, he was taciturn and withdrawn. An editor described him as "rather repellent to look at, a sort of squint, red face and slightly blotchy nose, but a fine figure of a man." Lloyd George has written of him that he had only "flashes of greatness. He was like one of those revolving lighthouses which radiate momentary gleams of revealing light far

---

[11] Austen Chamberlain, *Down the Years* (London, 1935), 111. A less than spirited defense of Asquith's leadership is offered in the authorized biography, J. A. Spender and Cyril Asquith, *The Life of Lord Oxford and Asquith* (2 vols.; London, 1932), especially II, 131. But even Grey, who was very fond of the Prime Minister, remarks in his *Twenty-five Years, 1892–1916* (2 vols.; London, 1925), II, 247: "He was not disposed to go to meet the occasion and take it by the forelock."

[12] C. E. Callwell, *Field Marshal Sir Henry Wilson: His Life and Diaries* (2 vols.; London, 1927), *passim;* London *Times, The History of the TIMES: The 150th Anniversary and Beyond, 1912–1948* (2 vols.; London, 1952), I, 353.

[13] *Lord Riddell's War Diary, 1914–1918* (London, 1933), 31.

[14] Sir George Arthur, *Life of Lord Kitchener* (3 vols.; London, 1920), III, 12–15; Churchill, *World Crisis,* II, 171–173.

out into the surrounding gloom and then suddenly relapse into complete darkness. There were no intermediate stages."[15] Having spent most of his life on foreign posts, he was uncomfortable in England and especially uncomfortable when seated at the long brown table in Downing Street. He is said to have confessed that he hesitated to reveal military secrets before a group of strangers.[16] He attended, therefore, to the business of the War Office and interfered as little as possible with Grey's diplomacy.

The First Lord of the Admiralty, Winston Churchill, was not powerful enough to oppose Grey effectively.[17] Quite the opposite of Kitchener, he allowed his imperious mind to roam far outside the narrow business of his department. It was as true of him at forty as at seventy that he regarded few matters as lying outside the spheres of his expertness. He enjoyed some popularity, too, as an early champion of naval preparedness, but his colleagues distrusted him. Not only was he a renegade Unionist, but as Home Secretary he had stood out against the navy bills, only to become their most ardent supporter when appointed First Lord. His earlier crusade to suppress anarchism had been conducted with undue zeal. Leading troops and cannon, he had besieged a tenement in Stepney that housed two Russian refugees. Despite his brilliance and charm, he was impotent to force decisions against the objections of the Foreign Secretary.

The final figure who might have opposed Grey was similarly handicapped, although only temporarily. The Chancellor of the Exchequer, David Lloyd George, was perhaps the most energetic and resolute member of the Cabinet. Certainly he was the most ambitious. A not unfair comparison between his traits and those of Joseph Chamberlain had been drawn earlier by the *Daily Mail:* "The same clear, low-pitched cruel voice; the same keen, incisive

[15] Lloyd George, *War Memoirs,* I, 194; the editor was Sir Edward Cook of the *Daily News,* quoted in J. W. Robertson Scott, *The Life and Death of a Newspaper* (London, 1952), 293.

[16] Spender and Asquith, *Asquith,* II, 124.

[17] His ambiguous position in the Cabinet is suggested even in his own *World Crisis,* but see Halévy, *History of the English People: Epilogue,* II, especially pp. 232–234.

phrases; the same mordant bitterness; the same caustic sneer; the same sardonic humour; the same personal enmity." [18] These qualities had led Lloyd George to leadership among radical Liberals and moderate pacifists, but the outbreak of hostilities checked his rise. His convictions and ambitions were soon to affect Cabinet policy, but the war's onset found him temporarily in eclipse.

Owing to both character and circumstance, Grey was in a position virtually to dictate the Cabinet's policies toward America. Asquith supported him, while Kitchener remained silent, Churchill lacked the power to raise effective opposition, and Lloyd George stood temporarily in the shadows. Since the relation of the United States to the war depended to a large extent upon the policies that Britain adopted, Grey bore chief responsibility at the outset for determining what that relation would be.

His ascendancy, it is true, lasted little more than nine months. When the war lengthened into a bitter and bloody stalemate, the House of Commons and the public grew restless. The Liberal government gave way to a coalition, and the new Cabinet was not only less susceptible to Grey's influence but also more responsive to pressures from newspapers and parliamentary factions. Grey's control depended on the temporary unity of the nation, and he was able to dominate the Cabinet and direct British policy only while public opinion permitted him to do so.

His ability to insist upon the preservation of American friendship also owed something to the way in which the war progressed. The truly crucial issues for Anglo-American relations were those of blockade policy: whether Britain should endeavor to stop all German imports, including those from the United States, or leave America's trade interests untouched. And these alternatives emerged only slowly. The first month of the war was taken up in futile expectation of decisive battles on land and sea. After it became evident that the struggle would not end in this fashion, another three months passed before Britain succeeded in clearing the oceans of

---

[18] This indictment is quoted by two of Lloyd George's friendly biographers: E. T. Raymond, *Mr. Lloyd George* (London, 1922), 69, and Thomas Jones, *Lloyd George* (Cambridge, Mass., and London, 1951), 28.

German warships. Only after December, 1914, was it plain, in the first place, that the war would be one of endurance and, in the second place, that Britain would have the naval capability to blockade Germany. During the first half-year of war, events were allies of Grey's ambition to preserve American good will.

During the first month of fighting, it was not even apparent that the United States would be a factor in the war. Almost everyone assumed that hostilities would be brief. Since modern combat was thought too destructive and expensive to be long-lasting, it was reckoned that Germany would attack France, fail to capture Paris, and be forced to make peace when she ran out of men and money. This illusory expectation was blasted toward the end of August when the British commander-in-chief, Sir John French, suddenly reported that the key fortress of Namur had fallen in a day and that his own troops were retiring from Mons under fire. Planners in the Admiralty began to think of the Cotentin peninsula as a place where future British armies might land to rescue France.[19] Although the German attack stalled after the battle of the Marne in early September, confidence in a short war and a swift peace dwindled.

The interval of false hope saw relatively few questions affecting the United States. The Admiralty developed some concern about German merchantmen in American ports. Some of these ships were outfitted with gun mountings and high-speed engines for conversion into auxiliary cruisers, and they represented a genuine threat to the North Atlantic trade routes.[20] Naval authorities were worried lest the United States permit these auxiliary cruisers to leave her ports, and, though the question lay less clearly within their professional province, they were fearful lest the United States buy part of Germany's idle merchant fleet, thus providing the enemy with money

[19] Churchill, *World Crisis*, I, 290; Historical Section, Committee of Imperial Defence, *History of the Great War, based on Official Documents: Military Operations:* J. E. Edmonds, *France and Belgium, 1914* (2 vols.; London, 1922), I, 471–475.
[20] Committee of Imperial Defence, *History of the Great War: Naval Operations:* C. E. Fayle, *Seaborne Trade* (3 vols.; London, 1920–1924), I, 104–114.

to carry on the war. Aside from the inevitable question of contra-band definitions, these seemingly minor problems were the only ones to touch Anglo-American relations.

The Admiralty stressed in each case the importance of protecting British shipping. When it was rumored that the United States had allowed auxiliary cruisers to take the seas, an officer hurried to the American embassy. As the ambassador summarized his message for the Department of State, "German ships are leaving American ports constantly, provisioned and armed to prey on British commerce, and . . . British Government will undoubtedly claim full value for vessels destroyed or captured by such German ships. Such a claim may run into enormous sums." [21]

When the United States gave notice that no armed ships would be allowed to leave port, the Admiralty insisted that this rule should not be applied to British vessels armed for defense. Although satis-fied that the German auxiliary cruiser threat was checked by this decision, the First Lord protested against the comprehensiveness of the American declaration. "I should be so glad if you could see your way to making a strong stand against this . . . ," he wrote to Grey. "It is only when merchant ships are armed and commissioned as auxiliary cruisers, not for purposes of self-defence, but for those of commerce destruction, that we claim they should be treated as ships of war. . . . I would earnestly ask . . . that very great pressure should be exerted." [22]

On the danger of America's buying German ships, the First Lord was equally explicit, also writing to the Foreign Secretary:

The second point that I hope you will be able to fight is: no trans-ference after the declaration of war of enemy's ships to a neutral flag. . . . We cannot recognise such transferences, which are plainly, in the nature of things, designed to enable the transferred ship to obtain under the neutral flag an immunity from the conditions created by the war. . . .

[21] Page to Bryan, Aug. 6, 1914, United States Department of State, *Foreign Relations of the United States, Supplement: The World War, 1914* (Washington, D.C., 1928), p. 596.
[22] Churchill to Grey, Aug. 19, 1914, *World Crisis*, I, 574.

I venture to suggest to you that this position ought to be fought up to the point of full publicity, and by every means and influence at our disposal, before we are forced to consider the various inferior alternatives which no doubt exist.[23]

Under the illusion that the war would be short, Grey deferred to the recommendations of the Admiralty. He made representations on his own account in order to prevent the sailing of auxiliary cruisers. When Churchill asked him to protest the American ruling against the sailing of any armed ships, Grey obliged by writing Washington. Similarly, he notified the American government of Britain's strong objections to any transfer of German merchant ships to the American flag.[24] His actions, in each case, corresponded with those urged, on military grounds, by the Admiralty.

Even in these confused and hectic first weeks of the war Grey ✓ did not lose sight of the importance of preserving American friendship. On the day of Britain's declaration of war, he called in the American ambassador, Walter Hines Page, to explain the Cabinet's decision, to ask for sympathetic understanding, and to request "the courtesies of neutrality." [25] Although he did as the Admiralty proposed on the questions of auxiliary cruisers, armed vessels, and ship transfers, he acted with the utmost courtesy. Discussing the latter issue with Page, for example, Grey suggested that the United States might remove British objections by promising to use the purchased ships only for non-European trade. He was willing, he indicated, to consider any reasonable plan.[26] Conversing with Page on other points of possible friction, Grey strove to seem equally flexible and cordial.

That military considerations nevertheless stood uppermost in his

[23] *Ibid.*

[24] Barclay to Bryan, Aug. 4, 1914 (two memoranda), *Foreign Relations, Supplement: 1914,* pp. 593–595; Spring-Rice to Bryan, Sept. 4, 1914, *ibid.,* 606; Page to Bryan, Aug. 21, 1914, *ibid.,* 489–490.

[25] Burton J. Hendrick, *The Life and Letters of Walter Hines Page* (3 vols.; New York, 1922–1926), I, 315.

[26] Page to Bryan, Aug. 21, 1914, *Foreign Relations, Supplement: 1914,* pp. 489–490.

mind is suggested by the one decision that was to provoke genuine irritation in Washington. On August 20 the Cabinet voted not to abide by the Declaration of London, the unratified code for maritime warfare which had been drawn up in 1909, partly at Grey's instance. An order-in-council issued at the outbreak of war had conformed to this code, without mentioning it by name. The United States had promptly suggested that all the belligerents explicitly agree to abide by the Declaration, since it professed to "correspond with the generally recognized principles of international law." [27] It also allowed great freedom for neutral trade and specifically exempted from seizure as contraband certain important American exports, in particular copper ore and cotton. To reject the Declaration was, therefore, to risk irritating some very sensitive American interests.

The recommendation to reject it did not come, in this case, from the Admiralty. It came instead from two committees, one sitting in London and the other in Paris. Made up of naval officers and international lawyers, these two committees had been formed to consider legal questions rising out of the war. The American proposal had been referred to them, as had an earlier French suggestion that the Declaration of London be proclaimed, subject to "the right to modify it according to the lessons obtained from experience." Both committees advised rejecting the American proposition by proclaiming the Declaration to be in effect, subject to certain modifications and exceptions. This advice was based on military rather than legal grounds. Food and other supplies were coming into Rotterdam, a neutral port, and passing immediately to the German armies in Belgium. If the Allies agreed to be bound by the Declaration of London, they would find it difficult to stop these shipments. Warning of this likelihood, the two committees reported unfavorably on the American proposal. The Russian government agreed to be bound by whatever its allies did, and the French and British cabinets de-

---

[27] Page to Bryan, Aug. 5, 1914, *ibid.*, 215; Bryan to Page, Aug. 6, 1914, *ibid.*, 216. The quotation is from the preamble to the Declaration, which is published in full in *Foreign Relations, 1909*, pp. 318-333.

cided to follow the advice of their committees.[28] Asquith noted in his diary, "A rather long Cabinet this morning, all sorts of odds and ends about coal and contraband." [29]

Although Grey had not forgotten the importance of Anglo-American friendship, he apparently made no objections to these decisions of expediency. Anticipating a prompt end of the war, he gave relatively little attention to the possible repercussions of the Cabinet's decisions. He was absorbed, furthermore, in emergency tasks. The effort to prevent Turkish intervention involved intricate negotiations with all the Balkan states. The danger that military logic might lead to political disaster was much less apparent in minor questions involving the United States than in the Admiralty's threats to make war on the Dutch, the Italians, and the Turks.[30] During the first months of hostilities, in any case, the preservation of American friendship was not a central aim of his wartime diplomacy.

After Mons and the Marne, the probability of a long and wearing war increased. [As it became apparent that Britain would be partly dependent on American supplies, American friendship acquired military value.] It was not yet clear whether a conflicting necessity would arise. The navy was strained to the utmost in preparing for a decisive sea battle, protecting the transit of troops, and guarding ocean commerce. Of the 102 vessels not belonging to the Grand Fleet, 86 were engaged in standing watch over British shipping or patrolling for German raiders, and it remained uncertain whether

---

[28] Archibald C. Bell, *Die englische Hungerblockade im Weltkrieg, 1914–1915* (German translation; Essen, 1943), 100–101; Louis Guichard, *Histoire du blocus naval (1914–1918)* (Paris, 1929), 22–24; Denys Cochin et al., *Les organisations de blocus en France pendant la guerre (1914–1918)* (Paris, 1926), 2–3; Sazonov to Isvolski, Aug. 6, 1914, F. Stieve (ed.), *Iswolski im Weltkrieg* (Berlin, 1926), no. 41. The Bell volume is part of a confidential history prepared for the British government, which was somehow pirated and published by the Germans. The Guichard volume, which draws upon French naval archives, has been translated into English as *The Naval Blockade* (London, 1930), but the translation is somewhat carelessly done.

[29] Aug. 20, 1914, Spender and Asquith, *Asquith*, II, 125.

[30] See Churchill, *World Crisis*, I, 240, 268–269, 361–362; Grey, *Twenty-five Years*, II, 168–169.

Britain would be able to blockade Germany.[31] For about three months, therefore, from the end of August until the beginning of December, there seemed to be no military need outweighing that of preserving American good will.

It was in this period that Grey was most confident of his own premises. He wrote to the ambassador in Washington in early September, "We wish in all our conduct of the war to do nothing which will be a cause of complaint or dispute as regards the United States Government; such a dispute would indeed be a crowning calamity . . . and probably fatal to our chances of success."[32] He took the view that America's friendship was more important than the interruption of German imports. When a Contraband Committee was formed, Grey addressed the Foreign Office members and "emphasised the vital importance of our relations with America. He recalled that in 1812 questions of neutrality had actually involved us in war with the United States, and that the surest way to lose this war would be to antagonise Washington. . . . 'Mind, therefore, you keep a sense of proportion.'"[33] He also indicated that he would not sacrifice American good will even for the sake of tightening the alliance with France and Russia. Count Benckendorff, the Russian ambassador, reported on a conversation with Grey in early October, 1914: "For England in the course of this war two conditions are necessary: the ability to carry on her trade and the preservation of good relations with the United States. Grey asks you to understand," Benckendorff wrote his Foreign Minister, "that these two conditions are vital to England and her military power."[34]

Nor was Grey alone in these thoughts. Even the First Lord acknowledged America's importance. He suggested recruiting vol-

[31] Committee of Imperial Defence, *History of the Great War: Naval Operations:* Sir Julian Corbett, *Naval Operations,* I (London, 1920), 436; Churchill, *World Crisis,* I, 471; E. Keble Chatterton, *The Big Blockade* (London, 1932), 36–39.

[32] Grey to Spring-Rice, Sept. 3, 1914, Trevelyan, *Grey of Fallodon,* 356.

[33] Memorandum by Alwyn Parker, *ibid.,* 347–348.

[34] Benckendorff to Sazonov, Oct. 7, 1914, Union of Soviet Socialist Republics, Historical Commission, Central Executive Committee, *Mezhdunarodnye Otnosheniya v Epoku Imperializma,* Series Three: 1914–1917 (10 vols. in progress; Moscow, 1930—), VI, no. 370. The first eight volumes have been translated as *Die internationalen Beziehungen im Zeitalter des Imperialismus* (Berlin, 1932–1936).

unteers from the United States. "Nothing," he commented, "will bring American sympathy along with us so much as American blood shed in the field." He also cautioned his own officers that it was unwise for patrols to hover too near American ports. "They should . . . discharge their duties with tact," he minuted, "remembering how greatly British interests are concerned in the maintenance of good relations with the United States." [35] So long as the fleet remained incapable of tightening a blockade around Germany, the Admiralty endorsed Grey's sentiment, and so, apparently, did other members of the government. During the autumn of 1914, therefore, the policy of preserving American friendship at almost any cost was not Grey's alone but that of virtually the entire government.

During this period, nevertheless, three serious issues arose. The first was raised by the United States herself. It developed, to be sure, from the earlier British refusal to be bound by the Declaration of London. The response to America's proposal had taken the form of a revised order-in-council, proclaiming the Declaration "subject to certain modifications and additions . . . indispensable to the efficient conduct of . . . naval operations." [36] Although little or nothing had as yet been done in contravention of the Declaration, Grey learned that the American government was preparing a hot protest against the "modifications and additions." "I saw it," reported the British ambassador, Sir Cecil Spring-Rice, "and was really astonished at the tone in one or two of the sentences. I merely remarked that if it went off as it was, there would be a big catastrophe equal to, or worse than, that brought on by Cleveland's Venezuela dispatch." Although the ambassador also related how the sending of the protest had been blocked by an Anglophile friend of the President, he remarked, "I fear we are not out of the wood yet." [37] The issues were for the moment only abstract questions of

[35] Churchill to Asquith, Sept. 5, 1914, *World Crisis*, I, 293–294; Churchill to the First Sea Lord, Oct. 26, 1914, *ibid.*, 575.

[36] Page to Bryan, Aug. 26, 1914, *Foreign Relations, Supplement: 1914*, pp. 218–220; Cochin, *Organisations de blocus*, 157–166.

[37] Spring-Rice to Grey, Oct. 1, 1914, Stephen Gwynn (ed.), *The Letters and Friendships of Sir Cecil Spring-Rice* (2 vols.; Boston, 1929), II, 233.

law, but the United States was threatening to challenge nothing less than Britain's ability to wage an economic war if she should find it desirable and practicable.

The United States asked that Britain accept the Declaration of London *in toto*.[38] If this request were met, the navy would be forced to pass some goods to neutral European ports and, more important, to allow unrestricted importation of articles on the Declaration's free list. Besides cotton and copper, which were constituents of cartridges and shells, that list included other items susceptible of military use, like raw textiles, convertible into uniforms, rubber for vehicle tires, hides for boots and cavalry saddles, and agricultural nitrates easily turned into explosives. It also included paper, the hemoglobin of a modern army. Were Britain to accept the Declaration, she would virtually forswear the use of economic weapons. Grey found before him, therefore, a most serious conflict between the interest of waging war, on the one hand, and, on the other, that of preserving American friendship.

He exerted himself to the utmost to find some satisfactory compromise. He proposed a substitute order-in-council which Washington rejected. Summoning Page for frequent conferences, he endeavored to explain all the reasons why the Declaration could not be accepted in its entirety.[39] Not only would it cripple Britain's ability to wage an economic war, but acceptance would probably result in the overthrow of the government. The Declaration had not commanded majority support even in peacetime, he explained, and its acceptance under wartime conditions was sure to provoke a furor among Tories, with loss of confidence elsewhere. To act as the United States proposed might even upset the great alliance, he said, for the French and Russians were apt to feel that Britain was fighting only a half-war. Not only did Grey bare his anxiety to Page, but he even wrote a letter for the President of the United States, declaring:

[38] Lansing to Page, Sept. 26, 1914, *Foreign Relations, Supplement: 1914*, pp. 225–232.
[39] Grey to Spring-Rice, Sept. 28, 1914, *ibid.*, 236–237; Page to Bryan, Oct. 19, 1914, *ibid.*, 253–254; Hendrick, *Page*, I, 381–383.

We are most anxious to come to an agreement with United States Government for otherwise we shall have to choose between a dispute with the United States Government or giving up all attempts to prevent Germany from getting free supplies for her army and materials for all munitions of war: either alternative would or might be fatal to our chance of success and insure ultimate German victory and disappearance of Great Britain as a fully independent Power in Europe.[40]

Through four weeks of proposals and counterproposals, the issue remained undecided. Grey was encouraged to hold out. He had the sympathies of Ambassador Page. Spring-Rice reported that other influential Americans saw his side of the case. Since all reports from the United States told of intense public sympathy for the Allies, it seemed probable that the American government would be unable to go to extremes. The successive propositions from Washington, moreover, became increasingly conciliatory. The most important, for example, was a suggestion that Britain proclaim her obedience to the Declaration of London and then issue supplementary decrees evading it. From this evidence of vacillation Grey could hope that the United States would ultimately give way.[41]

His patience was rewarded. The United States withdrew her demand and agreed to insist only upon Britain's observance of traditional international law. Although the American government warned of probable trouble each time its ill-defined rights were invaded, Grey's private secretary spoke to Page of the government's "infinite . . . relief," and the ambassador reported a "most admirable effect all around."[42]

The second issue was raised by Britain's allies. Both France and Russia asked for intensified economic pressure on Germany. The French wished cotton to be stopped, while the Russians proposed

[40] Grey to Spring-Rice, n.d., enclosed in Spring-Rice to Wilson, Oct. 15, 1914, *Foreign Relations of the United States: The Lansing Papers, 1914–1920* (2 vols.; Washington, D.C., 1939), I, 250–252.

[41] Gwynn, *Spring-Rice*, II, 239–250; Lansing to Page, Oct. 16, 1914, *Foreign Relations, Supplement: 1914*, pp. 249–250; see Marion C. Siney, *The Allied Blockade of Germany, 1914–1916* (Ann Arbor, Mich., 1957), 24–29.

[42] *Foreign Relations, Supplement: 1914*, p. 258; Hendrick, *Page*, I, 387; Page to Wilson, Oct. 28, 1914, Private Papers of Woodrow Wilson, Manuscripts Division, Library of Congress.

enlarged interference with German food supplies.[43] Neither ally was entirely happy about the British contribution to the war thus far. The Expeditionary Force in France numbered only four divisions, and there had inevitably been some friction between its commander and the French high command. Turkey's belated declaration of war, coupled with German control of the Baltic, had meanwhile severed most of the supply lines between England and Russia. Not only did it seem from the standpoint of her allies that Britain was feeble on land, but her exercise of sea power fell somewhat short of the spectacular. She had neither engaged the German battle fleet nor as yet swept the seas of enemy raiders, and she had proved unable to prevent two German cruisers, the *Goeben* and *Breslau,* from making through the Turkish straits and gaining control of the Black Sea. It was little wonder that both Paris and St. Petersburg should wish their ally at least to ensure that Germany should not receive essential imports.

The Russian proposal of a limited food blockade reached London while Grey was still waiting out negotiations over the Declaration of London. Calling in the Russian ambassador, Grey explained in detail why he could not accede. "He told me," Benckendorff reported to his Foreign Minister, "that he could not let you remain under the impression that he did not understand the earnestness of your objections or that he had it in mind to deal with this question on any other except grounds of the greatest moment." The American economy, Grey explained, was in an uneasy condition, and it might be seriously upset by a sudden depression in the grain trade. He hoped it might be possible to block other German imports, such as oil, which he understood to be in short supply, but, as the ambassador reported, "he felt it necessary to state again that it is impossible for England to quarrel with the United States, that it is, on the contrary, a necessity of the first order to maintain really good relations, no more in England's special interest than in those of her allies."[44] Since the Russian government was seeking a loan in

---

[43] Benckendorff to Sazonov, Oct. 7, 1914, *Mezhdunarodnye Otnosheniya,* Series Three, VI, no. 370; Bell, *Die englische Hungerblockade,* 102–103.

[44] Benckendorff to Sazonov, Oct. 7, 1914, *loc. cit.*

London and, at the same time, being urged to look to America for money and supplies, Grey heard no more from St. Petersburg.

The French request that cotton be put on the contraband list was a much more difficult proposition. The suggestion had first been made in mid-September, and the French had become increasingly insistent just as the British government became more and more embarrassed about its relatively ineffective support on the western front. A daring attempt by Churchill to reinforce Antwerp had ended in disaster. The Germans were at the Channel coast, with their submarines threatening the further transit of troops and supplies. The Allies were meanwhile firing more shells and cartridges than they had ever expected to, and the anticipated munitions shortage made it seem all the more serious that guncotton was reaching the enemy in unlimited quantity.[45]

The French were in a position, moreover, to meet arguments grounded on the importance of American good will. Their own experience suggested that the United States was indissolubly bound to the Allies. Americans in France, including diplomats, were wholeheartedly pro-French. The ambassador in Washington reported nearly universal sympathy for the Allies. And it was evident that the American economy was going to profit increasingly from Allied purchases. The United States government had just lifted an earlier ban on loans and allowed J. P. Morgan and Company to lend France $10,000,000. It was the view of President Raymond Poincaré that the United States should be regarded, like Italy and Rumania, as a nation committed to the Allies but opportunistically delaying its armed intervention. From the French standpoint, there appeared to be few reasons for sacrificing military advantages in order to spare American feelings.[46]

The French proposal, furthermore, had some backing among Englishmen. The British ambassador to France, Sir Francis Bertie, wholeheartedly agreed with its logic.[47] Although documents are

[45] Bell, *Die englische Hungerblockade,* 103.

[46] Albert Pingaud, *Histoire diplomatique de la France pendant la guerre* (2 vols.; Paris, 1938), II, 232–233; Raymond Poincaré, *Au service de la France* (9 vols.; Paris, 1925–1932), V, 318.

[47] *The Diary of Lord Bertie of Thame, 1914–1918* (2 vols.; London, 1924), edited by Lady Algernon Gordon Lennox, I, 16, 52–55.

lacking, it is not unreasonable to suppose that some of Bertie's friends in the Foreign Office were with him. Sir Arthur Nicolson, who was Grey's Permanent Undersecretary, had long been ranged with the ambassador in advocating closer cooperation with Paris. While Grey had been unwilling to treat the peacetime entente as a binding alliance, Nicolson, Bertie, and the Assistant Undersecretary, Eyre Crowe, had favored making every commitment the French suggested. Both Bertie and Crowe, moreover, were subsequently to oppose conciliating American trade interests.[48] It seems likely, therefore, that unless they were deterred by fear that the fleet could not do the job, they supported the French proposal on cotton. Outside the government, meanwhile, were Tory, Conservative, and even Liberal spokesmen who wished economic weapons to be used ruthlessly and who shared the French view that America was securely bound by emotional and economic ties. There was thus support for the French proposal from individuals in the government and from elements in public opinion.

Grey nevertheless rejected the French demand. While the Declaration of London negotiations were in progress, he had raised the question in the Cabinet and been authorized to promise that cotton would not be on the new contraband list. When a French delegation arrived in London, refusing to approve Grey's pledge, several days of negotiation ensued. Grey probably communicated with the French government, then in refuge in Bordeaux. From the War Trade Advisory Committee, headed by his old friend and political comrade, the Marquess of Crewe, he obtained memoranda indicating that additional cotton imports would not add materially to Germany's munitions stocks. But the French proved adamant.[49]

Grey appealed to the Cabinet for support. At a meeting on October 28, six days after the American concession, he was instructed to continue negotiations for another day and, if these failed, to consult the Cabinet again on the 30th. Although he had not secured a final vote on the issue, he had demonstrated to the French delegates that

[48] Gwynn, *Spring-Rice*, II, 317–318; see Chapter XIV below.
[49] Bell, *Die englische Hungerblockade*, 103, 280.

Fr. wanted cotton on contraband list; Grey refuses

he was prepared to carry the issue formally to their government. Confronted with his evident determination, the French elected to give in. That night Crewe was able to deliver the new order-in-council for the King's signature.[50] Despite pressures of circumstance and bureaucratic and public opinion, Grey had refused to yield. He had stood so firm, indeed, as to bring the western allies to the brink of serious friction. But he had won his point.

The third issue to arise during the autumn was potentially the most dangerous of all. Sometime in October, the Admiralty proposed sowing mines through the North Sea.[51] In order to carry out this measure it would be necessary to ask that neutrals use the Channel route instead of the north-about passage. Neutral ships, moreover, would have to take on Admiralty pilots to conduct them safely through the minefields. And these requirements meant that no neutral vessel could approach Scandinavian or German ports without first submitting to search for contraband. If, after mines had been laid, the United States refused to accept these restrictions, there would be serious dangers for American ships, cargoes, and passengers, with the likelihood of very grave issues rising between Washington and London.

The Admiralty plan nevertheless had strong arguments behind it. First and foremost was the growing insecurity of the fleet. Submarines operating from German-held ports had torpedoed four cruisers in September and a dreadnaught in October. Minefields would shield the weary Grand Fleet against future attacks. Secondly, they would provide some additional security against invasion, a possibility that had once again come to seem alarming to the War Office.[52] The new First Sea Lord, Sir John Fisher, did advance the thought that mining the North Sea might make it easier to intercept contraband.[53] But the proposal was made chiefly for the security of the fleet and the home island. Military concerns of the first impor-

---

[50] *Ibid.*, 280; Sir Almeric Fitzroy, *Memoirs* (2 vols.; London, 1925), II, 575.

[51] Spender and Asquith, *Asquith*, II, 130; Viscount Fisher of Kilverstone, *Memories and Records* (2 vols.; London, 1920), I, 135, 137, II, 218; Corbett, *Naval Operations*, I, 182–183.

[52] Churchill, *World Crisis*, I, 490.

[53] Fisher, *Memories and Records*, II, 226–228.

tance were thus placed in the balance against a possible risk of American anger.

Confronted with such a choice, Grey apparently chose to enter no objection. Very few United States ships used the north-about route. American goods and passengers rode on Scandinavian vessels, and the Scandinavian lines would submit to whatever regulations Britain proposed.[54] In view of the spirit of accommodation shown in the Declaration of London negotiations, furthermore, the Americans could be expected to compromise, and, as it turned out, the United States did not protest at all. American shippers quickly adapted to the Admiralty's regulations and stopped for naval pilots, and no American vessel went down. In view of the fierce reactions provoked later by Germany's submarine war zone decree, it is evident, nevertheless, that Grey had run some risk.

The three issues of the autumn had been met successfully. The Foreign Secretary had stood fast against the Declaration of London proposal without, in the end, losing American friendship. He had refused with equal obstinacy to accept the French recommendation for adding cotton to the contraband list and thus endangering Anglo-American relations. He had yielded to military insistence upon the proclamation of a mine war zone, but no friction resulted. In the months when the future of the economic war remained undecided, Grey had preserved Britain's ability to opt later for a blockade without in any way sacrificing American good will.

As autumn turned into winter, the situation changed once more. After prospects of swift victory in the west disappeared, there lingered some hope that Russia might overbear the enemy in the east. The defeats in August and September at Tannenberg and the Masurian Lakes diminished this hope. In November and December reports from the British military observer told of exhausted stores and worn and depleted Russian divisions. It became apparent that the war would last at least until the coming summer. The Admiralty began to lay plans for another full year of war, while the army commenced thinking of requirements for 1916 and beyond.[55]

[54] Fayle, *Seaborne Trade*, I, 299.
[55] Churchill, *World Crisis*, I, 289–304.

Early in December, furthermore, Admiral Doveton Sturdee trapped the German raider squadron off the Falkland Islands and destroyed all but one of its five cruisers. The German threat on the oceans diminished, and the Admiralty was able to recall warships to home waters. The eight aged vessels assigned to commerce patrol were all retired, and a new Tenth Cruiser Squadron was formed out of twenty-four new high-speed converted merchantmen.[56] With dawning certainty that the war would be long came, at last, assurance that the navy would have the power to strangle the enemy.

Interest in using this power naturally grew. Although the French had yielded to Grey's insistence in October, they continued to prod their ally. Lord Bertie remained convinced that the French logic was right, and he probably received increasing support among his friends at home. Within the War Office there arose the view that only exhaustion of the enemy would produce victory. An economic adviser to Kitchener, visiting Paris, spoke to Bertie of the military necessity for starving Germany. The Admiralty called for intensified economic warfare not only for its own sake but also in order to force the German navy into an engagement with the Grand Fleet. If the populace could be made to suffer, the admirals reasoned, the enemy would have no choice but to challenge Britain's command of the North Sea. These views came to be expressed with increasing vigor at sessions of the Cabinet and of the smaller War Council formed in November.[57]

Public opinion favorable to a thoroughgoing blockade of Germany also grew. Since many officers and officials enjoyed close relations with publishers, this movement need have been neither spontaneous nor coincidental. One of the newspapers to open agitation for intensified economic warfare was the London *Morning Post*. A principal leader writer for the *Post* was Henry Spenser Wilkinson, a brother-in-law and intimate friend of Eyre Crowe.[58] There was a sudden movement in this direction on the part of other Tory

---

[56] Corbett, *Naval Operations*, II, 8, 50–51; Chatterton, *The Big Blockade*, 53–54, 58 ff.

[57] *Diary of Lord Bertie*, I, 52–53; Bell, *Die englische Hungerblockade*, 203–204.

[58] See Hale, *Publicity and Diplomacy*, 286.

journals. The *Saturday Review,* for instance, commented in its issue of November 7, 1914, on the importance of giving every considera-tion to the United States. Only two weeks later, on November 21, it called for less milk and water in the treatment of neutral trade.[59] Although there is no evidence that the Tory leadership had elected to press this issue, it is clear that some unrest was stirred in the House of Commons. Both Asquith and Churchill felt obliged during November to speak reassuringly about the extent to which Britain was curbing German supplies.[60]

Advocates of blockade did not challenge Grey's premise. When Bertie and the War Office economist discussed the desirability of starving Germany, they acknowledged that it could not be done unless some means were found for circumventing American ob-jections. The Admiralty likewise took this need into account.[61] And Tory journals defended their proposals by arguing that American emotions and interests were identical with those of the Allies. The *Spectator* published regular letters from the United States telling of ardent pro-Ally feeling in such unlikely places as the oil fields of Texas and the logging camps of California. The *Saturday Review* insisted that there would be no real injury to American interests or sympathies if Britain imposed a blockade.[62] Although individuals were apprehensive of possible trouble, the mood of the demand was one of complacency about the future of Anglo-American relations.

The entire Cabinet sympathized, of course, with the motives that produced the blockade agitation. Asquith noted in his journal dur-ing the Declaration of London negotiations, "The Americans are raising difficulties . . . . We naturally do not want to have a row with them, but we cannot allow the Germans to be provided for." [63] Grey accepted every proposal that did not threaten Anglo-American accord. In the course of his discussions with the French in October,

[59] *Saturday Review,* CXVIII (Nov. 7, 1914), 478–479, (Nov. 21, 1914), 523.

[60] *Parliamentary Debates: Commons,* 5th Series, LXVIII, pp. 315–317, 1603–1605.

[61] *Diary of Lord Bertie,* I, 53; Churchill, *World Crisis,* II, 284.

[62] *Spectator,* CXIII (Oct. 17, 1914), 524, (Nov. 14, 1914), 664; *Saturday Re-view,* CXVIII (Dec. 26, 1914), 643.

[63] Lord Oxford and Asquith, *Memories and Reflections, 1852–1927* (2 vols.; London, 1928), II, 42.

for instance, he agreed that certain pressures could be applied to neutral states neighboring Germany. As early as November 3 he directed a circular to the Dutch, Norwegian, Swiss, and Italian capitals. If these states were voluntarily to stop the exportation of contraband, he suggested, their own importers might find it somewhat easier to obtain goods. Costly delays for visit and search might well be reduced to a minimum, and opportunities for selling in Allied markets might be enlarged.[64] Convinced by intelligence reports that Germany was obtaining oil and copper through dummy firms, particularly in Italy, Grey permitted the fleet to halt shipments, even from the United States.[65] As much as the Bertie–Nicolson–Crowe group, the War Office, the Admiralty, and the Tories, the Foreign Secretary and the Prime Minister wished to sever Germany's supply lines.

The distinctive element in Grey's view was an absence of any complacency about the United States. The Declaration of London negotiations had indicated the tenacity with which Americans would defend international law when it coincided with American interests. Spring-Rice continuously cautioned Grey of the hold that exporting interests had over the Wilson administration. Warning against undue interference with copper, for instance, the ambassador wrote, "The copper interests here are very powerful as the exports for last year were valued at nearly thirty million sterling, and at the present moment the mining districts are in a very dangerous situation. We shall have to find some means of crippling Krupp without ruining the mining states here who possess the ear of the Secretary of State and have a commanding influence in the Senate." [66] Grey knew, too, that the United States economy stood at the edge of depression and that, although the war had brought some revival, it was still far from flourishing.[67] He was keenly alert therefore to the dangers involved in tampering with American business.

He felt reason, furthermore, to be fearful of German influence in

[64] Siney, *Allied Blockade*, chapter III, *passim*.
[65] Bell, *Die englische Hungerblockade*, 142–144.
[66] Spring-Rice to Grey, Oct. 5, 1914, Gwynn, *Spring-Rice*, II, 237–238.
[67] Benckendorff to Sazonov, Oct. 7, 1914, *loc. cit.*

America. The number of voters of German and Irish inheritance was in itself disturbing, and the autumn and winter of 1914 brought news of organized pressure by these groups. Calling for an embargo on munitions, which would, of course, be injurious solely to the Allies, they succeeded in getting bills before Congress. Although the administration openly opposed these bills, the Foreign Secretary's informants were not altogether certain that they would be defeated.[68] Certainly the agitation for peace had spread in the United States, and British officials believed German agents to be encouraging it. The mediation ambitions of the President and his Secretary of State were undoubtedly sincere and well-intended, but they were full of danger for Anglo-American relations. Peace negotiations were virtually impossible so long as the Germans remained in the posture of victors, and talk of peace was hazardous since it might frighten one of the great allies into saving what she could by a separate treaty. German-led agitation in the United States could therefore jeopardize the moral foundations of Anglo-American friendship, and Grey felt it necessary to be additionally cautious in adding to the causes of complaint by the American public.

He may even have been fearful that German influence reached into high places. Several incidents had provoked other observers to alarm. The Department of State suddenly issued an order classifying ship manifests as confidential and forbidding their publication until thirty days after sailing time. Since British agents had theretofore been able to inspect manifests and alert patrols to suspicious cargoes, this order seemed a deliberate effort to hinder Britain.[69] The President himself cooperated in one instance with German agents. The Hamburg-America liner *Dacia* was ostensibly sold to American citizens who then loaded it with cotton and dispatched it to Rotterdam. The whole transaction seemed engineered to provoke an Anglo-American dispute, since Britain had announced her unwill-

[68] Spring-Rice to Grey, Dec. 29, 1914, Gwynn, *Spring-Rice,* II, 250; Theodore Roosevelt to Grey, Jan. 22, 1915, Elting E. Morison *et al., The Letters of Theodore Roosevelt* (8 vols.; Cambridge, Mass., 1950–1954), VIII, 876–881.
[69] Spring-Rice to Bryan, Nov. 23, 1914, *Foreign Relations, Supplement: 1914,* pp. 636–637; Page to Bryan, Jan. 19, Feb. 8, 1915, *Foreign Relations, Supplement: 1915,* pp. 7, 322; Hendrick, *Page,* III, 227.

ingness to recognize any transfers of German vessels. Yet the American government defended the *Dacia's* buyers and asked that the ship be allowed to pass.[70] In another instance, German agents hired the American-owned vessel, the *Wilhelmina,* loaded it with food, and sailed it for Hamburg. As Britain had begun to intercept all food bound directly for Germany, this case, too, had been carefully contrived. Its purpose was to attract public attention to the British starvation campaign. Yet the American government once again cooperated in the plot by asking that the *Wilhelmina* be granted safe passage.[71] Page reported suspicions of German influence high in his own government, and Tory journals commented on the administration's eagerness for German votes.[72] Although Grey may not have shared these suspicions, he may well have thought the American government obtuse to the point of being dangerous.

Far from complacent about American friendship, therefore, he continued his efforts to minimize friction. Arrangements were sought with United States shippers to permit pre-sailing inspections by British officials. Cargoes thus certified could be sped through the patrols with a minimum of delay. A special committee was set up in London to expedite the handling of ships that had not been previously searched. When Grey felt it necessary to seize goods, he endeavored to make full explanations and to relieve the potential injury to American interests. When halting copper, for instance, he offered to buy the shipments and, indeed, to purchase the whole export for 1915. Tirelessly meeting with Page and other American officials, he endeavored to reconcile the demands of the war with those of American commerce.[73]

He also sought conciliatory means of combating the apparent

[70] J. H. von Bernstorff, *My Three Years in America* (London, 1919), 72–73.

[71] Bernstorff, *My Three Years in America,* 76–77; *Foreign Relations, Supplement: 1915,* pp. 105–107.

[72] Rappaport, *British Press and Wilsonian Neutrality,* 17; Hendrick, *Page,* III, 227–228; Amy Strachey, *St. Loe Strachey: His Life and His Paper* (London, 1930), 326–329; *The Academy,* LXXXVIII (Jan. 2, 1915), 3.

[73] Page to Bryan, Dec. 6, 1914, *Foreign Relations, Supplement: 1914,* pp. 356–358; Page to Wilson, Nov. 30, 1914, Wilson Papers.

German influence in Washington. His dexterous defense against the mediation threat will be described later. His ingenious handling of the *Dacia* case is a familiar story. As Page's biographer relates, the inspiration came from the ambassador. Reminding Grey that Franco-American relations were relatively tranquil, Page suggested that the ship might be captured more happily by the French navy than the British. "A gleam of understanding immediately shot across Grey's face. . . . 'Yes,' he said, 'why not let the Belgian royal yacht seize it?' " And it was, in fact, taken in tow by a French patrol.[74] In the meantime Grey maintained a cordial correspondence with influential Americans, such as Theodore Roosevelt, sought in every way to put his views before the President, and, through a special bureau of the Foreign Office, endeavored to keep his finger on the pulse of the American press.[75]

No tactics by the Foreign Secretary, however, could achieve more than temporary success. Military insistence upon intensified economic warfare grew steadily. In late January, Admiral Fisher addressed a memorandum to the War Council observing that the laws which restricted interference with neutral trade· were "obsolete" and "based on the conditions of a century ago." When the Germans proclaimed a submarine campaign against merchant ships, the French and British admiralties, the French Foreign Ministry, and a majority in the British Cabinet all called for retaliation by blockade. Agitation on the part of the Tory press meanwhile increased, and Conservative and Liberal organs began to join in.[76] Grey's efforts to limit interference with American trade could be, at best, delaying actions.

The spring of 1915 brought still other changes. Grey lost the ability to impose on British policy his own evaluation of American good

[74] Hendrick, *Page*, I, 395.

[75] H. C. Peterson, *Propaganda for War, 1914–1917* (Norman, Okla., 1939), 23ff.

[76] Spender and Asquith, *Asquith*, II, 130–131; Churchill, *World Crisis*, II, 304–306; Guichard, *Blocus naval*, 39–40; Cochin, *Organisations de blocus*, 7–8; Fayle, *Seaborne Trade*, II, 6; Poincaré, *Au service de la France*, VI, 66; Rappaport, *British Press and Wilsonian Neutrality*, 31; Irene Cooper Willis, *England's Holy War: A Study of English Liberal Idealism during the Great War* (New York, 1928), 195–206; *Blackwood's Magazine*, CXCVII (Feb., 1915), 274–277.

will. The circumstances that had given him ascendancy in the
Cabinet altered, and the Cabinet itself lost command of the country.
Uncertainties about the pattern of the war disappeared, making it
evident that remorseless economic pressures would have to be applied to the enemy. Before new policies came into effect, however,
the Germans had launched their submarine campaign, and hostility
had begun to grow between the United States and Britain's enemies.
The Germans, moreover, had rebuffed America's mediation overtures without the tact shown by the Allies. The moral bases of
Anglo-American friendship had been strengthened instead of weakened. Relations between the two countries after the spring of 1915
developed under a fresh set of conditions. But during the critical six
months before the German-American estrangement, Grey had ensured that it should be British policy to preserve the friendship
of the United States at almost any cost.

II

America's Benevolent Neutrality

When the war opened, the United States had no option but to be neutral. One or two people did suggest that she might, like Britain, intervene to punish the violation of Belgian neutrality, and public sympathy for Belgium ran hot. But the country generally simply felt astonishment and uncertainty, mingled with gratification that America was not involved. Owing to the large English and German elements in the population, government leaders assumed that the nation could never take part on either side without bringing on a civil war at home. The strength of these mixed loyalties, added to traditions of isolationism and pacifism, seemed to forbid intervention and, indeed, to preclude any aid of one side at the expense of the other. The United States government appeared to have no choice but impartial neutrality.

No other alternative could present itself until American interests became involved in the conflict. The government did have an overriding obligation to protect the business and the rights and safety of citizens. It would have been unfaithful to its trust, as well as to the national tradition, if it had failed to help Americans make money out of the war: "The new world," Jefferson had said, "will fatten on the follies of the old." [1] It would have been even more undutiful to disregard America's own security, her dominance in the Western

---

[1] Jefferson to Edward Ruttledge, July 4, 1790, P. L. Ford (ed.), *The Writings of Thomas Jefferson* (10 vols.; New York, 1892–1899), V, 197.

Hemisphere, and her prestige as a great power. But only when such an interest as trade, citizens' rights, security, or prestige came into jeopardy could the government even contemplate discrimination or retaliation.

It would not be true, however, to suggest that the government was wholly passive, even at first. The duties of rigid neutrality were by no means clear, and a number of minor, though potentially important, issues had to be resolved. German ships presented a problem, for release of auxiliary cruisers or purchase of idle ships would hurt the Allies. To pen them up, on the other hand, would hurt the Germans. Since all German cargo carriers disappeared from the seas, decisions affecting war trade presented similar difficulties. If the United States permitted the export of contraband, she benefited the Allies; if she forbade such trade, she greatly aided their enemies. If, similarly, the government insisted that Americans had a right to sell to Germans, it would ask the Allies to deny themselves the weapon of economic pressure, while if it conceded them the use of this weapon, it would be aiding in the strangulation of their enemies. Issues of this nature were hard to deal with in any case, and they became exceptionally difficult when subjected to the test of strict impartiality.

Circumstances gave an edge in each case to the Allies. Much of the information which reached the American government had a pro-Ally bias. Since the British government controlled the trans-Atlantic cables, news from Allied sources arrived freely and in quantity. Foreseeing an unbalance, the American government permitted two German radio stations to remain in operation in the United States. Some newspapers, moreover, maintained correspondents who relayed the German interpretation of events, and neither the government nor the public was deprived altogether of information from the German side. It would not be true, therefore, to state that Americans had a completely one-sided view of the war.[2] But it is true that American officials received enough from Allied sources

[2] See Arthur S. Link, *Woodrow Wilson and the Progressive Era* (New York, 1954), 146–148.

to give them a somewhat better understanding of the Allied perspective than of the German. Since most of the American diplomats
in Europe sympathized with the Allies, their reports helped to
deepen this understanding.[3]

Far more important was the government's estimate of public
opinion. Long before biased news or propaganda could possibly have
had any effect, the public had demonstrated its profound sympathy
for Belgium, and the Allied cause had come to seem righteous in
the eyes of a large number of Americans. The President himself
estimated 90 per cent of the people to be pro-Ally, and the German
chargé d'affaires described regretfully the "anti-German tide" in the
country.[4] This tendency in public opinion did not, of course, compel
policies favorable to the Allies, but it did weigh against decisions
that could be interpreted as injurious to them.

Neither of these circumstances ought to be exaggerated. That the
information available to policy-makers enabled them to understand
the Allied viewpoint did not ensure that their decisions would be
shaped to fit it. The indicators of public opinion that registered
sympathy for the Allies also showed a strong public attachment to
neutrality. There was no inconsistency between the President's estimate that most Americans were pro-Ally and the *Literary Digest*
poll in which 242 out of 367 newspaper editors described themselves
as favoring neither side.[5] It was thought possible to be sympathetic
yet completely neutral. Although resentment could be stirred by
decisions harmful to the Allies, even stronger emotions might be
called up by actions that seemed partisan or unneutral. While public
sympathy for the Allies, added to the character of the government's

---

[3] See, as examples, T. Bentley Mott, *Myron T. Herrick: Friend of France* (New
York, 1930), 115–217; Allan Nevins, *The Letters and Journals of Brand Whitlock*
(2 vols.; New York, 1936); Henry Van Dyke to Wilson, Sept. 10, 1914, Wilson
Papers; Thomas Nelson Page to Wilson, Nov. 7, 1914, *ibid.;* and Sir James Rennell
Rodd, *Social and Diplomatic Memories* (London, 1925), 229.

[4] Mark Sullivan, *Our Times: The United States, 1900–1925* (6 vols.; New York,
1926–1933), V, 50–59; Cedric C. Cummins, *Indiana Public Opinion and the
World War, 1914–1917* (Indianapolis, 1945), 13–15; Gwynn, *Spring-Rice,* II, 245;
Poincaré, *Au service de la France,* V, 529; Haniel von Haimhausen to Jagow, Aug.
8, 1914, German Foreign Ministry Archives (General).

[5] *Literary Digest,* XLIX (Nov. 14, 1914), 939–942.

information, gave a slight advantage to alternatives favoring the Allies, it gave no more than that.

Whether the government's interpretations of neutrality would help the Allies or the Germans depended less on circumstance than on the individual policy-makers and their notions of duty and national interest. During the early stages of the war, at least, the sources of American policy did not lie in intelligence reports or public opinion polls; they lay in the consciences of the Secretary of State, William Jennings Bryan, the Counselor of the Department of State, Robert Lansing, the President's friend and adviser, Colonel Edward M. House, and, above all, of President Woodrow Wilson himself.

The Secretary of State was almost a pacifist.[6] A heavy-set man with a broad, dignified smile and an Elizabethan fringe of hair around his bald crown, Bryan was by nature a crusader. His mighty voice and controlled but almost pathological energy had been thrown into nearly every Protestant reform movement of his lifetime. Along with the rural radicals who formed his electoral cadres, he had swung from the purifying jingoism of the Spanish war era into a form of patriotic pacifism. Since the first decade of the century he had been agitating for disarmament, arbitration, and for the mobilization of world opinion against war. He had himself conceived the idea of bilateral treaties binding all nations to impartial investigation of disputes before resorting to war. When his past leadership in the Democratic party entitled him to the first place in Wilson's cabinet, he made it a condition of his acceptance that the President should permit him to press this plan on other governments. Although he gave himself fully to the other business of his department, still he worked hardest in the interest of his "cooling-off period" treaties. Thirty were signed before he left office, and he looked upon them as among the administration's greatest achievements.[7]

As a near pacifist, Bryan viewed the European war with horror. He believed it America's duty to prevent hostilities from spreading.

---

[6] See particularly Merle E. Curti, *Bryan and World Peace* (Northampton, Mass., 1931).

[7] Bryan and Mary Baird Bryan, *The Memoirs of William Jennings Bryan* (Philadelphia 1925), 383–394.

He made a determined effort to neutralize eastern Asia, but his chief concern was to keep the war away from America.[8] He hoped that it would be possible to prevent public sympathies from attaching themselves too closely to either side. So that Americans might hear both points of view, he personally conducted the negotiations that kept the two German radio stations in operation.[9] He persuaded the President to discourage banks from lending money to belligerent governments. "[E]xpressions of sympathy are disturbing enough when they do not rest upon pecuniary interests," he wrote Wilson, "—they would be still more disturbing if each group was pecuniarily interested in the success of the nation to whom its members had loaned money." [10] From the very beginning, he regarded it as the paramount object of American policy to escape involvement in the conflict.

Lansing differed from the Secretary in both character and outlook. A trim and elegant New Yorker, just turned fifty, he had never been attached to any crusades. He had practiced law and developed some reputation as a scholar in the field of international law. His serene, handsome face and well-barbered grey mustache fitted a man who was married to the daughter of a former Republican Secretary of State, John W. Foster, and whose patron was Elihu Root, one of the deacons of conservative Republicanism. His inner values, too, were less those of the Democratic reformers around him than those of the legal guild and the New York business and financial community.[11] To him the object of diplomacy was not simply to keep the peace; it was, first of all, to uphold the purity of law and, second, to obtain advantages for American businessmen.

---

[8] See Ernest R. May, "American Policy and Japan's Entrance into World War I," *Mississippi Valley Historical Review*, XL (1953), 279–290.

[9] See *Foreign Relations, Supplement: 1914*, pp. 667–681; Haimhausen to Jagow, Aug. 8, 1914, German Foreign Ministry Archives (General); *Lansing Papers*, I, 152–157.

[10] Bryan to Wilson, Aug. 10, 1914, *Lansing Papers*, I, 131–132.

[11] See Lansing, *War Memoirs* (New York, 1935), the sketch by Julius W. Pratt in Samuel F. Bemis (ed.), *American Secretaries of State and Their Diplomacy* (10 vols.; New York, 1927–1929), X, 47–175, and especially Edward H. Buehrig, *Woodrow Wilson and the Balance of Power* (Bloomington, Ind., 1955).

His own sympathies lay entirely with the Allies, and he responded, in some degree, to considerations of national security and prestige. These acquired characteristics were to emerge more strongly as the war went on, but in its early months his interest lay chiefly in preserving the law and promoting business prosperity.

Colonel House's part in policy-making was large but not continuous. Holding no official post, the slight, taciturn Texan remained away from Washington much of the time, preferring New England in the summer and a New York apartment in the winter. Yet his influence was greater than that of any other individual.[12] With Wilson he sat for long hours, listening while the President exposed his mind. As a rule, he had already talked with others to find out what Wilson had been saying to them.[13] He gave Wilson the impression of being one with him in thought. "He had a way," Grey commented, "of saying 'I know it' in a tone and manner that carried conviction both of his sympathy with, and understanding of, what was said to him."[14] The colonel was able, therefore, to offer suggestions that seemed mere extensions of the President's thinking. Wilson often took these suggestions as his own ideas or trusted the colonel with blank commissions to act for him. In American diplomacy, the hand was sometimes the hand of Wilson while the voice was that of House.

The colonel's views on foreign policy were quite different from those of Wilson's official advisers. They may, indeed, have been quite unlike Wilson's own. With so adroit a dissembler as House, it is

[12] Editorial comment in Charles Seymour, *The Intimate Papers of Colonel House* (4 vols.; Boston, 1926–1928) offers the best discussion of House yet penned. See also Seymour, *American Diplomacy during the World War* (Baltimore, Md., 1934), Arthur D. Howden-Smith, *Mr. House of Texas* (New York, 1940), an unilluminating volume by the colonel's onetime secretary, George S. Viereck, *The Strangest Friendship in History: Woodrow Wilson and Colonel House* (New York, 1932), and Alexander L. and Juliette L. George, *Woodrow Wilson and Colonel House: A Personality Study* (New York, 1956).

[13] Memorandum of a conversation with Henry Morgenthau, Nov. 18, 1928, in the Private Papers of Ray Stannard Baker, Division of Manuscripts, Library of Congress.

[14] Grey, *Twenty-five Years*, II, 125.

difficult to distinguish what he said in earnest from what he merely said for effect. The total impression given by his voluminous diary is that he was much more European than American in his diplomatic thinking or, at any rate, more Rooseveltian than Wilsonian. Although he seemed to accept the President's vision of a world permanently at peace and steadily progressing, his private notations indicate that he conceived of rivalries and conflicts as inherent in international relations. He anticipated antagonism between Russia and the west, for example, if Germany should be wholly defeated, and he believed the United States to be protected from violence only by the coincidence of British and American interests and by the balance of power in Europe. How he arrived at this Metternichian conservatism from a background in cotton trading and county politics remains a mystery. A French writer has remarked that he is less accurately described as "the Talleyrand from Texas" than as one who would pass in Texas for a Talleyrand. An accomplished English diplomat, on the other hand, judged his "the best diplomatic brain that America has yet produced." [15] As a result of his almost European outlook, in any case, he saw his country's diplomatic objectives in wartime as, first, the preservation of Britain's friendship and, second, the enlargement of America's relative power and influence.

Wilson held, of course, the determining position. Whatever Bryan, Lansing, or House might advise, the President was usually the only one who could make a final decision. The mind of this frail, iron-jawed New Testament prophet was the most enigmatic of the four. He was at least as subtle and complex as House, and his character and outlook were full of paradoxes. With some of his associates he could be a cold, stern Presbyterian divine. With others he could be warm, jolly, and even romantically sentimental. In public life he could alternate between utterly unrealistic moral fervor and ruthless practicality. His leading biographer ends an extended character summary by writing, "Being neither mind reader nor psychiatrist, the biographer can only agree with Colonel House that Wilson

[15] Pingaud, *Histoire diplomatique,* II, 244; Harold Nicolson, *Peacemaking, 1919* (new edition, London, 1945), 11.

was 'one of the most contradictory characters in history.' " [16]

One central characteristic of his thought, clearly, was its moralism. He was, the same biographer writes, "not only a man of ideas; he was, even more importantly, a citizen of another invisible world, the world of the spirit in which a sovereign God reigned in justice and love. . . . Mankind, he felt, lived not only by the Providence of God but also under His immutable decrees; and nations as well as men transgressed the divine ordinances at their peril." [17] For Wilson, therefore, any policy had first to meet a stern test within his own conscience.

But rightness had many aspects for him. Like Bryan he believed peace to be a virtue, and a policy could seem just to him if it simply avoided war. Like Lansing he believed in commerce. He was to say in 1916, "There is a moral obligation laid upon us to keep out of this war if possible. But by the same token there is a moral obligation laid upon us to keep free the courses of our commerce and of our finance." [18] Like Lansing, too, he believed in law. As a nineteenth-century Liberal, schooled in the writings of Bagehot, he saw law and trade as symbols of progress and the rule of law as the only alternative to tyranny on the one hand or anarchy on the other. As a result, his conscience could find merit in a policy if it seemed to protect international law or to benefit the American economy. With House's guidance, he could also see virtue in enlarging America's prestige or, euphemistically, her power to do good. Although he judged alternatives first of all by a subjective test of rightness, he weighed them also against the hard coin of moral, political, and economic advantage.

During the first month or so of war, Americans assumed, as the English did, that the war would be short. Neutrality policies were

[16] Link, *Wilson: The New Freedom*, 70. In addition to the first two volumes of Link's monumental biography, see the penetrating sketches in John M. Blum, *Woodrow Wilson and the Politics of Morality* (Boston, 1956), and H. C. F. Bell, *Woodrow Wilson and His People* (New York, 1945).

[17] Link, *Wilson: The New Freedom*, 64.

[18] Address at Topeka, Feb. 2, 1916, William E. Dodd and Ray Stannard Baker (eds.), *The Public Papers of Woodrow Wilson* (6 vols.; New York, 1925–1927), IV, 91.

expected to have a brief life. The President not only failed to fore-see the importance of neutrality issues, but also remained preoccu-pied with domestic affairs and, just at the outbreak of the war, was personally shaken by the death of his wife. He left most decisions to the Department of State. Bryan was thus able to see to it that the United States set pacifist examples, as, for one, in forbidding loans. But he, too, regarded the technical issues of neutrality as unimportant, and he allowed Lansing to shoulder most of the re-sponsibility. America's early definitions of neutrality consequently reflected the Counselor's preoccupation with law and trade.

His decision on the German auxiliary cruisers was, to be sure, in favor of the Allies. He ruled that the ships could not sail, and orders were issued forbidding any armed vessel to leave port. When the British objected that his decision would affect some of their mer-chantmen as well, Lansing obligingly drew a distinction between offensive and defensive armament which narrowed the application of the order to German ships alone. In addition, he made another ruling which forbade colliers to leave port with coal for German warships. Even though it is true that Lansing would have had to strain his legal ingenuity to arrive at any other decisions, they were so distinctly favorable to the Allies in their results that Grey referred to them later as evidence of America's "benevolent neutrality." [19]

It seems unlikely, however, that Lansing's object was to aid the Allies. The decisions were fully justified within his own conceptions of strict neutrality. He had been warned that Britain would claim payment from the United States for any damage done by German auxiliary cruisers. Though doubting if such claims would be sus-tained, he was not certain, and since legal precedent permitted the rulings that he made, he simply chose the safest and least expensive alternatives. His decisions, furthermore, contributed to American prosperity, for the United States had an interest in keeping the trade lanes as free as possible from the interference of German raid-ing squadrons. American exporters relied on British and French ships to carry their goods to Europe, and the shortage of shipping

[19] Benckendorff to Sazonov, Oct. 7, 1914, *Mezhdunarodnye Otnosheniya*, Series Three, VI, no. 370.

was acknowledged to be the most serious economic problem before the country during the early days of the war.[20] Lansing's decisions were thus in accord with the law and, at the same time, of benefit to American trade.

In a second area where he decided American policy, his actions seemed much less favorable to the Allies. He initiated the proposal for general acceptance of the Declaration of London. Ignoring the probable interest of the Allies in cutting off German imports, he asked that they preserve this monument to the dream of a world ruled by law. At the same time, of course, he also asked that they permit Americans to fill Germany's demand for scarce war commodities like cotton and metal ores. The proposal was in the interest of law and business without being in the interest of the Allies.

Lansing may not have felt that it was prejudicial to the British and French. The Asquith Liberals, after all, had been among the Declaration's authors. When asking Parliament to ratify the document, they had contended that Britain had more to gain from being able to trade as a neutral than to lose from being unable to wage a starvation campaign as a belligerent. Expecting the war to be short, Lansing may have assumed that the Cabinet would retain this frame of mind. In view of Grey's undisguised interest in preserving American friendship, he could also expect Britain to recognize that the sharply defined rules of the Declaration would minimize friction over neutral rights. "Acceptance," said the message to London, ". . . would prevent grave misunderstandings which may arise." [21] Lansing need not, in other words, have regarded his proposal as unacceptable in London.

Mingled with his concern for law and trade, indeed, there may actually have been from the outset some interest in aiding the Allies, when it could be done legally and profitably. He clearly had no thought of ultimate intervention. It was he who suggested

---

[20] New York *Times*, Aug. 3–9, 1914; *Commercial and Financial Chronicle*, XCIX (Aug. 8, 1914), p. 375.

[21] Bryan to Page *et al.*, Aug. 6, 1914, *Foreign Relations, Supplement: 1914*, p. 216. The original is in decimal file 763.72112/48A, Archives of the Department of State, National Archives, Washington, D.C. Notations on it suggest that Lansing was the actual author of the proposal.

that the President call for public impartiality "in thought as well as in action," in order, probably, to discourage criminal acts that might lead to postwar claims.[22] But not only did he decide disputed issues in favor of the Allies, he also proposed that the United States voluntarily denounce the Germans. When the open city of Antwerp was bombed, Lansing recommended protesting in some fashion this "outrage against humanity." A future bombing might injure American citizens, he contended, and the government would be better prepared to claim an indemnity if it had stated a view at the outset.[23] Some trace of emotion crept into his advice on this matter, and it may also have insinuated itself into his reasoning on issues of neutrality. Even so, his decisions were perfectly adapted to the aims of safeguarding law and promoting prosperity.

Lansing's almost single-handed direction of American policy came to an end as soon as it became evident that the war would be long. The Antwerp issue, as a matter of fact, marked the transition. Lansing made his recommendation on August 28. Bryan intervened on the next day to block it, writing to the President, "I am so anxious that we shall avoid anything that can possibly bring us into collision with the beliggerent [sic] powers that I am not sure that we should make any protest at all." Wilson decided the dispute himself, ruling "that we ought to be very slow to make formal protests, chiefly because we shall no doubt be called upon by every one of the belligerents before the fighting is over to do something of this kind and would be in danger of becoming chronic critics of what was going forward." [24] He, too, had come to anticipate prolonged hostilities and to be concerned about the long-range consequences of American policies. Although it was some time before he began to concentrate on foreign affairs, he did interest himself in questions of neutrality, and Lansing ceased to formulate policies independently.

[22] Memo by Lansing, Aug. 9, 1914, *Lansing Papers*, I, 151–152.
[23] Lansing to Bryan, Aug. 28, 1914, *ibid.*, I, 29–30.
[24] Bryan to Wilson, Aug. 29, 1914, Private Papers of William Jennings Bryan, Division of Manuscripts, Library of Congress; Wilson to Bryan, Sept. 4, 1914, *Lansing Papers*, I, 33.

Despite general recognition that the war would be long, the tendencies in American policy continued to be the same. Among the decisions reached during the autumn were at least three that materially helped the Allies and correspondingly injured the Germans. One reversed the earlier ban on loans. By permitting the extension of commercial credit, the administration made it possible for the Allies to buy increasing quantities of war supplies. A second affirmed the liberty of Americans to make and sell almost any weapons that belligerents would buy. Since the Central Powers could not import arms, this decision meant that the United States could serve as an arsenal for the Allies. The third was to make no protest against Britain's mine war zone decree. In all three instances American policy benefited the Allies.

To an even greater extent than had been true during the first months of the war, these decisions were free of any deliberate unneutrality. Since the Secretary of State was away during much of the autumn, campaigning for Democratic Congressional candidates, he took only a small part in shaping these policies, but he approved each one. They satisfied his concern for the preservation of America's peace. Lansing, now aware that the war might continue for some time, suppressed all emotion and concentrated entirely on preserving international law and advancing American trade. Since Wilson had become aware that questions of neutrality might have some future importance, he superintended the Counselor's work, applying in each instance his own inner tests of righteousness.

The reversal of the loan ban seems to have originated with Lansing. Its object clearly was to help American business. The original ban had been imposed when the administration expected a short war. With prolonged fighting in prospect, it became evident that the belligerent governments would have to do some buying on credit. Even Bryan, who had sponsored the ban, came to recognize that its continuance might be economically harmful. Before leaving Washington he evidently murmured to the French ambassador that the government's answer might be different if it were asked once again to approve of loans to belligerent governments, and Lansing, as acting Secretary, put the issue squarely before the President. If the ban were not lifted, he warned, war orders would go to Canada, Australia, and Argentina instead of America. Wilson seems to have accepted this reasoning without hesitation.[25]

It was politically desirable, of course, to find a method of reversing the policy without seeming to do so. When hints to newspapermen failed to have any effect, Lansing resorted to an unusual device. He drew up a memorandum stating that the President felt the earlier ban did not apply to commercial loans. Wilson approved this memorandum, even though the text, signed by Lansing, declared, "The above are my individual impressions of the conversation with the President, who authorized me to give them to such persons as were entitled to hear them, upon the express understanding that they were my own impressions and that I had no authority to speak for the President or the Government." [26] When bankers called at the Secretary's office, they were shown this memorandum. They went away aware that they could now negotiate the loans that had earlier been forbidden, but the change of policy had not been publicly acknowledged. When German sympathizers later criticized the reversal, indeed, the administration went so far as to deny that there had been any change. The fact was, of course, that the original doctrine had been considerably diluted.

Despite this effort at disguise, the administration's motive seems to have been nothing more than to appear consistent. There certainly was no question of acting unneutrally. At the time, the Germans favored the change as much as the Allies. The National City Bank of New York, which represented German borrowers, had denounced the earlier ban.[27] Rumor had it, just before the change, that German agents were industriously seeking a fifty-

---

[25] Lansing to Wilson, Oct. 23, 1914, *ibid.,* I, 137–140; on Bryan's actions see Report of the Special Senate Committee on the Investigation of the Munitions Industry, 74 Cong., 2 sess., Senate Doc. No. 944, part 6, p. 16; New York *Times,* Oct. 15–16, 1914; Charles A. Beard, "New Light on Bryan and War Policies," *New Republic,* LI (June 17, 1936), 177–178.

[26] Memo by Lansing, Oct. 23, 1914, *Lansing Papers,* I, 140.

[27] Hassenberg to the Deutsche Bank, Sept. 3, 1914, German Foreign Ministry Archives (General).

million-dollar loan, and though the German ambassador exerted no influence to bring about the change he was notified in advance, and he evidently raised no objection. He reported dispassionately to Berlin, "President Wilson has somewhat modified his policy on loans to belligerent governments. The realization is gradually dawning here that ready money for big trade is not to be had abroad, and that it will therefore be necessary to advance it by means of loans."[28] In his view the action was only natural. Since there was no question of its legality, Lansing and Wilson had every reason to believe that America was serving her own interests without in any way failing to perform her duty as a neutral.

The policy of permitting unlimited manufacture and sale of munitions seemed equally proper, and its initial announcement was instinctive rather than calculated. Not only was it justified by nearly all the legal precedents, it was a tradition in American practice, and no German spokesman or sympathizer complained of the policy until after the battle of the Marne. Even then, the German government merely contended that America was prolonging the war by supplying munitions to the Allies, and German agents organized publicity for an arms embargo as a step to hasten peace.

This movement nevertheless gathered force. The German-language press began to campaign for an embargo; letters appeared in many metropolitan dailies; Congressmen heard from their German-American constituents; and distinguished German sympathizers, like Professor Hugo Münsterberg of Harvard, wrote directly to the President.[29] One result was the appearance in Congress of bills providing for an embargo. Another was rumored defection from the Democratic party by Americans of German de-

[28] Bakhmetev to Sazonov, Sept. 19, 1914, *Mezhdunarodnye Otnosheniya*, Series Three, VI, no. 279; Bernstorff to Jagow, Oct. 19, 1914, German Foreign Ministry Archives (General).

[29] *Foreign Relations, Supplement: 1914*, p. 647; Bernstorff, *My Three Years in America*, 34 *et seq.*; Carl Wittke, *German-Americans and the World War* (Columbus, Ohio, 1936), 57 ff.; Clifton J. Child, *The German-Americans in Politics, 1914–1917* (Madison, Wis., 1939), 42 ff.

scent.[30] These events necessarily compelled Wilson and Lansing to review their policy.

There could be no doubt that it served America's economic interests. Not only on the seaboard but in the interior as well, Allied purchases were contributing to a revival of business. St. Louis, for example, was beginning to fill orders for boots, saddles, canned meat, and flour, as well as for the chemicals and metals of the munitions industry.[31] An arms embargo would jeopardize the position of the United States as the chief supplier for the Allies. It would therefore run counter to the administration's necessary aim of promoting prosperity. Wilson commented to House that the proposal was "a foolish one as it would restrict our plants." [32] In taking account of the economic importance of continued arms sales, furthermore, the administration would in no sense be defying the neutralism of the public. According to the *Literary Digest,* at any rate, "The idea generally held is that we are not our brother's keeper. We can make and sell what any nation wishes to order. . . . If it happens that only certain nations control the Atlantic, . . . that is not our fault or concern. Both the United States and the Atlantic Ocean have been here for a considerable time, and if any nation has not taken them sufficiently into account, it is obviously that nation's fault." [33] [Wilson and Lansing had reason to believe, in other words, that the policy of permitting unrestricted trade in munitions was both in the national interest and, at the same time, in accordance with the public will.]

For Wilson, of course, it was not always sufficient that a policy be profitable and popular; it had also to be justified on legal and moral grounds. Despite his own feeling and despite the evidence of public approval, he still asked for lawyers' opinions on the policy, and he continued to meditate it within his own conscience. The

[30] Samuel Untermeyer to Wilson, Nov. 19, 1914, Wilson Papers; *Lansing Papers,* I, 161–165; Memo by Tumulty, Nov. 9, 1914, Wilson Papers.

[31] John C. Crighton, *Missouri and the World War, 1914–1917: A Study in Public Opinion* (Columbia, Mo., 1947), 38–42.

[32] Diary, Nov. 25, 1914, Private Papers of E. M. House, Yale University Library, New Haven, Connecticut.

[33] *Literary Digest,* XLIX (Dec. 19, 1914), 1208.

legal opinions given him were decisively in support of the policy. Lansing advised not only that toleration of the arms trade was lawful but that any contrary course would violate international practice. The United States, he contended, would be altering the conditions of war; it would, in a sense, be changing the rules in mid-game. When a group of distinguished New York lawyers expressed an identical view, the President wrote to Lansing, "I now feel fully fortified in the matter." After the German ambassador inadvertently admitted that the American policy was legally irreproachable, Wilson felt cleansed of any lingering doubt.[34]

He came, indeed, to find moral as well as legal justification for the policy. Although America's arms production went exclusively to the Allies, those nations were less prepared for war than were their enemies. If the United States were suddenly to cut off shipments, they would justly feel mistaken in having failed to arm in time of peace, and the example would be injurious to the cause of disarmament after the war.[35] Even in the short term, the fact of Allied unpreparedness seemed to lend virtue to the policy of permitting unrestricted trade in munitions. The suggestion of an embargo was, in fact, a proposal that the United States support the better armed belligerents against the less well armed, and not only Wilson and Lansing, but also Bryan, saw this point. When the Secretary was asked to comment on the embargo resolution pending before Congress, he wrote, "any action looking to interference with the right of belligerents to buy arms here would be construed as an unneutral act, not only because the effect of such action would be to assist one party at the expense of the other, but also because the purpose of the resolution is plainly to assist one party at the expense of the other." Wilson endorsed this argument wholeheartedly.[36]

Sure that it met the interests of the nation, that it commanded public support, that it conformed to international law, and that it

[34] *Lansing Papers,* I, 115–116, 166–182; *Foreign Relations, Supplement: 1914,* p. 647.
[35] *Lansing Papers,* I, 124–125; drafts in 763.72111 Em 1/25–33, State Department Archives.
[36] Bryan to Wilson, Jan. 6, 1915, Wilson Papers; Wilson to Bryan, Jan. 7, 1915, *Lansing Papers,* I, 116.

√ served moral ends, the administration could vigorously uphold the right of Americans to make and sell arms. The President and Secretary of State openly opposed Congressional moves for an embargo. They responded sharply to domestic attacks and replied with increasing heat to German and Austrian charges that the trade was one-sided.[37] They viewed their policy as right, lawful, and beneficial.

The third significant policy adopted during the autumn of 1914 was that of bowing to the British mine warfare decree. Even though Wilson and his advisers had come to expect a long war, they do not seem to have given much thought to the implications of this decree. The decision to enter no objection was made quickly, and no evidence suggests that it was ever seriously reconsidered. Although German sympathizers conducted an intensive letter-writing campaign in favor of a formal protest, the Department of State answered all such letters with stiff formality. Most of the letters were nearly identical in phrasing, and Department officials were undoubtedly suspicious of their spontaneity. Suggestions by other neutral governments of a possible joint protest were rejected with dispatch.[38] In seeking the motives for this decision, therefore, one is probably manufacturing arguments that the decision-makers themselves never bothered to work out.

It is worthwhile, nevertheless, to search out the possible motives, because this decision does contrast strikingly with that made later when the German government proclaimed a submarine war zone. On the surface the two decrees were similar. Both defined areas within which ships could not travel safely. The mine, like the torpedo, drew no distinction between contraband and non-contraband cargoes and none between neutral and belligerent status. Both decrees therefore affected the principle that neutral goods and persons should be able to move wherever they wished. Why then did Wilson and his associates take no action?

The answer probably is that acquiescence in the British decree

---

[37] *Foreign Relations, Supplement: 1915*, pp. 776–799.

[38] The letters are filed in 763.72, State Department Archives; *Foreign Relations, Supplement: 1914*, pp. 453–463.

seemed legally, morally, and economically justifiable, while acquiescence in the subsequent German decree did not. International
law with regard to mine warfare was unclear. Although the Hague
Conventions had restricted their use, mines had been recognized as
legitimate weapons. The British government might be charged
with violating the second Convention, it is true, on the ground that
it was mining the open sea, but British lawyers could contend that
this action was a mere adaptation of the Convention, intended to
make it applicable to modern warfare. There was room for argument, to be sure, but the legal issue was not so clear as it seemed
in the case of the submarine.

There was a prevailing belief, furthermore, that British morals
were better than German, at least under a Liberal government.
Wilson, Lansing, and others who might have influenced the decision were predisposed to trust Asquith and Grey, and Wilson was
to say several times that Anglo-American disputes turned solely on
matters of administration, not on questions of principle.[39] [Since
the President and his chief advisers could not view the Kaiser as
a fellow Liberal, it is not surprising that they should have felt
righteous anger at the submarine while feeling none at the British
mine.]

Yet another factor no doubt deterred a formal protest, for there
were practical disadvantages to be taken into account. Since no
tangible interests were imperiled by the mines, an American protest
would have been altogether gratuitous. It would have involved the
same risk of captiousness that Wilson had commented on when
declining to protest the German bombing of Antwerp. It might,
furthermore, have reduced America's power to defend real interests
and principles if they were subsequently endangered. A State Department official, whose views were distinctly not pro-British, advanced this argument when pressed by a Danish diplomat.[40] And
the administration also had to take account, of course, of the inher-

[39] Wilson to Lansing, Jan. 14, 1915, *Lansing Papers,* I, 266; diary, Jan. 9, 1915,
Private Papers of Chandler P. Anderson, Division of Manuscripts, Library of Congress.
[40] Memo by Brun, Dec. 28, 1914, quoting Cone Johnson, *Foreign Relations, Supplement: 1915,* p. 296.

ent dangers in challenging Britain. Wilson was mindful of 1812, and Lansing was already advising that irritation over invasions of neutral rights might reach serious proportions.[41] In contemplating any possible issue with Britain, it was necessary to look far ahead and think not only of risks to America's trade but of possible risks to her peace as well.

Of fundamental importance was the fact that American interests were not jeopardized by the British decree. The war zone was to embrace only portions of the North Sea where relatively few American vessels sailed and where American passengers were rare. Since the British government offered to safeguard ships on condition of their complying with British contraband rules, the economic and personal interests of the United States were virtually unaffected. The subsequent German decree, on the other hand, seemed to Wilson an "extraordinary threat to destroy commerce." [42] Legal and moral considerations undoubtedly had some part in causing him to respond differently to the British and German decrees. They may even have dominated his thinking. But it is still significant that the central difference in the two cases was a matter of national interest and not of either law or morality.

In all of these decisions, indeed, Wilson and Lansing could feel that they were serving the national interest and, at the same time, observing faithfully the dictates of law and morality. On one occasion, Wilson modified his policy on the munitions trade because of a legal or moral scruple. He chose to forbid the sale of disassembled submarines. Though Lansing contended that the transaction would technically be lawful, the President decided against it "in the *spirit,* at any rate, of the *Alabama* decision." [43] As a rule, however, neither Wilson nor Lansing nor even Bryan felt any doubts about the virtue and wisdom of these various policies.

This is not the place to deal with the question of whether these

---

[41] Diary, Sept. 30, 1914, *Intimate Papers,* I, 303–304; Lansing to Wilson, Sept. 27, 1914, *Lansing Papers,* I, 247–248.

[42] Wilson to House, Feb. 13, 1915, Ray Stannard Baker, *Woodrow Wilson: Life and Letters* (8 vols.; New York, 1927–1939), V, 252.

[43] *Lansing Papers,* I, 114–115.

decisions were, in fact, so calamitous as some later analysts have thought. It should be clear from the preceding chapter that they had relatively little effect on the British government. Grey did comment on the benevolence of American neutrality, but he was preoccupied with its unbenevolent aspects. He would certainly have found his own conciliatory policy more difficult to pursue if the United States had released German auxiliary cruisers, forbidden credit for Allied long-term purchases, or protested the mine war zone decree. Had the American government imposed an arms embargo, he might even have found it impossible to check a demand for some form of retaliation, and the tranquility of Anglo-American relations might have been dangerously altered. America's decisions thus contributed in some measure to the preservation of friendship. The accusation that Wilson's neutrality policies were baneful does not rest, however, on their influence in London but rather on their effect in Berlin, and appraisal of their relative insignificance in German policy must be deferred until later.

From the standpoint of American policy-makers, in any case, no ill consequences could be foreseen at the time. No one in the administration had reason to believe that it would be wrong for the new world to fatten on the follies of the old. The risk of discord with England was much more apparent than any danger of friction with Germany. It is hard to conceive of alternative courses that Wilson and Lansing might have followed in 1914 without sacrificing the national economic interest, violating their own moral codes, and deliberately rendering service to the Germans. It may not be too much to say, indeed, that the alternatives not only were unthinkable for the Wilson administration but would have been so for any other administration similarly situated.

III

The Shadow of 1812

Although there was some identity between the interests of the United States and the wishes of the Allies, the two were not always the same. Some American businessmen hoped to preserve their trade with Central Europe, and some were eager to fulfill Germany's increased wartime demand. Others wished to take advantage of Britain's preoccupation by attracting her former customers in Latin America, Asia, and neutral Europe. The administration not only felt duty bound to protect these businessmen but also to aid in enlarging American commerce. The President thought it a prerequisite to expand the merchant marine, and only Germany's idle cargo vessels were available. The aim of buying these ships and that of securing the utmost freedom for neutral commerce were both in conflict with the objectives and policies of the Allies.

The first run-in between American interests and Allied policy resulted from Britain's refusal to accept the Declaration of London. Lansing, who had sponsored the original proposal, endeavored to force the Declaration upon the British government. In the complicated exchanges of September and October, 1914, his first object was to preserve the Declaration, both as a symbol of legal progress and as a safeguard for American trade. When he found that Britain simply would not accept the Declaration in its entirety, he next tried to obtain maximum concessions for American business. Though he did not wish to anger Britain, his efforts to conserve

Anglo-American friendship were not sufficiently energetic to suit Colonel House. The colonel intervened to advise the President against being overlegalistic and to recommend that, if necessary, minor trade interests should be sacrificed; it was more important, he contended, to keep the good will of Britain. Since Wilson, from his own standpoint, was anxious lest a legal or commercial controversy arouse the public, he heeded the colonel's advice, and in the end the United States abandoned the Declaration. The episode needs, however, to be recounted in some detail.

When the United States asked for general adherence to the Declaration of London, it will be remembered, the British government had agreed, subject to "certain modifications and additions which they judge indispensable to the efficient conduct of their naval operations." According to lawyers in Washington, these modifications made deep inroads, not only into the principles of the Declaration but also into the customary rules of maritime warfare. A special secret committee, the Joint State and Navy Neutrality Board, reported that one of these reservations virtually abolished the important distinction between absolute and conditional contraband, while another applied the doctrine of continuous voyage "in an extreme form." [1] Someone in the Department of State proceeded to draw up a strong indictment of the British order-in-council, couched as an instruction for Ambassador Page, and Lansing approved it, probably after editing it himself.[2]

It was this draft instruction that Spring-Rice considered worse than Cleveland's Venezuela note, but it was, in fact, much less explosive than the sensitive ambassador thought. While it declared that the United States could neither assent to the order-in-council nor "submit to its enforcement," it threatened only claims for pay-

[1] Memo by the Joint State and Navy Neutrality Board, Sept. 5, 1914, 763.72112/184½, State Department Archives. Years later Cone Johnson told Ray Stannard Baker that he had been directed by Wilson to compose a note "with teeth in it." But this distant recollection seems doubtful since the President had as yet shown little interest in any neutrality issue. Cone Johnson to Baker, Oct. 15, 1932, Baker Papers, quoted in Baker, *Wilson*, V, 205.

[2] *Foreign Relations, Supplement: 1914*, pp. 225–232; Lansing to Wilson, Sept. 27, 1914, *Lansing Papers*, I, 247–248; Lansing, *War Memoirs*, 118–120.

ment of damages. Aside from legal arguments, furthermore, it appealed primarily to the hope of preserving Anglo-American friendship, warning of "possible misunderstandings . . . especially at the present when the relations of the two countries are so cordial and when their friendship rests upon the secure foundation of the mutual esteem and common ideals of their respective peoples." Nor was the instruction intended necessarily as a public protest. Page was to communicate its contents to Grey and leave a copy, if Grey desired, but the document was to remain merely an instruction for Page's guidance. Lansing evidently believed that the United States could make a strong plea on legal grounds, assert the hope of protecting American trade, and count on Britain to recognize the importance of being conciliatory.

House, however, disliked the Counselor's tactics. He happened to be dining with the President when the draft instruction arrived at the White House. Since Lansing asked that it be returned if possible in time for the next day's diplomatic pouch, Wilson invited the colonel to help him. As House subsequently noted in his diary:

Lansing's letter of instruction to Page was exceedingly undiplomatic, and I urged the President not to permit it to be sent. I also urged him, in spite of Lansing's protest that the letter must go at once, not to send it until further thought and a better understanding could be had on the subject. I suggested that he call Lansing over the telephone and find out something further about it. He did this but did not get much satisfaction, and he directed Lansing to send Page a despatch and later, instructions. In other words, he was sparring for time.

I then suggested that he permit me to have a conference with Sir Cecil Spring-Rice and get at the bottom of the controversy. He expressed warm approval of this plan. After this we went to bed, pretty tired and somewhat worried.[3]

On the following day, House and Wilson canceled the proposed instruction. After exhibiting it to Spring-Rice and discussing its flaws with the ambassador, House returned to the President. He had made arrangements with the White House usher for Lansing to be kept waiting in an anteroom while he gave Wilson the benefit

[3] Diary, Sept. 27, 1914, House Papers.

of his conversation with Spring-Rice. Pointing out the objectionable matter in the draft instruction, House suggested that a telegram be substituted, "giving the general heads for a friendly discussion." [4] After House had slipped out again, Wilson talked with Lansing, directing him to hold up the instruction and draft such a telegram. The Counselor returned to his office and followed the President's bidding. Asking Wilson then to examine the draft telegram, Lansing observed, "I confess I am not satisfied with it, because there seems so much to say which is not said." The President, nevertheless, endorsed the telegram after recasting it.[5]

In his emendations, Wilson sought to eliminate all threats and to re-emphasize America's desire for a friendly settlement. He stressed anew, however, the warning that American public opinion might be aroused if Britain carried out her order-in-council, and he did nothing to modify the proposal that she accept the Declaration of London without qualification. One quotation will suffice to show the character of Wilson's changes. Lansing had closed the telegram, "In presenting the substance of this instruction to Sir Edward Grey you will assure him that it is done in the most friendly spirit"; Wilson amended it to read, "you will assure him of the earnest spirit of friendship in which it is sent. The President is anxious that he should realize the terms of the Declaration of London represent the limit to which this Government could go with the approbation and support of its people."

The result of House's initial intervention was thus simply a change in the method of opening negotiations. Lansing had originally asked Wilson to approve a long instruction, itemizing the legal arguments against the order-in-council. House objected to its tone, persuaded Wilson to cancel it, and opened the negotiations informally by showing Spring-Rice the draft. Directed by Wilson to prepare a substitute, Lansing drafted a telegraphic instruction, and Wilson rounded it off with a virtual demand for acceptance of the

[4] Diary, Sept. 28, 1914, House Papers.
[5] Lansing to Wilson, Sept. 28, 1914, *Lansing Papers*, I, 248–249; Wilson's changes are evident on the file copy in 763.72112/359, State Department Archives, and in the final text, *Foreign Relations, Supplement: 1914*, pp. 232–233.

Declaration of London. The only immediate effect of all this activity was removal of the State Department's long brief. The colonel's action may have had indirect effects. It may, for example, have persuaded Spring-Rice that Britain had a friend at court; it may also, conceivably, have awakened in Wilson some distrust of Lansing's judgment. So far as the negotiation with Britain was concerned, the episode was inconsequential. The United States took precisely the position that the State Department had recommended. Objecting to the order-in-council, the government called for unconditional acceptance of the Declaration of London.

From the outset, nevertheless, the Americans made it clear that they did not intend to press this demand to the point of alienating Britain. Not only did House so assure Spring-Rice, but Lansing, in negotiating with the ambassador, took pains to show a conciliatory disposition. In all his conversations with Spring-Rice, he complained of the order-in-council because it "menaced the friendly relations existing . . . . and . . . might change the sentiment of the American people." [6] When Page and Grey agreed upon a formula that abridged the free list, it is true, Lansing found it "objectionable" and "obnoxious." [7] But Wilson refused to fight, even for the free list. He had already declared to the British ambassador, "a dispute between our two nations would be the crowning calamity," [8] and he grew restless over the dragging pace of Lansing's negotiations. He thought of 1812, when popular feeling, he believed, had made it impossible for Madison to do what he thought wisest.[9] Wilson wanted the negotiations to end before demagogues began to rant about free ships and free goods.

He had reason to believe, furthermore, that Grey was as desirous as he of an agreeable settlement. Spring-Rice had written him, "My government is doing all in its power to avoid interference with neutral trade, especially with the trade of the United States." [10] The

[6] Memo by Lansing, Sept. 29, 1914, *Foreign Relations, Supplement: 1914,* pp. 233–235; *ibid.,* 238–242; Gwynn, *Spring-Rice,* II, 235–236.

[7] *Lansing Papers,* I, 252–255.

[8] Spring-Rice to Grey, Sept. 3, 1914, Trevelyan, *Grey of Fallodon,* 355–356.

[9] Diary, Sept. 30, 1914, *Intimate Papers,* I, 303–304.

[10] Spring-Rice to Wilson, Oct. 15, 1914, *Lansing Papers,* I, 250–251.

ambassador had also conveyed Grey's personal assurance of Britain's anxiety for the maintenance of American friendship. So impressed was the President with this assurance that he immediately sent a copy of Grey's letter to Lansing. "The tone of it is so candid and sincere, and so earnest that I am sure you will wish to send our reply at once." [11] The President then summoned Lansing to the White House and guided him in the next and final stage of his negotiations with Britain.

At Wilson's direction, Lansing cabled London a summary of objections to the proposed new order-in-council, accompanying this summary with an explicit declaration of American policy. "This Government," he commented, ". . . is not disposed to place obstacles in the way of the accomplishment of the purposes which the British representatives have so frankly stated." He also remarked on how much the United States appreciated "the staunch friendship of Great Britain . . . , which it hopes always to deserve." If Britain were but to declare her nominal adherence to the Declaration of London, he went on, she would find the United States willing to accept any number of practical modifications. England could, for example, extend the definition of absolute contraband almost indefinitely. If she wished to impede a neutral's trade with Germany, she had but to proclaim that neutral's ports bases of supply for the enemy. While this latter doctrine was admittedly unprecedented, Lansing remarked, its application "would meet with liberal consideration by this Government and not be the subject of serious objection." Grey indicated a full understanding of these proposals when he exclaimed to Page, "Do you mean that we should accept it and then issue a proclamation to get around it?" [12]

This "dishonorable proposal," as Page viewed it, represented Wilson's effort at a compromise. The draft remaining in the State Department's archives indicates that the President personally wrote more than half the dispatch to London.[13] Urging Page to press

[11] *Ibid.*, 252.
[12] *Foreign Relations, Supplement: 1914*, pp. 250–252; Hendrick, *Page*, III, 182.
[13] The draft is printed in *Lansing Papers*, I, 253–255; cf. the final version, *Foreign Relations, Supplement: 1914*, pp. 250–252.

the proposal forcefully, Wilson declared, "all the British government seeks can be accomplished without the least friction with this
government and without touching opinion on this side the water
on an exceedingly tender spot. I must urge you to realize this aspect
of the matter and to use your utmost persuasive efforts to effect an
understanding, which we earnestly desire, by the method we have
gone out of our way to suggest, which will put the whole case in
unimpeachable form." [14] That Wilson was the author of this proposal was learned by Spring-Rice from Lansing, and the ambassador
wrote the President, thanking him and commenting that "the spirit
. . . will I am sure be fully appreciated by my government." [15]
Wilson had thus taken in hand the negotiations, spurred Lansing
to additional compromises for the sake of harmony, and offered
to accept the letter rather than the substance of the London rules.

It was at this point that Grey candidly unfolded to Page all the
factors making Britain's adherence to the Declaration nearly impossible. The Foreign Secretary offered his final draft of an order-
in-council, containing many concessions to American demands.
Page reported these concessions to be all that Britain could yield.
In an urgent message, "to be deciphered Lansing alone and
shown to the President," the ambassador warned that persistence
by the United States would "alienate the two Governments and
peoples for a generation." [16] In the meantime, Spring-Rice also
cautioned the President, "If the United States protest, we shall either
have to issue the proclamation in spite of the protest or abandon
all hope of carrying out measures which are absolutely essential to
our very existence." [17]

After Wilson had conferred with the Counselor about these
ominous messages, Lansing returned to his office and wrote regretfully:

It seems to me that in view of the rigid attitude of the British Government further attempts to obtain an agreement on the Declaration of

[14] Wilson to Page, Oct. 16, 1914, *ibid.*, pp. 252–253.
[15] Spring-Rice to Wilson, Oct. 16, 1914, Wilson Papers.
[16] Oct. 20, 1914, *Foreign Relations, Supplement: 1914*, pp. 255–256.
[17] Spring-Rice to Wilson, Oct. 20, 1914, Wilson Papers.

London would be useless. We must, therefore, stand on the rules of international law which have been generally accepted without regard to the Declaration. . . . The great loss is the failure to have a definite code, which will undoubtedly be the source of numerous controversies.

It is to be regretted that in spite of all that has been done, the purpose of the negotiation has failed.[18]

In a message to Page, approved by Wilson, the Counselor notified the British government that the United States would cease to uphold the Declaration of London and would in future insist only upon its rights under traditional international law.

In all of this negotiation the attitude of the United States was an uneasy amalgam of the views of Lansing, House, and Wilson. Though Lansing wished to avoid open conflict with Britain, he was willing to run the risk of controversy in the interests of law and trade. He felt that one decisive struggle at the outset was preferable to a number of little battles later on. House, on the other hand, opposed any open contest. It was his view that the preservation of Anglo-American friendship outweighed other considerations. Though Wilson seemed ultimately to take this latter view, he stressed throughout the danger of public excitement. Had it not seemed urgent to end the controversy before inflammatory speeches and editorials began to appear, he was prepared to press the British unrelentingly until they accepted the law, as he understood it, and agreed to spare American trade. Despite the sacrifice of the Declaration of London, which seemed to Grey so gratifyingly conciliatory, American maritime policy remained undefined and ambivalent.

The necessity for defining a policy became increasingly acute. Under the unrepealed contraband decrees, Britain held up a number of American cargoes. Copper destined for Italian ports was halted on the ground that the consignees were probably acting for the Germans. Meat products, stopped en route to the Netherlands, were held in Liverpool, where they slowly began to spoil. Alto-

---

[18] Desk diary, Oct. 20, 1914, Private Papers of Robert Lansing, Manuscripts Division, Library of Congress; Lansing to Wilson, Oct. 20, 1914, *Lansing Papers,* I, 255–256.

gether innocent cargoes were detained while British inspectors conducted a meticulous search for hidden contraband. All shippers
were inconvenienced by the Royal Navy's insistence on conducting
visit and search in British ports rather than on the high seas. Quite
apart from these acts of interference with American trade, the
British government was imposing a set of imperial embargoes on
strategic items like tungsten and graphite and thus was preventing
American manufacturers from obtaining essential imports. Though
the economic losses were offset by Allied purchases, it seemed that
American interests were being subjected to an unending series of
small injuries.

Not only was this damage enough in itself to provoke the government, but it gave rise to some public demand for action. Injured
exporters and shippers addressed vigorous complaints to the Department of State. The meat packers indulged in extensive telegraphic
protest. The copper interests were reported by the British ambassador to be very active in Washington. Nor were these business
interests alone, for German agents and German-Americans, frustrated in other aims, sought to create a public clamor for some
expression of resentment against England.[19] Within the administration it could be assumed that these outcries appealed to latent
Anglophobia in the public at large. Real and potential pressure
from public opinion thus contributed to a feeling that some action
was urgently necessary.

The only possible form for such action was a note of protest,
charging Britain with infringements of international law. The
method of pleading individual cases was tried without result. Not
even strong language availed. One message, for instance, described
British practices in visit and search as "wrongful and unjustifiable
[acts] . . . to which this Government explicitly objects and for
which it denies there is any international right." [20] But no satisfactory response emerged from London. Another method tried with-

[19] The packers' telegrams are in 300.115, State Department Archives; Spring-Rice
to Grey, Oct. 5, 1914, Gwynn, Spring-Rice, II, 237–238; Child, German-Americans
in Politics, 47.
[20] Foreign Relations, Supplement: 1914, pp. 353–354.

THE SHADOW OF 1812 63

out success was that of confidential negotiation, but the only compromise suggested by the Foreign Office involved surrender of the
claims of American shippers in return for a relaxation of the imperial embargoes.[21] Since neither device yielded any promise of
satisfaction for the injured parties or for public opinion, there remained only the recourse of a formal published protest.

The preparation of this protest brought out all the still unrecon-
ciled differences that existed within the administration. Lawyers
in the Department of State were willing to make sharp demands
on Britain. Solicitor Johnson evidently prepared a very strong indictment. Although his draft is missing from the archives, it seems
likely that Lansing edited it before it went to the White House.
It probably contained no threat except one of prolonged litigation,
but it appears nevertheless to have carried a sharp demand for
repentance and reparation. It seems, in other words, to have resembled earlier documents from Lansing's pen in that it aimed
chiefly at defending law and trade.

The first dissent was registered implicitly by the Secretary of State.
Though Bryan sympathized with the lawyers' indignation, he was
still more interested in peace than in either law or trade. Forwarding
the draft note to Wilson, he indicated some concern over the danger
that it might lead to serious controversy, and he all but apologized
for advising the President to approve it. "I think," he wrote, "in
view of the increasing tension there is on the subject it is well for
us to put this Government's views in definite form so that in case
inquiry is made as to what has been done it will be manifest that
we have exerted ourselves to the utmost to bring about a lessening
of the hardships imposed upon neutral countries." [22] He seemed
willing to enter a protest for the record but not to insist that its
demands be complied with.

The second dissent came from Wilson who, on this occasion,
intervened to protect Anglo-American friendship. Although House
was at his side once again, the President seems to have acted on his
own impulse. As the colonel recorded in his diary, Wilson received

[21] *Ibid.*, 356, 358.
[22] Dec. 17, 1914, *Lansing Papers*, I, 257.

the State Department draft and invited House to help him edit it:

> The despatch was crudely written, and . . . [the President] said, "I
> can see we will have to rewrite this." He took his pencil and began
> to make corrections. Before he had finished one page he became tho-
> roughly out of patience and threw his pencil down saying, "It is not
> right to impose such a task upon me. They have not written good and
> understandable English, much less writing it in a way to avoid giving
> offense." He sent the document back to the State Department, re-
> questing me to see Spring-Rice and attend to the note verbally, telling
> him that the despatch would follow later.[23]

To revise both the language and tone of the note required another
week. Lansing assumed responsibility for the changes, but he conferred with Bryan every day.[24] In the meantime, House followed
Wilson's instructions and talked with Spring-Rice, explaining Wilson's earnest wish to have Britain release American copper. Spring-
Rice thought it ironic, as he wrote later, that an "Administration,
which had survived the subjugation of Belgium and the ruin of
Mexico, should now be so completely upset by the capture of a
cargo of copper owned by Mr. Guggenheim." He thought release
of the cargoes might nevertheless be possible, and after discussing
with House the terms of the proposed State Department protest,
he indicated no apprehension for Anglo-American friendship.[25]
When Lansing sent Wilson a final revision of the note, the President made only a few textual changes and approved its dispatch.[26]

The note retained some vigorous arguments, but more striking
was its wordy cordiality. It was being sent "in the most friendly
spirit and in the belief that frankness will better serve the continuance of cordial relations between the two countries than silence."
The British government was assured that "It is with no lack of
appreciation of the momentous nature of the present struggle in
which Great Britain is engaged and with no selfish desire to gain
undue commercial advantage that this Government is reluctantly

---

[23] Diary, Dec. 18, 1914, House Papers.

[24] Desk diary, Lansing Papers.

[25] Diary, Dec. 18, 1914, House Papers; Gwynn, *Spring-Rice,* II, 250; Diary, Dec.
29, 1914, *Intimate Papers,* I, 314.

[26] 763.72112/545A, State Department Archives.

forced to the conclusion that the present policy of His Majesty's Government toward neutral ships and cargoes exceeds the manifest necessity of a belligerent." The United States made no demands on Britain but merely asked for information or recommended reconsideration of some British policies.[27]

Although the process of drafting this protest had brought the administration no nearer to a clear policy, the need for definitions became considerably less acute. Partly as a result of House's efforts, the British government received the protest without annoyance. The British press greeted it calmly and in some quarters even with approval. Since Grey proceeded to release detained cargoes, to purchase copper, and even to relax some imperial embargoes, the number of possible issues between Washington and London dwindled. When Grey eventually replied to the protest, Lansing advised a fresh American note, but Wilson thought otherwise. As he remarked to Chandler Anderson, another State Department lawyer, he saw "no very important questions of principle involved in the differences between the two governments." [28]

Anglo-American friendship seemed to survive in good health. Not even the carefully contrived *Wilhelmina* case disturbed the surface calm. The United States did ask that the ship be allowed to carry its cargo of foodstuffs to Germany, and this request represented a fundamental challenge to the Allied policy of starving the enemy. When the ship was captured, however, the British government cited a recent Prussian decree as evidence that all imported food was in fact treated as government property, and the United States accepted this argument and declined to make a public issue over the seizure.[29] Other issues had seemed similarly to settle themselves, and Wilson was convinced that little remained besides administrative problems. No one in the administration saw the differences with England as moral issues.

[27] *Foreign Relations, Supplement: 1914*, pp. 372–375.
[28] *Lansing Papers*, I, 261–266; diary, Jan. 9, 1915, Anderson Papers.
[29] *Foreign Relations, Supplement: 1915*, pp. 313–314, 317–318, 335–337; diary, Feb. 22, 1915, Anderson Papers; for details see J. C. Crighton, "The *Wilhelmina*: an Adventure in the Assertion and Exercise of American Trading Rights during the World War," *American Journal of International Law*, XXXIV (1940), 74–88.

The apparent tranquillity of British-American relations was obviously due to many causes. Colonel House's periodic interventions undoubtedly contributed toward preventing friction. Of at least equal importance was the predisposition of both Wilson and Lansing to trust the British Liberals and to give them the benefit of any moral or legal doubts. Of even more importance, perhaps, was Wilson's fear that a controversy might inflame the public and generate pressures which he would be unable to control. This fear, which was more than shared by his Secretary of State, induced the President to procrastinate, compromise, and avoid hard and fast declarations that might produce later trouble. The result was that Anglo-American issues were not settled; they simply were not sharply drawn.

It is hard to escape the conclusion, however, that the primary cause for this apparent tranquillity was the fact that Britain did so little damage to Americán interests. It was possible for Wilson to view legal differences as technicalities, to trust in British morality, and to evade public controversy because he was so rarely confronted with a serious threat to American trade. Grey's insistence on minimum interference with American commerce, his provisions for expeditious handling of American cargoes, and his policy of buying suspected contraband instead of merely seizing it, achieved their intended effect. Although other factors contributed to the preservation of Anglo-American friendship, none was more important than the conciliatory policy of the British government.

That controversies involving more important American interests might have led to dangerous friction is evidenced by the one issue that did cause serious dispute. The possibility of America's buying German merchant vessels, it will be recalled, had caused the British government some concern during the war's earliest weeks. It was feared not only that such a transaction might help Germany financially but that a government-owned ship of the United States might run afoul of the Royal Navy and thus create a very dangerous political issue. Grey felt it necessary to oppose any move toward purchase of German ships. Wilson, on the other hand, became in-

creasingly eager to form a government-owned merchant marine and
to enlarge the amount of tonnage available to American exporters.
In his enthusiasm he disregarded international law, discounted
moral aspects of the question, and focused almost entirely upon the
twin objects of frustrating domestic opposition and increasing national prosperity. The result was an issue between the British and
the United States more serious than any other that arose during the
first year of war.

Wilson was naturally concerned over the war's effect on American trade. He recognized at the outset of the war that the economy
was menaced by a sudden shortage of shipping. The largest part
of America's exports was normally carried by foreign vessels, and
pre-emption by belligerent governments, added to the timidity of
shipowners, reduced the number of available bottoms. The shortage
came, furthermore, at a critical time, for the summer harvests were
just beginning their journey to the European market. Fifty million
bushels of wheat were reported to have piled up at Atlantic wharves
during the first weeks of the war.[30]

Although the shortage of vessels was temporary, it was followed
by an equally serious surplus of tonnage, accompanied by sharp
fluctuations in freight rates and insurance premiums. Shipowners
had hesitated at first to load their vessels, and uneasy underwriters
had set high rates. When the British and American governments
swiftly offered cheap war risk insurance and the British fleet swept
the seas of commerce raiders, these shipowners lost their hesitancy
and began to pile cargoes on board. In the meantime, competition
arrived. Ships that ordinarily carried war goods like coal began to
load wheat and cotton; others came from the Baltic and North Seas
to the Atlantic, looking for new business. As a British naval historian writes, "The result was a glut of tonnage both on the Welsh
and American freight markets. . . . Not only were charters difficult
to obtain, but freights fell to such an extent that many owners began
to lay up their vessels on arrival as an alternative to running them
at a loss." [31] Alternations between shortage and plenty and unpre-

[30] New York *Times*, Aug. 14, 1914.
[31] Fayle, *Seaborne Trade*, I, 194.

dictability in freight rates provided unsatisfactory conditions for the growth of American war trade.

The President looked about for measures that might remedy this situation. Confronted with the initial shortage, he proposed the expedient of permitting re-registration under the American flag of vessels owned by American citizens which had theretofore flown foreign flags.[32] Although this proposal was enacted into law, the number of ships affected proved to be relatively few. In the meantime, the long-range problem had become apparent, and the Secretary of the Treasury had suggested an altogether different approach. He recommended that the President ask for legislation creating a government corporation to build and buy ships and to operate these at fixed minimum rates.[33] The immediate purpose of this legislation would be to permit purchase of the fifty-four German ships lying idle in American ports. Wilson, indeed, referred to these as "probably the only ships we could buy for the service." [34] Yet he responded enthusiastically to the Secretary's suggestion and promptly arranged for introduction of an appropriate bill.

The ship purchase bill met serious resistance. The British and French governments made their opposition vehement and explicit. Private shipping corporations and their financiers denounced the bill as socialistic. On Capitol Hill, Republicans and dissident Democrats organized an effective opposition.[35] So effective was it, indeed, that the bill failed to come to a vote before the autumn adjournment. Although the President pleaded for its passage at the next session of Congress, he was unsuccessful. The House approved it 215–121, but filibusters and similar tactics prevented its success in the Senate.[36] Not until September, 1916, more than two years

[32] Baker, *Wilson*, V, 107–112; W. G. McAdoo, *Crowded Years* (Boston, 1931), 294–297.

[33] McAdoo to Wilson, Aug. 14, 1914, Wilson Papers.

[34] Wilson to McAdoo, Nov. 8, 1914, *ibid.*

[35] *Foreign Relations, Supplement; 1914,* pp. 485–503; Baker, *Wilson*, V, 113–115; New York *World*, Aug. 22–25, 1914; John A. Garraty, *Henry Cabot Lodge* (New York, 1953), 307–308; Elihu Root to Lord Bryce, March 1, 1915, quoted in Charles C. Tansill, *America Goes to War* (Boston, 1938), 568.

[36] New York *Times*, Jan. 5, Jan. 22, Jan. 24, Jan. 28, Feb. 2, Feb. 10, Feb. 12, Feb. 17–20, 1915; Baker, *Wilson*, V. 120–137.

after Wilson's initial proposal, was a ship purchase law enacted.

Owing to this obstruction of the President's wishes, the diplomatic issue never became so acute as it might have. The British government was not placed in the position of having to seize a vessel owned by the United States government. The only near crisis occurred when Britain refused to allow free passage for the *Dacia,* but the danger was averted by Grey's expedient of having the vessel seized by the French. Grey's apprehensions, nevertheless, were entirely justified, for Wilson was, in fact, committed heart and soul to the ship purchase plan. The President did offer some comfort to those who expressed fear of a diplomatic controversy. "[W]e are very keenly alive to the difficulties we might get into if ships were purchased from the belligerents," he wrote to one, "and shall be very slow to do anything that involves such dangers."[37] And he allowed House to reassure Spring-Rice that the United States would not transfer money directly into the German war treasury. The plan, House reported, was to buy ships with long-maturing Panama bonds.[38] In all his statements, however, the President dealt only with the abstract question of transfer of ownership, declaring repeatedly that the ship purchase plan involved no greater risks than had the earlier re-registry plan. He did not touch upon the danger of a government-owned vessel's being seized, thus creating an issue that could neither be postponed nor compromised.

The President firmly upheld the right of the government to own and operate an ex-German ship. If the British were to seize such a ship, he declared, they would be guilty of "unjustifiable and highhanded action."[39] Despite conflicting opinions from his legal advisers, he insisted that America's right to buy German ships was "susceptible of clear establishment in any impartial tribunal."[40] Nor did he look upon it as a legal issue alone, for he regarded it domestically as a question which divided true Americans, on the one hand, from selfish reactionary interests, on the other. He de-

[37] Baker, *Wilson,* V, 130.
[38] Diary, Sept. 20, 1914, House Papers.
[39] Wilson to Lansing, Aug. 22, 1914, Baker, *Wilson,* V, 114.
[40] Wilson to C. W. Eliot, Feb. 18, 1915, *ibid.,* 131.

nounced opponents of his plan for seeking "to defy the nation and prevent the release of American products to the suffering world which needs them more than it ever needed them before." [41]

Though Wilson employed these legal and moral arguments to reinforce his stand, he placed chief emphasis upon the fact that his ship purchase plan would serve America's economic interests. Exhorting the Congress, he declared, "The government must open these gates of trade and open them wide." The want of a government merchant marine, he wrote to the Speaker of the House, was a "great impediment to the shipment of our goods." And he lamented that the consequence of the Senate's inaction was "infinite damage to the business of the United States, to farmers, to laborers, to manufacturers, to producers of every class and sort." [42] It was the national economic interest that Wilson wished to serve, and the legal or moral issues were subsidiary.

On an issue thus involving the nation's economic interests, Wilson was willing to risk controversy with the Allies. Before making his second appeal to Congress, it is true, he had been advised by Lansing that the British government would probably yield. [43] When he discovered that Lansing had been in error, however, he did not in any way diminish his effort to obtain passage of the law. Nor was he deterred by other lawyers who insisted strongly that the ship purchase plan was contrary to international law. He seemed, indeed, to resent such legal advice. [44] Assuming his plan to be very much in the national interest, he tended to disregard its legal aspects, and he was willing to risk exciting public passions.

It is pointless to speculate on the possible consequences had Wilson secured his law and had it created specific issues between the United States and Britain. The situation would at least have been

[41] *Public Papers*, III, 241–242.
[42] *Ibid.*, 220; Baker, *Wilson*, V, 120, 133.
[43] *Lansing Papers*, I, 107–109.
[44] Lansing to Wilson, Oct. 19, 1914, enclosing memoranda by C. Johnson, E. Wambaugh, and the Joint State and Navy Neutrality Board, 195.1/148½, State Department Archives; desk diary, Oct. 20, 1914, Lansing Papers.

charged with uncertainty, for Wilson would already have staked America's prestige on a successful outcome. The possibility of procrastination, compromise, or evasion would have been much less than was the case in maritime issues that did arise. In any event, the risk was there, and Wilson was prepared to chance it in order to further the nation's economic interest. The episode reinforces the impression that Anglo-American friendship was protected by Grey's policy of safeguarding American trade. Although it does not in any sense demonstrate that friendship was preserved by Grey alone, it does suggest that the other factors making for harmony might have been ineffective if American interests had been allowed to suffer greater injury.

IV

A Healing Peace

One American policy had little or no relation to economic interests. The United States government wished to help restore peace.
Wilson earnestly wanted to mediate. House shared and encouraged
this ambition, while the Secretary of State became almost obsessed
with it. Although Lansing was less keen than his associates, he kept
his reservations to himself.[1] Mediation came, as a result, to seem
a cherished aim of America. Since the Allies were in no position to
cooperate, there was continuous danger of a moral falling-out. If
the British should seem to oppose peace, the President's trust could
be irreparably shaken. Disputes over trade might turn into issues
of principle, and relations between Washington and London might
become very sore indeed.

It was nearly two years, however, before the peace issue began
to impair cordiality. In the interval the American ambition served,
paradoxically, to maintain harmony rather than to disturb it. Colonel House was partly responsible, for the President made him his
principal agent. The colonel so defined his mission as to put the
preservation of Anglo-American friendship ahead of the achievement of peace. Grey meanwhile handled both the Americans and
the Allies with dexterity, candor, and subtlety. More important still,
the German government discouraged American mediation and thus

[1] He did confide in his father-in-law, former Secretary of State John W. Foster,
for Foster wrote him on Sept. 16, 1914: "I agree with you that the Allies will not
agree to any peace negotiations unitl Germany is beaten so thoroughly that she
cannot again be the disturber of the peace of the world." Lansing Papers.

sacrificed its opportunity to drive a wedge between the United States and Britain.

It was some time before Colonel House became the director of America's mediation effort. At the outbreak of hostilities the President tendered his good offices, even though the colonel advised against it.[2] Wilson was disappointed by the rejection of his offer, but he did not lose hope. Bryan meanwhile remained watchful for any opportunity to mediate, and the President allowed him virtually a free hand. Just as during the early weeks maritime matters remained in the hands of Lansing, so peace questions were largely left to Bryan.

America's policy, as Bryan defined it, was simply to help restore peace. He did not believe that the terms should concern the United States, nor did he care whether the peace preserved a balance of power or left one nation dominant over the others. His government's only interest, he held, was to bring the bloodshed to an end as quickly as possible, restore peacetime conditions for American business, and remove from his countrymen the temptation of emotional involvement. His aim was to bring peace at any time and on any terms.

He made his first practical attempt in September, 1914, when the war was in its second month. The German ambassador, Count von Bernstorff, had remarked that his government stood ready to consider a peace proposal. Oscar S. Straus, a former ambassador to Turkey, heard Bernstorff make this statement in the course of a dinner party. He asked if he could relay it to Bryan. When the ambassador consented, Straus went immediately to the Secretary. Bryan thereupon called in Bernstorff and asked for confirmation. When the ambassador repeated his declaration, Bryan went at once to the White House, where the President gave him permission to communicate with the American representatives in Berlin, London, and Paris, to determine if there existed, in fact, any opportunity for mediation.[3]

[2] *Intimate Papers*, I, 278–279, 282–283.
[3] Oscar S. Straus, *Under Four Administrations* (Boston, 1922), 379–386; Bernstorff, *My Three Years in America*, 58; diary of the White House usher, Wilson Papers; Bryan to Gerard, Sept. 7, 1914, *Foreign Relations, Supplement: 1914*, p. 98.

Bryan handled the affair with surprising caution. Instead of sending an appeal for peace, he merely reported the facts, commented on the President's willingness to act, and asked for the ambassadors' opinions. In the meantime he conferred with the British and French representatives in Washington, asking them to outline the Allied terms of peace. He tried, too, to keep rumors of these queries from leaking out. Since reporters infested not only the corridors but even the mail and cable rooms of the State-War-Navy Building, he was unsuccessful, and hints did reach the newspapers.[4] He had done his best, however, to act quietly and tactfully.

The entire effort failed. It had started from a false premise, since the German ambassador had not been acting under instructions. Though Bernstorff had encouraged Bryan, he had not even reported the fact to Berlin. He cabled only, "Straus sounded me out on an American mediation attempt. . . . I contained myself without refusing, for I wanted the odium of refusal to fall upon our enemies."[5] As a result, Bryan's messages not only drew disappointing responses from London and Paris, but they also brought from the German Foreign Office a declaration obviously intended to close off further discussion. Although the Secretary contemplated going on with the effort, Wilson and Lansing judged it best not to do so.[6]

When no subsequent opportunity developed, Bryan began to urge the President to take the initiative. He suggested an open appeal. Neither side could win, he wrote; all accused their enemies of starting the war; all professed a desire for peace. Wilson ought therefore to proclaim, "the responsibility for *continuing* this war is just as grave as the responsibility for *beginning* it," and ask for immediate peace talks.[7] Undiscouraged by the President's gentle rejection of

[4] Gwynn, *Spring-Rice*, II, 221–223; Bryan to Wilson, Jan. 31, 1915, Correspondence between Secretary of State William Jennings Bryan and President Woodrow Wilson, State Department Archives; New York *Times*, Sept. 8, 1914.

[5] Bernstorff to Jagow, Sept. 7, 1914, German Foreign Ministry Archives (Secret Mediation).

[6] *Foreign Relations, Supplement: 1914*, pp. 100–101, 104; Wilson to Lansing, Sept. 17, 1914, *Lansing Papers*, I, 8; Lansing to Wilson, Sept. 18, 1914, *ibid.*, 9.

[7] Sept. 19, 1914, Bryan Papers.

this proposal, Bryan continued to suggest a peace appeal. He spoke of it publicly on October 15, a day of prayer for peace set aside by Wilson at Bryan's instance, and he sent an abstract of his speech to the White House.[8] When various Latin American representatives began to talk of joint mediation, the Secretary asked the President if he wished to make an appeal on his own or in company with other governments. Although Wilson replied that he wished to wait until his good offices were requested by the belligerents, Bryan did not abandon the idea that the United States ought to press for peace negotiations.[9]

On December 1, well after the Congressional election, he addressed a fresh exhortation to the President. In addition to being desirable in itself, he contended, the restoration of peace had come to be necessary as a matter of national interest. The war was injuring the cotton trade and disrupting business. It was also interfering with the administration's domestic missions. "Delicate questions are constantly arising in connection with our efforts to preserve neutrality," wrote the Secretary. "These may not only affect our relations with the belligerents but they disturb political conditions in this country and threaten to turn attention from our economic problems." It was unwise to wait for a call from the warring nations, he argued; the President should demand peace at the earliest possible moment, no matter what the terms might be.[10]

After the Straus affair, Wilson ceased to be exclusively dependent on Bryan. Colonel House told him that Bryan had mismanaged that negotiation, and some newspapers ridiculed the Secretary.[11] When the colonel suggested undertaking private talks with the various ambassadors, the President approved. House also proposed writing to an acquaintance in Germany. He had received a letter from Arthur Zimmermann, the German Undersecretary of State, acknowledging a prewar note to the Kaiser, and the colonel asked Wilson if this letter might not be answered in such a way as to

[8] Oct. 4, 1914, Wilson Papers.

[9] Bryan to Wilson, Oct. 7, 1914, *Lansing Papers*, I, 9; Wilson to Bryan, Oct. 8, 1914, Baker, *Wilson*, V, 291.

[10] Wilson Papers. A slightly different version is printed in *Lansing Papers*, I, 10–11.

[11] Diary, Sept. 28, 1914, House Papers; New York *World*, Oct. 9, 1914.

encourage future correspondence about mediation. The President not only consented but encouraged his friend to do so. "He thought," House noted in his diary, "to emphasize his mediation proposal and let . . . [Zimmermann] know that we stood ready at any time. He planned to get in direct touch with the Kaiser through Zimmermann, thinking perhaps, the Kaiser would prefer to reach the President in an unofficial way through me rather than through our Ambassador." [12]

Not only did Wilson approve of private negotiations by House, but he helped to conceal them from the Secretary of State. After House had composed the letter to Zimmermann, the President forwarded it to the Department of State, asking that it be sent in a diplomatic pouch. He sent it under seal, writing only, "This is a letter from Mr. House to Herr Zimmermann. Mr. House met Herr Zimmermann when he was abroad this summer and promised to write to him." [13] Somewhat later Wilson confessed to House that he had not been open with the Secretary of State. "The President said," noted the colonel, "that he, Mr. Bryan, did not know that he, the President, was working for peace wholly through me, and he was afraid to mention this fact to him for fear it would offend him. He said Mr. Bryan might accept gracefully, but not being certain, he hesitated to tell him." [14]

As the President came more and more to rely on House rather than on Bryan, he accepted implicitly an entirely different concept of mediation. It is not certain that he was aware of the change. His own ideas were still far from precise. Among his papers, indeed, there is a startling document reflecting the state of his thought as of November, 1914. It is his reply to a letter from Page summarizing the peace terms talked of among British officers: Alsace-Lorraine to France, Schleswig-Holstein to Denmark, South Germany to Austria, the Austrian Slavs to Russia, indemnity for Belgium, and the German colonies "as pawns to trade in working out the details of the bargain." Wilson observed:

[12] Diary, Aug. 30, 1914, House Papers.
[13] Wilson to Bryan, Sept. 16, 1914, Wilson Papers.
[14] Diary, Dec. 3, 1914, House Papers.

My only comment at present is that what they suggested seems to me a programme which needs as its premise the practically complete defeat of Germany and not merely a stand-off fight, because it involves to a very considerable degree a dismemberment of the German Empire. But, after all, it is not the details that interest me, but the general judgment as to the prospects of the war and the general principle involved in the outline settlement.[15]

It is evident from this document that Wilson had not yet concentrated his intellect on the problem of peace.

House, on the other hand, had already developed quite definite ideas. He was convinced, for instance, that a victorious Germany would be a menace to the United States, and he sought to impress this view on Wilson. On one occasion, as he noted in his diary, "I again insisted that Germany would never forgive us for the attitude we have taken in the war and, if she is successful, she will hold us to account. I told him that I had it on fairly good authority that the Kaiser had it in mind to suggest to us that the Monroe Doctrine extend only to the Equator, which would leave Germany free to exploit Brazil and the other South American countries."[16] The colonel did not, however, favor total Allied victory. He thought that in the event of German defeat, Russia might prove a new menace. He went so far as to warn Spring-Rice "that if the Allies won and Germany was thoroughly crushed, there would be no holding Russia back."[17] He could, it is true, waver from this certainty. He once confided in his diary that mediation was best not pressed against the wishes of the Allies. "I feel," he wrote. "they are determined to make a complete job of it while they are in it, and I also feel in my heart that it is best for Germany, best for Europe and best for all the world, to have the issue settled for all time to come."[18] When Spring-Rice expressed reluctance to enter on discussions of peace, giving as his reason the advantageous military position of Germany, House set aside the objection: "In my opinion it would be a mistake to concede that Germany had any advantages

---

[15] Hendrick, *Page,* III, 166–169; Wilson to Page, Nov. 10, 1914, Wilson Papers.
[16] Diary, Nov. 25, 1914, House Papers.
[17] Diary, Sept. 20, 1914, *Intimate Papers,* I, 328.
[18] Diary, Dec. 14, 1914, House Papers.

whatsoever, and it seemed to me the proper attitude to assume was one of absolute confidence in the ultimate defeat of Germany." [19] It was House's general view, nevertheless, that the United States would profit from a peace which reduced Germany's strength but left her a power.

House believed that he had impressed these ideas upon Wilson. After describing his exhortation on the German peril, he noted in his diary that Wilson had "replied that the war was perhaps a God-send to us, for if it had not come we might have been embroiled in war ourselves." [20] He also recorded that they discussed Bryan's proposal for a public appeal for peace and considered whether American interests did, in fact, call for peace on any terms. As House's diary reports this highly important conference:

The President read a memorandum which Mr. Bryan had given him which he said he had saved to read with me. It was an earnest argument for the President to again offer his services as mediator. I was certain it would be entirely footless to do this, for the Allies would consider it an unfriendly act, and further it was not good for the United States to have peace brought about until Germany was sufficiently beaten to cause her to consent to a fundamental change in her military policy. . . . He agreed to this. [21]

House may, of course, have misinterpreted the President. Certain of Wilson's later acts suggest that he departed from these views if, indeed, he ever accepted them at all. In relation to the peace efforts of 1914–1915, however, the extent of his comprehension is immaterial. His independent thoughts were shapeless at best, and he relied on House to forward his vague but powerful ambition to mediate. In this area, the policies of House were the policies of the United States, and House took the view, in the first place that peace should not be pursued as an end in itself and, in the second place, that the aim of mediation ought to be subordinated to that of preserving Anglo-American friendship.

House was anxious, nevertheless, to bring about mediation. When

[19] Diary, Dec. 23, 1914, House Papers.
[20] Diary, Nov. 25, 1914, House Papers.
[21] Dec. 3, 1914, House Papers.

an opportunity arose to discuss peace with the belligerents, he decided to visit London, Paris, and Berlin. Despite his own views, he created a situation in which the Allies might have been forced to proclaim their opposition to the President's ambition. He also presented the Germans with an opportunity to build a moral tie between themselves and the United States.

House's expedition was prompted, like Bryan's earlier proposal, by the German ambassador in Washington. Bernstorff told him that his government was willing to encourage mediation.[22] Although the colonel recognized the reluctance of the Allies, he saw no option but to press them. When he received lukewarm encouragement from Grey, who cabled that England could not stand out against a reasonable proposal, the colonel decided to embark for London.[23] He made this decision, even knowing that it would be unwelcome. He told Wilson that he would have to use tact with the British ambassador. "I thought it was best," he noted, "to tell him I wanted to try out the Germans, and the President said, 'Of course, if you stop over in London and see the British Government in the meantime, that would be expected and could not offend the sensibilities of the British Ambassador.'" [24]

House did endeavor to smooth his reception in the Allied capitals. He held several conferences with Spring-Rice and even met on one occasion with the ambassadors of all three great Allies. The Russian described this meeting in a dispatch to St. Petersburg. In view of the paucity of documents paralleling the House diary, it is worth quoting at length. Bakhmetev wrote:

We remarked to him that a proposal to end the war through a restoration of the "status quo ante," with no reparation or guarantee, could hardly be taken under consideration, for it would only give Germany a breathing spell in which to recover from the unsuccessful war and prepare for a new one. Thereupon House replied very naïvely, he hopes to obtain a promise from the Chancellor that Germany will give up her militarism, and thus the danger of a new conflict with her will be

[22] *Intimate Papers,* I, 329, 331–332, 340–341.
[23] Diary, Dec. 23, 1914, House Papers.
[24] Diary, Jan. 13, 1915, *Intimate Papers,* I, 351.

entirely removed. Here we reminded him, if Bethmann-Hollweg has called treaties "scraps of paper"—how much trust can be put in his words, if he conveys them through a third and unofficial and personally unanswerable individual? He appeared embarrassed and assented to all we said; finally he explained it to be his mission at the desire of the President to become acquainted with "the true feelings of Germany." . . . I finally declared to him that if Germany really wants peace, she knows the way by which she can attain it—through a direct approach to the allied powers, and not through private talks and empty promises.[25]

House's own record reads:

It was rather awkward at first. Both Jusserand and Bakhmetieff were violent in their denunciation of the Germans and evinced a total lack of belief in their sincerity. They thought my mission would be entirely fruitless.

Later, I brought them around to the view that at least it would be well worth while to find how utterly unreliable and treacherous the Germans were, by exposing their false pretenses of peace to the world. That suited them better, and it was not a great while before we were all making merry and they were offering me every facility to meet the heads of their Governments.[26]

The difference between these two documents does not suggest that House's diary is an inaccurate record, but it does indicate that the colonel is not always to be trusted as an interpreter of others' moods and thoughts. In any case, the colonel had made his effort and thought he had succeeded.

He not only had to seek a friendly reception, of course, but he also had to be sure of remaining Wilson's spokesman while negotiating abroad. The obstacle was Bryan, who stood for an altogether different policy and who remained the President's official adviser. When first discussing the mission with Wilson, House advised the President to tell Bryan of the plan "and to do it with all the emphasis possible in order that Mr. Bryan might feel the impact of it and keep the matter secret." [27] When Bryan expressed disappointment

[25] Bakhmetev to Sazonov, Jan. 14, 1915, *Mezhdunarodnye Otnosheniya*, Series Three, VII, no. 8.
[26] *Intimate Papers*, I, 352.
[27] Diary, Dec. 20, 1914, House Papers.

that he had not been chosen instead, the colonel reported this reaction to the President. According to House's diary, Wilson was disturbed by Mr. Bryan's ambition, and said he believed he (Bryan) would prefer not to have peace if it could not be brought about through himself. He corrected himself after making this statement and said it was unfair to Mr. Bryan, but what he meant to say was that Mr. Bryan was so anxious to do it himself that the idea obsessed him. He declared that if necessary he would allow Mr. Bryan to resign from the Cabinet before he would let him undertake such a delicate mission, for which he felt he was so unfitted.[28]

After hearing this outburst the colonel could feel reasonably sure that the President would not desert him.

On January 30, 1915, he embarked for England on the *Lusitania*.

House's mission was recognized in London to be a serious threat to Anglo-American friendship. The earlier expressions of America's mediation policy had not been so menacing. France and Russia, to be sure, had taken offense at them. Bryan's proposal in September had provoked the French Foreign Minister to comment, "France, who has bound herself to conclude no separate peace, can for her part only greet with refusal the attempt of the German Government to bring about mediation by the United States, for this attempt proceeds either from a desire to win the sympathies of Americans or from the exhaustion which Germany begins to feel." The Russian Tsar had emphatically seconded this sentiment.[29]

The British government had not been so offended by America's early mediation efforts. Grey had welcomed them at first. Expecting the war to be short, he had written to Washington, "At the first moment . . . that it could be stopped honourably on fair terms we should like it to be stopped . . . . What terms of peace would be fair would depend upon how things went." [30] By the time of Bryan's proposal, he had come to anticipate a longer war, but he was still willing to encourage the United States. "As to mediation,"

[28] Diary, Jan. 13, 1915, House Papers.
[29] Isvolski to Sazonov, Sept. 11, 1914, *Mezhdunarodnye Otnosheniya*, Series Three, VI, no. 247.
[30] Grey to Colville Barclay, Aug. 7, 1914, Grey, *Twenty-five Years*, II, 163.

he noted saying to Page, "I was favourable to it in principle, but the real question was: on what terms could the war be ended? If the United States could devise anything that would bring this war to an end and prevent another such war being forced on Europe I should welcome the proposal." [31]

When House began to talk of visiting Europe, Britain's situation had altered considerably. Grey had come to be troubled by the danger of disunity among the great Allies. Russia's sufferings had created some sentiment there for a separate peace, and the aged Count Witte was reported to be marshaling the old Germanophile faction.[32] Friction between London and Paris had meanwhile grown, and Frenchmen were reportedly jesting that Germany would fight to the last German and England to the last Frenchman.[33] There had developed the danger that if Britain encouraged the United States, she might seem to be deserting her allies, and they in turn might hasten to negotiate separately with the enemy.

Britain's own peace terms, moreover, had grown ‚increasingly numerous and complex. Not only had Britain's allies begun to talk of dividing up German and Austrian possessions, but Englishmen themselves were speaking of new colonies and reparation payments. Asquith noted that he and Grey seemed the only ones in the Cabinet who wanted no new territory for Britain.[34] Apart from postwar ambitions, furthermore, the British government had also to consider the intricate and unpleasant negotiations required by military plans. As Grey summarized for the benefit of the Russian government, "It is essential to secure the participation of Rumania and Greece in the war, if Germany and Austria make preparations for a new and stronger attack on Serbia, for she cannot defend herself alone. In addition it is necessary that the attitude of Bulgaria should be

[31] Grey to Spring-Rice, Sept. 9, 1914, *ibid.*, 119–120; cf. Imperiali to Sangiuliano, Sept. 4, 1914, *I documenti diplomatici italiani*, Series 5: 1914–1918 (1 vol. in progress; Rome, 1954—), I, no. 571.

[32] Buchanan to Grey, Nov. 12, 1914, *Mezhdunarodnye Otnosheniya*, Series Three, VI, no. 501.

[33] *The Academy*, LXXXVIII (Jan. 16, 1915), p. 33.

[34] Asquith, *Memories and Refl   ions*, II, 82.

friendly and actively helpful." [35] To attain these ends the Foreign
Secretary had to offer the property of Austria-Hungary and Turkey.
To purchase Italy's alliance he had to employ similar coinage. It
was no longer possible for Grey to state categorically that Britain's
only peace terms were reparations for Belgium and disarmament.

When Grey learned of the colonel's proposed visit, he had reason
to feel some alarm. The President obviously supported House. In
his annual message in December, Wilson had expressed hope for
"an opportunity such as has seldom been vouchsafed any nation, the
opportunity to counsel and obtain peace in the world and reconcili-
ation and a healing settlement of many a matter that has cooled
and interrupted the friendship of nations." [36] Although Page opposed House's mission just as he had earlier opposed Bryan's overtures, this fact held little consolation for Grey. The colonel's voice
was presumably that of the President himself.

Grey failed to fend off the colonel. Endeavoring to do so, he sent
a sequence of messages for House.[37] One warned the colonel against
being entrapped by German propaganda; Bernstorff, he cautioned,
could not be sincere. Another declared that whatever the Foreign
Secretary's own terms, he could not speak for the Cabinet or for the
Allies. But these gestures neither appeased nor deterred the colonel.
Germany seemed sincere, House advised, and was probably on the
verge of opening a peace drive. "[I]t would create a profound
impression," the colonel warned, "and if it was not met with sympathy by the Allies, the neutral sentiment, which is now almost
wholly against the Germans, would veer toward them." [38] Already
uncertain about the constancy of American sympathy, Grey could
hardly ignore House's determination. Nor could he disregard the
possibility that Germany meant, in fact, to sue for peace.

Grey faced a predicament. Forced to take the American overtures

[35] Buchanan to Sazonov, Jan. 20, 1915, *Mezhdunarodnye Otnosheniya*, Series
Three, VII, no. 41.
[36] *Public Papers*, III, 225.
[37] Grey to Spring-Rice, Sept. 18, 1914, Grey, *Twenty-five Years*, II, 121; diary,
Dec. 20, 1914, *Intimate Papers*, I, 341; House to Wilson, Dec. 27, 1914, House
Papers; House to Wilson, Jan. 8, 1915, *ibid.*
[38] House to Page, Jan. 4, 1915, Hendrick, *Page*, I, 424–425.

seriously, he discussed them with the Prime Minister, the British ambassador in Paris, and even with the War Office.[39] While he wished above all else to keep the United States friendly, he feared that American mediation might have dreadful results. If successful, it might produce an inconclusive peace, requiring Britain to remain forever in arms against renewed aggression by Germany. If unsuccessful but dexterously managed by German propagandists, it might generate a revulsion of feeling toward the Allies. Spring-Rice evidently stimulated his concern on this score. The ambassador's Russian colleague reported, at any rate:

> The English ambassador . . . is a very fretful and nervous man and thinks of only one thing, not to lose completely the traditional brotherly sympathy of the Americans, for he clearly perceives that the English are here the least loved of all the Allies, and it always seems to him as if the German ambassador will be able to persuade the government and public opinion that Germany is peaceful while the Allies are warlike, and that he will be able thereby to turn sympathies to Germany, and that we must, in consequence, do all that is possible to keep blame off of us.[40]

Faced with House's evident determination to visit London and Berlin, Grey found himself ensnarled. At one and the same time, he had to convince the American government of Britain's love for peace, convince allies and prospective allies of her opposition to any inconclusive peace, and convince Germans that she was willing to listen to any reasonable offers. The predicament was one that would have tried the artfulness of a Talleyrand.

Grey sought first to acquaint the American government with some of Britain's problems. Convinced that House was bent on a trip to Europe, he unfolded some of the Allies' added conditions for peace. In addition to his personal conditions, he had Spring-Rice warn House, France might want part of Lorraine and Russia would like Constantinople. But the colonel replied obtusely. "I thought that

[39] *Diary of Lord Bertie*, I, 78; Asquith, *Memories and Reflections*, II, 61; Gerald French (ed.), *Some War Diaries, Addresses, and Correspondence of the Earl of Ypres* (London, 1937), 173.

[40] Bakhmetev to Sazonov, Jan. 14, 1915, *Mezhdunarodnye Otnosheniya*, Series Three, VII, no. 8.

was something to be threshed out later," he recalled saying to the ambassador, "and that the conversations should begin upon the broad lines of an evacuation and indemnity for Belgium and an arrangement for a permanent settlement of European difficulties, including a reduction of armaments." [41]

Despairing of subtlety, Grey called in Chandler Anderson, who had been assisting Page and who was about to sail for the United States. He outlined for Anderson the problems before the British government. Asking him to carry the message to Wilson and House, Grey explained that France would require Alsace-Lorraine and also a money indemnity from Germany and that Russia would require Constantinople and the Dardanelles. [42] He did not tell Anderson that Britain had already endorsed Russia's ambition, but he indicated the strong likelihood that she would do so during the peace negotiations. Although these conditions went far beyond any which Grey had mentioned earlier, Wilson and House took them in without blinking. Wilson intimated to Anderson, indeed, that the Russian conditions pleased him. He "said in regard to Constantinople," Anderson noted, "that he had anticipated that it would either be neutralized or would be taken by Russia, and that in his opinion Great Britain's traditional policy against permitting Russia access to the Mediterranean was based on theoretical rather than practical dangers to British interests." [43] Wilson and House did not see Britain's new peace conditions as obstacles to the permanent peace for which they hoped.

Grey's second task was to prepare his allies for House's coming and for the rumors of peace that were bound to attend it. All of the Allies, of course, had heard about House's plans from their representatives in Washington. But Grey notified the French and Russians of Bernstorff's maneuvers as if disclosing fresh information. He explained the replies made through Spring-Rice: "for any negotiations about peace, the conditions are, that Belgium regain her independence and integrity and that she be paid a suitable indem-

[41] Diary, Dec. 23, 1914, *Intimate Papers*, I, 342.
[42] Diary, Jan. 9, 1915, Anderson Papers.
[43] *Ibid.*

nity. . . . His Majesty's Government also holds it essential that any
final peace must be such that it will secure not only Great Britain
but also her allies against any future attack on the part of Germany.
Finally, England would naturally have to question her allies concerning any conditions which they might impose." [44] Although
discounting Bernstorff's statements as propaganda maneuvers, Grey's
notification went on:

> Sir E. Grey is far from a desire to discourage any overture made in
> a sincere manner, which offers a promise of leading to the conclusion
> of a satisfactory peace; and if any satisfactory assurance at all is given
> that Germany truly shows a desire for peace, Sir E. Grey would then
> observe that conditions would have to be agreed upon by the Allies.
> In this case Great Britain would discuss this with Japan . . . as well as
> with France and Russia. . . . The information which has come to His
> Majesty's Government from neutral sources concerning the true opinion
> of official circles in Berlin does not testify to its peaceful character. Sir
> E. Grey is of the opinion that so long as this state of mind persists, the
> continuation of the war with the greatest possible zeal is the only sub-
> ject about which there is any useful purpose to be served by discussion.

With candor, Grey sought thus to deaden suspicions that might
arise when House came to London. He assured the Allies of
Britain's willingness to continue the war while preparing them for
any gestures he might feel obliged to make in response to pressure
from House.

As a final precaution, Grey reached a confidential understanding
with the major allies. The French government asked that the Allies
agree to reject any proposal for negotiation coming through a third
party, no matter how trustworthy. Overcoming French objections,
Grey obtained consent to the following text: "If the three allied
powers are informed by a duly authorized intermediary that Germany and Austria-Hungary genuinely desire to conclude peace, the
three powers will reply that they will consult one another in order
to settle on the conditions which they hold necessary for a suspension
of hostilities and for the restoration of a lasting peace, and that they

[44] Buchanan to Sazonov, Jan. 12, 1915, *Mezhdunarodnye Otnosheniya*, Series
Three, VI, no. 759.

will communicate directly with the German and Austro-Hungarian government [*sic*], as soon as the latter have made formal overtures for peace." [45] Although partially armed against House's visit by these agreements and by his disclosures to House and Chandler Anderson, Grey still awaited the colonel's visit with some trepidation.

To his delight, none of his fears proved justified. He had met the colonel once before and knew that he had been of some service to Spring-Rice. But Grey was surprised, on closer acquaintance, to find "combined in him in a rare degree the qualities of wisdom and sympathy." As Grey wrote later, "House left me in no doubt from the first that he held German militarism responsible for the war, and that he regarded the struggle as one between democracy and something that was undemocratic and antipathetic to American ideals. . . . I felt sure that he did not differ much from Page in his view of the merits of the war." [46] Instead of finding him an antagonist in a fencing bout over mediation, Grey discovered in House a strong partner in the effort to preserve Anglo-American harmony.

Grey felt able to disclose to House all the considerations that stood as bars to mediation. He explained the situation in the Balkans and his hope of luring Greece, Rumania, and perhaps Bulgaria and Italy into the Allied camp. Not only did House sympathize with Grey's problems, but he even mourned with him when dispatches suggested that Bulgaria might slide the other way. Grey felt able to disclose to House all his fears about Dominion conditions for peace. The Union of South Africa would probably want German colonies, he predicted, and Australia would certainly desire the German islands in the South Pacific. Although House hoped for a statement of some Allied conditions, he neither deplored nor condemned these ambitions.[47] "His judgment of men and things," Grey later observed, "was both keen and detached." [48]

Grey found, too, that the colonel was no zealot whose enthusiasm

[45] *Ibid.*, no. 764, and note 4 containing the French draft; *ibid.*, VII, no. 2.
[46] Grey, *Twenty-five Years,* II, 124–125.
[47] *Intimate Papers,* I, 363–382.
[48] Grey, *Twenty-five Years,* II, 125.

for peace might shiver the trans-Atlantic friendship. Within hours of his arrival, as House wrote in his diary, he let Grey know he "had no intention of pushing the question of peace, for . . . it could not be brought about, in any event, before the middle of May or the first of June. I could see the necessity," he noted, "for the Allies to try out their new armies in the Spring, and I could also see the necessity for Germany not to be in such an advantageous position as now, for the reason she would be less likely to make terms that would ensure permanent peace." [49] Rejoicing at the colonel's statement, Grey was able to notify his allies that the danger had proved an illusion. Since the French Foreign Minister was in London discussing the Balkan situation, Grey told him in person. He telegraphed St. Petersburg, "Colonel House does not intend to mediate, but wishes merely to obtain information about the prospects for peace." [50]

There still remained the possibility that House might go to Berlin and be there beguiled by some German peace propaganda, but the colonel soon dispelled even this fear. Lest he destroy his future usefulness, he had said at first, he ought to travel to Berlin quickly.[51] Grey and Asquith advised against too early a journey. Germany was opening an offensive in Russia, they explained, hoping to sway the Balkans; the Allies, meanwhile, had plans afoot for reinforcing Serbia and for assaulting the Dardanelles. Until the results of the German and Allied campaigns were known, they advised, House was more likely to find the Germans in a hopeful mood than in the despairing mood essential for a peace overture. He accepted their counsel and delayed for several weeks his departure from Britain.[52] When Wilson admonished him not to go too far in letting the British government plan his movements, House returned an eloquent letter. Germany was not ready to indemnify Belgium and disarm, he declared. Nor were France, Russia, and the British

[49] Diary, Feb. 11, 1915, House Papers.
[50] Buchanan to Sazonov, Feb. 14, 1915, *Mezhdunarodnye Otnosheniya*, Series Three, VII, no. 190.
[51] Diary, Feb. 13, 1915, *Intimate Papers*, I, 372.
[52] *Intimate Papers*, I, 378–380.

Dominions prepared to accept those terms alone, even if Germany consented to them. Should he leave too promptly, he warned, Britain "will probably cease to consider you as a medium." His remaining in England, he added, helped to repair British opinion of the United States. The President objected no more.[53] House postponed his departure until Grey and Asquith agreed that the time had come.

House's mission thus helped to strengthen Anglo-American friendship. Despite the direct conflict between the Allied policy of continuing the war and Wilson's eager ambition to mediate, this fact did not come sharply into view. House was managing the President's efforts, and he set the preservation of accord above the promotion of peace. Grey's skill ensured that the antagonism between Allied and American policies was not disclosed in full to Wilson. The threat of a moral breach between Washington and London was thus circumvented, but the underlying difference remained, and it was to trouble Anglo-American relations in the future.

[53] Wilson to House, Feb. 15, 1915, Baker, *Wilson*, V, 311; House to Wilson, Feb. 22, Feb. 23, 1915, Wilson Papers.

V

Germany and American Mediation

During the first months of the war the German government need not have concerned itself about the United States. Although Wilson's neutrality policies were irritating, since they made America an arsenal for the Allies, little could be done by Germany to change them. Practically the only possibility of bettering relations and perhaps acquiring American diplomatic support arose from Wilson's ambition to mediate. By encouraging this ambition the imperial government might have divided the United States from the Allies and created a basis for German-American cooperation. The possibility was remote, to be sure, but not inconceivable.

To understand why the German government made no effort to exploit Wilson's mediation ambitions it is necessary first to comprehend the peculiar structure within which policy was made. Unlike the decision-making apparatus in London and Washington, with which English and American readers are familiar, the machinery of the German imperial government is not well remembered, even in Germany. The formal powers of deciding foreign and military policies lay altogether with the executive. They were, indeed, semidivine properties of Wilhelm II, either as King of Prussia or as German Emperor. Had Wilhelm actually been such an impetuous and resolute personality as he pretended to be, he could have overridden ministers, legislative bodies, the kings and princes of the German states, and popular opinion. In foreign affairs he was limited only by the consultative powers of the

Bundesrat, and as King of Prussia he controlled twenty-one of that body's sixty-one votes.[1] As Emperor he possessed absolute control of the navy, and as Supreme Warlord he held wartime command over all German armies.

But Wilhelm was, in fact, a timid and indecisive ruler. In the *Daily Telegraph* affair of 1908, his rashness had created a threat of constitutional revolution. He suffered, as Erich Eyck puts it, an inner collapse (*seelischer Zusammenbruch*).[2] The crown had been criticized and even reprimanded by the representatives of the people. It was almost as if a pope had met contradiction from a lay convocation of Catholics, and thereafter Wilhelm lived in continuous dread of losing his prerogatives, if not indeed his throne. He virtually ceased to have a will of his own, and his thoughts came to be those of the last strong man to see him.

Chief among those under him was the Imperial Chancellor, Theobald von Bethmann Hollweg. Possessing wide executive powers under the constitution, the Chancellor also had continuous access to the throne. All departmental ministers were his subordinates and, in theory, could see or report to the Kaiser only if he approved. Nearly all diplomatic correspondence and ministerial memoranda filtered through his hands. So long as the Kaiser declined to exercise his own will, Bethmann possessed great power, but, unlike the Emperor, he suffered from an undefined dependence on parliaments and public opinion. He felt it necessary to command support in the popularly elected Reichstag, among his fellow delegates in the Bundesrat, and also at home in the Prussian Landtag. It is true that, since his policies were nominally the Kaiser's, they had some hedging of divinity. Since he himself belonged to no party, he was less open to attack than were western premiers. After the outbreak of war, moreover, it verged on the unpatriotic to criticize him or his actions. But he was still subject to the pressures and vagaries of domestic politics.

---

[1] Prussia in her own right had only seventeen votes, but the King also had the power to cast the three votes of Alsace-Lorraine, where his appointee served as governor, and the one vote of Waldeck, which he controlled under an agreement of March 2, 1887.

[2] Erich Eyck, *Das persönliche Regiment Wilhelms II: politische Geschichte des deutschen Kaiserreiches von 1890 bis 1914* (Zürich, 1948), 498–500.

By temperament, however, Bethmann was not much more ready than the Kaiser to exercise imperial authority. A ruddy, awkward giant, with a short spade beard and a misleadingly satanic face, he loved the outdoors and often fled Supreme Headquarters for his estate at Hohenfinow. It was the hunt rather than the bird covert that drew Bethmann, but his affinity for the country grew, like Grey's, from a distaste for power. He confessed to agonizing over decisions and to procrastinating because of a "deadening sense of responsibility." His memoranda were long, thoughtful, and pedantic, exhausting all possible alternatives. He impressed many as an unworldly idealist, *"einen weltfremden Philosophen."*

Like Grey and Wilson, the German Chancellor was an idealist with a hard grasp of practical politics. He did not, it is true, possess the arts of mass appeal. Otto Hammann, who was press officer for both Bethmann and Prince Bülow, has compared the two as orators:

Bethmann Hollweg was certainly in speech . . . no less powerful than his predecessor. But he consciously and deliberately avoided all that had made the speeches of Prince Bülow so popular: the rhetorical trimmings. While Bülow frequently broke the progress of a speech with a striking sally, a clever *bon mot,* Bethmann Hollweg disclosed his thoughts in more depth and with the utmost dignity. . . . With Bülow everything depended on the stirring effect of his words on the audience, whereas his successor seemed to speak to meditative readers.[3]

In intimate conferences with party politicians, Bethmann could, like Wilson, be both charming and convincing. But his career had

[3] Otto Hammann, *Bilder aus der letzten Kaiserzeit* (Berlin, 1922), 69–70. Hammann's sketch, pp. 66–78, is the most penetrating and sympathetic character study I have seen. Bethmann's own *Betrachtungen zum Weltkriege* (2 vols.; Berlin, 1919), of which only the first volume, *Reflections on the World War* (London, 1920), has been translated, exposes only the meditative and pessimistic side of his mind. For its other aspects one must follow his memoranda, letters, and memorials printed in various places. The most extensive treatment of his policies is confined to the pre-war period: Walter Koch, *Volk und Staatführung vor dem Weltkriege* (Stuttgart, 1935). There are vivid but somewhat superficial sketches of him in Johannes Ziekursch, *Politische Geschichte des neuen deutschen Kaiserreiches* (3 vols.; Frankfurt am Main, 1925–1930), III, 218–220, and in Eyck, *op. cit.,* 539–540. Hans, Count von Liebig, *Die Politik von Bethmann Hollwegs: Eine Studie* (3 vols.; Munich, 1919), is a diatribe written during the war by one of the Anti-Semitic leaders, but it is rich in documentary material.

been in the Prussian civil service, and his arts were those of a royalist bureaucrat. His skill lay in playing on individual and departmental interests, manipulating the handful of men who formed the imperial government, and obtaining decisions from the capricious will of the Kaiser. Despite his awkwardness with the public and the Reichstag, he knew few masters in the craft of household politics.

He was able to see to it that most of the information and advice reaching the Emperor should support his own recommendations. The Foreign Ministry was under his personal supervision, and the colorless Gottlieb von Jagow, who nominally headed it, served merely as an adjutant for the Chancellor. The official who presented dispatches and memoranda to the Kaiser was Colonel Karl Georg von Treutler, the Foreign Ministry representative at Supreme Headquarters, to whom Bethmann issued orders directly. Although the other civil departments, such as Interior and Treasury, stood less immediately under the Chancellor's hand, their communication with the Emperor was carefully guarded by him.

Even more important than his control over the ministries was his close alliance with the Cabinet chiefs. The three Cabinets, Military, Naval, and Civil, were archaic survivals of Frederick the Great's autocracy. They belonged to the King of Prussia rather than to the German Emperor, and their formal function was simply to advise him on appointments and promotions. But the Cabinet chiefs saw the Kaiser almost daily and, by volunteering advice, could exercise a powerful influence. The wartime Chief of the Military Cabinet chose to remain obscure and silent, but not so his two colleagues. The Chief of the Civil Cabinet, Rudolf von Valentini, was a close friend of Bethmann's, who helped the Chancellor whenever he could. The Chief of the Naval Cabinet, Admiral Georg Alexander von Müller, usually saw eye to eye with Bethmann and matched him in aptitude for intrigue.[4] The Chancellor thus had at

[4] The fundamental study of the Cabinet system is Rudolf Schmidt-Bückeburg, *Das Militärkabinett der preussischen Könige und deutschen Kaiser* (Berlin, 1933), which deals with all the Cabinet chiefs. Müller himself responded to the charges in Tirpitz's and Bülow's memoirs with three articles, one in *Grenzboten*, LXXIX (April 14, 1920), p. 16, "Meine Stellungnahme zu den Tirpitz-Erinnerungen," in

his disposal powerful levers for moving the Emperor's mind.

What the Chancellor lacked was control over the armed services. The Chief of the General Staff and the Chief of the Naval Staff had direct access to the throne. Since the Kaiser chose to superintend the war himself from a Supreme Headquarters near the field, the army chief was often personally at his side. The Chief of the Naval Staff remained at his office in the Leipziger Platz, but he could write to the Kaiser or visit him, subject only to the approval of Müller, the Naval Cabinet chief. The War and Navy Ministers were quite separate from the staffs, although the offices of War Minister and Chief of Staff were for a time held by the same man. The Navy Minister was theoretically subordinate to the Chancellor, but, in fact, he acted quite independently.

The Navy Minister was Grand Admiral Alfred von Tirpitz, a white-bearded, fiery veteran of many budgetary campaigns. Those, like the Chancellor, who differed with him he viewed as misguided and as probably disloyal to Germany. In seeking to overturn their opposition, he scrupled at no method. He invoked support from the royal family and from the courts of other German states. He maintained close ties with right-wing leaders in the Reichstag and never hesitated to arouse parliamentary agitation in his behalf. Through a well-organized press bureau in the Navy Ministry, he fed information to friendly newspapers and sought to create appearances of public support for his ideas.[5] The only member of the

Jahrbuch für Deutsche Politik, IV (1919), 655-662, and "Fürst Bülow und die Marinefragen," in Friedrich Thimme (ed.), _Front wider Bülow: Staatsmänner, Diplomaten und Forscher zu seinen Denkwürdigkeiten_ (Munich, 1931), 183–193, but these articles are pleas of injured virtue which cannot seem convincing to anyone who has read the minutes of imperial councils.

[5] Tirpitz is amply shown in his own _Erinnerungen_ (2 vols.; Berlin, 1919), translated as _My Memoirs_ (2 vols.; London, 1919), and in his _Politische Dokumente_ (2 vols.; Hamburg and Berlin, 1926). Among biographies of him are: Ulrich von Hassell, _Tirpitz: sein Leben und Wirken mit Berücksichtigung seiner Beziehungen zu Adalbert von Stosch_ (Stuttgart, 1920), Adolf von Trotha, _Grossadmiral von Tirpitz, Flottenbau und Reichsgedanke_ (Breslau, 1933), by an officer who served him for many years, and Waldemar Müller-Eberhart, _Tirpitz—Dollar und Völkertragödie_ (Leipzig, 1936). A not altogether convincing discussion of the Navy press bureau and its relation to Count Ernst zu Reventlow of the _Deutsche Tageszeitung_ is printed as Appendix II in _Politische Dokumente,_ II, 628–633.

imperial government who was truly adept in manipulating parliamentary and public opinion, Tirpitz was a formidable antagonist
for the Chancellor.

In the narrow arena of the imperial household, however, Tirpitz
was much less powerful than the quiet, ascetic, energetic general
who controlled the army. Erich von Falkenhayn was War Minister
at the outbreak of hostilities. After the Marne reverse he was appointed also to the more important office of Chief of Staff. He
possessed full authority thus to advise the Kaiser on the requirements for victory and on the needs of the army. Since the army, as
the foundation of the state, was a first concern for Prussian monarchs, Falkenhayn's advice could nearly always rule the Kaiser's
mind. He was prevented from dictating policy, as Ludendorff was
to do later, only by the insecurity of his control over the army. At
fifty-two, he was the youngest among the ranking generals. Since
he had neither risen through the Schlieffen school nor attached
himself to any cliques within the army, he was continually threatened by intrigues, and he depended altogether upon the continued
confidence of the Emperor. A second restraint, of course, came from
within, for Falkenhayn, as a model Prussian officer, held a narrow
view of his own professional competence. He declined to engage
in politics and deferred to the political wisdom of Bethmann and
the civilians.[6]

The handful of men who formed the imperial executive were in
some ways more insulated from outside pressures than their counter-
parts in England and America. For information they had to rely

[6] Falkenhayn himself wrote *Die oberste Heeresleitung 1914–1916 in ihren wichtigsten Entschliessungen* (Berlin, 1920), translated as *The German General Staff
and Its Decisions, 1914–1916* (London, 1920), and there are two biographies:
Adriano Alberti, *General Falkenhayn: die Beziehungen zwischen den Generalstab-
schefs des Dreibundes* (Berlin, 1924), which is interesting but sketchy, and Hans
von Zwehl, *Erich von Falkenhayn* (Berlin, 1926), an informative defense of the
general. Impressions of him are recorded also in Joseph, Count Stürgkh, *Im deutschen Grossen Hauptquartier* (Leipzig, 1921), 25–26, and in August von Cramon,
Unser österreichischer-ungarnischer Bundesgenosse im Weltkrieg (Berlin, 1920),
22–23. Helmuth von Wienskowski, *Falkenhayn* (Berlin, 1937), is almost entirely
a professional critique, as is Hans Delbrück's celebrated and penetrating *Ludendorff,
Tirpitz, Falkenhayn* (Berlin, 1920).

almost exclusively upon the bureaucracy. The press was not an important source of foreign intelligence. The extent to which the semi-official Wolff Bureau relied on Reuters and Havas had been a matter of complaint before the war, and the foreign representatives of individual newspapers were rather occasional correspondents than reporters.[7] Diplomats therefore provided most of the government's knowledge about foreign events and attitudes. With regard to the United States, crown officials were almost exclusively dependent on dispatches from Bernstorff and the military and naval attachés in Washington and on infrequent letters from consuls and German sympathizers in America. Weighed and commented on by inexpert officials or by occasional outsiders with some experience of the United States, these selective and incomplete reports formed the basis for all calculations involving America. The foundations of a policy could shift like sand according to the pessimism or optimism of a handful of distant correspondents.

The government was not insulated, however, from public opinion. Although the monarchy did not have to win votes, its ministers were at least as sensitive to popular moods as were elected officials in other countries. Policies had to be gauged with an eye to probable responses in the Reichstag.

The government had to be especially solicitous of the Conservative parties. Absolutist, imperialist, opposed to reform of any kind, their ethos is indicated by an article that appeared in the *Kreuzzeitung* during the war:

> The war, properly considered, has been Germany's salvation. Pacifism, internationalism, anti-militarism and all the other noxious weeds of modern times had reached such a flourishing stage that the stupid German Michael was at the point of being fatally infected with these diseases.

Then came the war, and through it our Kaiser saved, not the people only, but the old German nobility, from certain ruin. That nobility has nothing to fear from the war, for even in the event of defeat, the

---

[7] Otto Groth, *Die Zeitung* (4 vols.; Mannheim, 1928–1930), I, 527–547; Oron J. Hale, *Publicity and Diplomacy, with Special Reference to England and Germany, 1890–1914* (New York, 1940), 70–80. On the relations between the press and political parties, see Groth, *op. cit.*, II, 370–620.

people, grateful for the heroic efforts of its noble leaders, will not rise against the aristocracy.

It will be far otherwise. . . . We shall yet be absolute masters of the world. All the chimerical ideas of democracy will be driven forth forevermore. . . . The great task . . . when the war shall have terminated will be to purge our land of revolutionary ideas, so that our nobility may recover its splendor, power, and ancient authority.[8]

The Conservative parties held only seventy-two seats in the imperial Reichstag, but they controlled the Prussian Landtag. The Kaiser as King of Prussia and the Chancellor as Prussian Minister President needed Conservative support there. These parties, moreover, represented the economic and social caste for which the monarchy was primarily responsible and to whose interests it was most sensitive. The Conservatives spoke for the nobility, the great landholders, aristocratic society, and the officer corps. It was impossible for crown officials to disregard the views of the Conservatives, or even to take them lightly.

No Chancellor could govern, however, with the support of the Conservative parties alone. Even when they held more of the Reichstag's 397 seats, their support had been undependable. In the last years of peace, the *Zentrum* and its Catholic allies and the National Liberal party, which represented German heavy industry, had been the two firmer legs beneath the government. *Zentrum* and National Liberal leaders had come to assume that their wishes would be consulted, and, indeed, it was almost as necessary for the Chancellor to take account of them as of the Conservatives. He had at least to be tender of their respective economic interests, prejudices, and passions.

The war made it necessary to do more. At its outset the Emperor proclaimed the *Burgfrieden,* a truce in party conflict. "I no longer recognize parties," he declared, "I only recognize Germans."[9]

[8] *Kreuzzeitung,* Aug. 30, 1915.

[9] Viktor Bredt, *Der deutsche Reichstag im Weltkrieg,* 51. Bredt's book is volume VIII of Das Werk des Untersuchungsausschusses der Verfassunggebenden Deutschen Nationalversammlung und des Deutschen Reichstages, 1919–1926; *Die Ursachen des Deutschen Zusammenbruches im Jahre 1918,* Zweite Abteilung: *Der innere Zusammenbruch* (12 vols.; Berlin, 1925–1929).

Bethmann made it one of his central objects to preserve this *Burgfrieden,* the national unity, the *union sacrée,* of Germany. To this end he sought to placate the Progressives and Social Democrats. The socialist, Philipp Scheidemann, was invited to a meeting with the Kaiser; he was frequently consulted by Bethmann; his comrades were given government posts and expense-paid tours of the battle-front.[10] When the first flush of patriotic unity began to pale, Bethmann felt obliged to go farther still and to promise the Social Democrats and Progressives a postwar reorientation (*Neuorientierung*) in domestic policy.

The *Burgfrieden* had two sides. On the one hand, as Arthur Rosenberg has pointed out, it increased the power of the government. The Reichstag yielded such authority as it had won in the past, allowing the Kaiser's ministers to rule by martial law, decree, and fiat. On the other hand, it deprived the government of any flexibility or initiative. Few issues, it is true, could unite the Chancellor's bloc of Conservatives, National Liberals, and Centrists, but no issues whatever could make all parties one. As Scheidemann remarked, "Bethmann Hollweg was in a fearful position, for he had to be silent or else lose us or the people of the right." Dealing with any pressing issue, such as constitutional reform or war aims, the Chancellor had no choice but to avoid taking a stand. As he put it himself, he was compelled to follow a "diagonal policy."[11]

The press, of course, was as important as the Reichstag. The *Burgfrieden* aimed as much at unity among the nation's editors as among party leaders in the Reichstag. Half of the 3,000 newspapers in Germany were, in fact, party organs, and all but a few of the remaining 1,500 were trade or business journals, purely local sheets, or *Käseblätter,* tabloids useful chiefly for wrapping cheese. Otto

---

[10] See Bethmann's speeches of Aug. 4 and Dec. 2, 1914, in Friedrich Thimme (ed.), *Bethmann Hollwegs Kriegsreden* (Stuttgart, 1919), 3–23; Bethmann, *Betrachtungen,* II, 25–37; Philipp Scheidemann, *Der Zusammenbruch* (Berlin, 1921); and Scheidemann's testimony in *Die Ursachen des Deutschen Zusammenbruches,* vol. VII, part 1, pp. 274–277. See also Carl E. Schorske, *German Social Democracy, 1905–1917* (Cambridge, Mass., 1955), 290 ff.

[11] Bethmann, *Betrachtungen,* II, 35; Arthur Rosenberg, *The Birth of the German Republic* (English translation; London, 1931), 77.

Groth, in his exhaustive four-volume study of the German press, devotes only eight pages to non-partisan papers.[12] If the government could keep the backing of party leaders in the Reichstag, it could also limit criticism in the public prints.

The government could do more with the press, however, than with parties in the Reichstag. The power of censorship was broad. No newspaper was allowed, for example, to predict the probable duration of hostilities or to comment on war aims. If one violated this edict, it was placed under preventive censorship and had to submit its copy for approval. If it erred again, it was promptly suppressed. The censors were military officials, not directly under the Chancellor, but Major Deutelmoser, the chief censor, conferred often with Hammann and Alfons, Count Mumm von Schwarzenstein, the press officers for the Chancellery and the Foreign Ministry. Early in the war, moreover, the Interior Ministry directed officials in provincial towns to establish close relations with one or more local newspapers, giving them exclusive information in return for influence over their news columns and editorial opinions.[13]

The government could also make use of the handful of independent newspapers in the country. The *Norddeutsche Allgemeine Zeitung* was, of course, an official journal in all but name; it was given over almost exclusively to government releases. The *Kölnische Zeitung,* though free of any direct control, had long served for the publication of inspired news and comment, and its connection with the Foreign Ministry was so close that it was thought semiofficial in character. Hammann and Mumm held frequent conferences, in addition, with Theodor Wolff of the *Berliner Tageblatt,* Baron von Behr of the Berlin *Lokal-Anzeiger,* and August Stein of the

---

[12] Groth, *Die Zeitung,* II, 532–541; Wilhelm Nicolai, *Nachrichtendienst, Presse, und Volksstimmung im Weltkrieg* (Berlin, 1920), 167–168; Paul Roth, *Die Programme der politischen Parteien und die politische Tagespresse* (Halle, 1913); Hale, *Publicity and Diplomacy,* 50–59.

[13] Nicolai, *Nachrichtendienst, Presse, und Volksstimmung,* is the reminiscence of Deutelmoser's successor; Hammann, *Bilder aus der letzten Kaiserzeit,* 118–121, prints a letter from Mumm describing one instance in detail. The Interior Ministry order was first disclosed in *Vorwärts,* Oct. 25, 1915, and it was frequently discussed in the Reichstag.

Frankfurter Zeitung.[14] These newspapers helped, to some extent, in explaining the Chancellor's policies and encouraging the public to support them.

Bethmann thus possessed considerable power. Not only was he skilled in the arts by which decisions were wrung from the Emperor, but he was supported by the civil ministries and by the Cabinet chiefs. The *Burgfrieden* reduced the risk of partisan attack, and the government's many controls over the press enabled it to give some direction to public opinion. But the Chancellor was restricted by the necessity of preserving the *Burgfrieden,* by his lack of control over the military and naval services, and by the Kaiser's volatile will. Despite his power, therefore, Bethmann was not in a position easily to reach decisions. He was compelled often to follow not only a diagonal but a sinuous policy. The acts by which the German government alternately rebuffed and threatened the United States were not always the results of decisions; they were sometimes the consequences of indecision.

The rejection of American mediation overtures followed from the refusal of the government to define war aims. There would have been objections, in any event, to the use of American good offices. Bethmann outlined some of them when commenting to the Austrian government on House's proposed mission to Europe:

In American mediation *I see a danger* in that it would presumably lead to an international congress. In such a congress our position, two great powers against three, would be disadvantageous. Turkey has traditionally a weak role in congresses, and to the triple alliance belong Japan, Serbia, and Montenegro. If we could ignore Belgium as no longer existing, still her interests would be upheld by our enemies and to a certain extent also by the neutrals. Certainly, also, the neutrals (for example, Italy) would advance more demands against us than against

[14] Nicolai, *Nachrichtendienst, Presse, und Volksstimmung,* 172–176; Hamman, *Bilder aus der letzten Kaiserzeit,* 55–56, 120–121; Groth, *Die Zeitung,* II, 217–260; Bernhard Guttmann, *Schattenriss einer Generation, 1888–1919* (Stuttgart, 1950), especially pp. 107 ff. Cf. Johannes Lehmann, *Die Aussenpolitik und die Kölnische Zeitung während die Bülow-Zeit, 1897–1909* (Bleichrode, 1937).

our enemies. And from the American side we could expect, from the known do-good [*weltbeglückenden*] tendencies of Wilson and Bryan, the introduction of a batch of questions (disarmament, arbitration treaties, world peace), the more difficult to negotiate the more utopian they are.[15]

But these objections could have been overcome. Had Bethmann and his associates decided to negotiate for restoration of the *status quo ante,* they might have found it useful to cooperate with Wilson. Had they even decided to seek a separate peace with England, they might have encouraged him. But they did neither.

They chose not to encourage American mediation even though many high officials believed either result to be desirable. Although Bethmann uttered a wide variety of opinions, his personal view seems actually to have been what he recalled when writing his memoirs. From the very beginning, he declares, he hoped for nothing more than a peace of Hubertusburg. If Germany could but convince the Allies that she was not to be beaten, she would have won enough. Foreign Minister Jagow is said to have lamented within two days after Britain's declaration of war, "it must be the aim of German foreign policy to get out of this dismal war entirely as quickly as possible." Since Falkenhayn asserted time and again that Germany's sole realistic object was to prove that she could not be exhausted, he may be assumed to have shared this view.[16] Even a separate peace with England would have been welcome. Her intervention had not been entirely expected, and Bethmann seems to have hoped for some months that she might be induced to reconsider and withdraw from the fighting.[17]

[15] Bethmann to Leopold, Count von Berchtold, Nov. 23, 1914, German Foreign Ministry Archives (Secret Mediation).

[16] Bethmann, *Betrachtungen,* II, 18; testimony of Baron von Richthofen, *Die Ursachen des Deutschen Zusammenbruches,* VII, pt. 1, p. 215; Falkenhayn, *General Staff,* 25–26, 43–44, 173–174, 330; Zwehl, *Falkenhayn,* 61–64.

[17] For Bethmann's expectations, see Karl Kautsky *et al., Die deutschen Dokumente zum Kriegsausbruch* (2nd ed., revised; 4 vols., Berlin, 1928), II, 125, 136, 177; IV, 128–129. On his interest in a separate peace with England, see memo of Aug. 8, 1914, in Hugo von Pohl, *Aus Aufzeichnungen und Briefen während der Kriegszeit* (Berlin, 1920), 7–8, and the suspicious notes in *Politische Dokumente,* II, 95, and Tirpitz, *Memoirs,* II, 228, 230. Bethmann's alleged restraint of the navy is

Yet the Chancellor was almost incapable of seeking a negotiated peace, through the good offices of the United States or in any other fashion. Had he done so he would have met resistance within his own entourage. Tirpitz would have fought any move to stop the war before victory had been achieved in the west, and the Grand Admiral would have had allies throughout the government. The Naval Staff believed that if Germany were to be secure from future attack she needed permanent control over bases on the Belgian and French coasts. Many officers in the army General Staff, differing with Falkenhayn, felt sure of triumph and insisted that Germany should annex Belgium and hold the entries to France. Civilians in the Interior and Colonial Ministries argued that peace should bring, at the very least, economic domination of Belgium and the transfer of Belgian colonies in Africa.[18] Had the Chancellor elected to disclose his own views to potential mediators he would have shattered the unity of his own administration.

What really restrained him from taking any steps toward peace was the division in public opinion. During the earliest days of hostilities, the country appeared unanimous in believing the war to be defensive, forced upon Germany by the enemy. The triumphs of the army in Belgium, France, Galicia, and Poland produced a euphoric faith in ultimate victory. There arose discussion of the terms that might be imposed in order to ensure that the Entente should never again disrupt Germany's peace. Socialists, on the other hand, remained as firmly opposed to conquest as they had been earlier to imperialism. Annexationist and anti-annexationist factions emerged and swelled in strength.

The right-wing and bourgeois parties moved toward annexation-

---

detailed in *Politische Dokumente*, II, 43–45; the Chancellor's own explanation that the admirals made the decision is presented in his *Betrachtungen*, II, 8–9. There is no record in the Mediation or Secret Mediation files of the Foreign Ministry Archives of any official effort to approach England about a separate peace. Such evidence as exists is discussed in Kent Forster, *The Failures of Peace* (Washington, D. C., 1941), 3 ff.

[18] E. O. Volkmann, *Die Anexionsfrage des Weltkrieges* (which is vol. XII, part 1, of *Die Ursachen des Deutschen Zusammenbruches*), appendices 11 and 12, pp. 187–199; *ibid.*, 37; Hans W. Gatzke, *Germany's Drive to the West: A Study of Germany's Western War Aims during the First World War* (Baltimore, 1950), 8–17.

ism. There had for a long time been a small but influential group of imperialists, organized in the Pan-German League, the Defense Society, the Navy League, the Colonial Society, and, to some extent, the Society for Combatting Social Democracy. With the outbreak of war, these organizations gradually formed a solid front with the parties of the far right. Kuno, Count Westarp, explains in his massive memoir on Conservative politics why his party deserted its earlier view that Germany had reached a saturation point:

[I]t seemed a duty . . . , in order to strengthen the fighting spirit and perseverance of the troops, to set before their eyes the positive goal of a better and more secure future for themselves and for coming generations. The monarchist had to fear that the growth of radicalism, which is to be expected as a result of any war, would reach alarming proportions if the homecoming soldiers were to find as the reward for their heroism only an increased tax bill and were to become convinced that the government of the *Kaiserreich* had not understood how to profit from success in military operations.[19]

In October, 1914, the Conservative leadership joined forces with representatives of the Central Union of German Industrialists, the Agrarian League, and the Pan-German League to draw up a statement of war aims. It proved impossible to secure any common formula, but all accepted at least some of the terms that Heinrich Class had outlined in his Pan-German pamphlet, *Zum deutschen Kriegsziel:* in the west a frontier running from Boulogne to Belfort, taking in the Channel coast, Belgium, and segments of France; in the east a line from Lake Peipus to the mouth of the Dnieper, bringing in the Baltic provinces, Poland, and the Ukraine; partition of the British Empire, restricting Great Britain to England and Scotland; and the transfer of Siberia to Japan. Although individual differences, particularly over Polish annexation, prevented the publication of any precise summary of Conservative aims, the party leadership made sure that Bethmann knew the general outlines of their thought.[20]

[19] Kuno, Count Westarp, *Konservative Politik im letzten Jahrzehnt des Kaiserreiches* (2 vols.; Berlin, 1935), II, 40.

[20] *Ibid.*, 41–44.

Nor were the Conservatives alone. The Central Union of German Industrialists had National Liberal ties, and the National Liberal leadership became fanatically annexationist. Ernst Bassermann, one of the party chieftains, established a working alliance with Westarp and Heydebrand und der Lase, the Conservative strategists. By the end of the first winter, the Class program had been accepted in principle, though not in detail, by his party and by all of the six great economic associations, which included, in addition to the Central Union of Industrialists and the Agrarian League, the German Peasants League, the League of Industrialists, the Hansa League, and the German League of Middle Class Citizens.[21] Since the Pan-German organization included many intellectuals, annexationism may be said to have swept over the wise, the rich, and the well-born.

It made inroads, too, into the middle parties. Peter Spahn, a conservative *Zentrum* elder, ranged himself with the annexationists.[22] Matthias Erzberger, the bustling leader of the left Centrists, circulated a statement of war aims in September, 1914, calling for annexation of Belgium, the Channel coast, the French coal and iron regions, and the Congo, for partition of Russia, and for the exaction of enormous reparations. In the same month the two leading Centrist journals, the *Kölnische Volkszeitung,* representing Rhenish Catholics, and *Germania,* the Berlin organ, both condemned the idea of American mediation, writing of the necessity to guarantee Germany's future security and to carry on the war until the enemy had been reduced to impotence.[23] Even the leftist Progressives (the *Fortschrittliche Volkspartei*) were divided among

---

[21] *Ibid.,* 42–43; Volkmann, *Die Anexionsfrage,* 50; S. Grumbach, *Das annexionistische Deutschland* (Lausanne, 1917), 43–92; Ebba Dahlin, *French and German Public Opinion on Declared War Aims* (Palo Alto, 1933), 13–61; Gatzke, *Germany's Drive to the West,* 20–62.

[22] Frida Wacker, *Die Haltung der Deutschen Zentrumspartei zur Frage der Kriegsziele im Weltkrieg, 1914–1918* (Lohr am Main, 1937), 4–5.

[23] *Ibid.,* 4, quoting *Kölnische Volkszeitung,* Sept. 17, 1914, and *Germania,* Sept. 21, 1914. On Erzberger, see Wacker, 6–11, Volkmann, *Anexionsfrage,* 37, 67, and Klaus Epstein's biography, which has not yet been published.

themselves.[24] The enthusiasm for conquest ran through a broad segment of the German political spectrum.

The widespread annexationism did not, in itself, prevent Bethmann from encouraging neutral mediation. He knew of the vast dreams which bemused the right and center of the Reichstag, and he discussed with colleagues various peace terms that might placate them. The Briey and Longwy region of the Moselle valley, with its substantial coal and iron deposits, he thought, might be annexed, and Belgium might conceivably be tied to the German economy even while left politically independent.[25] The Chancellor appears to have felt that minor territorial gains might satisfy public opinion. Right-wing leaders warned him against negotiating any peace except on a basis of Allied surrender, but he was evidently willing to bargain for less, if the Allies should simply confess that they could not triumph.

What deterred him from taking active steps toward peace was not so much the strength of Pan-Germanism as the ferocity of public feeling on war aims. The annexationism of the right was matched by the equally violent anti-annexationism of the left. The Social Democrats opposed any conquest. Some did so for pacifist reasons; some because the acquisition of new territory would strengthen the ruling classes and hence postpone the socialist triumph; still others because the issue served to divide the nation, weaken the government, and advance the revolution. The bases for the party's policy were many and varied, but with its tradition of solidarity, it presented a united front against annexationism.[26] If Bethmann hinted at a peace without conquests, he would seem to be allying himself with the left. The result was likely to be not only complaint

[24] Hermann Ostfeld, *Die Haltung der Reichstagsfraktion der Fortschrittliche Volkspartei zu den Anexions- und Friedensfrage in den Jahren 1914–1918* (Kallmünz, 1934), 10–11.

[25] Volkmann, *Anexionsfrage*, 35–38; Westarp, *Konservative Politik*, II, 48–50; Gatzke, *Germany's Drive to the West*, 15–16.

[26] Volkmann, *Anexionsfrage*, 58 ff.; Schorske, *German Social Democracy*, 294–307; *Vorwärts* editorials in Ralph H. Lutz, *The Fall of the German Empire* (2 vols.; Palo Alto, 1932), I, 305–311; additional documents in Grumbach, *Das anexionistische Deutschland*, 429–460.

but open opposition from a majority of the Reichstag—an intolerable situation for a Chancellor who had to preserve the fiction that the imperial government was subject to no legislative control.

At the same time, Bethmann could not afford to alienate the Social Democrats and those who shared their views. He could not speak of specific territorial aims. In private conversation, on the one hand, he had to assure Scheidemann, the socialist, that he opposed any but the most modest extensions of territory while, on the other hand, he had to tell Westarp and Bassermann that he would settle for nothing less than the domination of Belgium and permanent security for Germany. The mention of peace terms in speeches, diplomatic notes, and even inspired news stories had to be vague and ambiguous.

In no way thus could the Chancellor seek to build a moral tie with the United States by fanning Wilson's mediation hopes. In public he could neither indicate a willingness to accept the *status quo ante* nor outline the terms of a victor's peace. Even in the secrecy of diplomatic communication he could do no more than pursue his diagonal policy. Any disclosure of terms would certainly become known to annexationists in the government and, through them, to the Reichstag and public. When speaking with a Danish peace envoy, known to be friendly to Germany, Bethmann could say no more than that "Germany did not go to war with any idea of territorial expansion. . . . But the later course of events has been such that the German people would find it difficult to be content with a peace which brought Germany no compensation for her great sacrifices, and he feared that the Belgian question was freighted with great difficulties and the German people would be hard to console for the injuries which they had suffered, especially from the British nation." [27] He could not speak with more precision to Gerard or House. For reasons of internal politics the Chancellor was precluded from encouraging American mediation and thus attempting to draw the United States away from the Allies.

[27] Memo by H. N. Andersen, n.d., *Mezhdunarodnye Otnosheniya*, Series Three, VII, no. 384.

The American overtures were rejected tactfully but firmly. Wilson's initial tender of good offices was brought directly to the Kaiser by the American ambassador, James W. Gerard, and the reply was composed on the spot by Wilhelm, scribbling on the back of a telegraph blank.[28] When the second offer was made, as a result of the Straus-Bernstorff conversation, Bethmann's answer was drafted by the annexationist Undersecretary for Foreign Affairs, Zimmermann. "The American ambassador earlier indicated to me . . . ," Zimmermann wrote to the Chancellor,

that . . . we should make peace as soon as possible after we have taken Paris. We could then impose an immensely high indemnity on France and take as many of her colonies as we wanted. I answered him that Germany desires, above all else, to conclude the war with a lasting peace. That wish would unquestionably not be fulfilled at the present moment by an arrangement in the pattern unfolded by him; its fulfillment requires a reckoning not only with France but also with Russia and England. Otherwise we would, in my opinion, have to expect within a few years a new war with the Entente Powers. . . . No one would understand it if the government wished now to call forth the mediation of the United States in order to bring about a peace on the basis sketched by him. . . . On the broader question of when in my opinion we would be ready for mediation I replied that in the event our enemies should request the intervention of the United States and should offer us suitable terms through Washington, the government would certainly take them under serious consideration.[29]

Zimmermann asked if he could answer the new proposal in the same fashion. Although Tirpitz suspected Bethmann and Jagow of having prompted the American overture, they were, in fact, as surprised as he and as disdainful as Zimmermann. The Undersecretary was permitted, therefore, to answer the Americans as he desired.[30]

When House entered the field, the Chancellor was compelled to

---

[28] Gerard, *My Four Years in Germany*, 199–202; *Foreign Relations, Supplement: 1914*, pp. 60–61.

[29] Memo by Zimmermann, Sept. 9, 1914, German Foreign Ministry Archives (Secret Mediation).

[30] *Politische Dokumente*, II, 122.

clarify his attitude toward the American ambition. The principal reason was that House had not only written to Zimmermann and talked with Bernstorff, but had also communicated with the Austrian ambassador in Washington, Constantin Dumba. The Austrian Foreign Minister therefore asked for Bethmann's comments on House's scheme and especially on the terms which the colonel outlined: evacuation of Belgium and general disarmament. To this inquiry Bethmann felt obliged to reply at length.[31] "We must avoid the appearance of being on principle for a continuation of the war *à outrance*," he wrote. "On the other hand, I have no hope of success from American interposition. America, because of her trade, is interested above all in a cessation of the war between England and us and therefore will do her best to obtain it. A bad peace with England could only mean the continuation for years of a latent war." He thought of adding, "England is our mortal enemy and a peace now can hardly lead to a positive result." Remembering the anxiety of the Austrian ally, he struck out this uncompromising line but went on to declare:

As to the individual points of House's offer, they seem to me all to be dictated by such an impractical enthusiasm for peace that it would be difficult for a *Realpolitiker* to give them a precise answer. . . . However, since I agree with you completely that we cannot reject the American offer on principle, it seems to me necessary to find a form for the answer that will . . . give the impression of a sympathetic reception.

By the time of House's arrival in Berlin in March, 1915, even the possibility of a pretended sympathy had largely vanished. Bethmann had by then been compelled to make annexationist sounds in public.[32] More important, the submarine campaign had opened, and Germany and the United States were already in potential enmity. Beyond commenting to House that the time for peace nego-

---

[31] Jagow to Foreign Ministry, Nov. 15, 1914, German Foreign Ministry Archives Secret Mediation); Bethmann to Berchtold, Nov. 23, 1914, *ibid*.

[32] In his speech of Dec. 2, 1914, Thimme, *Bethmann Hollwegs Kriegsreden*, 14–15. Shortly afterward, furthermore, Westarp compelled him to put on paper, though confidentially, a pledge that Belgium would not be surrendered: Bethmann to Westarp, April 8, 1915, Westarp, *Konservative Politik*, II, 48–49.

tiations might ultimately arrive, neither Bethmann nor Jagow felt able to offer any encouragement. When the colonel suggested that "freedom of the seas" might be incorporated in the peace settlement, thus guaranteeing Germany's maritime commerce, they were willing to approve the notion in principle. Even on this point, however, Jagow thought it necessary to qualify. "Whether we could agree to the specific provisions," he recorded saying, "I could not say without knowing them." [33] The result was that House brought away from Berlin a reinforced conviction that the Germans were "narrowly selfish in their purposes and have no broad outlook as to the general good of mankind." [34]

The German government made no use of its one opportunity for improving German-American relations and perhaps obtaining Wilson's diplomatic support. But the arguments against exploring this opportunity were overwhelming. Not only did the United States seem unsuitable as a mediator, but the government dared not speak of a negotiated peace, even with England alone. To have done so might have shaken the unity of Germany and deprived the government of public support.

[33] Memo by Jagow, March 23, 1915, German Foreign Ministry Archives (Secret Mediation).

[34] *Intimate Papers*, I, 414.

PART II

The Tightening of
German-American Tensions

VI

The U-Boat Campaign

Far more important than the rebuff to Wilson's mediation hopes
was the German decision to open a submarine campaign against
merchant shipping. Other acts might have aroused moral disapproval by the United States, but little else could have generated
a genuine antagonism. There were no American interests within
reach of German land forces. The one method by which Germany
could stir the United States to threaten war was by ordering submarines to attack neutral ships and belligerent passenger carriers.
Yet the German government chose to issue such an order.

Unlike the decision to reject mediation, this action was only
partly a product of necessity. It came about almost accidentally.
Submarines achieved surprise successes at a time when no other
German forces were making news. Certain naval officers elected to
champion wider use of the weapon, deliberately stirring public
hopes. Since other officials failed to look deeply enough into the
implications of these proposals, the publicity was allowed to run
unchecked. As a result of its success, coupled with the relative
absence of reflective opposition, a decision in favor of a submarine
campaign was taken almost in a fit of absence of mind.

The process that led to this decision commenced in September,
1914. Early in the month a submarine chanced upon the British
cruiser *Pathfinder* and sank her.[1] In the latter part of the month,

[1] Vice Admiral Eberhard von Mantey (ed.), *Der Krieg zur See herausgegeben
vom Marine-archiv*: Capt. Otto Groos, *Der Krieg in der Nordsee* (5 vols.; Berlin,
1920–1925), I, 7.

a combination of bad weather and administrative inefficiency in the British Admiralty threw three more cruisers into the path of a U-boat. The aged vessels *Cressy, Hogue,* and *Aboukir Bay* were torpedoed off the Broad Fourteens by the small, slow U-9, a gasoline-burning submarine already considered obsolete.[2]

One consequence of these accidental successes was an arousal in the navy of enthusiasm for wider use of U-boats. Theretofore the vessels had been regarded as experimental and, at most, as auxiliary arms of the fleet.[3] Hardly anyone had conceived of the U-boat as an independent weapon operating against enemy commerce. After the September exploits, this novel idea began to spread through the fleet. Tirpitz and various officers in the Navy Ministry became interested. By early November the Chief of the Naval Staff had decided to urge such a course upon the Chancellor and the Emperor.[4] By the turn of the year nearly all the higher ranks of the navy had become engaged in energetic agitation for a U-boat campaign.

It is easy to understand this emergent enthusiasm. The navy had been useless in the early stages of the war. The High Seas Fleet had stood inactive while Britain cleared the oceans and established her dominance over the North Sea. While the army struggled to preserve and increase the Fatherland, the navy remained merely decorative, and its officers felt wounded not only in pride but also in hope. "If we come to the end . . . without the fleet having bled and worked," wrote Tirpitz, "we shall get nothing more for the fleet, and all the scanty money that there may be will be spent on the army. The great efforts of His Majesty the Emperor to make Germany a naval power will have been all in vain."[5] The September triumphs awakened hopes that the navy might be able, after all, to help win the war.

How these natural feelings overcame the judgment of so many

---

[2] *Ibid.,* I, 49; Churchill, *World Crisis,* I, 351–352.
[3] Mantey, *Krieg zur See:* Rear Admiral Arno Spindler, *Der Handelskrieg mit U-Booten* (3 vols.; Berlin, 1932–1934), I, 148–157.
[4] *Ibid.,* I, 1–10, 26–34; *Politische Dokumente,* II, 281–286.
[5] Tirpitz to Pohl, Sept. 6, 1914, *Politische Dokumente,* II, 105.

officers is somewhat harder to understand. The U-boats available
for operations in the North Sea area were but twenty-one in number.
Twelve of these were slow, gasoline-powered, and capable of operating only in the Channel region. Only nine were diesel craft that
could reach England's western coasts, and the largest carried but ten
torpedoes.[6] In view of the quantity of British shipping, it required
considerable imagination to envision a successful blockade. The
only prewar estimate, indeed, called for a force of two hundred
and twenty-one submarines equipped with devices not yet designed.[7]
Some officers remained aware of the discrepancy between the idea
and the means available to execute it.[8]

But the majority submerged their doubts. Neutral shipowners,
they reasoned, would be frightened away from English ports. If
the campaign were masked as retaliation against British interference with trade, neutral governments might even cooperate in the
blockade.[9] A few sinkings would meanwhile strike such terror into
English shippers as to halt sailings. Many officers relied on a hypo-
thetical account, printed before the war, of England's strangulation
by a handful of submarines. This confidence-inspiring estimate had
appeared in *The Strand* magazine over the name of Sir Arthur
Conan Doyle. When an admiral was asked after the war to explain
the Naval Staff's miscalculations, he indicated blushingly that the
navy had put too much faith in Sherlock Holmes.[10]

From this irrational enthusiasm in the navy grew a public cry
for the opening of a submarine campaign against British commerce.
The idea was thrown dramatically into the public arena by Tirpitz.
In an interview with an American journalist, Karl von Wiegand,
the Grand Admiral declared, "England wants to starve us. We can
play the same game. We can bottle her up and destroy every ship
that endeavors to break the blockade." When asked if Germany

[6] Spindler, *Handelskrieg*, I, 148–176.
[7] *Ibid.*, I, 153–154.
[8] *Politische Dokumente*, II, 285–286, 288–289, 298–299, 307.
[9] Tirpitz so declared to Bethmann in an interview of Jan. 27, 1915, *ibid.*, II,
301–303.
[10] Testimony by Admiral von Capelle, Carnegie Foundation, *Official German*

had enough U-boats, he replied vehemently and misleadingly, "Yes, we are superior to England in submarines of the larger types."[11] Published in late December, this interview attracted wide notice. The idea of striking England's vitals with the U-boat weapon had received the authoritative imprimatur of the navy's elder statesman.

The seed dropped by Tirpitz rooted in fallow ground. It is unlikely that the desperate frustration of the government was widely shared. Few knew the extent to which operations in the west had failed. Official reports had so disguised the importance of the Marne engagements that they had passed almost unnoticed.[12] The clamor aroused by Tirpitz's interview was probably not spontaneous; the newspapers that most strongly supported his plan were those most closely identified with the Navy Ministry.[13] But a feeling must have been growing that moated England was responsible for the war's prolongation. There was thus a favorable atmosphere for a secret weapon delusion.

The Grand Admiral's proposal soon found support among party leaders. It appealed to the Anglophobia of the right. Offering also a promise of swift triumph, it fitted in with annexationist dreams.

Documents Relating to the World War (2 vols.; New York, 1920), I, 594. The publication is a translation of the reports and proceedings of certain investigating committees created after the war by the German National Assembly. The largest part is a translation of Stenographische Berichte über die öffentlichen Verhandlungen des Untersuchungssausschusses, 2. Unterausschuss (Berlin, 1920), and Aktenstücke zur Friedensasktion Wilsons: Beilagen zu den stenographischen Berichten des Untersuchungsausschusses, 2. Unterausschuss (Berlin, 1920).

[11] Text in Politische Dokumente, II, 623–627. It was somehow softened before being published in the United States. The version given to Americans read: "We can play the same game. We can bottle her up and torpedo every English or Allies [sic] ship which nears any harbor in Great Britain thereby cutting off large food supplies." New York Sun, Dec. 23, 1914, cited in Tansill, America Goes to War, 227. Tirpitz's original statement read simply: "Wir können dasselbe Spiel treiben, England einschliessen und jedes Schiff verstören, dass die Blockade zu durchbrechen versucht."

[12] Ziekursch, Politische Geschichte, III, 327–328. Bethmann was responsible for suppressing news of the setback: Reichsarchiv and Reichskriegsministerium, Der Weltkrieg, 1914 bis 1918, bearbeitet und herausgegeben von der Kriegsgeschichtlichen Forschungsanstalt des Heeres: Die militärischen Operationen zu Lande (15 vols. in progress; Berlin, 1925—), V, 14–15.

[13] Editorials reproduced in Spindler, Handelskrieg, I, 243–250.

When the government seemed to delay adopting the proposal, vexation developed. Even Erzberger, the left Centrist, published a pamphlet, *No Sentimentality,* calling for immediate institution of a ruthless submarine blockade.[14] When Bethmann visited Berlin, he found deputies accusing him of pro-British leanings.[15] And not even the left socialists opposed this clamor. By the spring of 1915, there seemed to have risen a U-boat fervor comparable to the annexationist passion.

The government was not so powerless before this movement as it was before the annexationist fever. The Foreign Ministry had an opportunity to kill the Tirpitz interview, which it blunderingly failed to seize. The text was sent to the Ministry for censorship. When the responsible officer, Count Mumm, read it through, he received the impression that Wiegand had already cabled it to America. It had, in fact, gone in a diplomatic pouch, and its publication could still have been stopped. But Mumm assumed that it would be printed overseas and therefore could not be kept from German editors. After telling Zimmermann about it, he authorized its release to the press.[16]

Even after the interview's publication, there remained some chance of cooling public enthusiasm. The truth about Germany's limited capabilities could have been spread before party leaders as it was later. But Bethmann and his associates did not oppose the movement, partly from mistaken information, partly from irresolution, but largely from simple failure to foresee its consequences.

Chance played a part, too, in the ultimate approval of the blockade plan, but Bethmann was alerted by this time to the need for careful calculation. Every political aspect of the proposal was surveyed, at least superficially, in the Foreign Ministry and the Chancellery. On various grounds Bethmann postponed its adoption.

[14] Published in Feb., 1915; extensive extracts will appear in Epstein's "Erzberger."
[15] It was Zimmermann's recollection in 1928 that Bethmann had complained of this on Feb. 1, 1915, Spindler, *Handelskrieg,* I, 79–80.
[16] *Politische Dokumente,* II, 621–627; Bethmann, *Betrachtungen,* II, 121; memo by Jagow, Jan. 17, 1915, German Foreign Ministry Archives (U-boat War).

He was concerned, first of all, about possible effects on neutrals, especially those of southern Europe. Should a submarine campaign pit Germany against all neutrals, Italy and the entire Balkan peninsula might fall into the Allied camp. Since the army General Staff held that Germany could not stand such an addition to the number of her enemies, this possibility threw a dark shadow over the Chancellor's thoughts on U-boat warfare.[17]

The United States was secondary in his thinking. Bernstorff and his aides had faithfully reported America's strong sympathy for the Allies. They had also made clear her dedication to profitable trade. From Wilson's legalistic pronouncements against interference with business, Bethmann might foresee an American outcry against a submarine decree, but he had little reason to fear war. "President Wilson said to me," wrote Bernstorff in his first personal report to Bethmann, " 'We must be absolutely neutral, because otherwise our mixed population would fall into another war.' "[18] The ambassador stressed time and again America's consuming desire for peace,[19] and he reported continual though slight improvement in America's attitude toward Germany, crediting the improvement to fear of Japan, to Britain's heavy-handed censorship, to the mine war zone decree, and to the achievements of German arms: " 'Nothing succeeds like success' is still a fundamental principle of Americans, and he who has success will always find friends." Receiving this report in late December, Bethmann read it carefully and underlined sections.[20] It suggested that a successful blockade of Britain might turn American sympathies toward Germany. But the United States remained a question mark.

[17] Memo by Bethmann, Dec. 27, 1914, *Politische Dokumente*, II, 293–295; memos by Pohl of conversations with the Chancellor, Jan. 7, Jan. 23, 1915, *ibid.*, 297–298, 300; memo by Tirpitz, Jan. 27, 1915, *ibid.*, 301–303; Count von Quadt, Minister in Athens, to Jagow, Jan. 26, Jan. 28, 1915, German Foreign Ministry Archives (Secret).

[18] Bernstorff to Bethmann, Sept. 6, 1914, German Foreign Ministry Archives (Outbreak and Mediation).

[19] Bernstorff to Jagow, Sept. 21, 1914, *ibid.;* Bernstorff to Jagow, Sept. 22, 1914, German Foreign Ministry Archives (General); Bernstorff to Jagow, Oct. 4, 1914, *ibid.* (Outbreak and Mediation); Bernstorff to Jagow, Oct. 14, 1914, *ibid.*

[20] Bernstorff to Bethmann, Nov. 20, 1914, *ibid.* (General).

Rendering his preliminary verdict on the blockade plan, Bethmann gave more weight to uncertainty about the neutrals than to arguments advanced by the admirals. Shortly after receiving the first recommendation from Admiral Hugo von Pohl, the Chief of the Naval Staff, he asked the Foreign Ministry for an estimate of neutral reactions and received a further warning that the small neutrals, Italy, and the United States were all unpredictable. The submarine blockade should be instituted, he was advised, only if the military situation were so favorable as to make it folly for any neutral to take the Allied side.[21] Answering Pohl, the Chancellor gave due regard to this advice. Though conceding the desirability of striking England with any and all weapons, he detailed the possible political consequences. Italy and Rumania might declare war, and all the European neutrals might halt exports to Germany. "Although America, because of its lack of military forces, can hardly declare war on us," the Chancellor stated, "still it is capable of proclaiming a trade boycott against us, like that of England, as well as pushing forward, to some extent officially, the export of war material to our enemies." American antipathy toward Japan would no longer hinder the Allies from bringing Japanese troops to Europe, and the United States might join the campaign to destroy German commerce. "The thoughts of the Foreign Office," Bethmann assured Pohl, "are not of a legalistic nature, but they result from considerations of military-political opportunity. The question is not *if*, but *when* the measure may be taken without harm to our situation. . . . This moment seems today still not to have arrived."[22]

Bethmann clung to these doubts throughout most of January. Arguing the question before the Kaiser on January 9, Bethmann presented his case "very aptly and calmly." Although Pohl contested each of the Chancellor's reservations, he failed to overcome them. The Kaiser ruled, "U-boat commerce war shall for the time being be postponed, until the present uncertainty of the political situation has cleared. Then shall the All-Highest be asked anew for a decision. In the meantime the U-boats are to be readied for

---

[21] Zimmermann to Bethmann, Nov. 30, 1914, Spindler, *Handelskrieg*, I, 53–54.
[22] Memo by Bethmann, Dec. 27, 1914, *Politische Dokumente*, II, 292–295.

commerce warfare." [23] Bethmann was not fighting the admirals as he was to do later. He was simply holding them back until a propitious time.

Although the political air failed to clear, Bethmann's doubts began to yield. Italy and the Balkan governments grew steadily less friendly, and it came to seem as if restraint on Germany's part would not, in any case, hold them back from war. The United States meanwhile issued its protest against British interference with trade. Reports from Washington indicated a widening breach between the Allies and the United States.[24] The pro-German Queen of Sweden urged the Kaiser to declare a U-boat blockade, and the Naval Staff passed on intelligence reports indicating passivity, if not enthusiasm, in Norway and the Netherlands.[25]

Pressure on the Chancellor meanwhile grew fierce. It came, first of all, from the Naval Staff. Growing more and more insistent, Pohl proclaimed that the blockade had to come at once. England had only six or seven weeks of food supplies, he declared, but she would soon begin to receive Argentine grain. Once this grain was in her warehouses, England could hold out indefinitely against a blockade.[26] Germany's own food stocks were meanwhile dwindling. The Interior Ministry had grossly overestimated the harvest, making it necessary for the government to ration food.[27] Economists joined with the admirals, therefore, in urging a submarine blockade of

[23] Memo by Müller, Jan. 9, 1915, ibid., 190–192; memo by Pohl, Jan. 9, 1915, Pohl, Aus Aufzeichnungen und Briefen, 100–101.

[24] Bernstorff to Jagow, Jan. 25, 1915, German Foreign Ministry Archives (General), predicted a conflict over the shipping bill. Bernstorff to Jagow, Feb. 1, 1915, ibid., commented optimistically on the impression made by the German-American rally in Washington. The two messages were received respectively on Jan. 27 and Feb. 3.

[25] Reichenau, Stockholm, to Jagow, Jan. 6, 1915, German Foreign Ministry Archives (Secret); memo by Pohl, Jan. 20, 1915, Spindler, Handelskrieg, I, 66–67; memo by Jagow, Jan. 20, 1915, German Foreign Ministry Archives (U-boat War).

[26] Spindler, Handelskrieg, I, 67–74; Pohl, Aus Aufzeichnungen und Briefen, 101–105.

[27] Helmuth von Moltke, Erinnerungen, Briefe, Dokumente, 1877–1916 (Stuttgart, 1922), 399–406.

Britain, just as Zimmermann and others of the Foreign Office ceased to advise against it. Impressed also with the enthusiasm of the public, Bethmann felt unable to resist any longer.

He capitulated quickly. After conferring with Tirpitz, he met with Pohl, Zimmermann, Falkenhayn, and Interior Minister Clemens von Delbrück. All insisted that the submarine blockade be imposed as soon as possible. Bethmann still worried whether Germany had enough U-boats for the purpose, but Pohl assured him categorically that the fleet was ready. The Chancellor felt concern about Belgium. If American relief shipments were halted, Germany would have to feed the Belgians from her own slender stocks. Delbrück eased his mind on this score, and Bethmann went home from this conference with most of his doubts suppressed.[28] On the following day, February 2, his reservations broke entirely. After a conference with Zimmermann and the Treasury Minister, Karl Helfferich, he telephoned Pohl and told him to go ahead and submit to the Kaiser a decree declaring all the waters around Britain a submarine war zone.[29]

Since Pohl was leaving the Naval Staff to take command of the High Seas Fleet, he moved quickly to secure the Kaiser's consent. He wanted the decree to be his last official act. The imminence of his departure from the Naval Staff had, in all probability, spurred him during the entire month. It certainly led him to evade routine in approaching the Emperor, for he did not clear the decree with Tirpitz as he should have. Nor did he permit the cautious Chief of the Naval Cabinet to hear of it. At Wilhelmshaven, where the Kaiser came on February 4 to install Pohl in his new command, the admiral cornered the Emperor in the bow of a motor launch. With Tirpitz, Müller, and the rest of the imperial entourage sitting in the after-part of the boat, unable to hear above the motor's roar, Pohl asked the Kaiser to approve a war zone decree. The Emperor

---

[28] Memo by Tirpitz, Jan. 27, 1915, *Politische Dokumente*, II, 300–303; memo by Pohl, n.d., *ibid.*, II, 303; Spindler, *Handelskrieg*, I, 78–84.

[29] Memo by Pohl, n.d., *Politische Dokumente*, II, 303; Spindler, *Handelskrieg*, I, 85.

nodded his consent.[30] Pohl published a notice that day, over his own signature, and the Foreign Office sent a prearranged dispatch to the neutral capitals.

The waters around Great Britain and Ireland, declared the Navy and Foreign Ministries, were to become a war zone on February 18. Germany "will endeavor to destroy every enemy merchant ship that is found in this area of war," the dispatch warned, "without its always being possible to avert the peril, that thus threatens persons and cargoes. Neutrals are therefore warned against further entrusting crews, passengers and wares to such ships." Since English vessels sometimes hid under neutral flags, the warning went on, neutral ships ought not to enter the war zone. "[T]heir becoming victims of torpedoes directed against enemy ships cannot always be avoided. . . . The German Government . . . ," the dispatch concluded, "may expect that the neutral powers will show no less consideration for the vital interests of Germany than for those of England and will aid in keeping their citizens and the property of the latter from this area. This is the more to be expected, as it must be in the interest of the neutral powers to see this destructive war end as soon as possible." [31]

The decree of February 4 had been issued without full consideration of possible American reactions. When Wilson denounced it, the government suddenly realized the danger of drawing America into the war. Although the admirals expressed willingness to run this risk, Bethmann disagreed, holding American intervention to be a calamity which Germany should industriously avoid, and there commenced the running battle that was to continue for two years.

The issue arose almost as soon as the decree had been published, for dispatches from all neutral capitals indicated vexation and, in some cases, outrage. The Italian foreign minister spoke gravely to the German ambassador. From Norway, the Netherlands, and Denmark came reports of angry press comment and grim official

---

[30] Memo by Müller, Feb. 4, 1915, Walther Hubatsch, *Die Ära Tirpitz: Studien zur deutschen Marinepolitik, 1890–1918* (Göttingen, 1955), 128; *Politische Dokumente*, II, 306, 314.

[31] *Foreign Relations, Supplement: 1915*, pp. 96–97.

silence.[32] Bernstorff warned of anger in the United States, cabling *"A mistake could have the most serious consequences."* [33] Hard on the heels of this message came the American note calling attention "very candidly and earnestly, to the very serious possibilities of the course of action apparently contemplated." Should American ships or lives be lost as a result, the United States "would be constrained to hold the Imperial German Government to a strict accountability." [34] Despite some friendly embroidery, the note had the stiff texture of an ultimatum.

Before Bethmann thus loomed the contingency which he had foreseen but discounted. Recognizing the enormous economic power of the United States, he realized belatedly that her hostility could be the worst of all events for Germany. Italy, the Balkan states, and even the northern neutrals might follow the United States in a declaration of war, and the American protest note sounded like a preface to such a declaration.

He and Jagow at once concluded that the decree had been a mistake and ought to be revoked. With the help of Johannes Kriege, the Foreign Office's legal expert, they hastened to draw up a soothing reply to the American note, designed to reassure Wilson that Germany intended no harm to neutrals and that, if necessary, U-boats would be ordered not even to molest neutral ships carrying contraband. Since danger to American vessels rose solely from Britain's misuse of neutral flags, they also wished to declare, Germany was delighted that America had concurrently protested to London against this practice. If Britain yielded to this demand, they were prepared "to assert conditionally a guarantee that merchant ships sailing under American flags will not be attacked." [35] The Chancellor and Foreign Minister were ready thus to suspend the decree insofar as it affected the United States.

[32] Bülow to Jagow, Feb. 4, 1915, German Foreign Ministry Archives (U-boat War); Lucius to Jagow, Feb. 9, 1915, *ibid.* (Secret); Kühlmann to Jagow, Feb. 9, 1915, *ibid.*; Rantzau to Jagow, Feb. 8, 1915, *ibid.* (U-boat War).

[33] Bernstorff to Jagow, Feb. 11, 1915, *ibid.* (U-boat War).

[34] *Foreign Relations, Supplement: 1915,* pp. 98–101.

[35] German Foreign Ministry Archives (U-boat War) contains several drafts. One is printed in Spindler, *Handelskrieg,* I, 110–114.

The admirals, however, opposed. Learning somehow of the draft note, the Naval Staff objected with sailorly vigor. To frighten the neutrals was a chief object of the war zone decree, the staff insisted, and an exemption for American ships would vitiate the entire plan. "I am of the opinion," wrote Admiral Bachmann, the new Chief of the Naval Staff, "that the assurance asked for by the American government can in no wise be given, for such an assurance makes *absolutely ineffective* the U-boat action ordered." Tirpitz supported him, and so did Pohl, now Chief of the High Seas Fleet. Seeking to protect his earlier accomplishment, Pohl telegraphed: "Respect for the navy will in my opinion suffer terribly, if this loudly publicized undertaking, which has aroused great hope among the people, should be ineffectively carried out. Please present my opinion to His Majesty." [36] With one voice they insisted on ruthless prosecution of the U-boat war.

In view of the gravity of the issue, it seems extraordinary that the admirals should have taken such an uncompromising stand. Pohl, of course, felt some natural pride of sponsorship. Already a dying man, he may not have been entirely sound in mind. Bachmann and Tirpitz, on the other hand, remained healthy, and both confessed to private doubts as to the workability of the whole plan. Although Tirpitz had incited agitation in favor of U-boat warfare, he had advocated a scheme somewhat different from Pohl's, and he had been in favor of postponing operations until sufficient submarines could be built. When Pohl recklessly pushed through his own plan, Tirpitz was so infuriated that he considered resigning.[37] No less disturbed was Bachmann, who thought it almost inconceivable that any real success could be achieved with only twenty-one U-boats.[38] But he and Tirpitz chose, nevertheless, to disguise these doubts and make a resolute defense of Pohl's decree.

Having elected to defend the decree, they felt it necessary to fight against any compromise with the neutrals. Since the twenty-one

[36] Bachmann to Bethmann, Feb. 14, 1915, *Politische Dokumente*, II, 309–310; Pohl to Bachmann, Feb. 15, 1915, *ibid.*, 311.

[37] Memo by Tirpitz, Feb. 6, 1915, *ibid.*, 307.

[38] Bachmann diary, Feb. 15, 1915, Hubatsch, *Die Ära Tirpitz*, 128.

submarines would not be able to sink many ships, any real reduction in British imports would have to result from fear on the part of shipowners. As soon as the decree was issued, therefore, Tirpitz and Bachmann commenced a drive to terrify neutrals. The Grand Admiral called Gerard into a clandestine meeting where he warned of the terrible danger that American ships would run by entering the war zone.[39] Bachmann brought about the dispatch of a supplementary note to neutral capitals, declaring: "[T]here can be no further assurance for the saftey of neutral shipping in the English naval war zone. . . . Neutral vessels must therefore again be *most earnestly* warned against venturing into this area." [40] When Bethmann and Jagow proposed assuring the United States that neutral ships would not be damaged, the admirals naturally fought against them.

When the issue was brought before the Kaiser, Wilhelm solicited the views of Falkenhayn. Colonel Treutler, the Foreign Ministry's representative at Supreme Headquarters, and Admiral Müller, the Chief of the Naval Cabinet, were present. Treutler took it upon himself to represent the Chancellor's viewpoint. As he subsequently reported to Bethmann:

I declared that a promise of concession in the note was absolutely necessary, for no one could give assurance that America would not, upon receiving a firm response, have recourse immediately to strong measures against us. The stakes in this game are too high for any risk to be taken that is not absolutely necessary.

Herr v. Falkenhayn agreed and declared, under all circumstances it must be assured that America should not enter the war, so long as England is not subdued or else until our position is secure. He proposed in this connection that the question . . . be placed squarely before the Naval Staff, to what degree it would give assurance that England could be brought to modify her attitude within about six weeks. . . . His Majesty thereupon ordered . . . that the note . . . should be sent when and if the Naval Staff, as he could not but take for granted,

[39] Gerard, *My Four Years in Germany,* 217–218.
[40] Bachmann to Jagow, Feb. 10, 1915, Spindler, *Handelskrieg,* I, 101–103; memo by Foreign Ministry, Feb. 11, 1915, *Foreign Relations, Supplement: 1915,* pp. 104–105.

should admit that it could not guarantee such a prompt modification on the part of England.[41]

Falkenhayn had thus intervened to support the Chancellor.

The result, nevertheless, was a compromise, for Tirpitz and Bachmann evaded the question. Receiving a telegraphic inquiry from the Emperor, they put their heads together. They were expected, obviously, to state that the U-boat could not work its magic within six weeks. To Tirpitz's suspicious mind, the inquiry seemed a trick. Bethmann meant to secure a bald admission from the navy, the Grand Admiral believed, and use it as evidence to support some timid policy. Tirpitz and Bachmann framed their answer, therefore, with a view to blocking the Chancellor. "A silly question," remarked the Grand Admiral's deputy, "deserves a silly answer," and the admirals telegraphed the Kaiser, "Secretary of State and Chief of Naval Staff are convinced that England will modify attitude within six weeks of opening of new campaign if all available forces be energetically employed from start." Although the Kaiser noted on the margin of the telegram, "richly hedged," he directed the Foreign Office to recompose the note to America in collaboration with Tirpitz and the Naval Staff.[42]

Germany's reply to the United States, as a result, blended unassimilated strains. Although asserting the exclusive intention of damaging British commerce, the German government reiterated its earlier warning. Neutral shippers who ventured into the war zone assumed the responsibility for any accidents. Although submarine commanders had been instructed "to abstain from violence to American merchant vessels when they are recognizable as such," still American ships could be safe only if they avoided the war zone or proceeded through it under convoy.[43] Three-fifths of the note exhaled the dusty doubts of the Chancellery and Foreign Office; the remainder snorted with quarterdeck determination.

[41] Treutler to Bethmann, Feb. 15, 1915, *Politische Dokumente*, II, 313–315.

[42] Tirpitz, *Memoirs*, II, 149–150; Bachmann diary, Feb. 16, 1915, Hubatsch, *Die Ära Tirpitz*, 129; Tirpitz and Bachmann to Müller, Feb. 15, 1915, *Politische Dokumente*, II, 313; Müller to Tirpitz, Feb. 16, 1915, *ibid.*, 316.

[43] *Foreign Relations, Supplement: 1915*, pp. 112–115.

Hardly had Germany's civilians and admirals put together this note before they faced the same questions once again. A message from the United States suggested a possible compromise between Germany and Britain. In order to protect the interests of neutrals, the German government was to withdraw its decree and refrain from submarine attacks on merchantmen, while the British in return were to suspend orders which prohibited foodstuffs from reaching Germany.

The proposal aroused enthusiasm in the Foreign Office. Distressed by a continuing flow of ominous dispatches from Washington and Rome, Jagow exulted, "It would constitute a moral victory over England's pretended mastery of the sea. In addition we would ensure the provisioning of Germany." For bargaining purposes, the Foreign Minister wished to ask that Britain admit raw materials as well as food and, at the same time, give up the use of neutral flags and the arming of merchantmen. But he was willing to settle for the compromise as proposed and to abandon submarine warfare altogether.[44]

The admirals, of course, opposed such a compromise. In this case, however, they employed somewhat subtler tactics. Instead of attacking the proposal outright, they merely insisted on the addition of impossible conditions. The admission of raw materials as well as food should be demanded, not merely suggested, and Britain should be required to permit idle German merchantmen to take the seas under neutral flags and carry wares to German ports. Differing basically with the Foreign Minister, the admirals contended that Germany would give up an extraordinary advantage if she restricted her U-boat campaign and that the compensation had to be equal to the sacrifice.[45] To Bethmann and Jagow, the sacrifice already seemed bearable.

Once again, naturally, the civilians and admirals had to offer up their quarrel into the irresolute hands of the Kaiser. Bethmann, Jagow, Tirpitz, Bachmann, and Müller gathered with the Emperor at Schloss Bellevue in Berlin. The Chancellor opened the debate

[44] Memo by Jagow, n.d., *Politische Dokumente*, II, 320–321.
[45] Bachmann to Jagow, Feb. 27, 1915, *ibid.*, 321–322.

by asserting that all the conferees agreed in not wishing simply to reject the American proposal. The admirals, he intimated, had less desire than he to ask a genuine compromise, and their conditions were impossibly high. Arguing the case for a conciliatory answer to America, Bethmann "emphasized the necessity for us to bring in food and fodder from outside, even if only in small volume." Against the Chancellor stood Tirpitz and Bachmann. "The U-boat war," the Grand Admiral proclaimed, "was perhaps the only effective weapon we had against England."

Viewing this sharp conflict, the Kaiser wavered. He "declared that our entire people urgently demanded the U-boat war. The Chancellor had to reconcile himself to that." He "was obviously hesitating as to how he should decide," noted the admirals, and he turned to Müller, asking the Cabinet chief's advice. When Müller explained regretfully that he had to go against his uniform and side with the Chancellor, the Kaiser followed suit. He permitted Bethmann and Jagow to answer the compromise proposal as they desired.[46]

Nothing came of this victory, since the British government rejected the compromise and the Americans declined to press the question. Submarines continued to operate under the decree of February 4. Although the Chancellor had acknowledged the importance of keeping America out of the war, he had tried but feebly to halt the U-boat campaign. It was his policy to impose only such limitations as the United States insisted upon and to do this only when it was necessary to prevent war. His attitude was largely governed, therefore, by estimates of neutral attitudes, and these estimates were determined in turn by the information that came through official channels.

During the spring of 1915 Bethmann's concern about the U-boat problem temporarily eased. He practically ceased to worry about adverse effects on the south European neutrals. Whether Russia's advance against the key Carpathian fortress of Przemyśl could be checked or not seemed much more likely to determine their atti-

---

[46] Memo by Tirpitz and Bachmann, Feb. 28, 1915, *ibid.*, 322–326; Tirpitz, *Memoirs*, II, 299–301.

tudes.[47] Since his concern over the United States rose partly from fear lest her policies influence those of European neutrals, his interest in America also waned. In any case, dispatches from Washington indicated that American antagonism toward the U-boat had ebbed. Bernstorff radioed quotations from the Washington *Post,* a newspaper hostile to Britain, thus giving the impression that Americans had forgotten the submarine in a new preoccupation with the British blockade. "Our diplomatic situation here has significantly improved in recent days . . . ," cabled the ambassador shortly after the English blockade announcement, "commercial circles begin to realize that England menaces American trade more than we, and, conclusively, commercial interests are always decisive here." [48] Backing up the ambassador's estimate were reports from the military attaché, Captain Franz von Papen, who also described America's attitude as harmless. "It is above all pleasing," wrote Papen in early March, "to note how after 7 months of warfare, democratic heads begin at last to wonder whether the hated Prussian militarism has not borne a share in the marvelous blossoming of the German people and the marshaling of all moral and economic forces for the maintenance of our existence. . . . [C]ontinuous propaganda has succeeded in offsetting the prejudices of the independent press in this country, and the lessons of German successes on land and water will also triumph here, slowly but surely!" [49] When the United States then hesitated to make representations about the sinking of an American ship, the estimates of Bernstorff and Papen seemed to be confirmed. A German auxiliary cruiser halted and sank the *William P. Frye,* a grain ship bound for Queenstown, Ireland.

[47] Bethmann to Falkenhayn, March 17, 1915, German Foreign Ministry Archives (Secret).
[48] Bernstorff to Jagow, April 6, 1915, *ibid.* In a message bearing no date, but received in Berlin on Feb. 18, 1915, German Foreign Ministry Archives (General), Bernstorff had commented on the excitement roused by the question of British use of neutral flags. In a message of Feb. 19, 1915, *ibid.,* he observed that the torpedoing of an American vessel might be settled peaceably by appeal to the Hague Conventions and protracted litigation. He passed on a friendly editorial from the Washington *Post* in a cable of Feb. 22, 1915, *ibid.*
[49] Papen to War Ministry, March 7, 1915, German Foreign Ministry Archives (Secret).

According to Bernstorff's dispatches, Wilson and Lansing wanted to settle the question informally, and their eventual note to Berlin asked only compensation for the shipowner.[50] Such courtesy seemed evidence that earlier fears of the United States had been chimerae.

When House appeared in Berlin late in March, his soft language strengthened disbelief in American enmity. Seeking to redeem Wilson's reputation as an impartial mediator, the colonel underplayed all points of German-American contention. Attacking the chief complaint against the United States, the colonel explained away the munitions trade. "Mr. House declared the following:" noted Jagow, "America has almost no government munitions factories (or none at all), and for her army in case of a war, she will have to rely upon private industry. Should the President now forbid exports, he would ruin the domestic munitions and arms factories. That would constitute a danger for the State." Without explaining the Pan-American pact that he and Wilson had been discussing, House mentioned one of the articles envisioned for such a treaty. "Mr. Wilson has thought of declaring," Jagow further paraphrased, "that the State would take over the private factories. Then the export could be prohibited." Should this socialization of the munitions industry not occur, House explained, it would be the fault of Congress and not that of the President.[51]

House endeavored thus to make Wilson appear a friend of Germany, and by talking of freedom of the seas, he made it seem possible that the United States and Germany could team up against England. In his effort to show a friendly disposition, he went so far as to suggest that German-American understanding need not be hindered even by the Monroe Doctrine. Talking with the Minister for Colonies, House advised economic but not political colonization of Brazil.[52] Whether or not the colonel's pleasing words rebuilt

[50] Bernstorff to Jagow, March 12, March 23, 1915, German Foreign Ministry Archives (General); Bryan to Gerard, March 31, 1915, *Foreign Relations, Supplement: 1915*, p. 357.

[51] Memo by Jagow, March 23, 1915, German Foreign Ministry Archives (Secret Mediation).

[52] Diary, March 23, 1915, House Papers.

Wilson's status as an impartial mediator, they certainly blurred any image of the United States as a potential enemy.

Relieved of their momentary fright, German officials became sneeringly critical of the United States. They badgered every available American on the subject of the arms trade. "It seems that every German that is being killed or wounded is being killed or wounded by an American rifle, bullet, or shell," House wrote wryly from Berlin, "I never dreamed before of the extraordinary excellence of our guns and ammunition. They are the only ones that explode or are so manufactured that their results are deadly." [53] This criticism of America's arms trade appeared in public statements from Supreme Headquarters.[54] Reading one of Bernstorff's dispatches, the Kaiser himself vented extreme annoyance. The ambassador had written, "The policy of the American government is dominated by the sole idea of becoming enmeshed in no complications whatever. 'We want to stay out of everything' is the single rule." "*Then stop the ammunition!*" scrawled the Kaiser on the margin. "*Peace at any price,*" he added.[55]

Even Bethmann fell into this prevailing mood. In early April he met with the Bundesrat Committee on Foreign Affairs, whose members were ministers president from other German states. Before this select and discreet audience he asserted, "The United States of America would be able to play an influential role if imaginative and strong men were at her head. That is not the case. The American politicians limit themselves to paper protests even against Japan in order that their businessmen may enrich themselves. American public attitudes toward Germany have improved but without attaining influence on policy." [56] The respect and fear briefly inspired by the strict accountability note had soured into scorn.

[53] House to Wilson, March 26, 1915, *Intimate Papers*, I, 404; Gerard wrote of a "hate campaign" based on the munitions traffic, *Foreign Relations, Supplement: 1915*, pp. 103, 138.

[54] Gerard to Bryan, March 11, 1915, *ibid.*, p. 138.

[55] Bernstorff to Jagow, April 6, 1915, with marginal notes by the Kaiser, German Foreign Ministry Archives (General).

[56] Report on the session of April 7, 1915, Ernst Deuerlein, *Der Bundesratsausschuss für die Auswärtigen Angelegenheiten, 1870–1918* (Regensburg, 1955), Appendix VI, pp. 280–281.

Partly as a result of this changed feeling, the U-boat offensive increased its tempo. Under the influence of Wilson's protest, the Kaiser had first postponed the offensive and then permitted it to go ahead under severe restrictions. Only ships positively identified as enemy were to be destroyed; "in no circumstances are ships under neutral flags to be attacked." [57] As the likelihood of any real American opposition seemed to diminish, admirals began to find the Kaiser more attentive when they suggested giving a freer hand to the U-boat commanders. When the U-29 was rammed and sunk because of the restrictive order, the admirals believed it time to demand a change. Going directly to the Kaiser, Tirpitz and Bachmann asked him to approve a new directive. The Kaiser did so, instructing U-boat commanders to make their first concern thenceforth not the safety of neutral shipping but the security of their own boats. Although this new directive in no way repealed earlier orders to spare neutrals, it provided a wider margin for error and unchained the zeal of U-boat commanders.[58] Sinkings rose to more than one a day, and accidental torpedoings of neutral ships became common occurrences. Supporters of the navy expressed their enthusiasm, and even Tirpitz felt content.[59] The leash of strict accountability had frayed and snapped.

The U-boat commanders themselves had chafed under the earlier orders. Although they had succeeded in sinking about 132,000 tons of shipping during February and March, their achievement represented a dent of less than a quarter of 1 per cent of the United Kingdom's shipping. The cost in U-boats, furthermore, had been fearful. Four out of the twenty-one failed to return, and the surviving commanders welcomed as only right the new imperial

---

[57] Spindler, *Handelskrieg*, I, 135.

[58] *Politische Dokumente*, II, 328–329.

[59] Operations of all U-boats are described in Spindler, II, 16–55, from logs and operations reports. The total tonnage sunk by U-boats dropped appreciably after the new decree, largely because U-boat commanders spent their small stocks of torpedoes more freely, firing them against fishing boats and sailing vessels. The U-33, for example, fired two of its six torpedoes into the *Paquerette*, a French schooner of only 399 tons. But this drop in tonnage sunk seems to have gone almost unnoticed. See Albert Ballin, Director General of the Hamburg-American line, to Tirpitz, April 16, 1915, *Politische Dokumente*, II, 330–332.

order to pay more regard to their own vessels than to neutral flags.

Although the new order also gave them more discretion, the commanders still felt hampered by the duty of sparing neutrals. Hardly one had returned from a voyage without reporting the English approaches to be filled with neutral flags, nearly all concealing British ships. On board genuine neutral vessels, furthermore, search parties from submarines had invariably found contraband. Were it not for political restrictions, they declared, each submarine could sail to its assigned ground, discharge its torpedoes quickly into a sea of profitable targets, and shunt back to port for a reload. The potentialities of U-boat warfare seemed fully demonstrated. In the Dover Straits on February 24, the U-8 sent to the bottom three English ships totaling 11,047 tons. On March 12, the ill-fated U-29 repeated the exploit, sending down three ships off the Scilly Islands, and the U-28 matched this score on March 27. If given a free hand, the U-boat commanders felt, they could fulfill even the rash promises made by Germany's admirals.

Talk around submariners' wardrooms undoubtedly turned to the folly of weakling politicians in Berlin. Despite the quantity of newspaper comment on U-boat prospects, the submarine captains must have felt that the civil government was insufficiently aware of the U-boat. It does not seem far-fetched to suppose that conversation touched on the possibility of some dramatic awakening. It had taken the U-9's successful sinking of three British cruisers, after all, to open the eyes of big-ship admirals. If some new coup could be brought off, it might stir even the politicians. Suppose, for example, that the pride of England's merchant marine, the giant luxury liner *Lusitania,* should be sent to the bottom; would that not show the government, and the world, how powerful was this weapon which Germany held in her hand?

The possibility of an attack on the *Lusitania* had certainly been a subject of comment elsewhere. As early as August 5, 1914, a Manhattan newspaper had described the belligerent vessels in the port of New York. The German auxiliary cruiser *Vaterland* was flashing a light around the harbor, wrote an imaginative reporter for the New York *Herald,* and stopping it at intervals "to dwell covetously on the trim stern of the *Lusitania*." A German diplomat wrote to an influential American in March, 1915: "If one of our submarines should get the *Lusitania*, either under English or American flag, she would sink her, if she could, without a moment's hesitation." [60] Since the possibility was also a common subject of horrified speculation in Washington and London, it seems not at all improbable that it provided matter for enthusiastic discussion among German submarine commanders.

One who could discuss the subject with realism was Lieutenant Commander Schwieger. An articulate champion of U-boat warfare, Schwieger commanded the late model, long-range U-20. In January he had sailed out to intercept troopships entering Le Havre. He sank three English vessels without warning and damaged a fourth, which turned out to be a privileged hospital ship. During February he simply moved his boat from Wilhelmshaven to the advanced base at Zeebrugge. In port most of the time, he had plenty of opportunity to hear superior officers in the fleet and staff damn the blindness of politicians. During March, he was out for about two weeks, rounding Land's End and sailing as far north as the Firth of Clyde. He torpedoed one fair-sized English steamer deep in the mouth of the Bristol Channel, another off the Liverpool lightships, and a third on the way home. Before he set out again late in April, he had returned to Wilhelmshaven, learned of the Kaiser's new orders, and received a much broader directive. He was to return to Irish waters and the St. George's Channel area. His orders were simply "to attack: transports, merchant ships, warships." No caution about neutral flags or passenger-carrying vessels inhibited his initiative.

Knowing these waters to be the routes for the *Lusitania* and her sister, the troopship *Mauretania*, Schwieger may have made an inward promise to keep a weather eye open for a four-stack silhouette. Rounding the Orkneys and coming down west of the Hebrides, he failed to spot a worthwhile target. Northwest of Ireland he

[60] Unsigned letter to John Callan O'Laughlin, March 25, 1915, copy enclosed in O'Laughlin to Wilson, April 16, 1915, Wilson Papers. O'Laughlin, the editor of the Chicago *Herald*, described the writer as "a German who is a Minister in the diplomatic service of Germany and is aiding Prince von Bülow in Italy."

launched a torpedo against a ship under Danish flag, but the shot missed and the ship skittered out of harm. His first real victim was a tiny sailing boat caught outside of Queenstown on May 5. The next day's bag was considerably more satisfying: two English steamers totaling almost 12,000 tons. But the sea was rough and the fog heavy. He crept back to the Old Head of Kinsale, preparing to vacate the St. George's Channel in hope of clearer targets west of Ireland. The sight of a cruiser forced him under water and caused a delay in his departure. At 1:45 P.M. he surfaced to find the weather clearing. At 2:30 he sighted on the horizon a silhouette with four stacks and four masts.

Since the silhouette was moving diagonally across the U-boat's bow at 14 knots and the U-20's highest submerged speed was only 9½ knots, Schwieger's chances seemed slight. But the giant target suddenly began swinging to starboard, toward Queenstown and the U-20's track. As six bells sounded in his tiny control room, Schwieger ordered the engines to stop. At 3:10 he signaled away one torpedo. It spun through the water and struck amidships, just aft of the bridge. A spraying explosion followed. Wreckage lifted into the sky, higher than the ship's tallest mast. "Boiler or coal or powder?" jotted Schwieger in his log. The giant vessel heeled and began to settle. Watching it, Schwieger decided not to expend another torpedo. The ship was going under, and his binoculars could make out on the sinking stern which of the sisters he had sunk. The golden letters spelled out *Lusitania*. Schwieger set a course for Wilhelmshaven, to report his triumph.[61]

The *Lusitania* was carrying 1,959 persons. The voyage across the Atlantic had been uneventful. Thinking of the passengers' comfort, the captain had been careful not to remind them of the war. He had

---

[61] Spindler, *Handelskrieg*, I, 63–64, II, 86–88 and Map 4; Spindler, "The *Lusitania* Case," *Berliner Monatshefte*, XIII (1935); Thomas A. Bailey, "The Sinking of the *Lusitania*," *American Historical Review*, XLI (1935–1936), 54–73, and "German Documents relating to the *Lusitania*," *Journal of Modern History*, VIII (1936), 320–337. Notable among recent contributions to the voluminous literature on the *Lusitania* are Oscar Handlin, *Chance or Destiny* (Boston, 1956), 143–166, and A. A. and Mary Hoehling, *The Last Voyage of the Lusitania* (New York, 1956).

maintained a moderate speed and steered a straight course. The 18-knot speed and zigzag course prescribed by Admiralty warnings would have upset glasses in the parlors and interfered with deck games and promenades. It might also have alarmed some of the hundreds of women and children on board. For these reasons the *Lusitania*'s side had glided so easily into the path of Lieutenant Schwieger's torpedo. The point of impact chanced to be some vulnerable point. It may have been a bunker; it may have been a cargo space stored with cartridges or fuses; or the torpedo may have penetrated to a midships boiler. Whatever the case, the explosion shuddered the entire ship. Passengers leaped from their bunks or deck chairs, and panic swirled across the decks. In the next eighteen minutes, nevertheless, more than seven hundred went over the side into boats. The trained crew of an amphibious transport can hardly do better. But many could not be saved. When the ship sank, 1,198 passengers and crew went down with her. Of these, 128 were United States citizens. The submarine had thus created a real issue between the United States and Germany.

VII

Strict Accountability

Tension between Berlin and Washington did not result altogether from uncertainties in German policy. Wilson decided to take a stand against the submarine when he could conceivably have accepted the German decree as he had earlier the British mine-laying proclamation. He then elected to separate his demands upon Germany from any made upon Britain, insisting that the Germans obey international law regardless of what their enemies did. And he chose to threaten war if Germany failed to comply. In each case he had at least one alternative, usually one recommended to him by Bryan as more apt to preserve peace. He rejected these options, not through any want of eagerness to avert war, but because he suffered a profound sense of responsibility—for his party, for his country's interests and prestige, and for mankind. The tragedy was not a tragedy of errors. His decisions seemed the only ones that he could make.

The first important decision was, of course, that taken during the first week after publication of the German decree. The response, if any, to be made by the United States was the subject of much study in the Department of State. The question was thoughtfully explored by Wilson, Lansing, and Bryan. The Counselor's desk diary records no fewer than eight conferences between himself and one or both of the others during a five-day period. The German decree was even the topic of at least one cabinet meeting. The resultant note declaring that any injury to American vessels or citizens would be "an indefensible violation of neutral rights" for which the United States would demand "strict accountability," was thus a product of careful deliberation.

It is evident that the decision drew upon moralistic and legalistic sentiments. The U-boat campaign threatened to shred what Wilson called "the fine fabric of international law," since submarines were to sink without visit and search, without drawing any distinction between contraband and non-contraband, and without taking precautions for the safety of non-combatants.[1] Unable to risk these amenities, owing to their boats' thin hulls and slow speeds, the German captains would menace innocent cargoes and lives. Even Bryan, the least legalistic of the policy-makers, was thunderstruck at the sweeping violations of international law contemplated. He "was at first incredulous;" the German ambassador records, "he believed a submarine campaign of this nature to be unthinkable, and my statements to be merely bluff." [2]

It was also evident that the German decree represented a threat to important American economic interests. Orders from the Allies for war goods, food, and other supplies were lifting the United States out of the near depression in which she had languished during the earlier months of the Wilson administration. Instead of disrupting business, as had at first been feared, the war had brought a restoration of confidence and optimism. Newspapers gave full publicity to monthly export-import statistics showing ever more favorable balances of trade. New plant construction was reported from all industrial sections of the country. Machine-tool manufacturers and other capital-goods suppliers were reported working overtime. Wheat futures reached a new high in January, 1915. And most of this new flush of economic health seemed attributable to the prospect of Allied demand.[3] Since the German decree called upon American shippers to halt war trade, it jeopardized this new prosperity.

---

[1] Wilson used the phrase in his open letter to Senator Stone, Feb. 24, 1916, *Public Papers*, IV, 123.

[2] Bernstorff, *My Three Years in America*, 111.

[3] New York *Times*, Jan. 25, 1915; *Literary Digest*, L (Feb. 6, 1915), 287; *ibid.* (March 6, 1915), 459-461; Crighton, *Missouri and the World War*, 41-47.

Cabling to House, the President referred to it as an "extraordinary threat to destroy commerce." [4]

Confronted with this menace not only to morality and law but to American interests as well, the administration possessed two broad options. One was to enter a protest calling upon the Germans to withdraw their decree. The other was to refrain from comment, as had been done earlier with regard to the bombardment of open cities, where, similarly, the threat to American lives was not yet actual. Such inactivity could have been justified on the ground suggested editorially by the isolationist Washington *Post:* "The stress and excitement of war, however great, are not sufficient to lead [Germany] to outrage the friendship of the United States . . . . we may be sure that extreme care will be taken . . . to avoid the destruction of American ships." [5] The policy would have been, in other words, to wait and hope that no specific case arose.

This alternative was, in fact, canvassed. Lansing suggested it to the President. After reacting angrily to first reports of the decree, the Counselor received an Associated Press report of an explanatory statement by the German Foreign Ministry. There it was asserted that German naval forces had orders to avoid violence to neutral ships insofar as they could be recognized as such. Perhaps relying on this statement, Lansing wrote Wilson, "The memorandum impresses me as a strong presentation of the German case and removes some of the objectionable features of the declaration. . . . In my opinion it makes the advisability of a sharp protest, or of any protest at all, open to question." [6]

But this alternative was rejected. Lansing went to see Wilson at the White House, subsequently telephoned Bryan, and started work the next morning on a formal note. [7] The basis was a draft which Lansing had composed during his earlier heat and which Wilson had carefully edited. The decision had thus been taken by the President, probably with the concurrence of Lansing and Bryan,

---

[4] Wilson to House, Feb. 13, 1915, Baker, *Wilson,* V, 252.
[5] Washington *Post,* Feb. 7, 1915.
[6] Lansing to Wilson, Feb. 7, 1915, Baker, *Wilson,* V, 247.
[7] Desk diary, Lansing Papers; 763.72/1434, State Department Archives.

to state immediately the moral and legal objections to Germany's decree.

There is, unfortunately, little record of the reasoning that under-lay this choice. One may infer that Wilson was prompted by a feeling that the Germans, being morally obtuse, responded best to the language of force. An eminent New York lawyer advised, "a clear and firm declaration in advance generally tends to obviate such extreme action as will force a collision, while on the other hand a failure so to do often brings about the very thing that we most desire to avoid." Wilson commented that this observation was "exactly in line with the facts and the right way of dealing with them." [8]

Yet another possible motive was the President's sense of public opinion. He had already reached the conclusion that 90 per cent of the people were unsympathetic toward Germany. This impression, created by popular reactions to the invasion of Belgium, was re-inforced when the public seemed to grow even more angry at acts like the burning of Louvain and alleged atrocities by German troops. Some Republican leaders had already charged timidity and im-morality in the failure to denounce the invasion of Belgium. It had been alleged that the ship purchase plan, being deliberately favorable to Germany, was a bid for hyphenate votes.[9] Had the administration failed to denounce the submarine decree, these attacks might have swelled into major partisan issues, jeopardizing Wilson's domestic leadership and at the same time increasing the difficulty of calming public passion and preserving neutrality. It may have been to thoughts of this nature that the President was referring when he wrote a friend on February 14:

The last two weeks have been like a fever . . . no one who did not sit daily here with me, each anxious twenty-four hours through, could possibly realize the constant strain upon our vigilance and upon our

---

[8] J. M. Dickinson to Lansing, Feb. 6, 1916, *Lansing Papers*, I, 196–198; Wilson to Lansing, Feb. 11, 1915, *ibid.*, 195, note 32.

[9] Gwynn, *Spring-Rice*, II, 245; *Intimate Papers*, I, 196–198; Cummins, *Indiana Public Opinion*, 24–33; Garraty, *Lodge*, 306–308; Philip C. Jessup, *Elihu Root* (2 vols.; New York, 1938), II, 321–322; Robert E. Osgood, *Ideals and Self-Interest in America's Foreign Relations* (Chicago, 1953), 138–139; New York *Times*, Nov. 29, Dec. 5, Dec. 7, Dec. 18, 1914, Jan. 8, Jan. 17, Feb. 6, Feb. 7, 1915.

judgement entailed by the rapidly varied conditions both "on the Hill" (that is, in Congress) and in the war area. . . . To keep cool heads and handle each matter composedly and without excitement as it arises, seeking to see each thing in the large, in the light of what is likely to happen as well as in the light of what is happening now, involves a nervous expenditure such as I never dreamed of. . . . I go to bed every night absolutely exhausted, trying not to think about anything, and with all my nerves deadened, my own individuality as it were blotted out.[10]

In any case, the agony had brought forth a decision in favor of announcing clear-cut opposition to the submarine.

In the announcement there was one ambiguity. It was not plain from the note of February 10 whether the United States demanded that Germany merely spare neutral ships or spare all American passengers, even if traveling on English and French liners. Since the latter question subsequently formed the issue upon which Wilson took his stand, some students have been led to conclude that it was an afterthought, that Wilson did not intend originally to call for strict accountability for American lives lost on belligerent vessels.

Some contemporary observers believed that this principle had been omitted from the note. One wrote Lansing, asking him about the omission, and Lansing replied: "I think if you will read the note again, you will find that it is open to interpretation so far as American lives are concerned." [11] The unpublished diary of Chandler Anderson has since revealed the reason behind this ambiguity. "Mr. Lansing took the view," noted Anderson,

that . . . if this proposition had been flatly stated, we could not consistently have addressed a note to Great Britain objecting to the use of the American flag on British ships. In fact, we should have had to approve the use of American flags on British ships for the purpose of giving notice that American citizens were on board. . . . This inconsistency would have stood in the way of sending a note to Great Britain about the flag contemporaneously with the note to Germany about the

[10] Wilson to Mary A. Hulbert, Feb. 14, 1915, Baker, *Wilson*, V, 253–254.
[11] Lansing to Floyd Clarke, Feb. 16, 1915, Lansing Papers.

war zone, and the Department was exceedingly anxious to balance its protests in this way in order to avoid an appearance of partiality.[12]

The note to Britain, as a matter of fact, added to the ambiguity. It employed gentler language. Whereas the note to Germany rang with phrases like "serious impossibilities" and "critical situation which might arise," the message to London expressed only "anxious solicitude." Through House, furthermore, the President softened it still further, cabling to the colonel, "I regretted the necessity of sending this note about the unauthorized use of our flag, but it could not be avoided, for sooner or later the use of the flag plays into the hands of Germany."[13] By sending the two notes simultaneously, nevertheless, the government did suggest that it might consider Germany justified in carrying out the submarine decree if British ships failed to abandon the practice of flying neutral flags.

This impression was also given by the compromise proposal shortly put forward. Bryan, who was probably responsible for the balancing note to Britain, sponsored this move. Troubled by loose talk of war in the American press, and, according to Gerard, in the German press as well, he wrote to Wilson, "The situation is growing more and more delicate and under the proposed war zone plan we are liable, at any time, to have a disaster over there which will inflame public opinion. . . . I am led to believe from Conversations with the German and Austrian Ambassadors that there would be a chance of securing the withdrawal of the military zone order in return for favorable action on the food question." German willingness to permit distribution of foodstuffs by American agencies, observed Bryan, "takes away the British excuse for attempting to prevent the importation of food. . . . If I am not mistaken the efforts to bring this 'economic pressure'—as they call it—upon women and children of Germany will offend the moral sense of our country." The United States ought, therefore, to propose a swap. Britain should raise her ban on foodstuffs, and Germany should retract her war zone decree. "If we can secure the withdrawal

[12] Entry for "January 4–February 13, 1915," Anderson Papers.
[13] *Foreign Relations, Supplement: 1915*, pp. 98–101; Wilson to House, Feb. 13, 1915, Baker, *Wilson*, V, 252.

of these two orders," wrote the Secretary, "it will greatly clear the atmosphere and if we cannot do it I believe that we are approaching the most serious crisis that we have had to meet."[14]

Fresh dispatches from Europe supported the Secretary's argument. Replying to the American protest note, the German government indicated a willingness to withdraw its decree should the United States induce Britain to mend her ways. Gerard interpreted this statement as an offer to trade submarine warfare for food and raw materials. When Bryan prodded Page, he even received some encouragement from London. After discussing these dispatches with Lansing, Bryan wrote hurriedly to Wilson, declaring that a "ray of hope" had appeared. Authorizing the Secretary and Counselor to compose a formal compromise proposal, Wilson replied, "I am cheered to see the 'ray of hope' and we must follow it as best we can."[15]

Although Wilson approved this proposal of Bryan's, Lansing did not. He was convinced that Germany had no serious need for imported food and that she would never accept a genuine compromise.[16] He was also troubled by the danger of creating ill-feeling in London. As Chandler Anderson noted in his diary, "We agreed that great care must be taken . . . in order not to put Great Britain in a false position, if she was unwilling to agree to Germany's proposal."[17] Great Britain and Germany were both to resign the use of floating mines, the use of submarines for attacks on commerce, and the flying of false colors on merchant vessels. Germany was to entrust the distribution of food imports to American agencies, and Britain was, in turn, to allow food shipments to these agencies.

Wilson, on the other hand, was enthusiastic. He backed up the formal proposal with a long cable to House. "Please say to Page," instructed the President, "that he cannot emphasize too much . . . the favorable opinion which would be created in this country if the British government could see its way clear to adopt the suggestions

[14] Bryan to Wilson, Feb. 15, 1915, *Lansing Papers*, I, 353–354.
[15] *Foreign Relations, Supplement: 1915*, p. 111; *Lansing Papers*, I, 361–363.
[16] Memo by Lansing, Feb. 15, 1915, *Lansing Papers*, I, 367–368.
[17] Diary, Feb. 19, 1915, Anderson Papers.

made there. Opinion here is still decidedly friendly, but a tone of great uneasiness is distinctly audible now and the events and decisions of the next few days will undoubtedly make a deep impression." [18]

The effort proved a dismal failure. On the very evening of the formal proposal, a dispatch from London darkened the ray of hope. "The English," declared Page, "will show the greatest courtesy and consideration to us but none henceforth to the Germans." House wrote to Wilson on the same day, "While I was urging Grey to bring about such a compromise, and while he regarded it with some favor, I thought it could readily be seen that the Naval and Military Departments would most likely veto it, and the chance of successful negociation was slender." [19] After the formal proposal, nevertheless, Page still described Grey as personally favorable to the compromise, and Bryan kept at Spring-Rice about the immorality of a starvation campaign. Gerard meanwhile shocked the Secretary by suggesting that the United States compel British acceptance by threatening an embargo on arms. "I presume it was not his own idea," Bryan commented to Wilson, "for he could hardly expect a threat as effective in securing any understanding." [20]

Whatever hope or illusion remained was smashed by Germany's formal reply. It will be remembered that Bethmann and Jagow, overcoming the admirals, had composed an answer which they believed to embody acceptance of the compromise proposal. But it was not so read in Washington. Official German translates harshly, and the conditions which Jagow had intended as trading points were taken by Wilson, Lansing, and even Bryan, to be demands. When the British declared that the Germans had made a mockery of the compromise proposal, the American government was prepared to accept this judgment. Though Bryan was tempted to con-

[18] Wilson to House, Feb. 20, 1915, Baker, *Wilson,* V, 313; the text received by House, House Papers, differed in some particulars.

[19] *Foreign Relations, Supplement: 1915,* pp. 118–119; House to Wilson, Feb. 20, 1915, Wilson Papers.

[20] *Foreign Relations, Supplement: 1915,* p. 122; Gwynn, *Spring-Rice,* II, 256; Gerard to Bryan, Feb. 27, 1915, *Foreign Relations, Supplement: 1915,* p. 126; Bryan to Wilson, March 1, 1915, Wilson Papers.

tinue correspondence, Wilson and Lansing discouraged him.[21]

Despite the futility of both the balancing note to Britain and the compromise proposal, they indicate the extent to which American policy remained unclear. Wilson had, to be sure, chosen to denounce the German decree, but he had not decided whether he meant to hold his ground or not. So long as he dealt conjointly with German and British infringements of international law, he was in a position to back down from his insistence that Germany should mend her ways. It would still be possible for him to declare that he could not endeavor to coerce both parties and, as a practical matter, to yield before both.

Nor had he decided as yet what he meant by "strict accountability." He was to assure Bryan that it meant only judicial accountability and that he did not intend to press for immediate settlement of any case. Speaking of the British blockade order, furthermore, he used the very same phrase. America should hold Britain, he declared, to "a strict accountability for every instance of rights violated and injury done." [22] In this case it seems highly unlikely that he thought of going so far as to threaten war. In application to Germany the meaning of the phrase remained uncertain.

During the spring of 1915, there were thus two critical decisions to be made. The United States might choose to continue coupling

---

[21] As translated by the clerks of the American Embassy in Berlin, the key passage read: "The Imperial Government must, however, in addition [attach importance to] having the importation of other raw material used by the economic system of noncombatants including forage permitted. To that end the enemy Governments would have to permit the free entry into Germany of the raw material mentioned in the free list of the Declaration of London . . . ."; *Foreign Relations, Supplement: 1915,* pp. 129–130. The German text reads: "Daneben muss aber die deutsche Regierung Wert darauf legen, dass ihr auch die Zufuhr anderer der friedlichen Volkswirtschaftdienenden Rohstoffe einschliesslich der Futtermittel ermöglicht wird. Zu diesem Zweck hätten die feindlichen Regierungen die in der Freiliste der Londoner Seekriegsrechtserklärung erwähnten Rohstoffe frei nach Deutschland gelangen zu lassen . . . ."; *Norddeutsche Allgemeine Zeitung,* March 3, 1915. Bryan to Wilson, March 2, 1915, Bryan-Wilson Correspondence, State Department Archives; desk diary, Lansing Papers.

[22] Wilson to Bryan, March 24, 1915, *Lansing Papers,* I, 289.

German and British infringements of law, or might separate them, declaring that what was demanded of Germany was altogether independent of any demands upon the Allies. Similarly, America might elect to define "strict accountability" in terms of postwar judicial claims or might back its demands with a threat of war.

The less risky alternative was advocated in each case by Bryan. He had already shown some disagreement with Lansing as, for example, in vetoing the Counselor's proposed protest against the bombing of Antwerp. He had come to differ with Wilson over the tactics to be employed in seeking peace. Although he had evidently accepted the necessity of protesting the submarine decree, he remained convinced that virtually no law, no moral principle, and no national interest were worth the risk of war. As incidents grew out of the German submarine campaign, his fears quickened, and he came to plead with the President for a policy of appeasement.

The first incident arose late in March, when a U-boat sank the British steamer *Falaba*. Among the victims was Leon C. Thrasher, a second-class passenger who happened to be an American citizen. Lansing contended that the death had resulted from an illegal act by the German captain. Law required a naval commander to ensure the safety of passengers before sinking a prize. But a firm protest, the Counselor acknowledged, would be an attack on the entire submarine campaign, and the consequences might be "most momentous." [23]

Bryan was profoundly disturbed by this likelihood. He searched his imagination for arguments in mitigation of the German act. If the *Falaba* had been armed, he suggested, then the U-boat commander might have been justified in firing without warning. It might also be reasoned, he wrote Wilson, that Thrasher had voluntarily risked death. "I cannot help feeling," he observed, "that it would be a sacrifice of the interests of all the people to allow one man, acting purely for himself and his own interests, and without consulting his government, to involve the entire nation in difficulty

[23] Lansing to Bryan, April 2, 1915, *ibid.*, 365–366; Lansing to Bryan, April 5, 1915, *ibid.*, 369–370.

when he had ample warning of the risks which he assumed." He advised against taking issue with Germany over the case.[24]

When Wilson reached a contrary decision, Bryan became almost frantic. The President had hesitated for three weeks, consulting his cabinet and other advisers, before ruling reluctantly in favor of a "solemn and emphatic protest against the whole thing, as contrary to laws based, not on mere interest or convenience, but on humanity, fair play, and a necessary respect for the rights of neutrals." Bryan objected forcefully. He warned that such a note as Wilson proposed would certainly bring on a crisis. Germany and her partisans could charge the American government with failure to protest against the food blockade and to press Britain on her use of neutral flags. While a charge of unneutrality would be unjustified, he believed, still it would be leveled against the administration, and the whole atmosphere was dark with omens of war. So dangerous did the predicament seem to Bryan, indeed, that he proposed a desperate escape. Instead of protesting the death of Thrasher, Bryan wrote earnestly to Wilson, the United States should speak in behalf of "the tens of thousands who are dying daily in this 'causeless war.'" The President should make a public appeal for the acceptance of mediation.[25]

As a result of this eloquent appeal, Bryan won his point. The President rejected his suggestion of a peace appeal; such a bid, he commented, "would be futile and would probably be offensive. We would lose such influence as we have for peace." Nevertheless, he yielded to the Secretary's insistence on the Thrasher case. "Perhaps," he wrote to Bryan, "it is not necessary to make formal representations . . . at all." [26]

Discussion of the Thrasher case had been amiable. Not until the very end had any conflict developed. The fundamental differences between Bryan, on the one hand, and Lansing and Wilson, on the other, had nevertheless begun to emerge. When fresh incidents occurred, these differences sharpened. On the day following Wil-

[24] Bryan to Wilson, April 7, 1915, *ibid.*, 374–376.
[25] Wilson to Bryan, April 23, 1915, *ibid.*, 377–378; Bryan to Wilson, April 23, 1915, *ibid.*, 378–380 (the text in the Wilson Papers is somewhat different from the printed version, though in no important respects).
[26] Wilson to Bryan, April 28, 1915, *Lansing Papers*, I, 380.

son's retreat on the Thrasher question, a German plane dropped two bombs on the American freighter *Cushing*. Three days later, on May 1, a submarine attacked the American tanker *Gulflight* without warning. Two American sailors leaped overboard and drowned. Before full reports on these incidents reached Washington, the *Lusitania* had gone down.

These incidents increased Bryan's anxiety. His mind was temporarily eased by Wilson's assurance that the settlement of issues could be deferred until after the war's end. After the Secretary had heard this declaration from the President, he wrote in great relief, "it is the *possibility* of *war* from which I shrink and I think we have a good excuse for asking that the disputes be settled when reason reigns." [27] But this cheerful feeling soon faded.

The *Lusitania*'s sinking required a note of protest. Bryan did not deny its necessity, for the loss of one hundred and twenty-eight innocent American lives simply could not be overlooked. But he was desperately unhappy, writing to Wilson: "I join in this document with a heavy heart." "As the days wore on," writes his wife, "his sleep became broken. He would lie awake three and four hours at a time, tossing, jotting down memoranda for the next day's work, etc." [28]

In succeeding weeks he advanced one proposal after another in the hope of forestalling a crisis. When sending out the note to Germany, he suggested that the President make a statement softening its effect. To discourage jingoes in the United States and to reassure the Germans, Wilson should declare that accountability might be strict without necessarily being immediate, and he should make it plain that the United States always approved of investigation and arbitration. When Wilson finally turned down this proposal, Bryan replied that he was "very sorry. . . . I fear the use the jingo element will make of the German note." [29] He did not lose faith in Wilson's

[27] Bryan to Wilson, May 5, 1915, Baker, *Wilson*, V, 326.

[28] Bryan to Wilson, May 12, 1915, Wilson Papers; Bryan, *Memoirs*, 421.

[29] Bryan to Wilson, May 12, 1915, *Lansing Papers*, I, 400–401; Wilson to Bryan, May 12, May 13, 1915, *ibid.*, 401–402; Bryan to Wilson, May 13, 1915, Wilson Papers; Wilson to Bryan, May 13, 1915, *Lansing Papers*, I, 403; Bryan to Wilson, May 13, 1915, *ibid.*, note 60.

determination to postpone a final settlement, but he wanted this purpose made plain.

Bryan also desired action to prevent any new issue from arising. Rather than depend on Germany to abate her submarine warfare, he believed, the United States ought to ensure for herself that German torpedoes created no more potential crises. He advocated a warning to American citizens not to travel on belligerent vessels while negotiation with Germany was in progress. After discussing this idea with Wilson, he directed Lansing to draw up such a warning. At the same time, he strongly urged a protest to Britain against interference with American trade. The warning, he believed, would not only prevent crises but also exhibit America's peaceful intentions, while the note to Britain would demonstrate American impartiality. But the President rejected both of these suggestions.[30]

In all of these specific suggestions, Bryan was not only advocating that the United States place its peace above all other interests, he was also pleading with the President to keep the initiative in his own hands. Explaining his later opposition to the second *Lusitania* note, he said, "It will be Germany's turn to make the next move. If it were our turn, I could trust the President to find a way out. It is virtually placing the power to declare war in the hands of another nation."[31] To the ends of preserving the peace and keeping the initiative, he advocated holding open an escape route by continuing to couple German and British violations of law. He also urged public assurances that issues would not be pressed to the point of war.

Hardly any of the President's other advisers favored these alternatives. Although House was still abroad, his advice came in by letter and cable, and he, too, favored resolute opposition to Germany. After the *Lusitania*'s sinking, he cabled Wilson predicting war and suggesting that war might not be a bad result. "[I]t will not be a new war," he declared, "but an endeavor to end more speedily an old one. Our intervention will save, rather than increase, the loss

---

[30] Bryan to Wilson, May 14, 1915, *ibid.*, 406; Wilson to Bryan, May 14, 1915 (two letters), *ibid.*, 406–407.

[31] Bryan, *Memoirs*, 422.

of life." [32] The colonel was told that Wilson had read the message to the cabinet; if this was so, it undoubtedly awakened some sympathy there. The Postmaster General and the Secretary of the Navy did seem to lean toward Bryan's view, but they were willing to abide by the President's decisions. Insofar as the views of other secretaries have been recorded, they tended in the direction of House's.[33] Lansing had differed with the Secretary from the outset. Trying to estimate German policy, he had concluded at the very beginning of the submarine campaign that the German government had no fear of a war with the United States. He interpreted the submarine campaign as deliberate provocation. "Everything seems to point," he wrote even before the *Lusitania*'s sinking, "to a deliberate effort to affront this Government and force it to open rupture of diplomatic relations." [34] As a result, he opposed any measures of appeasement, reasoning that they would ultimately be unsuccessful and merely cause the United States humiliation, lessened prestige, and reduced internal unity. He argued for a stiff protest in the Thrasher case, opposed any intimation that the United States might postpone settlements till after the war, and drafted resolute notes in connection with the *Lusitania*.[35]

The choice between appeasement and defiance lay, of course, with Wilson, and it is evident that he suffered great uncertainty. When the Thrasher case arose, he waited three weeks before deciding to protest and then changed his mind when Bryan objected. He spoke on his own initiative of deferring settlements till after the war, and he seriously considered issuing a statement to that effect along with the first *Lusitania* note. It was only insistence by Lansing, Tumulty, and the Secretary of War, supported by information from a newspaper reporter, that led him to change his mind. When he did so,

[32] House to Wilson, May 9, 1915, *Intimate Papers,* I, 434.

[33] House diary, June 20, 1915, *ibid.,* II, 5; L. M. Garrison to Baker, Nov. 12, Nov. 30, 1928, Baker Papers; desk diary, Lansing Papers; David F. Houston, *Eight Years with Wilson's Cabinet* (2 vols.; Garden City, New York, 1926), I, 135 ff.; John M. Blum, *Joe Tumulty and the Wilson Era* (Boston, 1951), 96–98.

[34] Memo by Lansing, Feb. 15, 1915, *Lansing Papers,* I, 367–368; Lansing to Bryan, May 1, 1915, *ibid.,* 382.

[35] *Ibid.,* 395–398, 407–408, 417–418, 426, 440–445, 449–450.

furthermore, he apologized to Bryan. "I was as sorry as you can have been to withdraw the 'statement' which we had intended for the press. It cost me a struggle to do so." [36]

Before sending the *Lusitania* note, as a matter of fact, Wilson went through another long period of inner debate. For three days after the sinking, he isolated himself. Having to appear in public in order to address a group of newly naturalized citizens, he gave voice to some of his own uncertainty. A citizen, he declared, had "not only always to think first of America, but always, also, to think first of humanity." Yet, as he went on to say, "The example of America must be the example not merely of peace because it will not fight, but of peace because peace is the healing and elevating influence of the world and strife is not. There is such a thing as a man being too proud to fight. There is such a thing as a nation being so right that it does not need to convince others by force that it is right." [37]

Sometime during the month after the *Lusitania*'s sinking, however, Wilson made up his mind on the two crucial issues remaining. He decided to separate his demands upon Germany from any made upon Britain. When Bryan advocated that a note should be sent to London protesting the blockade in order to offset the stern note to Germany, Wilson replied, "[W]e cannot afford even to seem to be trying to make it easier for Germany to accede to our demands by turning in similar fashion to England concerning matters which we have already told Germany are none of her business. It would be so evident a case of uneasiness and hedging that I think it would weaken our whole position fatally." [38] The President had elected to close off this avenue of retreat.

He also decided to back up his demands on Germany with an implied threat of war. It is not evident, to be sure, that he had made up his mind to carry out this threat if the Germans defied him. Down to the day in 1917 when he asked Congress to declare war, he

---

[36] Wilson to Bryan, May 14, 1915, *Lansing Papers*, I, 404; desk diary, Lansing Papers; Blum, *Tumulty and the Wilson Era*, 96–97; Garrison to Baker, Nov. 12, 1928, Baker Papers.

[37] Baker, *Wilson*, V, 330–335; New York *Times*, May 11, 1915; *Public Papers*, III, 318–322.

[38] Wilson to Bryan, May 20, 1915, *Lansing Papers*, I, 411.

remained unsure in his own conscience whether it would be right to take such action. Nevertheless, he did conclude in 1915 that he could not compel Germany to respect American interests and obey the law unless he confronted her with the menace of force. As a result he spurned Bryan's suggestions of appeasement. "It is hard to turn away from any suggestion that might seem to promise safety for our travellers," he wrote after Bryan had proposed warning Americans off belligerent ships, "but what is suggested seems to me both weak and futile. To show this sort of weak yielding to threat and danger would only make matters worse." [39] And he abandoned his earlier notion of promising to postpone settlements until after the war.

The logic behind these two decisions is no easier to document than that behind the strict accountability note. It is, however, somewhat easier to infer. Wilson had been warned often and authoritatively that British opinion was volatile and dangerous. If he condemned the blockade at the same moment that he damned the submarine, he might find himself in Madison's predicament of being at odds with everyone. Bryan could take a different view because he had great confidence in the cooling-off period treaties, one of which he had negotiated with England. Since Wilson probably did not share the Secretary's faith in these treaties, he would have acted irresponsibly if he had created trouble in London while the submarine issue remained unresolved.

His decision to threaten war was also affected, no doubt, by sensitivity to public opinion. Despite his self-enforced isolation, he cannot have remained unaware that the *Lusitania*'s sinking had created an apparent surge of nationalism. Press surveys indicated a widespread desire for some vigorous response on the part of the government. [40] Not only Theodore Roosevelt, who condemned the sinking as an "act of piracy," but other Progressives and Republicans stood ready to marshal this sentiment against Wilson if he chose to be less than

[39] Wilson to Bryan, May 14, 1915, *ibid.*, 406.

[40] New York *Times*, May 11, 1915; New York *World*, May 12, 1915; St. Louis *Globe-Democrat* survey of May 16, 1915, cited in Crighton, *Missouri and the World War*, 83–84; *Literary Digest*, L (May 29, 1915), 1262–1264; see Link, *Wilson and the Progressive Era*, 164–165.

resolute and unyielding. It would not be true, of course, to say that the President's mind was overcome by fear of public feeling. He wrote to a friend, "I am deeply touched and rewarded . . . by the extraordinary and generous support the whole country has given me in this German matter. . . . I know, moreover, that I may have to sacrifice it all any day, if my conscience leads one way and the popular verdict the other." [41] Yet the pull of public passion, threatening his domestic leadership and, indeed, his ability to maintain executive supremacy, must have exercised some influence over his judgment.

It is finally by no means insignificant that Wilson knew his country's prestige to be involved. When he rejected Bryan's proposals as "weak" and "yielding," he did not have reference only to the reactions they might evoke in Berlin. Walter Page warned that a conciliatory policy would "forfeit European respect," and Wilson commented, "It is a very serious thing to have such things thought, because everything that affects the opinion of the world regarding us affects our influence for good." [42] Not only economic and moral interests, but also the intangible political interest, a great power's prestige, seemed at stake.

Wilson chose, in any case, to reject the alternatives advocated by Bryan. He did so in letter after letter, turning down specific suggestions from the Secretary, but he did not finally commit himself until it became necessary to send a second note on the *Lusitania* issue. Germany's long delayed reply to the first communication challenged the facts stated by the United States and invited protracted debate. It yielded none of the principles insisted upon by the President and offered little or no abatement of the submarine campaign.

Wilson promptly informed the cabinet of the policies upon which he had settled in his own mind. He read to the assembled secretaries a note which he had drafted on his own typewriter, strongly worded and demanding that Germany give up her submarine campaign. When one member asked about a protest to England, several objected. Material interests, they said, ought not to be considered at

[41] Wilson to Nancy Toy, May 23, 1915, Baker, *Wilson*, V, 347.
[42] *Foreign Relations, Supplement: 1915*, pp. 385–386; Wilson to Bryan, May 10, 1915, *Lansing Papers*, I, 387.

the same moment with "a grave matter involving human lives."
This brought Bryan upright. As Secretary Houston recorded afterward:

> Bryan got excited. He said that he had all along insisted on a note
> to England; that she was illegally preventing our exports from going
> where we had a right to send them; and that the Cabinet seemed to be
> pro-Ally. . . . The President sharply rebuked Bryan, saying that his
> remarks were unfair and unjust. He had no right to say that any one
> was pro-Ally or pro-German. Each one was merely trying to be a good
> American. We had lodged a protest with England and might do so
> again at the proper time, but this would be a singularly inappropriate
> time to take up such a matter with her. . . . Certainly, in any event,
> when we had before us a grave issue with the Germans, it would be
> folly to force an issue of such character with England. We were merely
> trying to look at our duty and all our problems objectively. He added
> that certain things were clear and that as to them his mind was
> made up.[43]

For the next few days, Bryan continued his efforts to block or
soften action that might bring on a clash with Germany. When
Wilson asked him to put his suggestions in writing, he responded
with several long and forceful letters. But the suggestions he made
were the same ones he had made in April and May. Wilson had
rejected them before, and he did so again. Bryan urged delay on
the ground that "time itself is a factor of no mean importance."
Wilson replied, "I think that time . . . is of the essence in this
matter in order that the German Government should be made to feel
that we regard it as pressing." [44]

Bryan repeated his pleas again and again. On the morning of
June 3, he sent Wilson a long letter arguing for arbitration. On the
afternoon of the same day, he sent another letter, pleading that citizens be forbidden to travel on ships carrying contraband. When the
cabinet session on the following day showed Bryan that he was
almost alone in opposing a new note, he bundled all his arguments
into one earnest appeal. This letter, sent to Wilson on June 5, urged

[43] Houston, *Eight Years with Wilson's Cabinet*, I, 135–139.
[44] *Lansing Papers*, I, 419–420; Wilson to Bryan, June 2, 1915, *ibid.*, 421.

arbitration, restriction of passenger traffic on belligerent ships, and the dispatch of a protest against Britain before a new note was sent to Germany.[45]

The President rejected all Bryan's pleas. Arbitration, he said, could not be suggested "without hopelessly weakening our protest." An order concerning passengers and contraband, though desirable, was "clearly impossible . . . before the new note goes to Germany." And he wrote, "I think that our object with England can be gained better by not sending a note in connection with this one than by sending it." Although the President said he rejected Bryan's advice "with deep misgiving," he rejected it firmly and completely.[46] On the following day Bryan informed the President that he had decided to resign.

On June 9 the second *Lusitania* note was dispatched. Since it merely restated the points made in the first note, many observers were at a loss to understand why Bryan had given up his office. From the correspondence that has since come to light, it is evident, of course, that the Secretary's position had simply become untenable. After his victory in preventing a protest in the Thrasher case, not a single one of his major recommendations had been accepted. Wilson told House that when Bryan gave notice of his intention, "he had remarked with a quiver in his voice and of his lips 'Colonel House has been Secretary of State, not I, and I have never had your full confidence.' "[47] But the Secretary's resignation was not a mere product of pique or of a sense of uselessness.

It was one symbol, indeed, of the administration's gradual shift from indrawn pacifist reformism to Progressive nationalism. Bryan had been a spokesman not only for appeasement but for isolationism. He had contended that the United States should not defend any interest at the risk of war, and he had argued for policies that would leave the power of decision in Washington—that would, in other words, permit the United States to make concessions without complete humiliation. It was these policies, as well as his specific recom-

---

[45] *Ibid.*, 422–426, 427–428, 436–438.
[46] Wilson to Bryan, June 5, 1915, *ibid.*, 438.
[47] Diary, June 24, 1915, House Papers.

mendations, that the President had rejected, and Bryan resigned because Wilson had chosen to close the avenues of retreat, to threaten war, and to stake America's prestige on the success of his diplomacy.

The fact that America's prestige was thereafter at risk is obvious. It is of such importance in understanding the relative inflexibility of American policy after June, 1915, however, that the point deserves to be stressed. The logic of the strict accountability and *Lusitania* notes, of course, remained active. Submarine warfare posed a constant threat to cherished rules of international law and to the interests of humanity, as Wilson interpreted them. Increasingly, too, it menaced the American economy. As Wilson himself remarked in 1916, foreign trade had ceased to be marginal to America; it had become vital.[48] Since the largest part of America's expanding export trade continued to be carried in British and French ships, a submarine campaign would result in serious losses to American traders, even if attacks were restricted to Allied vessels. Any effective campaign, furthermore, would also injure American prosperity by raising freight rates and decreasing the amount of available tonnage. The United States retained an important, if not vital, interest in maintaining its ground.

If only moral principles and economic interests had been at stake, there might have been some possibility of compromise. Passenger travel, for Americans at least, might have been restricted to vessels certified as carrying no contraband and plainly marked. Although the definitions of contraband were becoming increasingly uncertain, some arrangement might also have been made for shipping noncontraband items separately. It needs to be remarked that no such compromise would have had the slightest chance of lasting success. The German submarine enthusiasts wanted to stop all shipping from entering British and French ports, and the Chancellor was checking their desires only at the point where America threatened war. Had the United States retreated from the positions of the strict accountability and *Lusitania* notes, she would soon have found herself pressed for still further concessions, until there remained no

---

[48] Address at Detroit, July 10, 1916, *Public Papers*, IV, 228–230.

choices except to make war or to give in altogether. But Wilson and his advisers were, at best, only dimly certain of what German policy would be. What deterred them, more than anything else, was a recognition that America would sacrifice prestige if she hedged, compromised, or retreated.

Each of the three leading policy-makers conceived of America's prestige in slightly different terms. To House it involved primarily the nation's standing among the powers. It was this international status to which he was referring when he advised Wilson, "Your first note to Germany after the sinking of the *Lusitania* made you not only the first citizen of America, but the first citizen of the world. If by any word or act you should hurt our pride of nationality, you would lose your commanding position overnight." [49] During the *Sussex* crisis in 1916, he noted in his diary, "What I tried to impress upon him was that if he failed to act he would soon lose the confidence of the American people and also of the Allies, and would fail to have any influence at the peace conference. I tried to make him see that we would lose the respect of the world unless he lived up to the demands he has made of Germany regarding her undersea warfare." [50] And he expressed the same thought when speaking to the German ambassador. "I made it clear to him," House wrote Wilson, "that if you did not take a strong stand in regard to submarine warfare as conducted by Germany you would not have the slightest influence in bringing about peace. The Allies would consider this country impotent to either help or hurt, and they would look upon us as they look upon the South American republics." [51] Although the colonel could speak in the same breath of the President's status among the American people, he was chiefly concerned with the nation's reputation abroad.

Lansing, who succeeded Bryan as Secretary of State, looked upon domestic and international prestige as two sides of the same coin. It was necessary, he felt, to keep an appearance of resoluteness and strength, not only for the sake of being listened to in foreign capitals

[49] House to Wilson, Aug. 22, 1915, *Intimate Papers*, II, 30.
[50] Diary, March 30, 1916, *ibid.*, 228–229.
[51] House to Wilson, April 22, 1916, House Papers.

but also to retain the confidence of people at home. He nearly always coupled the two, writing, for example, of the *Arabic* negotiations, "continued discussion of this subject would, I believe, be contrary to the dignity of the United States and would invite general criticism from the American people." [52] When advising Wilson to meet an Austrian submarine campaign with an ultimatum, he declared, "I feel fully the responsibility of sending it. But what other course is open to us if we wish to maintain our self-respect as a Government?" [53] When urging severance of relations over the *Sussex* case, he asserted, "The honor of the United States and the duty of the Government to its citizens require firm and decisive action." [54] To Lansing the avoidance of compromise was a necessary matter of duty, honor, dignity, and self-respect.

To Wilson, on the other hand, it was a moral question as well as a matter of pride. In this context he preferred the term, honor, to any other, and he maintained that it should be preserved for its own sake and not merely for appearances. Although he could be upset by reports of unfavorable or scornful comment abroad, he could also assert, as he did in a letter to Lansing, "what we are guided by is our sense of what is just and right and not our sensibility as regards what other nations think about us." [55] From some of his statements, it is true, one gets the impression that he was thinking of the nation's appearance in the eyes of moral men or perhaps of its reputation in history. There is, for example, another letter to Lansing in which the President declared that refusal to consider arbitration in submarine cases "would place us in a very difficult position to justify in the opinion of the rest of the world." [56]

Although the attitudes of the three were different, the practical result of their common concern was the same. All believed that any appearance of concession or compromise would taint the reputation, the dignity, or the honor of the nation. Despite the fact that Wilson's

---

[52] Lansing to Wilson, Sept. 11, 1915, *Lansing Papers*, I, 480.
[53] Lansing to Wilson, Dec. 17, 1915, *ibid.*, 499.
[54] Lansing to Wilson, March 27, 1916, *ibid.*, 539.
[55] Wilson to Lansing, Sept. 10, 1915, *ibid.*, 477.
[56] Wilson to Lansing, Dec. 27, 1915, *ibid.*, 507.

conception of prestige was the least substantial of the three, it was he who stated most eloquently and forcefully the reasoning that underlay the refusal to contemplate retreat from the positions taken in the strict accountability and *Lusitania* notes. Defending his diplomacy against pacifist attacks, he wrote to Senator Stone in February, 1916:

For my own part, I cannot consent to any abridgement of the rights of American citizens in any respect. The honor and self-respect of the nation is involved. . . . To forbid our people to exercise their rights for fear we might be called upon to vindicate them would be a deep humiliation indeed. . . . It would be a deliberate abdication of our hitherto proud position as spokesmen even amidst the turmoil of war for the law and the right. It would make everything that it has achieved during this terrible struggle of nations meaningless and futile. . . . What we are contending for in this matter is of the very essence of the things that have made America a sovereign nation. She cannot yield them without conceding her own impotency as a nation and making virtual surrender of her independent position among the nations of the world.[57]

[57] *Public Papers*, IV, 123.

VIII

Firmness and Patience

The United States had proclaimed its opposition to any effective
U-boat campaign. Wilson had chosen to make the issue one between
the United States and Germany alone, and he had implicitly threatened to use force if the Germans failed to yield. But his conditions
were not met. Germany sent litigious notes about the *Lusitania,*
refusing either to apologize or to pay reparations, and ships continued to be torpedoed. In view of his earlier decisions, the President
was constantly faced with the necessity of reviewing his position.
It was almost true, indeed, that he had to rethink his foreign policy
every morning before breakfast. His broad alternatives were always
the same. He could back down completely and adopt the policies
Bryan had recommended; or he could take steps to carry out his
implicit threats. In practice he did neither. Although he retreated
somewhat from the categorical demands of his *Lusitania* notes,
he stood firm on the essential requirement that submarine commanders spare neutral lives. In individual cases, meanwhile, he
offered the Germans opportunity and ample time to meet his contentions. He was at once firm and patient.

It was Wilson himself who insisted on patience. His chief advisers
urged him to be bolder and more aggressive, but his own inclination was to speak softly. When Germany replied to the second
Lusitania note, her communication seemed sarcastic in tone and
framed for consumption at home. Lansing, who had succeeded

Bryan as Secretary of State, advised answering it curtly, but Wilson chose instead to draft an argumentative, somewhat rambling reply. The President took the view, as he wrote House, that "the Germans *are* modifying their methods; they must be made to feel that they must continue in their new way unless they deliberately wish to prove to us that they are unfriendly and wish war." When Lansing sought to stiffen up the President's draft with "a veiled (rather thinly veiled) threat," Wilson excised it, commenting, "I do not think we need add *a sting*." [1] Although the final note marked no retreat from the demand that American lives be spared, it was so worded as to require no further correspondence. Wilson had meanwhile made every effort to create an impression that the crisis had passed.[2]

When the *Arabic* was sunk in August, 1915, he again held out against counsels of impatience. The incident was a clear affront to his principles, for a large, unarmed passenger liner had been torpedoed without warning, and two Americans had drowned. Colonel House wrote to him immediately, "Further notes would disappoint our people and would cause something of derision abroad. In view of what has been said, and in view of what has been done, it is clearly up to this Government to act." House recommended sending Bernstorff home or else summoning an emergency session of Congress. Though Lansing was less outspoken, he indicated that relations probably ought to be severed.[3] But Wilson tactfully rejected the counsel of both. He declined to summon even an emergency Cabinet meeting, and House noted in his diary, "I am surprised at the attitude he takes. He evidently will go to great lengths to avoid war." [4]

[1] Lansing to Wilson, July 14, 1915, *Lansing Papers*, I, 457–458; Wilson to Lansing, July 19, 1915, 763.72/1940, State Department Archives; Wilson to House, July 14, 1915, Baker, *Wilson*, V, 367; Lansing to Wilson, July 21, 1915, *Lansing Papers*, I, 463–464; Wilson to Lansing, July 21, 1915, *ibid.*, 464.

[2] *Ibid.*, 454–455; New York *Times*, July 13, July 15, 1915.

[3] House to Wilson, Aug. 22, 1915, Wilson Papers; Lansing to Wilson, Aug. 24, 1915, *Lansing Papers*, I, 470–471.

[4] Wilson to Lansing, Aug. 21, 1915, *ibid.*, 468; diary, Aug. 21, 1915, *Intimate Papers*, II, 32.

When Bernstorff displayed anxiety and eagerness to find some solution, Wilson encouraged Lansing to negotiate. The ambassador disclosed that his government had earlier ordered submarine commanders to obey prize rules, and he offered to recommend an open pledge that ships would not be sunk without warning. Wilson insisted only on a further promise that efforts would be made to provide for the safety of passengers and crews.[5] When Bernstorff published a declaration to that effect, the President had every reason to feel that his patience had been rewarded with success.

The *Arabic* crisis was not in fact so easily disposed of. The official German note explaining the sinking failed to confirm Bernstorff's declaration, and at almost the same time another torpedoing occurred. The westbound liner *Hesperian* went down, without, as it happened, loss of life. Lansing advised the President to threaten a break in relations unless Germany disavowed the *Arabic* sinking and formally endorsed the promises made by her ambassador. But Wilson insisted on waiting for all the facts and meanwhile encouraged House to talk informally with Bernstorff. The President suffered anguish in what he described as "the labyrinth made for us by this German 'frightfulness,'" and he was evidently willing to accept a compromise, if one could be devised. Tempted by the thought of arbitration, he turned away from it only out of fear that the public might view acceptance as cowardice. For much the same reason he felt it necessary to require disavowal by Germany of the submarine commander's act. He wrote to House, "Bernstorff is evidently anxious to get his government off from any explicit or formal disavowal of the *Arabic* offense; but I do not see how we can with self-respect do that. The country would consider us 'too easy' for words, and any general avowal of a better purpose on their part utterly untrustworthy."[6] But he was willing to accept no more than a disavowal coupled with a pledge that unarmed vessels would not be sunk without warning and precautions.

[5] Lansing to Wilson, Aug. 26, 1915, *Lansing Papers*, I, 471–473; Wilson to Lansing, Aug. 27, 1915, *ibid.*, 473.
[6] Lansing to Wilson, Sept. 11, 1915, *ibid.*, 478–480; Wilson to House, Sept. 7, 1915, House Papers; Wilson to Lansing, Aug. 9, 1915, *Lansing Papers*, I, 466; Wilson to House, Sept. 20, 1915, House Papers.

He might even have been willing to acknowledge Germany's right to sink armed vessels by surprise attack. Bernstorff explained away the *Hesperian* case by stating that the ship had been armed, and Wilson commented ruefully to Lansing that the ambassador was exploiting a mistake he himself had made earlier. In the first *Lusitania* note he had condemned attacks on "unarmed" ships while Lansing had recommended the term, "unresisting." [7] But he seemed willing to let the error stand, if the Germans pressed the question. In any case, he insisted on nothing more than disavowal of the *Arabic* sinking, and he carried patience to the point of waiting a full month for Bernstorff to extract the necessary note from his own government.

He ultimately won not only a disavowal but also a declaration that regulations for U-boat commanders were "so stringent that the recurrence of incidents similar to the *Arabic* case is considered out of the question." This pledge not only satisfied Wilson's immediate demands but also met the broader requirements that he had laid down in the *Lusitania* correspondence. If the German government had elected to fight out the distinction between unarmed and unresisting ships, Wilson might have retreated somewhat from the ground he had taken earlier, but the *Arabic* crisis was, as it turned out, a trial of his patience rather than of his firmness.

It was but one such test. Although German submarines ceased temporarily to create incidents, Austrian U-boats began to do so. In November, 1915, the *Ancona,* an Italian liner, was torpedoed without warning and without any precautions for saving lives. Of the twelve Americans on board, nine perished. When the State Department cabled inquiries to Vienna, it was told that the *Ancona* had attempted to flee and that deaths were due to "condition of panic incident to Latin blood." Although the Austrian government ultimately made a full apology, it was not long before yet another sinking occurred. The *Persia,* a P & O steamer bound for Alexandria, went down with at least two Americans on board, one of them

[7] Wilson to Lansing, Sept. 10, 1915, *Lansing Papers,* I, 477; *ibid.,* 396.

a consular officer. The German and Austrian governments both restated their willingness to be bound by international law, but both denied responsibility. "We are asked," the French ambassador observed, "to believe [the *Persia*] sank of its own accord, committing a kind of suicide." [8] Germany was still refusing, furthermore, to settle the *Lusitania* case, even though she had apparently accepted all of Wilson's contentions.

Equally trying to the President's fortitude was the mounting evidence of German espionage and sabotage in the United States. The papers of Dr. Heinrich Albert were picked up by a Secret Service agent, while the documents carried by an unofficial courier, James F. J. Archibald, were confiscated by the British and forwarded to Washington. Another agent, Dr. Joseph Goricar, deserted the Austrian service and published information about a 3,000-man network directed by the Austrian consul general in New York, Franz von Nuber, and by the German military and naval attachés, Captain Franz von Papen and Frigate-captain Karl Boy Ed. Goricar's testimony, added to the documents seized from Albert and Archibald, revealed organized attempts to spread propaganda, cause work stoppages in munitions plants, and derange America's chemical and metals industries.[9] Sufficient evidence was accumulated meanwhile to bring the conviction of one German for blowing up a bridge, the arrest of five others for conspiring to destroy munitions ships, and the indictment of yet another on a charge of violating American neutrality. Unaccountable explosions in factories, rumors of bomb plots, and examples of individual enterprise, like the attempt of Eric Münther to assassinate J. P. Morgan, generated widespread public alarm.[10] The evidence before the President was even more

[8] Penfield to Lansing, Nov. 23, 1915, *Foreign Relations, Supplement: 1915*, p. 619; Jusserand to Lansing, Jan. 22, 1916, *ibid.: 1916*, p. 149.

[9] New York *World*, Aug. 15–Aug. 21, 1915; *Literary Digest*, LI (Nov. 27, 1915), 1207–1208; New York *Times*, Oct. 2, Oct. 24–Oct. 31, Nov. 2–Nov. 7, Nov. 10–Dec. 31, 1915.

[10] New York *Times*, Dec. 18, Dec. 20, Dec. 21, Dec. 22, Dec. 28, 1915; *Literary Digest*, LII (Jan. 1, 1916), 7; Great Britain, Foreign Office, *American Press Resumé*, Sept. 10, 1915, cited in Peterson, *Propaganda for War*, 157; Cummins, *Indiana Public Opinion*, 137–141.

impressive, since he had learned, among other things, of conspiratorial dealings between German agents and Mexican revolutionaries.[11]

Faced not only with continued submarine activity but also with this proof of subversive activity, Wilson's patience seemed to falter. He allowed Lansing to write Vienna about the *Ancona* case in terms so peremptory as to constitute virtually an ultimatum. He instructed the Secretary of State to insist, furthermore, upon a *Lusitania* settlement and to tell Bernstorff, if necessary, that "a failure to settle this question in the same frank way that the sinking of the *Arabic* was settled would be little less than a repudiation of the assurances then given us and seem to lead back to the very crisis in our relations that was then so happily avoided."[12] Prompted by the mounting evidence of German conspiracies, he insisted that the principal Austrian and German agents be sent home. Nuber's exequatur was voided; Papen and Boy Ed were declared *personae non gratae;* and the Austrian government was asked to recall its ambassador. Although Lansing expressed doubts about the propriety of adding Dr. Albert to this list, Wilson replied that he wished to be rid of him, even if it were necessary to resort to technicalities.[13] He appeared to be trimming ties with the Central Powers and, at the same time, approaching an ultimatum on the submarine question.

In reality, however, the President was still far from forcing the Germans to a clear-cut choice or from taking the choice out of their hands. Determined though his actions appeared, he was, in fact, less vigorous than some of his counselors advised. House had recommended immediate severance of relations over the *Ancona* case, and Wilson had declined to do so.[14] When Lansing advised cutting off the correspondence with Austria and warning her of war, Wilson rejected this counsel as well. Instructing the Secretary to continue negotiations, he wrote, "how can we refuse to discuss the matter

[11] Diary, July 11, 1915, Lansing Papers; memo by Lansing, Dec. 1, 1915, *Lansing Papers*, I, 86; Lansing, *War Memoirs*, 75.
[12] *Lansing Papers*, I, 494, 497–498; Wilson to Lansing, Nov. 21, 1915, *ibid.*, 493.
[13] *Ibid.*, 80–90.
[14] House to Wilson, Nov. 21, 1915, *Intimate Papers*, II, 47.

with them until all the world is convinced that rock bottom has been reached?"[15] While he demanded a settlement of the six-months-old *Lusitania* case, he also insisted that conversations with Bernstorff be conducted with a minimum of publicity. House's discreet talents were enlisted for this work.[16] In acting against German and Austrian agents, furthermore, the President also stopped short of the measures urged upon him. McAdoo recommended adding Bernstorff to the list of *personae non gratae,* and it was House's view that the connection with the Central Powers should be cut to a single thread. Although Wilson believed Bernstorff to be as guilty as the others, he declined to send him home. He sought, too, to make the actual dismissals seem measures of law enforcement and nothing more. They "would have to be managed mighty well," he remarked to House, "if the implication of a diplomatic breach is to be avoided."[17]

Wilson had reason to feel, in the second place, that he was not forcing Germany's hand. The situation in the Balkans had not escaped his attention, and he recognized how preoccupied were the Central Powers with the delicate balances there. Bulgaria had just entered the war on their side. Two German armies under General August von Mackensen were acting in conjunction with Bulgarian forces in an effort to overwhelm Serbia. Although the Allies had made a landing at Salonika, their contingents were not large enough to affect the battle, unless Greece and Rumania should abandon neutrality and join them. Upon the wavering inclinations of these two Balkan neutrals depended the ability of Turkey to remain in the war and of Germany to continue checking reinforcement and resupply of Russia. It was obviously important to the Central Powers that Greece and Rumania be kept neutral, and it was apparent that a breach with America might affect the decisions of these unpredictable governments. House and Lansing both commented to Wilson on this fact, and the President himself remarked that he felt sure Germany would do nothing to make trouble with

[15] Wilson to Lansing, Dec. 29, 1915, *Lansing Papers,* I, 509.
[16] *Ibid.,* 494–496; Wilson to Lansing, Dec. 29, 1915, *ibid.,* 508–509.
[17] Baker, *Wilson,* V, 372; Wilson to House, Sept. 7, 1915, *ibid.,* 386.

the United States until the Balkan situation was settled.[18] His apparent tendency to become more firm was thus partly a result of sensitivity to changing conditions in the theaters of war. It reflected, in any case, no alteration in his fundamental policy of forbearance.

The *Sussex* crisis in March and April, 1916, was to be the ordeal of this policy, and even then the President was to allow Germany leisure to reach a clear-cut decision. His continued patience and procrastination meant not only that the choice between peace and war remained in Berlin but that Bethmann had time both for maneuver in imperial councils and for manipulation among domestic political groups. Wilson's patience was thus a factor of the first importance in the preservation of American-German peace.

In seeking to explain this policy of forbearance, one must look to the President himself. His chief advisers recommended that he follow more forceful tacks. There is no evidence that he differed much with their appraisals. Yet he rejected their counsel.

Lansing advised him to press for complete surrender on the U-boat issue, avoid prolonged correspondence, and openly threaten war. The Secretary based his stand, first of all, on the assumption that Germany would choose war or peace largely on the basis of her own hard calculations of probable gain and loss. He did not as a rule contend that America's action would have any material effect on Germany's decisions. He stood, secondly, on the belief that America should not flinch at the possibility of war. In his diary for July 11, 1915, he wrote:

I have come to the conclusion that the German Government is utterly hostile to all nations with democratic institutions because those who compose it see in democracy a menace to absolutism and the defeat of the German ambition for world domination. . . . Germany must not be permitted to win this war and to break even, though to prevent it this country is forced to take an active part. This ultimate necessity must be constantly in our minds.[19]

[18] Diary, Oct. 16, 1915, Anderson Papers; House to Wilson, Nov. 21, 1915, Wilson Papers; Lansing to Wilson, Nov. 24, 1915, *Lansing Papers*, I, 495.
[19] Lansing Papers.

Even this diary entry, it should be stressed, reflected a hope that the necessity for intervention might not arise, and Lansing noted additionally that American public opinion was not ready for combat. But the belief that war would not be an unmixed evil undoubtedly helped him to be stoical when contemplating the possible results of the policy he advocated.

House did not share Lansing's view that Germany could be influenced only slightly by America's actions. Having visited Berlin, he had a sharp awareness of German internal divisions. He recognized that some of her military and naval leaders were willing to risk war with the United States, but he thought the civil authorities anxious to keep the peace. It was his view that the United States by seeming resolute and willing to fight would strengthen the peace advocates against the war faction.[20] Arguing that greater firmness by Wilson would increase the chances of avoiding conflict, he gave much the same advice as the Secretary of State.

His basic assumption, in any case, was identical with Lansing's. Time and again he remarked to Wilson that if Germany were victorious, she would promptly turn against the United States. Speaking with the President during one period of Allied reverses, he commented, "it looked as if [Germany] . . . had a better chance than ever of winning, and if she did our turn would come next." [21] Like Lansing, too, he held that "It ought to be America's fixed policy not . . . to permit Germany to win if the strength of this country can prevent it," and he could see advantages as well as disadvantages if war should result from a policy of firmness.[22]

Wilson did differ with these advisers just as they differed with each other. He may, for instance, have continued to feel that Germany might respond to moral suasion. He did seem sometimes to agree with Lansing that the Germans acted solely from calculations of power. Complaining to House about the slowness of the *Arabic* negotiations, he remarked, "I am suspicious enough to think that they are merely sparring for time in order that any action we might

[20] See, as examples, *Intimate Papers*, I, 434, 469, II, 17–18, 21, 30.
[21] Diary, Oct. 8, 1915, House Papers.
[22] Diary, Dec. 15, 1915, *ibid*.

take may not affect the unstable equilibrium in the Balkans." [23] Although he received a good deal of intelligence from House, Gerard, and others about the political contests in Germany, he rarely, if ever, commented on them. When he spoke of influencing the Germans, he seems to have thought in terms of bringing them collectively to their senses, to a realization of moral obligations, and to a recognition of the interests of humanity.

He does appear, however, to have shared the view of Lansing and House that Germany was an enemy. He hoped that she might be too exhausted by the European war to turn immediately upon the United States, but he was not sanguine. Whenever House asserted that the Western Hemisphere would be her next target if she defeated the Allies, Wilson admitted the probability of this prediction.[24] His speeches advocating preparedness exhaled a deep apprehension for the long-range security of the Western Hemisphere. When Lansing sent him a memorandum arguing that war would have advantages as well as disadvantages, Wilson responded, "it runs along very much the same lines as my own thought." [25] He was thus at least willing to accept the premises of a policy of greater firmness.

Where he differed most from his two advisers was not in rationale but in emotion. Wilson retained an instinctive love of peace and horror of war. He could say eloquently, for example, that America ought to remain at peace in order to set an example for the world and be ready to use her influence when the war was over, and at the same time agree with House and Lansing that America's role in the postwar settlement would be greater if she joined in the fighting. The frightfulness of war weighed on his conscience. So did the sense that war was a release of passions—unreasonable, unhealthy, and impious. He was more in sympathy with pacifism than either of his chief advisers.

Wilson was also a cautious man. When the *Hesperian* was sunk,

[23] Wilson to House, Aug. 25, 1915, Baker, *Wilson*, V, 373; see also *ibid.*, 374–375, and diary, Dec. 2, 1914, Dec. 15, 1915, House Papers.
[24] *Intimate Papers*, I, 298, II, 84–85; diary, Sept. 22, Dec. 15, 1915, House Papers.
[25] *Lansing Papers*, I, 470–471.

the President refused to be drawn into a hasty judgment, even though it was only days since the German ambassador had given pledges that no further incidents would occur. "My thought just now is full, of course, of this *Hesperian* business," he wrote to House. "It looks, I fear, as if it were going to be extremely difficult to get at any real facts in the case; and yet the facts are essential to any intelligent handling of the case." [26] He felt a need to be certain of his ground.

He also had a deep sense of duty. As House recognized, "The welfare and happiness of a hundred million people are largely in his hands. It is easy enough for one without the responsibility to sit down over a cigar and a glass of wine and decide what is best to be done." [27] Wilson had to be clear in his mind and conscience that he was leading his nation wisely. "The country is undoubtedly back of me in the whole matter," he wrote to House during the *Arabic* crisis, "and I feel myself under bonds to it to show patience to the utmost." [28]

Although Wilson accepted the judgments of his advisers, he declined to follow their recommendations. His pacifist inclinations held him back. So did his native caution and his sense of duty. Where House and Lansing might conclude that all recourses had been exhausted, Wilson's instincts were to wait and hope for some miraculous deliverance. These traits of the President's thought and character were probably more important than any other single factor in producing the American policy of patience and delay.

The influence of public opinion upon the President ought not, however, to be overlooked. The American people were not united. At one extreme were pacifists, opposing war in any circumstances; at the other were chauvinists, advocating armed intervention. Although these terms ought not to be applied strictly, except to Quakers and left Socialists at one end, and to members of the

[26] Wilson to House, Sept. 7, 1915, House Papers.
[27] Diary, April 9, 1916, *Intimate Papers*, II, 235; cf. Anne W. Lane and Louise H. Wall, *The Letters of Franklin K. Lane* (Boston, 1922), 177.
[28] Sept. 20, 1915, Baker, *Wilson*, V, 374-375.

American Rights Committee at the other, it is not unfair to characterize as pacifists those who joined Bryan in pleading for any and all concessions in order to avoid war with Germany. Nor is it too great a distortion to apply the term, chauvinist, to Theodore Roosevelt and his following, who championed arming to the teeth, condemning Germany for aggression and atrocities, and defending American rights by the prompt use of force. These groups were not altogether pure in doctrine, since individuals, chiefly German and Irish, joined one or the other while actually hoping for a war between the United States and Britain. On the whole, however, the two extremes were relatively clearly delimited.

It is the great mid-section of the population that is hard to characterize. A very large number could be termed neutralist. The adjective is not a contemporary coinage; it was employed in 1916 by an acute correspondent of the British War Propaganda Bureau to describe the widespread feelings of disinterest in the war, disapproval of partisanship, concern for unity among America's mixed population, and "desire to avoid war, so long as it . . . [could] possibly be avoided." [29] But an equally large number, including many who were neutralist, could also be characterized as nationalists, eager that American rights and interests be defended, vexed if the government made concessions to foreigners, and, on the whole, favorable to spirited diplomacy.[30] There was no line between nationalism and neutralism. A large majority of the population took both positions at once or shifted easily from one to the other. The same British correspondent observed: "This neutralism . . . might quite conceivably be transformed into . . . chauvinism—if, for instance, Washington were to give the signal for a national outburst against some foreign Power. . . . The essence of the outburst would not be partisanship for any country except the United States.

[29] *American Press Resumé,* March 3, 1916, Peterson, *Propaganda for War,* 172.

[30] See Link, *Wilson and the Progressive Era,* chapters 7, 9, *passim;* Cummins, *Indiana Public Opinion,* 90 ff., 110 ff., 151 ff., chapter 7, *passim;* Crighton, *Missouri and the World War,* 117–121; Edwin Costrell, *How Maine Viewed the War* (Orono, Maine, 1940), 50–51; John Higham, *Strangers in the Land: Patterns of American Nativism, 1860–1925* (New Brunswick, N. J., 1955), 194–204; Richard Hofstadter, *The Age of Reform: From Bryan to F.D.R.* (New York, 1955), 270–277.

... The national spirit of the Americans would now, as always, be more at ease in chauvinism than in neutralism."

A half-moon chart of American opinion would show a narrow band at one end, representing pacifism, adjoined by a somewhat wider area of untinted neutralism. At the other end would be a thin strip, indicating chauvinism, bordered by a broader band of pure nationalism. The chief impression—and the true one—would be of a wide muddy zone, filling perhaps 100° of the 180°.

Wilson recognized this ambivalence in public opinion. When faced with Germany's evident desire to protract the *Lusitania* negotiations, he declared to Lansing, "Two things are plain to me, in themselves inconsistent, viz. that our people want this thing handled in a way that will bring about a definite settlement without endless correspondence, and that they will also expect us not to hasten an issue or so conduct the correspondence as to make an unfriendly issue inevitable." [31] As he summarized the dilemma when writing to one of his old friends, "The opinion of the country seems to demand two inconsistent things, firmness and the avoidance of war." [32] Both Lansing and House took the same view. They expressed it, indeed, in language almost identical with Wilson's.[33]

The President and his chief advisers were convinced that the country overwhelmingly opposed war. There is some evidence, to be sure, that they believed this feeling more prevalent in the Midwest and Far West than on the Atlantic seaboard.[34] But Lansing testified that anti-war sentiment was strong even among eastern businessmen, writing in his *War Memoirs,* "The majority of my callers during the summer and autumn of 1915, and for many months after that time, senators, representatives, and men high in financial and business circles, frankly said that they were against war, or else stated that, though they favored it, the bulk of the people with whom they came in contact were opposed to it." [35] But

[31] Wilson to Lansing, July 13, 1915, *Lansing Papers,* I, 456.
[32] Wilson to Melancthon W. Jacobus, July 20, 1915, Baker, *Wilson,* V, 364.
[33] Lansing to Wilson, July 14, July 15, 1915, *Lansing Papers,* I, 457–459; House to Page, Aug. 4, 1915, *Intimate Papers,* II, 60–61.
[34] *Ibid.,* 40, 50, 95.
[35] Lansing, *War Memoirs,* 24.

he, House, and Wilson distinguished anti-war sentiment, or neutralism, from pacifism, which the President and the colonel thought to be the stand of a small minority and which Lansing regarded as concealing pro-German sympathies.[36]

They were equally well aware of nationalist sentiment, which demanded stronger action against Germany even while hoping that peace could be preserved. Their comments on the submarine incidents of 1915 and 1916 reflected an unrelieved fear of public impatience. During the *Ancona* discussions, Wilson observed to the Secretary of State, "I think the public are growing uneasy because of our apparent inaction in what seems a very aggravated case." [37] Lansing wrote in connection with the revived *Lusitania* negotiations, "American public opinion is become more bitter and . . . this state of affairs cannot continue much longer without the gravest consequences." [38] All members of the administration were sensitive to the possibility of popular dissatisfaction over any appearance of weakness. But they drew a distinction in this case, too, between the large mass favoring more resolute diplomacy and the small group that was eager for war.

The contradictory tendencies in public opinion must, in any case, have exercised some influence on Wilson's diplomacy. Quite apart from his need to have a united country behind him when negotiating with Germany and Britain, he could not antagonize any large bloc without imperiling the legislative program that he was to put forward in 1916. Unlike Lansing and House, who could think primarily in terms of diplomacy, Wilson had to be concerned about Congressional votes on farm loans, child labor legislation, and a tariff commission. Since a presidential election was approaching, he had to think, too, of the Democratic party.

One hope of attracting fresh support for himself and his party lay in appealing to Progressive nationalism. He could do this mainly, of course, by championing new domestic aims. He embraced the New Nationalism of Theodore Roosevelt's 1912 campaign and

[36] Diary, Oct. 13, Oct. 25, 1915, House Papers.
[37] Wilson to Lansing, Nov. 24, 1915, *Lansing Papers*, I, 494.
[38] Lansing to Bernstorff, Dec. 20, 1915, *ibid.*, 502.

embodied much of it in his legislation for 1916.[39] He also abandoned his earlier anti-military doctrines and advocated a limited preparedness program. But in the winter of 1915–1916 it seemed not impossible that Roosevelt himself might be the Republican candidate for the Presidency and that he might pitch his campaign as one against a timid and pacifist administration.[40] The President could forestall such attack only by maintaining a constant appearance of vigor and resolution.

Though his diplomatic advisers were less immediately concerned than he with domestic politics, they helped to keep these considerations before his eyes. Lansing, for example, wrote to the President in November, 1915:

> From the selfish standpoint of politics I think that the people generally are very much dissatisfied with a continuance of negotiations, that, if our demands are not acceded to, they desire action in asserting our rights, and that if there is further delay, they will turn against the Administration. I believe the pro-German vote in this country is irrevocably lost to us and that, no matter what we do now, we can never win back any part of it. If this view is correct, we ought not from the political standpoint lose the support of the Americans hostile to Germany. And I am afraid we will do so if we are not rigid in our attitude.[41]

In Colonel House's diary there is a curious entry recording a conversation between himself and Lansing on possible tactics for the approaching election:

> I spoke of my advice to the President as to making "Americanism" the main issue of the 1916 campaign. [Lansing] . . . was heartily in favor of it, and he even goes so far as to say that we should restrict immigration for many years until we have assimilated that we already have, and he was in favor of discontinuing the teaching of German and French in our public schools. We agreed to get together . . . and outline some sort of program and submit it to the President.[42]

To both Lansing and House a bid for nationalist support at home

[39] Link, *Wilson and the Progressive Era*, chapter 9, *passim*.
[40] *Literary Digest*, LII (Jan. 1, 1916), 7; New York *Times*, Nov. 30, Dec. 4, Dec. 6, Dec. 17, Dec. 21, Dec. 25, 1915.
[41] Nov. 19, 1915, *Lansing Papers*, I, 491–493.
[42] Oct. 2, 1915, House Papers.

seemed an effective complement to resolute diplomacy abroad.

Wilson's dilemma was that he also needed the favor of neutralists who opposed war as strongly, or even more strongly, than they demanded defense of rights and interests. He even needed the backing of pacifists, for some of them were powerful Democrats, like Bryan and Claude Kitchin, majority leader in the House, capable of blocking his legislative program and disrupting the party.[43]

He had to court nationalism without alienating anti-war neutralism. Speaking for preparedness, he used the language of pacifist Progressivism. Peace, progress, reform, and the protection of individual liberties were his aims, he insisted, and the reserve army was to be, as nearly as possible, a democratic and civilian force.[44] Defending his diplomacy, he proclaimed that it had only peaceful ends. "You need have no fear," he wrote in one letter, "that the jingoes will force or even hurry me into anything." And he was always conscious of how his actions might seem in neutralist eyes. "Haste . . . ," he once wrote to Lansing, "would be likely to give the country the wrong impression, I fear with regard to our frame of mind." [45]

While the vigorous policy advocated by House and Lansing was consistent with Wilson's hope of winning nationalist support, it was inconsistent with his desire to hold the neutralists. To that end he needed to follow a policy of patience, tolerance, and procrastination. While one may find the deeper sources of this policy in Wilson's own mind and temperament, it is not unfair to say that it suited his domestic aims.

It would be an oversimplification, of course, to suggest that only personality and public opinion dictated a patient policy. At least two other factors affected Wilson's willingness to wait for a clear-cut decision by the Germans.

One was his sense of America's military weakness. Although his

[43] Alex M. Arnett, *Claude Kitchin and the Wilson War Policies* (Boston, 1937), *passim; Literary Digest,* LI (Nov. 20, 1915), 1143–1145, 1162, (Dec. 4, 1915), 1267–1268.

[44] Addresses on Preparedness, Jan. 27–Feb. 3, 1916, *Public Papers,* IV, 1–121.

[45] Wilson to Mrs. John W. Kern, Jan. 12, 1916, Wilson Papers; Wilson to Lansing, Aug. 21, 1915, *Lansing Papers,* I, 468.

preparedness campaign was partly political, it was also unquestionably a product of real concern over the nation's defenseless condition. The country, he believed, was not prepared to play a significant role in the war if Germany should force intervention. Nor was it ready to defend the Western Hemisphere if the Germans, victorious in Europe, should launch an attack across the seas. It was not even capable, he feared, of putting down the German-Americans if they rose to help their Fatherland. Many people believed that America had to be patient with Germany simply because she was not yet ready to fight. Cone Johnson, for example, made this point when arguing for a peaceful termination of the *Lusitania* negotiations. "War between the United States and Germany," he wrote to Lansing, "is not to be thought of now, for the reason, if no other, that such a war could not be conducted at this time."[46]

Wilson was conscious of this argument for patience. Once when House insisted that the United States would have to intervene to prevent a German victory, Wilson responded that the colonel was under an illusion. "His general idea," the colonel noted, "is that if the Allies were not able to defeat Germany alone, they could scarcely do so with the help of the United States because it would take too long for us to get in a state of preparedness. It would therefore be a useless sacrifice on our part to go in."[47] Although Wilson may only have been rationalizing his instinctive pacifism, he stood on solid ground. Army officials had estimated the requirement for effective military intervention as an expeditionary force of 500,000 backed by another 500,000 men in a ninety-day reserve.[48] Since Wilson decided that such a program would be politically undesirable and impractical, he may also have concluded that the United States simply could not be readied adequately for a war with Germany. The prestige of the nation, preserved by vigorous diplomacy, might be lost in a subsequent demonstration of military inefficiency and impotence.

[46] July 16, 1915, *ibid.*, 460.

[47] Diary, Dec. 15, 1915, House Papers.

[48] United States, War Department, *Statement of a Proper Military Policy for the United States* (Washington, D.C., 1915); Military Attaché to War Ministry, June 6, 1915, *Mezhdunarodnye Otnosheniya*, Series Three, VIII, no. 71; Bakhmetev to Sazonov, June 29, 1915, *ibid.*, no. 206.

In advocating a preparedness program considerably short of the planners' estimates, Wilson laid great stress on the necessity of protecting the Western Hemisphere. "Nobody seriously supposes . . . that the United States needs to fear an invasion of its own territory," he declared in one speech. "What America has to fear, if she has anything to fear, are indirect, round-about, flank movements upon her regnant position in the Western Hemisphere." [49] While it is true that this was a necessary argument, whether meaningful or not, there is no reason to suppose that Wilson was deliberately uncandid. There are entries in House's diary indicating that the President discussed the possibility of German action in the Western Hemisphere as a real danger. To Lansing he expressed alarm at reports of German influence in Colombia, and he pressed Congress to appropriate twenty-seven million dollars for pre-emptive purchase of the Danish West Indies.[50] It is not impossible that another reason for his reluctance to force Germany's hand was a real concern over America's inability to safeguard her "regnant position."

Yet another was the danger of action by German-Americans. In the early months of the European conflict, he was even worried over the possibility of civil war.[51] His fear ebbed, to be sure, as evidence came in to indicate that the German sympathizers were unpopular and few in number, but it was replaced by concern over the extent of German subversion. After reading the Albert and Archibald correspondence and the reports of the Secret Service, Wilson wrote to House that the country was "honeycombed with German intrigue and infested with German spies." [52] Apprehension of danger at home may have been an additional factor prompting him to go slowly in negotiating with Germany.

It seems unlikely, however, that concern over American unpreparedness was a major influence in Wilson's policy of patience. He would certainly not have been restrained by such thoughts if

[49] Address in New York, Jan. 27, 1916, *Public Papers*, IV, 9.
[50] Diary, Dec. 15, 1915, House Papers; Wilson to Lansing, March 1, 1916, *Lansing Papers*, II, 516; Baker, *Wilson*, VI, 92–94.
[51] Bernstorff to Jagow, Sept. 6, 1914, German Foreign Ministry Archives (Outbreak and Mediation).
[52] Wilson to House, Aug. 4, 1915, Baker, *Wilson*, V, 372.

he had concluded in his heart that Germany was willfully defying law and morality and recklessly attacking American interests. Nor is it probable that awareness of military weakness held in his thinking anything like the importance of preserving Congressional majorities and winning votes for the Democratic party. It was at most a subsidiary element in his reasoning.

An entirely different idea may have played a larger part in his thinking. The hope of serving as Europe's peacemaker still stirred in him. Peace would itself provide the best possible escape from foreign and domestic problems, and the image of himself as its restorer was one that actuated his deepest ambitions and promptings. He was to say time and again that the United States should keep herself pure and free from war in order to lead the nations of Europe back to health and tranquillity, and this conception formed a bridge between his conscious nationalism and his instinctive pacifism.[53] The hope that patience and delay in dealing with Germany might create an opportunity for mediation could have exerted a strong influence over Wilson.

During the winter of 1915–1916, furthermore, he was once more actively pursuing this will-o'-the-wisp. His new effort, which involved a fresh mission to Europe by Colonel House, is best detailed in the context of Anglo-American rather than American-German relations. It is enough to say here that House devised a complicated plan which appeared at once hopeful and practical. He outlined it for the President in October, 1915, not long after the *Arabic* settlement. In December he departed for London, and he did not return until March, 1916, on the eve of the *Sussex* crisis. The President seems to have hoped against hope that House would succeed, and this thought may have combined with his recognition of America's unpreparedness, his appreciation of the domestic political situation, and his personal inclinations to produce his policy of resiliency, patience, forbearance, and procrastination.

[53] See William L. Langer's essays in William L. Langer, Arthur S. Link, and Eric Goldman, *Woodrow Wilson and the World Today* (Bryn Mawr, Pa., 1957), and Arthur S. Link, *Wilson the Diplomatist* (Baltimore, Md., 1957).

IX

The Testing of Wilson's Policies

While it was not easy for the administration to remain patient, neither was it easy to stand firm, even on the farther ground that Wilson had taken in the *Arabic* crisis. During January and February, 1916, there arose a virtual rebellion by pacifist and neutralist members of Congress. No sooner had this uprising been quelled than Germany seemingly began to repudiate her pledges, and the American government faced the most serious crisis that had yet arisen. The two aspects of American policy, firmness and patience, were both put on trial in the winter and spring of 1916.

The difficulty of maintaining a firm but patient policy toward Germany became starkly evident when Congress reconvened at the end of 1915. Recognizing that issues of German-American relations were certain to excite debate, the administration prepared to fend off attacks from Republican chauvinists. Although the charge of weakness was raised, as expected, there also arose criticism from the other side. Democratic neutralists leagued in support of the policies that Bryan had advocated before his resignation, and the administration seemed compelled to seek means of appeasing this bloc. Its problem was to content them without offending nationalist sentiment and without sacrificing the objects of its diplomacy.

At the opening of the Congressional session there was every reason to fear an outburst of anti-German hysteria provoked by chauvinists. Anti-German feeling had been growing steadily. The *Lusi-*

tania sinking had been promptly followed by the issuance of a British official report on German atrocities. Though recounting almost incredible incidents of butchery and brutality, it was signed by the well-known and highly respected scholar and former ambassador, James Bryce, and a British agent reported to London: "Even in papers hostile to the Allies, there is not the slightest attempt to impugn the correctness of the facts alleged. Lord Bryce's prestige puts scepticism out of the question, and many leading articles begin on this note." [1] The German use of poison gas after the spring of 1915 also created feeling, as did Zeppelin raids on undefended British cities. In October, 1915, when nurse Edith Cavell was executed for helping Allied soldiers escape from German prison camps, the outburst rivaled that in the *Lusitania* case. [2] And the continuous exposure of espionage and sabotage activities kept alive the passions that these events had stirred.

Administration leaders were apprehensive lest these feelings be mobilized by the chauvinists. Theodore Roosevelt and his partisans had kept up a running criticism of Wilson's feebleness. Although conservative Republicans had been slow in adopting this line of attack, the beginning of 1916 saw leaders like Henry Cabot Lodge and Elihu Root raise similar charges. [3] Newspaper criticism meanwhile grew, highlighted by sarcastic editorials on the slow pace of the *Ancona* negotiations and on the failure of Wilson to send Bernstorff home after the espionage and sabotage disclosures. [4] The advo-

---

[1] *American Press Resumé*, May 27, 1915, Peterson, *Propaganda for War*, 58; Great Britain, Parliamentary Papers: Command 7894-7895, "Report of the Committee on Alleged German Outrages" (2 vols.; London, 1915).

[2] Tumulty to Wilson, Nov. 19, 1915, Blum, *Tumulty and the Wilson Era*, 102; *American Press Resumé*, Oct. 29, 1915, Peterson, *Propaganda for War*, 63; *Literary Digest*, LI (Nov. 20, 1915), 1139-1140; Cummins, *Indiana Public Opinion*, 28-29, 102, 136-137.

[3] New York *Times*, Jan. 23, Feb. 16, 1916; Garraty, *Lodge*, 319-321; Jessup, *Root*, II, 322-323.

[4] *Literary Digest*, LI (Nov. 20, 1915), 1139-1140, (Nov. 27, 1915), 1207-1208, LII (Jan. 1, 1916), 7; Crighton, *Missouri and the World War*, 86-87; Costrell, *How Maine Viewed the War*, 53; Harold C. Syrett, "The Business Press and American Neutrality, 1914-1917," *Mississippi Valley Historical Review*, XXXII (Sept., 1945), 222-223.

cates of more forceful diplomacy came to include anti-administration
Democrats as well as Progressives and Republicans. The National
Security League, an organization advocating all-out preparedness
for war with Germany, had as one of its co-directors Judge Alton
B. Parker, the Democratic presidential nominee of 1904, and in its
speakers' bureau was the opportunistic leader of the Boston Irish,
James M. Curley.[5] It was the view of many informed observers that
Wilson's opponent in the presidential election would be either
Roosevelt or someone endorsed by him and that Wilson stood little
chance of re-election.[6] At the beginning of 1916, therefore, one of
the major problems before the administration appeared to be a popular drift toward chauvinism.

Lansing and Wilson looked forward to the approaching session
of Congress with this thought uppermost in their minds. The
Secretary of State declared that the six-months-old *Lusitania* issue
had to be settled promptly, for "the present resentment of public
opinion in this country might cause a serious situation of affairs if
the matter was discussed in Congress; . . . it was even possible that
Congress, with whom the power rested, might declare war." [7]
According to the President's private secretary, Wilson himself was
no less apprehensive. Tumulty jotted down a memorandum on
January 4, 1916, in which he noted the President's saying:

[Y]ou may as well understand my position right now. If my re-
election as President depends upon my getting into war, I don't want
to be President. . . . I am more interested in the opinion that the country
will have of me ten years from now than the opinion it may be willing
to express to-day. Of course, I understand that the country wants action, and I intend to stand by the record I have made in all these cases,
and take whatever action may be necessary, but I will not be rushed
into war, no matter if every last Congressman and Senator stands up
on his hind legs and proclaims me a coward. . . . I believe that the
sober-minded people of this country will applaud any efforts I may

[5] Collection of National Security League pamphlets, Harvard University Library.
[6] *Literary Digest*, LII (Jan. 1, 1916), 7; House to Gerard, March 24, 1916, House
Papers; Henry Morgenthau, *All in a Life-Time* (New York, 1922), 235.
[7] Memo by Lansing, Nov. 17, 1915, *Lansing Papers*, I, 490–491.

make without the loss of our honour to keep this country out of war.[8]

Nor did this apprehension die down during the earliest days of the Congressional session. When the *Persia* went under, the Secretary of State became genuinely alarmed, telegraphing Wilson that "popular excitement . . . may manifest itself in Congress." [9] Capitol Hill did, in fact, reverberate with orations in which Germany's conduct was termed "monstrous" and "unspeakable." [10] Feeling ebbed when Germany, Austria, and Turkey all denied responsibility, and no proof emerged that one of their U-boats was culpable. It receded still further when Bernstorff issued a new pledge that U-boats would obey international law. Chauvinists in Congress meanwhile turned their criticism away from Wilson's European diplomacy to his inaction in Mexican affairs.[11] While conservative Republicans continued to drift toward chauvinism, the danger of a national outburst appeared to have diminished.

The political threat that came to preoccupy the administration was one that apparently had not been foreseen. It was a virtual rebellion on the part of neutralist Democrats. It commenced with opposition to the preparedness program. Though Wilson had thought at first that the whole country favored limited rearmament, he soon found against him a range of Progressives, Socialists, and, most disturbing of all, agrarian radicals from his own party. Not only did Bryan join in vigorously, but so did Congressional leaders like Kitchin, Warren Worth Bailey of Pennsylvania, and Clyde H. Tavenner of Illinois. Anti-preparedness resolutions adopted by farmer and labor groups, particularly in the Midwest and South, indicated neutralist and even pacifist strength among the enlisted ranks of the party.[12] So serious did this sudden opposition seem

[8] Memo by Tumulty, Jan. 4, 1916, Joseph P. Tumulty, *Woodrow Wilson As I Know Him* (New York, 1921), 249–250.

[9] Lansing to Wilson, Jan. 3, 1916, Wilson Papers.

[10] *Congressional Record*, 64 Cong., 1 sess., pp. 318–325, 416–426, 458–464.

[11] *Ibid.*, pp. 589–603.

[12] Wilson to Garrison, Aug. 16, 1915, Baker, *Wilson*, VI, 10–11; *Literary Digest*, LI (Nov. 20, 1915), 1143–1145, (Dec. 4, 1915), 1267–1268, (Dec. 11, 1915), 1356; New York *Times*, Oct. 16, Oct. 27, Nov. 16, Nov. 19, Nov. 23, Dec. 5, Dec. 6, Dec. 20, Dec. 28, 1915, Jan. 6, Jan. 19, 1916; Link, *Wilson and the Progressive Era*,

that the President hurriedly scheduled a week-long speaking tour into the Ohio and Mississippi valleys.

The neutralists who had begun to cluster against preparedness soon attacked on another flank, demanding that Wilson retreat from his rigorous opposition to the German U-boat war. While the *Persia's* sinking raised excitement among the chauvinists, it produced an opposite reaction among neutralists. Almost a dozen Senators rose to criticize the principle of risking war in order to protect Americans who chose to travel on belligerent vessels. Though some were Progressives and others, like O'Gorman of New York, were Democrats long at outs with the administration, the dozen also included men who had theretofore hewed to an administration line. Kern of Indiana and Hardwick of Georgia argued that Americans ought not to take passage on belligerent ships; Owen of Oklahoma contended that Congress ought to forbid them to do so; Gore, his colleague, presented a resolution to deny passports for such travel.[13] Stone of Missouri meanwhile went privately to the State Department in order to tell Lansing of his sympathy with these views.[14] On the issue of German policy as well as on that of preparedness, agrarian Democrats seemed to be lining up with pacifist Progressives in opposition to the President.

Wilson viewed this development with the utmost concern. By conferences with members of Congress he tried to re-establish his leadership.[15] In his speaking tour he endeavored to reach the broadest possible range of American opinion. He appealed to all but outright interventionists and what he called "out-and-out pacifists" —those who preached "the doctrine of peace at any price and in

---

180–183. Crighton, *Missouri and the World War*, 117–121, shows how the newspapers, the apparent indices of public opinion, registered support of preparedness in 1915 and how it was only at the end of the year that agrarian opposition began to show itself in strength.

[13] *Congressional Record,* 64 Cong., 1 sess., p. 495.

[14] Lansing to Wilson, Dec. 21, 1915, *Lansing Papers*, I, 221–222; Stone to Wilson, Dec. 13, 1915, Wilson Papers.

[15] Wilson to Lansing, Dec. 21, 1915, *Lansing Papers*, I, 222; Wilson to Tumulty, Jan. 3, 1916, Wilson Papers; diary of the White House usher, *ibid.;* Baker, *Wilson,* VI, 160–161.

any circumstances."[16] Speaking continually of America's desire for peace and disinterest in the outcome of the war, he pleaded with his audiences to realize that the United States was not always in command of her own destiny. It is undoubtedly significant that he made his strongest appeals to nationalism rather than to neutralism. In each of his speeches he stressed the necessity of being ready for battle if America's interests or rights were denied. At Topeka, Kansas, for example, he declared:

[I]t may be necessary to use the force of the United States to vindicate the right of American citizens everywhere to enjoy the protection of international law.... [T]here is a moral obligation laid upon us to keep out of this war if possible. But by the same token there is a moral obligation laid upon us to keep free the courses of our commerce and of our finance, and I believe that America stands ready to vindicate those rights.[17]

In retrospect it may seem that these speeches sounded a tocsin for a new coalition, one of Democratic stalwarts and nationalist Progressives. But Wilson's probable intention was simply to produce a demonstration of public opposition to pacifism.

While the President was attempting to undermine the neutralists in their home districts, Lansing made a clumsy effort to appease them by diplomatic maneuver. The evidence of their strength in Congress depressed the Secretary of State. In his diary for January 9, 1916, he wrote:

We are not yet ready to meet the submarine issue squarely. Our people are not aroused to a sufficient pitch of indignation at the barbarism of the Germans. It is hard to comprehend this apparent indifference, but the fact that it exists cannot be doubted. . . .

The first effort, in my opinion, should be to prevent, if possible, a situation arising which will force this Government into open hostility to the German Government. The time for that has not come. The people are divided in sentiment. I do not believe that Congress would favor drastic action and would be resentful if the President should act without their authorization. . . .

[16] Address at Des Moines, Feb. 1, 1916, *Public Papers*, IV, 72–73.
[17] Feb. 2, 1916, *ibid.*, 90–91.

I believe, therefore, that for the present we must endeavor to keep out of the war and avoid, if we can, being forced by German aggressions to employ severe measures. We must be patient and endure indignities and injustice until the people of this country realize that the German Government is the inveterate foe of all the ideals which we hold sacred. . . .

I dread the next few months, because, if Germany renews her barbarous submarine attacks and we fail to retaliate, this Government will be subject to violent criticism and outspoken contempt at home and abroad.[18]

Holding this pessimistic view, he hoped to defer a new submarine crisis until the people had become better educated.

His idea was that the United States should ask the Allies to disarm all merchant vessels. The chief argument employed by the Germans in defending surprise U-boat attacks was the vulnerability of the boats to ramming or to gunfire from armed merchantmen. Lansing suggested that the United States ask acceptance of a *modus vivendi*. If the Central Powers would renounce surprise attacks, the Allies should, in turn, remove the armament from their merchant vessels.[19] The idea won Wilson's approval. Not only had he already verged on admitting that Germany had a right to attack armed ships, but he saw the question as almost a moral one. "It is hardly fair," he had written House, "to ask Submarine commanders to give warning by summons if, when they approach as near as they must for that purpose they are to be fired upon."[20] Two weeks after Congress had begun debating foreign affairs the Secretary of State therefore proposed this *modus vivendi* in a confidential circular to the Allied capitals.[21] Promptly discovered by a reporter and published in the New York *Evening Post,* it received an exultant reception on Capitol Hill. Some Congressmen who had been openly critical now spoke up for the administration. Since the *modus vivendi* proposal demanded something of the Allies, it seemed evidence of American impartiality. Offering to deprive Germany of

[18] Lansing Papers.
[19] Lansing to Wilson, Jan. 7, 1916, *Lansing Papers,* I, 334–335.
[20] Wilson to House, Oct. 4, 1915, Baker, *Wilson,* VI, 159.
[21] *Foreign Relations, Supplement: 1916,* pp. 146–148.

any reason for renewing submarine attacks without warning, it promised also to dissipate the hovering cloud of war. As a maneuver in domestic politics, it seemed temporarily a marked success.[22]

As a diplomatic maneuver, it proved a startling failure. When, with some asperity, the Allies rejected the proposal, Lansing undertook to exert pressure on them. Told that Germany and Austria contemplated new orders to submarine commanders, permitting surprise attacks on armed vessels, Lansing said, "the sooner it was done the better." He may even have indicated that he would welcome such action.[23] Of his many possible motives, the most likely is that he wished the Central Powers to make such a declaration so that the Allies would agree to disarm their merchantmen.

This pressure failed to have the desired effect. The German government promptly declared that after March 1, armed merchant vessels would be sunk without warning.[24] Although this declaration made no reference to Lansing's *modus vivendi,* the tie seemed plain. Newspapers commented on the apparent German-American partnership. Since the State Department was on the verge of accepting some new words as sufficient apology for the *Lusitania,* the result of Lansing's maneuver was to create an impression that the administration had abandoned its earlier firmness toward Germany and contemplated a future policy of appeasement.[25]

This interpretation was not at all what Lansing intended or Wilson desired. Members of the cabinet bridled. Secretary Lane, for example, sent Lansing a newspaper clipping, commenting, "This is the sort of thing of which I was talking today, that we are accepting something that the Teutons have proposed."[26] Colonel House entered his dissent in a cable from London: "There are so many other issues involved in the controversy concerning armed merchant-

[22] *Literary Digest,* LII (Feb. 12, 1916), 364–365.

[23] *Foreign Relations, Supplement: 1916,* pp. 149–150, 151–153, 183–185; *Lansing Papers,* I, 337, 339–342; Zwiedinek to Burian, Feb. 20, 1916, German Foreign Ministry Archives (U-boat War); Bernstorff to Jagow, n.d. (c. Feb. 26, 1916), *ibid.*

[24] *Foreign Relations, Supplement: 1916,* pp. 163–166.

[25] *Literary Digest,* LII (Feb. 26, 1916), 490–491.

[26] Feb. 15, 1916, Lansing Papers.

men that I sincerely hope you will be able to hold it in abeyance until I return. I cannot emphasize too strongly the importance of this." [27]

Although the President was astonished that Lansing's maneuver had failed, he was willing to abandon the *modus vivendi* proposal without delay. It was far from his desires that the administration should come to be known as pro-German. His recently concluded speaking tour had, after all, been an appeal to the very sentiments that would be outraged if such an impression were to spread. The advice of his most trusted friend, furthermore, had rarely been so peremptory, and the strength of House's warning could be taken to signify that the hope of mediation hung in the balance. The President and the Secretary of State both decided, in any case, that a hasty retreat was in order.

After a cabinet meeting Lansing issued a statement to the press, declaring that the *modus vivendi* had been broached to the Allies alone and that it was up to them to accept or reject it. Although hoping yet that they would see fit to accept, he acknowledged their right to decline. If they did so, the rules would remain what they had been and German attacks on defensively armed merchantmen, carrying Americans, would constitute, the Secretary declared, "a breach of international law and the formal assurances given by the German Government." By announcing shortly afterward that an otherwise agreeable *Lusitania* apology could not be accepted on account of the new declaration, he made it quite clear that no new harmony prevailed between Berlin and Washington.[28]

The *modus vivendi* ultimately died a quiet diplomatic death, but the domestic repercussions of Lansing's maneuvers were to endure for months. Although the new German declaration had been greeted with some dubiety by newspaper editors and Congressmen, still there prevailed a general optimism that crises with Germany were things of the past. Lansing's statement to the press created fresh alarm on Capitol Hill. The Senators and Representatives who had

[27] House to Lansing, Feb. 14, 1916, House Papers.
[28] *Foreign Relations, Supplement: 1916*, pp. 170, 172.

fluttered banners of revolt in January now sprang to the barricades. Representative Jeff: McLemore of Texas introduced a resolution to prevent Americans from taking passage on belligerent ships. He and a score of other Democrats protested in long speeches that the torpedoing of an Allied vessel with Americans on board would not constitute sufficient cause for war. In the Senate meanwhile, even stronger voices were uttering the same protest. The Democratic floor leaders and the chairmen of the Foreign Affairs and Foreign Relations committees were among the discontented, and newspapers estimated that overwhelming majorities in both Houses would endorse resolutions like McLemore's.[29] The incipient rebellion of January had almost become a revolution.

Wilson managed finally to stem the uprising. No sooner had it begun than he called in the floor leaders and chairmen of the Foreign Relations and Foreign Affairs committees and explained the policies that he had defended during his western tour. As Stone summarized this explanation, asking for the President's confirmation, "you would consider it your duty, if a German war vessel should fire upon an armed merchant vessel of the enemy upon which American citizens were passengers, to hold Germany to strict account." Others present at the meeting interpreted "strict account" as meaning war.[30] Since these conferees warned Wilson of the trend in Congressional sentiment, the President promptly composed the open letter to Stone which has been quoted earlier. Discounting the probability of war, he commented on the German government's past good faith and fidelity to promises but declared that he could not "consent to any abridgment of the rights of American citizens in any respect." [31]

Although the President's views won acclaim throughout the

---

[29] *Congressional Record*, 64 Cong., 1 sess., pp. 505, 510, 2755–3130. The New York *Times*, Feb. 24, 1916, reported that the House Foreign Affairs Committee had informally advised the President that there was little chance of preventing the passage of the McLemore resolution.

[30] Stone to Wilson, Feb. 24, 1916, Baker, *Wilson*, VI, 165–166; New York *Times*, Feb. 24, March 3, 1916; Link, *Wilson and the Progressive Era*, 211.

[31] *Public Papers*, IV, 122–124.

press, Congress remained discontented.[32] Responding to a plea from Speaker Champ Clark, Wilson called yet another conference, this time with the Speaker, the House leader, and the Foreign Affairs Committee chairman. At this 9 A.M. meeting, later transformed by myth into a "Sunrise Conference," the President merely repeated what he had said to Stone. Despite the majority leader's errant and senile recollection that the President had said he wanted war, Speaker Clark was consoled by the President's stress on the probability of a peaceful arrangement with Germany. When Clark left the conference, indeed, he was prepared to postpone a vote on the hostile resolutions.[33] But Wilson, acting on the tactical advice of Tumulty and Burleson, wrote another letter, this time to the Chairman of the House Rules Committee. He asked for a prompt vote, and when this unusual request was granted, the McLemore and Gore resolutions were tabled.[34] The President seemed to have smashed the revolt.

It is clear that he had temporarily re-established his Congressional leadership. One well-informed journalist thought otherwise, reporting, "Congress believed the American people will not sanction war unless American territory is actually invaded; The President is to be permitted to conduct the nation's foreign affairs with that inhibition imprest on his mind."[35] But Kitchin, one of the rebel leaders, remarked glumly, "the President absolutely dominates Congress."[36] And the remainder of 1916 saw no fresh revolt on the same scale.

The movement had served only to demonstrate the strength of neutralist feeling, and to indicate that a large body of opinion might easily be swept by crisis not from neutralism to nationalism but from neutralism to pacifism. Another convincing evidence was the revived movement for an arms embargo. A petition nearly seven miles long, bearing a million signatures, was presented to the Senate

---

[32] *Literary Digest*, LII (March 18, 1916), 697–698.

[33] Baker, *Wilson*, VI, 169–171; Link, *Wilson and the Progressive Era*, 212–213.

[34] Baker, *Wilson*, VI, 171–174; Blum, *Tumulty and the Wilson Era*, 99.

[35] David Lawrence in the New York *Evening Post*, quoted in *Literary Digest*, LII (March 18, 1916), 697–698.

[36] Kitchin to C. Lauterback, Feb. 28, 1916, quoted in Tansill, *America Goes to War*, 471.

by an Ohio Progressive, and he was seconded by others from Minnesota and Michigan and by Democrats from Nebraska, Arkansas, and Arizona.[37] Yet more proof was to come as the campaign of 1916 got under way and neutralists registered victories over nationalists in primary elections not only in Michigan and Nebraska, but in New York State as well.[38]

Wilson might continue to belittle the latent pacifism of Congress and the public, but he could not ignore it. He felt obliged, for example, to compromise much of his army program, accepting authorizations that most military men thought wholly inadequate.[39] He also felt it necessary to promise that he would consult Congress before he decided to send an ultimatum.[40]

It is also true, of course, that Wilson was under political obligations to nationalist sentiment. He had promised to defend American rights and interests, and he had evidently decided that Democratic chances in 1916 depended upon convincing the people that he was as manly and resolute as Roosevelt. There was no less of a threat to his leadership from chauvinism than from pacifism. But the opposition of Senators and Congressmen in his own party and among the Progressives made his policy of firmness a very hard one to uphold. Open defiance by Germany could lead to a real crisis on Capitol Hill and place before the President the spectacle of a distraught and disunited republic.

While the Congressional revolt of January and February demonstrated the difficulty of maintaining firmness, the *Sussex* crisis of March and April indicated afresh the torment involved in remaining patient.

The possibility of new and alarming submarine incidents had not subsided. The German decree which Lansing had encouraged was issued in early February. Armed vessels were to be sunk on sight, whether they carried passengers or not. But no startling sink-

[37] *Literary Digest,* LII (Feb. 12, 1916), 365.
[38] Link, *Wilson and the Progressive Era,* 230–231.
[39] C. Joseph Bernardo and Eugene H. Bacon, *American Military Policy: Its Development since 1775* (Harrisburg, Pa., 1955), 344–346.
[40] Diary, April 11, 1916, House Papers.

ings occurred immediately, and, at the same time, optimistic reports reached Washington. Bernstorff indicated that his government might be awaiting the outcome of the *modus vivendi* negotiations.[41] More important still, Admiral Tirpitz resigned, thus removing from the Kaiser's councils, as Americans supposed, the demon behind the ruthless submarine agitation. But the mild euphoria created by this event was briskly dispelled.

From the middle of March on, the omens became increasingly black. Cables from Berlin told of powerful forces, especially in the Reichstag, working for new submarine violence. In mid-March came a frightening report from the Netherlands. The Dutch liner, *Tubantia,* had sunk in the North Sea, reportedly as a result of torpedoing. Two days later came a similar report. A Dutch vessel bound out of London for Java had also been sunk by a U-boat. Neither carried Americans, but on March 25 came the sinking of the channel steamer *Sussex,* reportedly with ninety casualties, some of them Americans.[42] The anticipated German-American crisis was at hand.

Wilson insisted once again on delay. Although Lansing urged immediate severance of relations, the President disagreed. He waited for conclusive evidence that a U-boat had been at fault. Convinced at last that he would have to address another note to Berlin, he took great pains in drawing it up. Draft after draft came to him from the Department of State and went back with cautious revisions, queries, and suggestions for change.[43]

All the time, he was contending against insistent pleas, not only from Lansing, but also from Mrs. Wilson and from House. The colonel, it is true, justified the President's course to Lansing's Counselor, Frank Polk. House noted that Polk, in the course of this discussion, "began to understand for the first time how anxious the President was not to break with the Central Powers." [44] In private audience with Wilson, House nevertheless

[41] *Foreign Relations, Supplement: 1916,* pp. 171–172, 181–182.

[42] *Ibid.,* 178–181, 186, 205–211, 214; Van Dyke to Lansing, March 20, 1916, 763.72/2515, State Department Archives; *Lansing Papers,* I, 537–539.

[43] *Lansing Papers,* I, 539–543, 546–547, 549–551.

[44] Diary, April 1, 1916, House Papers.

argued that the United States had no choice but to accept the German challenge. When the President answered with an appeal to their mutual hope of peace, the colonel rejoined that if Wilson "failed to act he would soon lose the confidence of the American people and also of the Allies and would fail to have any influence at the peace conference. I tried to make him see," House added, "that we would lose the respect of the world unless he lived up to the demands he has made of Germany regarding her undersea warfare." [45] But the President refused to be rushed into action.

Before Wilson responded to the German challenge, he made one direct effort to obtain an Allied request for his mediation. Regarding the hope of such a request as the President's chief reason for temporizing, House had recommended a cablegram to Grey, "asking him whether or not it would be wise to intervene now rather than permit the break to come." [46] The President personally drew up such a cablegram, suggesting that Grey consult the Allies and act at once to request an American peace demand. Otherwise, a break with Germany over the submarine seemed inevitable, and "if this country should once become a belligerent, the war would undoubtedly be prolonged." [47] House followed up this cablegram with a letter, offering further explanation, "the President and I both think if we are once in the war it will lengthen it indefinitely. . . . We have another reason . . . and that is we are not so sure of the support of the American people on the submarine issue, while we are confident that they would respond to the higher and nobler issue of stopping the war." [48]

Although the President undoubtedly held some hope that the threat of war might be lifted by the opening of peace negotiations, it is more likely that he remained patient because of the division in public opinion and, of course, because of his own horror of war. There was no telling how many of the neutralists recently in arms for the Gore and McLemore resolutions might turn to intransigent

[45] Diary, March 30, 1916, *ibid*.

[46] House to Wilson, April 3, 1916, *Intimate Papers*, II, 229.

[47] Diary, April 6, 1916, House Papers; House to Grey, April 6, 1916, Wilson Papers.

[48] House to Grey, April 7, 1916, House Papers.

pacifism in the face of precipitate action on the President's part. Wilson refused to make the note to Germany as peremptory as his advisers desired. He so edited Lansing's drafts as to produce a bill of indictment satisfactory to both the Secretary and Colonel House, but he declined to demand compliance within a specified time or to close the door on further negotiation. Instead, he threatened to sever relations unless Germany declared her intention to abandon the practice of torpedoing without warning. In response to House's suggestion, he stiffened the note by asking that Germany make this declaration immediately, and he later accepted an amendment by Lansing in order to leave less opportunity for protracted debate.[49] But he declined to make the note a sharp ultimatum lest he have to carry out his promise and invite the Congress to approve or disapprove in advance.

He may have been emboldened to action finally by evidence that opinion outside of Congress was predominantly nationalist. The press, at any rate, exhibited patriotic anger at Jagow's official note disclaiming responsibility for the *Sussex*. "A long black vessel," the German Foreign Minister admitted, had, indeed, been torpedoed at roughly the time and place where the *Sussex* suffered misadventure, but the U-boat commander was sure that it had been a minesweeper. The *Sussex* must therefore have struck an English mine. According to surveys of the American press, this German explanation was almost universally regarded as an insult to America's intelligence. Even the near-pacifist New York *Evening Post* declared, "We have had something too much of all this, ever since the day of the monstrous crime of May 7, 1915; the time has come for making an end of it." The Chicago *Tribune,* reputed to be pro-German, printed a cartoon of a spear-helmeted German bowing apologetically, with his helmet point prodding the midriff of Uncle Sam. It was evident that the press, at least, was ready for such a cautious ultimatum as Wilson had upon his desk.[50]

On April 17, therefore, he authorized Lansing to send the final

---

[49] Diary, April 11, 1916, *ibid.*; *Lansing Papers,* I, 546, 549, 551.

[50] *Foreign Relations, Supplement: 1916,* pp. 227–229; *Literary Digest,* LII (April 22, 1916), 1129–1130.

version of the note to Berlin, and on the 19th, he appeared before Congress to explain his action. After rehearsing the long record of his efforts to secure abatement of the submarine menace, he declared that he had threatened to sever relations unless Germany renounced attacks without warning on passenger and cargo vessels. The Congress and the press received the message gravely but, on the whole, with approval. Although the Republican floor leader accused Wilson of seeking a war in order to get himself re-elected, this charge was generally deprecated. Treating the President's message with due solemnity, the majority of newspapers devoted their editorial pages to affirmations of national unity. Even the German-Americans, while appealing agonizedly for peace, saw fit to declare that they would prove loyal if war came.[51] The domestic ordeal, therefore, passed quietly.

Wilson felt compelled to restate his decisive opposition to any effective U-boat campaign. The *Sussex* torpedoing, followed by the sinkings of other liners, the *Englishman, Manchester Engineer, Berwindvale,* and *Eagle Point,* had left him no alternatives except to confess impotence or to deliver a virtual ultimatum. In the face of chauvinist and nationalist excitement throughout the country, he may have felt, indeed, that he would court political disaster if he failed to act. His foreign policy advisers were unanimous on this score. And fearful though he might be of latent pacifism, he could not but believe that surrender would be politically disastrous. It was in many ways even more difficult for him to remain patient in dealing with Germany than to remain firm.

The German government, as it turned out, renewed its pledges against illegal submarine attacks. Its communications were so ill-tempered that there remained some doubt as to whether the crisis had really passed. But when sinkings stopped, most of the nation breathed relief. Although the President's policy of firmness and patience had undergone a severe ordeal, it had not been put to the final test to determine whether patience meant appeasement or firmness meant war.

[51] *Ibid.* (April 29, 1916), 1201–1204; Cummins, *Indiana Public Opinion,* 196–197; Wittke, *German-Americans and the World War,* 80–81.

PART III

Germany's Dilemmas

X

Bethmann and the Admirals

After the spring of 1915, the burden of choice between war and peace lay upon the German government. Wilson had apparently threatened war if U-boats were allowed to attack passenger liners. By declaring that his demands on Germany were quite independent of any made upon Britain, he encouraged no hope that the threat might be lifted. Germany had to deny herself the use of the weapon in order to keep the peace or else strike at England and risk war. Chancellor Bethmann Hollweg had no doubt that the more important aim was to keep America neutral, and he was prepared to sacrifice the U-boat campaign or any part of it in order to keep the peace. Neither the Navy Ministry nor the Naval Staff agreed with him; the admirals insisted that the submarine weapon should be used to the full, come what might, and their pleas were supported by powerful blocs among the Reichstag and the public. It was necessarily Germany's policy, therefore, to carry on the U-boat war at whatever pitch the United States would allow. The result, both internationally and internally, was a rising rhythm of lull and crisis.

To temporize was, of course, Bethmann's way. He was scarcely a figure of fire and granite. But circumstances made it literally impossible for him to choose one of the drastic alternatives. He could not decide to abandon the submarine permanently. The Kaiser probably could not have been brought to approve such a policy, and, in any case, the decision would have shaken the unity of the nation, cut the Chancellor off from the Reichstag and the country, and perhaps imperiled the foundations of the Empire. Nor, on the other hand, could Bethmann bring himself to opt for an unrestricted U-boat campaign. Neither his conscience nor his political judgment would allow him to do so.

He was convinced that the submarine could not achieve decisive results in the war with England. "A peace forced upon England by the U-boat war," he wrote, "would be equivalent to public acknowledgment that England's supremacy at sea had been destroyed by Germany's sea power. Before England would make up her mind to make such an acknowledgment, she would sacrifice the last man and the last penny." [1] The best impartial advice given him was to the effect that, in the first place, the submarines could stop only a fraction of Britain's imports and, in the second place, that ruthlessness on Germany's part merely intensified the English will to fight.[2]

He was also certain that an all-out U-boat campaign would bring the United States into the war, with disastrous results for Germany. "It is absolutely beyond doubt," he said to the Reichstag budget committee, "that if today I proclaim a ruthless U-boat war, tomorrow America will have broken with us." [3] The effect of such a break, he believed, would be to bring all the European neutrals into the war on the Allied side. The newspapers of the Netherlands, the Scandinavian states, and even Switzerland, indicated that their governments would follow America's lead.[4] Bethmann predicted that the Dutch would enter the war as soon as Germany and the United States broke relations; the Allies not only would obtain reinforcement from Holland's small but well-trained army but, even

[1] Memo by Bethmann, Jan. 29, 1916, German Foreign Ministry Archives (GHQ—Amerika); also in *Official German Documents*, II, 1130–1139.

[2] *Ibid.*; Jagow to Treutler, April 21, 1915, German Foreign Ministry Archives (Secret Mediation); Ballin to Wilhelm II, Jan. 10, 1916, Bernhard Huldermann, *Alfred Ballin* (Berlin, 1922), 248–249.

[3] Westarp, *Konservative Politik*, II, 135, quoting the *Protokolle Haushaltsausschuss*, which were never available to the public and which appear to have been largely destroyed during World War II. Westarp's book is now practically the only source for the proceedings of the budget committee.

[4] *Literary Digest*, L (Feb. 27, 1915), 419, quoting Amsterdam and Rome newspapers and the *Neue Züricher Zeitung*.

more important, would gain access by sea to the rear of the German lines.[5] Among the crucial Balkan states, too, he found the American question almost decisive. "The attitude of the United States toward us," he declared during the *Arabic* crisis, "causes every other possible state to stiffen against us; it is, for example, an unmistakable barometer for the attitude of the Balkan states." [6]

Quite apart from its effect on European neutrals, the intervention of the United States would in itself, Bethmann thought, have cataclysmic results for Germany. There is a memorandum in the Secret File of the Foreign Ministry Archives which, if not Bethmann's, at least reflects his views. Itemizing the probable results of armed intervention by the United States, it mentions the financing of Germany's enemies, a doubling of their munitions imports, a reinforcement of Allied armies by the enlistment of American volunteers, "liquidation of the Balkans," and privations for Germany herself.[7] Intervention by the United States, the Chancellor did assert, would prolong the war by two years, and unlimited U-boat war was therefore the *ultima ratio*. "It represents such a challenge," he declared in 1916, "that it [could] . . . signify *finis Germaniae*." [8]

Holding such views, Bethmann could not bring himself to sanction a defiant submarine campaign. Although he was temperamentally disinclined to battle for convictions, he could not allow the admirals to ignore political considerations, to bet on their optimistic estimates of the U-boat's capabilities, and to make war on the United States. He felt obliged to fight with every resource against a decision in favor of an unlimited U-boat campaign.

At the same time, he was almost incapable of forcing a decision to abandon the weapon. The admirals would not accept his reasoning. Tirpitz and the successive Chiefs of the Naval Staff staked their experience and professional reputations upon the prediction that an

[5] Bethmann to Treutler, May 30, 1915, *Politische Dokumente*, II, 345.

[6] Minutes of a conference between Tirpitz and Bethmann and of a conference with the Kaiser, Aug. 26, 1915, *ibid.*, 404.

[7] Unsigned memo, Aug. 25, 1915, German Foreign Ministry Archives (Secret).

[8] Note of May 9, 1916, in Konrad Haussmann, *Schlaglichter, Reichstagsbriefe, und Aufzeichnungen* (Frankfurt am Main, 1924), 61; memo by Holtzendorff, Jan. 8, 1916, Spindler, *Handelskrieg*, III, 75.

all-out campaign would bring England to her knees before American intervention could affect the outcome of the war. Bethmann could caution the admirals of dangers, but he could not change their minds. He was continually in the position of seeming to place political ahead of military considerations.

As one result, he depended very heavily on the support of the army, although the army did not accept all his premises. Falkenhayn thought the navy's proposals untimely rather than pernicious. Eager to believe the admirals' prophecies, he said repeatedly that submarine commanders should be given their freedom as soon as the military situation permitted. The general did not share Bethmann's dread of the United States herself. He feared only the Dutch and the Balkan states, who might break his western line or cut the link with Constantinople. Falkenhayn would vote for postponement of an all-out U-boat campaign but not for abandonment. Had the Chancellor sought a drastic decision, the army would probably have joined the navy in opposing him.

Outside imperial councils, moreover, a decision to give up the U-boat would have met opposition in the Reichstag and among the public. The right-wing parties were fanatical in their enthusiasm for unrestricted U-boat war. Not only did they disagree with the Chancellor's reasoning, but they chafed at his temporizing policy and criticized it as openly as the *Burgfrieden* and the German political tradition permitted. In this attitude they were supported by a large segment of the *Zentrum* and even by Progressives.

The right-wing press challenged all the Chancellor's premises. It insisted, in the first place, that the U-boat could bring England to her knees. When a retired admiral published an article declaring that the submarine could not win the war, the journals that deigned to notice it commented with derision. The Hamburg Chamber of Commerce passed a resolution of condemnation, and two of the city's newspapers, the *Nachrichten* and the *Fremdenblatt,* denounced such writing as treasonable.[9] When Captain Persius, the respected naval expert of the *Berliner Tageblatt,* suggested that the claims of U-boat

---

[9] H. von Truppel, "Deutschland und Amerika," *Der Tag,* July 4, 1915; *Daily Extracts from the Foreign Press,* July 16, July 26, 1915.

enthusiasts might be exaggerated, even this modest warning provoked scorn and anger.[10] Conservatives, Free Conservatives, National Liberals, and right Centrists would hear no denial of the U-boat's effectiveness.

They insisted, too, that no serious consequences were to be feared from war with the United States. At the time of the strict accountability note the *Berliner Zeitung* declared of America, "She has no army, and her fleet would not dare to approach nearer our shores than does the English. The expulsion of Germans from America would mean her ruin. America's threats are simply ridiculous, and it is more than ridiculous to take them in earnest." [11] The Conservative *Tägliche Rundschau* declared that Germany had nothing to lose except the nice new ships sitting idle in American harbors, and a writer in *Der Tag* pointed out contemptuously that the United States had shown herself too feeble even to deal with Mexico.[12]

Nor was such comment confined to journals of the far right. The *Kölnische Volkszeitung,* a Centrist organ, declared that Americans would not go to war because they lacked the martial virtues, and war "requires so many sacrifices and destroys business." The Progressive *Vossische Zeitung* printed an article by the eminent classical scholar, Eduard Meyer, asserting that Wilson would not be able to go to war if he wanted to.[13] Even the Social Democratic *Vorwärts,* which commented skeptically on Meyer's prediction, suggested that American pacifism was probably powerful enough to prevent armed retaliation against a German U-boat campaign.[14] And challenges to this complacency were usually either mild, like the *Münchener Neueste Nachrichten*'s observation that Germany should keep the peace in order to protect German-Americans, or else bore the marks of official inspiration. Anton Meyer-Gerhardt, who had been one of Bethmann's agents in the United States, advertised the dangers of

[10] *Berliner Tageblatt,* July 12, 1915; *Deutsche Tageszeitung,* July 14, 1915.
[11] Quoted in the *Literary Digest,* L (Feb. 27, 1915), 418.
[12] *Ibid.* (June 26, 1915), 1525–1526.
[13] *Ibid.* (May 22, 1915), 1207; *Vossische Zeitung,* quoted in *Daily Extracts from the Foreign Press,* Aug. 12, 1915; see also Redaction des 'Documents sur la guerre,' *Résumé de la presse allemande,* no. 14 (c. Dec. 1, 1915).
[14] *Vorwärts,* July 15, July 29, 1915.

war, and the semiofficial *Kölnische Zeitung* warned against complacency.[15] Although it would not be true to suggest that the public, as a whole, was nonchalant about America, it is the case that very few people outside the government appeared to share the anxieties of the Chancellor.

The right-wing press claimed, as a result, to speak for the mass of German opinion. Ernst Reventlow of the *Deutsche Tageszeitung* asserted during the *Lusitania* crisis:

It is not too much to say that a profound and widespread excitement has seized the German people at the very suggestion that the German Empire can be expected to abandon the submarine war or to let it become an empty form. . . . We have innumerable proofs of the existence of this deep excitement in Germany. . . . Rarely has a measure of war been greeted with greater satisfaction and watched with more lively sympathy than the submarine war against Great Britain's commerce.[16]

Count Westarp asserted that the leaders of all parties except the Social Democrats were united in opposition to any limitation of the submarine war, and Centrist and Progressive leaders went to the Chancellery with Conservatives and National Liberals to express support for the admirals.[17] The dissent of the Social Democrats was relatively mild. Reprinting a declaration somewhat like Reventlow's, *Vorwärts* commented, "A large number of people are, as is well known, of quite another opinion." [18] Even among Social Democrats, the U-boat fever had made inroads. When Scheidemann spoke in the Reichstag, defending concessions to the United States, he began by saying:

Gentlemen, the enemy powers rest their hopes on our economic exhaustion. England's effort is, with all means, to carry out the starvation

[15] *Münchener Neueste Nachrichten*, cited in *Résumé de la presse allemande*, no. 14, p. 14; Meyer-Gerhardt, "Deutschland—Amerika," *Der Tag*, June 29, 1915; *Kölnische Zeitung*, Aug. 3, Aug. 26, Sept. 9, Nov. 3, 1915.

[16] *Deutsche Tageszeitung*, July 2, 1915.

[17] Memos by Zentralbureau des Reichsmarineamts, June 30, Aug. 10, 1915, *Politische Dokumente*, II, 373–374, 400; Westarp, *Konservative Politik*, II, 110.

[18] *Vorwärts*, July 14, 1915, commenting on an article in the *Berliner Neueste Nachrichten;* cf. memo by Zimmermann, March 1, 1915, German Foreign Ministry Archives (U-boat War).

war against our people. Against this attempt to strangle us, which is prosecuted without regard to international law and the rights of neutrals, a sharp defense is called for ("Very true!"—from the right). Here we fight for our existence ("Very true!"—from the left). We have the right on our side if we reply to the English hunger blockade with the U-boat war ("Very true!"—from the Social Democrats). No one can complain of that ("Very true!"—from the right).[19]

Bethmann, in any case, accepted the Conservative estimate. "Our public opinion is 'whipped up,'" he complained to navy leaders. "It is absolutely criminal how . . . [the people] have behaved in this matter."[20]

Confronted with such a state of parliamentary and public opinion, Bethmann could not easily carry a proposal to abandon the submarine weapon. He felt obliged, indeed, to make a public pretense of sympathy with the U-boat enthusiasts. At the outset of the *Lusitania* crisis, the official *Norddeutsche Allgemeine Zeitung* promised, "Every means that art and nature offer to overpower the enemy we shall inexorably and remorselessly employ."[21] The Chancellor's collaborator, Foreign Minister Jagow, asserted before the budget committee of the Reichstag in August, 1915, that restriction of the U-boat campaign could never be considered by the government. And Bethmann himself assured the Conservative leaders, "what is necessary will, without any hesitation, be done."[22]

The Chancellor could only attempt to moderate the public agitation. The press censors watched for articles directly critical of the government's policy, and several numbers of the Conservative *Kreuzzeitung* and *Deutsche Tageszeitung* were suppressed as a result.[23] In official, semiofficial, and friendly newspapers, meanwhile,

[19] *Stenographische Berichte der Verhandlungen des deutschen Reichstages*, XIII. Legislaturperiode, II. Sess., vol. CCCVII, 39 Sitzung (April 5, 1916), p. 858.

[20] Memo by Bachmann, June 22, 1915, *Politische Dokumente*, II, 365.

[21] *Norddeutsche Allgemeine Zeitung*, May 17, 1915.

[22] Westarp, *Konservative Politik*, II, 111; memo by Westarp, May 13, 1915, *ibid.*, 37.

[23] See Gerard to Lansing, June 22, June 25, 1915, *Foreign Relations, Supplement: 1915*, pp. 450, 454; Westarp, *Konservative Politik*, II, 109, 180–182; Liebig, *Die Politik von Bethmann Hollwegs*, III, 391–393.

the government's policy was supported and justified. Defending censorship of the *Deutsche Tageszeitung,* the official *Norddeutsche Allgemeine Zeitung* declared:

In the first place the impression was given that official circles, simply for the sake of peace with America, contemplated abandoning the great power of the U-boat weapon, and, in the second place, the absurd statement was unhesitatingly made that the accession of America to the ranks of our enemies would be a matter of no consequence. . . . Those who bear the responsibility and who must balance danger against advantage are immune to taunts of timidity, feebleness, or cowardice. . . . But for the dignity of the nation and in the interests of foreign policy, this propaganda must be brought to an end.[24]

The semiofficial *Kölnische Zeitung* introduced the public to the arguments that had been found effective with the General Staff, asserting during the *Arabic* crisis, for instance, "It must be emphasized once more that our most pressing problem is a free road to Constantinople, and we cannot get there if we burden ourselves with a new enemy."[25] Similar words appeared in newspapers whose editors or correspondents were intimate with officials of the Foreign Ministry. The *Berliner Tageblatt,* the Berlin *Lokal-Anzeiger,* and the *Frankfurter Zeitung* aided in the effort to abate public excitement.[26]

In order to prevent an unrestricted U-boat campaign, however, the Chancellor had to rely primarily upon maneuver and intrigue within the government. He could do no more than appease the public and the Reichstag. He could not appeal to them if a decision went against him in one of the Kaiser's councils. His antagonists, on the other hand, could always be consoled in defeat by the conviction that public opinion would ultimately bring them victory. Although circumstances gave to Germany the decision between peace or war for the United States, the German government did not in fact

---

[24] *Norddeutsche Allgemeine Zeitung,* June 21, 1915; cf. Gerard to Lansing, June 22, 1915, *Foreign Relations, Supplement: 1915,* p. 450.

[25] Sept. 3, 1915.

[26] See *Résumé de la presse allemande,* no. 7 (Sept., 1915), no. 9 (Oct., 1915), no. 10 (Oct., 1915).

possess the power to choose peace. The Chancellor could at best only postpone the decision for war.

The *Lusitania* issue pitted Bethmann for the first time against the admirals and the implacable force of public opinion. In modifying the original war zone decree, he had merely been checking the navy. It had been his intention to allow an unfettered U-boat campaign as soon as the air cleared, and he had, in fact, approved a modest extension after the United States ignored the *Falaba* sinking. But the result had been a series of sinkings, which included the Norwegian ship *Belfridge,* the Dutch *Medea* and *Katwijk,* and the American freighter *Nebraskan.* Even before the *Lusitania's* sinking, he had become alarmed at the possible consequences, writing to the Chief of the Naval Staff, "In the tense situation in which the whole policy of the Empire now stands, I cannot undertake to be responsible for a further worsening of relations with neutral powers through the conduct of the U-boat war in the present fashion." [27] But the *Lusitania* protest from the United States created a fresh necessity, for he now had to stop attacks not only on neutral flags but also on enemy ships carrying neutral passengers.

The task was one requiring great delicacy. The *Lusitania's* sinking had delighted the navy and been acclaimed by the public. Not only Conservative organs like the *Kreuzzeitung* and *Deutsche Tageszeitung* applauded, but so did the Centrist *Germania* and *Kölnische Volkszeitung* and the independent *Frankfurter Zeitung.*[28] If the Chancellor should propose apologizing for the act and forbidding U-boats to repeat the exploit, he was sure to provoke the admirals into anger and even, perhaps, into public opposition. A mere assurance to the American ambassador that neutral ships would not be sunk intentionally had drawn a vexed letter from Admiral Bachmann, the Chief of the Naval Staff.[29] Worse still, the navy's advocacy of widening rather than limiting the U-boat war was rumored

[27] Bethmann to Bachmann, May 6, 1915, *Politische Dokumente,* II, 333.
[28] See *Literary Digest,* L (May 22, 1915), 1206.
[29] Bachmann to Jagow, May 13, 1915, *Politische Dokumente,* II, 336.

to have support in the army. A General Staff officer proclaimed the *Lusitania* a great diplomatic victory, since it showed America that Germany was in earnest; more *Lusitania*s, he thought, would ultimately make the United States pro-German.[30] It was evident that Bethmann had to move slowly and cautiously.

Confronted with America's first protest, Bethmann procrastinated. Both Tirpitz and the Naval Staff held that the torpedoing should be defended as unexceptionable both in law and in ethics. It required all the suavity of the Chancellor's friend and ally, Admiral Müller, the Chief of the Naval Cabinet, to explain why some less provocative answer had to be returned. Neutral governments had already been advised that the *Lusitania* was fair game, Müller assured Tirpitz, but the case had a "reverse side." Italy still balanced on a knife-edge, held there partly by the Pope, and Italian demagogues should not be enabled to picture Germany as unrepentantly immoral and un-Christian. Müller succeeded in reconciling the navy to an expression of regret at the deaths of innocent passengers, and Jagow, the Foreign Minister, was allowed to reply to the United States inviting further discussion of the case.[31]

In the time gained through Müller's stratagem, the Chancellor set about to rally strength for a face-to-face test with the navy. Jagow stood with him, and so did the adroit and influential Müller, Valentini, the Civil Cabinet chief and Colonel Treutler, the Foreign Ministry representative at Supreme Headquarters. To win a decision from the Emperor, Bethmann needed additionally the support of Falkenhayn. He delegated Treutler to approach the general and say to him in the Chancellor's behalf:

If America joins our enemies, even if not immediately with arms, then the little neutrals will soon follow. In *Holland* there has emerged great uneasiness over the results which the annexation of Belgium by Germany would have on Holland's future. The danger arises that Holland would probably not oppose an attack by our enemies through

[30] *Ibid.*, 343–344.

[31] Tirpitz to Müller, May 9, 1915, *ibid.*, 335; Müller to Tirpitz, May 12, 1915, *ibid.*, 335–336; Jagow to Gerard, May 28, 1915, *Foreign Relations, Supplement: 1915*, pp. 419–421.

Dutch territory and would herself very likely join in it. I do not believe that we could withstand such an attack militarily. . . .

Your Excellency will discuss the foregoing with General Falkenhayn
and leave it to him, in case he shares the anxiety I feel about our military situation in the event that Holland abandons her neutrality, to put
the U-boat campaign into the proper perspective from the military
standpoint. In any event I ask you to tell the general definitely that with
a continuation of the U-boat war in its present form I can no longer
undertake to guarantee the attitudes of the neutrals.[32]

Knowing Falkenhayn's view that the army was already strained to
the utmost, the Chancellor was sure of making an impression on the
general, and he was, in fact, rewarded almost at once. Falkenhayn
paused only to ascertain that Admiral Müller concurred before
throwing in his lot with the Chancellor.[33]

Having won the general's support, Bethmann was ready for a
second maneuver. He accepted Müller's proposal of a conference
before the Kaiser where some of his differences with the admirals
might be ventilated. Neither Tirpitz nor the Chief of the Naval
Staff would agree to guarantee the safety of neutral flags, much less
that of neutral passengers on enemy ships. Admiral Bachmann had
declared, "One of the principal aims of the proclamation of February 4 was, by a stern warning of the war zone's perils, to frighten
neutral ships away from trade with England. This was not only
required in order to sharpen the effect upon England but was also
necessary, above all, to eliminate the possibility of causes for conflict
with neutral powers." [34] If pledges were given for the safety of
neutral vessels, the admiral felt, the result would be to increase the
amount of shipping to England and, correspondingly, the danger of
accidents and incidents. Since Bethmann had won the army Chief
of Staff to his view that concessions had to be made, he was prepared
to ask that the Kaiser overrule the admirals and order U-boat commanders not to attack vessels under neutral flags. In a debate before
the throne, he would have much more chance of winning on this

[32] Bethmann to Treutler, May 30, 1915, *Politische Dokumente,* II, 344–345.
[33] Note attached to above, *ibid.,* 345.
[34] Bachmann to Jagow, May 26, 1915, *ibid.,* 337.

issue than on a more comprehensive proposal to spare enemy passenger liners as well.

The imperial council of May 31 proved, nevertheless, to be an ordeal.[35] Treutler, Müller, and Falkenhayn spoke for the Chancellor. The minutes do not indicate that Bethmann himself uttered a word, and he may, in fact, have chosen to be absent in order that a second council might be summoned if the Kaiser ruled in favor of the navy. The Chief of Staff, in any case, took the lead in countering the arguments of Tirpitz and Bachmann, and, in doing so, he almost blundered into introducing the more delicate question of enemy liners. Referring to the *Lusitania,* he asserted, "no matter how right we were in the sinking . . . , still the question of power is decisive, and we could not bear to have America intervene on the side of our enemies." The Kaiser sat up at this and observed, "then the U-boat war must be stopped altogether, and for this step, which would excite the general anger of the people, the Chancellor must take responsibility." Müller felt compelled to interject soothingly, "The Chancellor certainly does not want to allow the U-boat war to stop altogether, and there could very well be devised to the satisfaction of the Chancellor an order for the U-boats which would— insofar as human foresight permits—take care of the political situation."

But the Kaiser was not altogether appeased. According to Tirpitz's notes, "His Majesty waved aside the objections, saying they were all 'humbug'; here it is the issue whether the U-boat war will be given up or not, and if the Chancellor is not willing to give it up, then it stays as it is under the decree. A draft bringing together all the earlier restrictions should be laid before him as soon as possible." Since a total abandonment of the U-boat campaign was almost out of the question, it might have seemed that Bethmann had lost his cause.

The reverse was the case, however, for the Kaiser had left the decision to the Chancellor. When the conference adjourned and

[35] Memo by Tirpitz and minutes by Müller, both May 31, 1915, *ibid.,* 346–347; Treutler to Bethmann, May 29, 1915, German Foreign Ministry Archives (U-boat War); Falkenhayn to Bethmann, May 31, 1915, *ibid.*

the admirals departed for their respective headquarters, Bethmann and Müller composed a new general order for U-boat commanders and quickly secured the Emperor's signature. Much more than a mere summary of old orders, it directed submarine captains not only to spare neutral ships but to resolve all doubts by inaction: "In doubtful cases it is better to let an enemy merchantman pass than to sink a neutral." [36] In the mists of the Kaiser's mind, this order may have seemed consistent with his resolution of the previous day. What it reflected, of course, was the fact that the Chancellor could exercise the royal power so long as the Emperor declined decisively to override him. The real test in any imperial council was not, as a rule, on the issue debated. It was rather on the ability of the Chancellor to retain his freedom of action. Since Bethmann had not been overruled by Wilhelm, he had won his point.

He had also won, therefore, on the more difficult question of enemy passenger liners. He was able to go to the Kaiser on June 2, the very next day, and ask for a further order, forbidding attacks on any large passenger ships. While the negotiations with the United States continued, he declared, it was necessary to prevent any fresh *Lusitania* incidents. He had deliberately skirted this question before, even giving Tirpitz and Bachmann the impression that he did not contemplate any such proposal. Having obtained the Emperor's vote of confidence, albeit on a different issue, he was temporarily secure in his power, and Wilhelm signed the order.[37]

Bethmann had thus emerged victorious in the first serious contest over war with America. Tirpitz and Bachmann fumed at his deceitful triumph. They composed a joint telegram to the Kaiser, declaring, "Through such an order Germany loses her last weapon against England and suffers in the eyes of her enemies and of the neutral powers a loss of military respect which can never be made good. . . . It can only be taken by our enemies, by the neutrals, by our own people, and by our own navy, as a dangerous sign of weakness." But the Emperor reaffirmed the order, making but one concession to the

---

[36] *Politische Dokumente,* II, 348.

[37] *Ibid.,* 348–349; Treutler to Bethmann, June 2, 1915, German Foreign Ministry Archives (U-boat War); Treutler to Jagow, June 3, 1915, *ibid.*

navy. He did add an insistence that the order be kept absolutely secret. Tirpitz and Bachmann offered their resignations, but the Kaiser hotly refused. "No!" he wrote, "the gentlemen have to obey and remain. A regular military conspiracy! Brought about by Tirpitz."[38] The Emperor's pride and the agility of Bethmann and Müller combined thus to prevent both a decision for war with America and a public contest that might have compelled such a decision.

The second *Lusitania* note almost forced Bethmann to fight for complete termination of the U-boat war. Each day's news strengthened the Chancellor's conviction that a rupture with the United States would be disastrous. The Balkan states were reported as willing to follow America's lead. If they did, the route to Constantinople would be cut and Turkey almost certainly overpowered. Austria would have to withdraw troops from the Russian front, and the Austrian Emperor might even lose his nerve and sue for terms. Falkenhayn insisted meanwhile that it was imperative to seek a separate peace with Russia, and such hopes as the Chancellor had would certainly be blasted if the Allies were reinforced.[39] Bernstorff reported the United States to be at the threshold of war. Wilson's real object, the ambassador advised, was "complete cessation of the submarine war, and . . . smaller concessions on our part could only be regarded as half-measures."[40] Bethmann thus had to contemplate the fearful possibility of asking the Kaiser to stop the U-boat campaign altogether.

Since he still held the support of Falkenhayn, he could at least consider such a proposal. The general remained alive to the perils of American intervention. At Müller's instance, he talked with the Chief of the Naval Staff, declaring that

[38] *Politische Dokumente*, II, 350–351; Treutler to Bethmann, June 6, 1915, German Foreign Ministry Archives (U-boat War).

[39] Treutler to Bethmann, June 3, 1915, German Foreign Ministry Archives (Secret); Reichsarchiv, *Der Weltkrieg*, VIII, 604.

[40] Bernstorff to Jagow, June 2, 1915 (received June 6, 1915), German Foreign Ministry Archives (Secret Mediation); Bernstorff, *My Three Years in America*, 128–130.

the navy must undertake to guarantee that through the U-boat the United States of America will not be brought into the ranks of our enemies. In the opinion of the political officials of the imperial government this was greatly to be feared if the U-boat war were continued in the same fashion as before the *Lusitania's* sinking. He, as Chief of the General Staff, could no longer in such circumstances take upon himself responsibility for the conduct of the war: not because of the armed might of the United States, but because the moral effect of its enmity on the other neutrals, above all on Rumania, Bulgaria, and Holland, would be fatal.[41]

If Bethmann felt obliged to act, Falkenhayn would at least support a temporary cessation of the U-boat campaign.

The Chancellor had no desire, however, to bring the issue to a head. Procrastinating, as was his habit, he summoned the Chief of the Naval Staff to an informal conference. For support he brought along Jagow and Meyer-Gerhardt, who had just returned from America. Over beer and cigars on that hot Tuesday evening, he asked Bachmann if the Naval Staff could possibly accept a proposal by Meyer-Gerhardt. U-boats would be pledged to follow the traditional rules of visit and search, providing only that Britain agreed to cease flying neutral flags over her own ships. As the Chancellor anticipated, Bachmann categorically refused. To make such a promise, the admiral quite accurately asserted, would be to abandon the entire campaign. Bethmann's attempt to reason with the admiral was thus a total failure.[42]

The conference, indeed, revealed the canyon that lay between the Chancellor's views and those of the navy. Bethmann asked if the admiral could not at least assent to the principle of making concessions to the United States. Bachmann retorted that he could never agree to a public declaration that Germany meant to spare passenger liners. According to the admiral's notes, the Chancellor responded, "It would be impossible for me to take such an attitude of blunt refusal; we *must* make concessions; otherwise we will have war

[41] Memo by Bachmann, June 17, 1915, *Politische Dokumente*, II, 359–360.
[42] Memo by Bachmann, June 22, 1915, *ibid.*, 364–366.

with America or—what is even worse—a break in diplomatic relations. I have to grant, furthermore, that the United States has a
right to expect something of us." When Bachmann blurted his outrage at any suggestion that Germany had done wrong, Jagow came
to the Chancellor's defense. "Even if the United States has no *right*
to lay such claims, still she has a strong *justification*. What would
we say, indeed, if in a war between other nations a ship with 1,500
innocent German passengers was sunk?"

Returning to the issue, Bethmann declared, "Concessions have to
be made, for apart from questions of *right* lies the power question.
We require of our allies, Austria and Hungary, heavy concessions
to the other powers in order to keep these out of the war. Our allies
have a right to demand of us that we make concessions to the Americans in order to keep them out of the ranks of our enemies." When
Bachmann stamped away, the Chancellor came to the doorway and
pleaded with him to think of the good of the whole and resign
himself to "temporary concessions." After six or eight weeks, Bethmann said, the situation might be better and U-boat operations
might be resumed. But the admiral was implacable. From his standpoint a sacrifice of the submarine war, even for a time, would endanger not only the hope of victory but the life of the nation.
To Bethmann, on the other hand, the U-boat seemed, in every
sense, a liability. There was no bridge between these two positions.

Despite the support of Falkenhayn, moreover, Bethmann had no
reason to feel confident. The Kaiser had already shown himself to
be frightened by the state of public opinion, and right-wing leaders
had since intensified their propaganda. The six powerful agrarian
and industrial associations had indicated their firm opposition to
any further limitation of the U-boat war. Reichstag leaders had
called on the Chancellor to voice concern lest fresh concessions be
made to the United States, and the right-wing press had grown as
clamorous as circumstances permitted. The *Kreuzzeitung* printed
no fewer than five editorials on the U-boat war within a space of
two weeks, and the *Deutsche Tageszeitung* grew so outspoken that
its publication was temporarily stopped. Indicating the breadth of
sympathy with the right wing, moreover, was the wave of criticism

reportedly provoked by this action. It was evident, as Bethmann confessed, that public opinion was in a high state of excitement.[43] Had the Chancellor been compelled to summon an imperial council, he might well have found himself unable to prevent an adverse decision.

As it turned out, he was spared the necessity of a test. Bernstorff's dispatches suddenly took a turn for the better. "The political outlook in America appears at present as calm as a summer's day . . . ," the ambassador wrote, "it may now be regarded as certain, that neither the President nor the American people want a war with Germany." [44] When an English mule ship went down with twenty-one American crewmen, the United States disregarded the incident on the ground that the ship had resisted search. Ambassador Gerard meanwhile indicated that his government might be satisfied with something far short of total surrender. Gerard suggested, indeed, that peace might be preserved if Germany allowed one English passenger vessel a week to pass unharmed. His own government would promise in return, he thought, to guarantee that such liners carried no contraband.[45] The Chancellor found it possible, as a result, to placate both the Naval Staff and the public.

He allowed Foreign Ministry representatives and naval officers to work out the reply to America's second *Lusitania* note. While it included Gerard's fatuous proposal, it embodied no concessions and implied no new change in the U-boat campaign. The press, as a whole, applauded the final note. Some Conservative journals still lamented compromises made in the past, but most expressed satisfaction at its apparent firmness. The Progressive *Vossische Zeitung*,

[43] Westarp to Heydebrand, June 17, 1915, *Konservative Politik*, II, 109–110; *ibid.*, 108, note 3; Gerard to Lansing, June 25, 1915, *Foreign Relations, Supplement: 1915*, p. 454; memo by Bachmann, June 22, 1915, *Politische Dokumente*, II, 365.

[44] Bernstorff to Jagow, June 9, 1915, German Foreign Ministry Archives (General); Bernstorff, *My Three Years in America*, 134–136.

[45] On the *Armenian: Foreign Relations, Supplement: 1915*, pp. 457–459, 463; on Gerard's activity: Gerard to Lansing, June 24, June 26, June 30, July 3, July 4, July 5, 1915, *ibid.*, 453, 454, 457–462; *Politische Dokumente*, II, 375; memo by Karl Bachem, July 31, 1915, from the Bachem manuscripts in Cologne, cited in Epstein's "Erzberger."

for example, summarized it as rejecting "every foreign attempt to dictate the weapons we may employ in defeating the English starvation plan." [46] Bethmann was thus spared temporarily both a new crisis within the government and, perhaps, a crisis outside of it.

Neither the firmness of the navy nor the excitement of the public convinced him that he should abandon all thought of ending the U-boat war. The reported relaxation in America's stand made the issue less pressing. A third *Lusitania* note did arrive, of course, and it demonstrated that Gerard had been wholly wrong in predicting a softening of Wilson's demands. The Kaiser read the American note and scrawled on its margin: "This is the most shameless thing in tone and bearing that I have had to read since the Japanese note of last August. It ends with a direct threat." Bethmann referred to it wryly as a "very coarse note," and he was told that the Reichstag and press wanted him to answer it sharply and provocatively. Bernstorff advised, however, that it could safely be left unanswered, and Bethmann was glad to do so. [47] In the meantime he continued to mull over the possibility of proposing that the U-boat campaign be abandoned completely.

In early August he circulated among his associates a long and thoughtful memorandum by the Treasury Minister, Karl Helfferich, an economist of pugnacious vanity, great ambition, and undeniable brilliance. Helfferich suggested that Germany's entire policy toward the United States ought to be reassessed. Instead of worrying about her on account of the Balkans and the Netherlands, he believed, the government ought to think of her economic strength. America could finance the Allies forever, he warned; the Central Powers would no longer be on the same footing with their enemies, and the Allies could simply wait out Germany's financial collapse. Helfferich contended that the government should seek to avoid a rupture

[46] Jagow to Gerard, July 8, 1915, *Foreign Relations, Supplement: 1915*, pp. 463–466; *Literary Digest*, LI (July 24, 1915), 149; *Aachener Allgemeine Zeitung, Magdeburgische Zeitung*, and *Vossiche Zeitung*, quoted in *Daily Extracts from the Foreign Press*, July 25, 1915.

[47] Marginal notes by the Kaiser on the U.S. note of July 23, 1915, German Foreign Ministry Archives (GHQ—Amerika), printed in *Politische Dokumente*, II, 378–380; memo by Tirpitz, Aug. 7, 1915, *ibid.*, 395.

with the United States not only because of its attendant effects but also because, in itself, it could be disastrous for Germany.

The minister went even farther, for he also pointed out the immense advantages that might be reaped if the United States could be drawn onto the German side. Not only could the Central Powers obtain money, but they might also hope for much-needed imports. Hostile sentiment toward Britain, he argued, was widespread in America, especially among the cotton growers of Wilson's own party, and the United States might be led to break the British blockade. All that Germany had to do was to abandon the U-boat for a few weeks or, at most, for three months, meanwhile joining Wilson in insistence on "freedom of the seas." The inherent conflict between American and British interests would accomplish the rest. Just by putting aside the U-boat weapon, whose effectiveness was at best uncertain, Germany could gain a decisive ally. "Press and public opinion," Helfferich added, "must not be allowed to weigh in the balance when such great stakes are in the game." [48]

Although Bethmann expressed neither approval nor disapproval of Helfferich's proposals, there is evidence to suggest that he did more than merely take them under advisement. If one could assume that he was responsible for inspired releases appearing in German newspapers during early August, it would be possible to conclude that he adopted the minister's ideas as his own. There appeared, in the first place, a number of attacks on the Conservative doctrine that England was the chief enemy. Many had no apparent official inspiration; a number came from provincial Catholic clergymen; but others did appear in journals like the *Frankfurter Zeitung* and the *Berliner Tageblatt,* which were sometimes used by the Chancellery.[49]

[48] Helfferich to Bethmann, Aug. 5, 1915, *ibid.,* 385–395; Karl Helfferich, *Der Weltkrieg* (3 vols.; Berlin, 1919), II, 318–323; the original letter is in German Foreign Ministry Archives (U-boat War).

[49] Hanover *Deutsche Volkszeitung, Das Forum, Frankfurter Zeitung, Kölnische Volkszeitung,* cited in *Literary Digest,* LI (Aug. 7, 1915), 242, (Aug. 28, 1915), 409; *Berliner Tageblatt,* Aug. 10, 1915; *Kölnische Zeitung,* Aug. 11, 1915; Karl Bachem, *Vorgeschichte, Geschichte, und Politik der deutschen Zentrumspartei* (8 vols.; Cologne, 1927–1931), VIII, 229.

Coupled with this challenge to the premise of the U-boat policy went, in the second place, a new line of attack upon Great Britain. The *Frankfurter Zeitung,* the *Berliner Tageblatt,* and the semi-official *Kölnische Zeitung* all took occasion to editorialize on England's injuries to neutral trade. The interests of Germany and such neutrals as the United States, said writer after writer, were in fact identical. Their common object was "freedom of the seas." Bethmann himself joined in, declaring in the *Norddeutsche Allgemeine Zeitung,* "the peace for which we strive must guarantee to all people the freedom of the seas and open to all nations the possibility of competing freely in the effort for material and moral progress." In his speech to the Reichstag on August 19, he placed freedom of the seas among the foremost war aims of the Empire.[50] These declarations and the attendant press campaign suggest that the Chancellor may have given very serious thought indeed to the Helfferich proposals.

If so, nothing came of it. The navy refused to accept a particle of Helfferich's reasoning. Tirpitz commented, for example:

A strengthening of sentiment for us in the United States and a turning of the American government against England I hold to be *impossible.* There is too much big capital invested in the munitions industry. *Our overthrow is in America's interest, in the first place because Germany did not go into the Anglo-American-Belgian-French trust bloc, and in the second place because America needs England for her position against Japan.*[51]

If there were any chance of turning America away from England,

[50] *Frankfurter Zeitung,* Aug. 7, 1915, quoted in Gerard to Lansing, Aug. 9, 1915, *Foreign Relations, Supplement: 1915,* pp. 506–507; *Berliner Tageblatt,* Aug. 1, Aug. 5, Aug. 19, 1915; *Kölnische Zeitung,* Aug. 3, Aug. 18, 1915; *Kölnische Volkszeitung,* cited in *Daily Extracts from the Foreign Press,* Sept. 3, 1915; *Aachener Allgemeine Zeitung,* cited ibid., Sept. 4, 1915; Ludwig Quessel in the *Sozialistische Monatshefte,* summarized at length in *Résumé de la presse allemande,* no. 1, pp. 7–8; *Norddeutsche Allgemeine Zeitung,* Aug. 12, 1915; Thimme, *Bethmann Hollwegs Kriegsreden,* 37–60.

[51] Notes on a meeting with the Chancellor, Aug. 7, 1915, entered as marginal comments on the Helfferich memo, *Politische Dokumente,* II, 385-395.

said the Grand Admiral, it would rise out of the U-boat war. If Germany could so damage trade that Britain became unable to pay the interest on her debts, then American hearts might change. As for the Helfferich proposals, they were unrealistic and unacceptable. If they were put forward by the Chancellor, Tirpitz indicated, he would feel compelled to resign and perhaps carry the issue to the press and public.

The potential popular opposition continued meanwhile to find expression. Conservative Berlin sheets, like the *Kreuzzeitung,* the *Tägliche Rundschau,* the *Morgenpost,* and the *Börsenzeitung,* all insisted that the United States was already Britain's ally and Germany's enemy. Reventlow commented that the freedom of the seas could be achieved only if the U-boat were allowed to destroy British sea power. The *Berliner Tageblatt,* for all its contribution to the free seas campaign, observed editorially that the United States wanted abandonment of the U-boat war, "and if Americans will not see that we cannot do that there is nothing to be done." Even the socialist *Münchener Post* raised its voice against termination of U-boat warfare. The English desired it, said a socialist writer, because they themselves wished to abandon the blockade; it was England's plan to allow unlimited food shipments so that commodity prices would fall and German agrarians would lose interest in continuing the war. [52] Had the Chancellor elected to press the Helfferich program, he would have risked both his own power and the continuance of the *Burgfrieden.*

Even if consideration of the Helfferich plan had not been barred by official and public opposition, it would have been blocked by events. On August 19 came the sinking of the *Arabic.* Lieutenant Schneider of the U-24 precipitated a new international and internal crisis. Operating off the mouth of St. George's Channel, only a few miles from the spot where the *Lusitania* went down, he was pre-

---

[52] *Résumé de la presse allemande,* no. 14; *Morgenpost* and *Börsenzeitung,* cited in *Literary Digest,* LI (Aug. 7, 1915), 242; *Deutsche Tageszeitung,* Aug. 3, 1915; *Berliner Tageblatt,* July 18, 1915; *Münchener Post,* reported in *Daily Extracts from the Foreign Press,* July 30, 1915.

paring to fire on a freighter when a grey hulk loomed on the eastern horizon. Ordering his boat under water, Schneider set a course to intercept, but the target obligingly turned toward the freighter. As Schneider awaited its arrival, he scanned its sides but found the markings and flag invisible. When about four miles away, it began to shift course. The turn brought it bow-on toward the submarine, and Schneider instantly concluded that it meant to ram him. Only five days before he had been attacked in such fashion. Without hesitating, therefore, he ordered the crew on number two torpedo tube to fire. Forty seconds later the missile struck a side conveniently exposed by another shift in course. The ship sank swiftly, but Schneider saw fifteen or more lifeboats go over its sides. Since he never saw the markings, he set it down in his log as an unknown freighter, of approximately 5,000 tons, probably carrying passengers. It was, of course, the 16,500-ton White Star liner, *Arabic,* and 44 of its passengers drowned, including two Americans.[53]

The *Arabic* incident forced the Chancellor to stop the U-boat war, not permanently, of course, and not for such positive ends as Helfferich had outlined, but merely in order to stave off catastrophe. Bernstorff radioed ominously, "I fear I cannot prevent rupture this time if our answer in the Arabic matter is not conciliatory." [54] The general situation meanwhile had grown even more delicate than it had been earlier, during the *Lusitania* crisis. Dutch newspapers had commented unfavorably on the Chancellor's recent speech, declaring that Germany's war aims threatened the independence of Holland. The risk of Dutch intervention on the side of the Allies was thus as great as ever.[55] Nor had the Balkan situation improved.

[53] Spindler, *Handelskrieg,* II, 261, 269–270; *Foreign Relations, Supplement: 1915,* pp. 516–520; U.S. Department of State, *Diplomatic Correspondence Relating to Neutral Rights and Duties* (European War, No. 3, Aug. 12, 1916), pp. 199–215, 219–227.

[54] Bernstorff to Jagow, Aug. 20, 1915 (received Aug. 25), German Foreign Ministry Archives (Secret); Bernstorff, *My Three Years in America,* 146.

[55] *Amsterdamer Allgemeen Handelsblad* and *Amsterdamer Telegraaf,* described in Eduard Engel, *Ein Tagebuch . . . 25. Mai 1915 zum 24. Mai 1916* (Berlin, 1916), pp. 1347–1348.

Falkenhayn was readying a massive offensive against Serbia, intended to secure the route to Constantinople. His plans required that Bulgaria join the Central Powers before the autumn, but Bethmann's promising negotiations with the Bulgarians suddenly stalled when the *Arabic* went down.[56] In order to protect the western and Balkan fronts, as well as to prevent American intervention, Bethmann had to act and act swiftly.

His first step was to ensure that there should be no more incidents while the *Arabic* question remained aflame. Somehow he managed to secure two successive orders by the Chief of the Naval Staff. The first directed U-boat commanders to be governed strictly and in all cases by their prior directives to spare large passenger liners. The second declared that until the situation cleared, no further U-boats should be sent into the war zone.[57] In the meantime, Jagow conferred earnestly with Gerard, endeavoring to prevent any hasty action by the Americans. A newspaperman reported that officials in the Foreign Ministry were behaving as if they had lost their heads, and the Foreign Minister, when speaking with the ambassador, almost went so far as to violate the Kaiser's earlier order. The Emperor had directed that no disclosure be made of the order to spare large passenger vessels. Jagow told Gerard, nevertheless, that he did not understand the *Arabic* sinking; if it was torpedoed, the submarine commander had disobeyed instructions.

"What were the instructions?" asked Gerard.
"Not to torpedo without notice."
"You mean passenger ships?"
Jagow fell silent.[58]

The Chancellor's second step was to arrange for a new imperial

---

[56] Reichsarchiv, *Der Weltkrieg*, IX, 149–163; memo by Tirpitz of a meeting with the Chancellor, Aug. 26, 1915, *Politische Dokumente*, II, 404.

[57] Orders of Aug. 24, Aug. 27, 1915, *ibid.*, 402.

[58] Gerard to Lansing, Aug. 24, 1915, *Foreign Relations, Supplement: 1915*, pp. 525–526; *Politische Dokumente*, II, 408.

council. Owing to the extremely delicate Balkan situation, he was certain of Falkenhayn's support. As before, he sought to ensure that the council should deal with a lesser issue, where he would have the advantage in argument. Summoning Bachmann and Tirpitz to Pless in advance of the council, he put before them a proposal that the secret orders of the preceding June should be made public, thus demonstrating to the United States that the *Arabic*'s sinking had, in fact, been accidental. Bachmann was willing to fight this proposal, but Tirpitz refused to be drawn onto such narrow ground. The Americans already knew, he asserted, that such orders were in effect; the fact that no liners had been sunk during June and July had told them that. The torpedoing of large passenger ships could not be prevented with certainty, he declared, unless U-boats were ordered not to operate in the war zone. The entire campaign would have to be abandoned, "so long as preventing a conflict with America matters to us." The Grand Admiral would not agree to debate anything less than the main issue.[59]

The subsequent council was therefore trying and uncertain. Bethmann spoke first, again proposing only that the secret order of June 6 should be disclosed. Falkenhayn backed him to the limit, declaring, "everything must be done which will forestall a conflict with the United States." But the Chief of the Naval Staff made a surprise move, producing a dispatch just received from Berlin which asserted that the situation in the United States had greatly improved. Tirpitz followed up by repeating the statements he had made earlier to the Chancellor. The admirals' speeches must have made a visible impression on the Kaiser, for Müller intervened to prevent the council from reaching any decision. It might be best, he suggested, to await the return of Lieutenant Schneider, so that the facts of the *Arabic*'s sinking might be obtained. "Should a declaration then prove to be necessary, it will have to be drawn up between the Chancellor and the navy in a form satisfactory to both." Treutler indicated that the Foreign Ministry would be willing to make an effort, and the Kaiser ruled, "the Chancellor should, in conjunction

[59] Notes by Tirpitz, Aug. 26, 1915, *ibid.*, 404–406.

with the navy, prepare a draft of a declaration *eventually* to be sent to the United States, and lay it before him." [60]

Bethmann had almost lost. Only the agile intervention of Müller, apparently, had restrained the Kaiser from deciding in favor of the admirals. The Chancellor spoke bitterly to Bachmann, saying that "he had become encircled on all sides, like the Russians. . . . He would not, however, capitulate like the Russians. He would not go away from Pless until His Majesty had ruled in his favor." [61] Or, he might have added, until the Kaiser assented to his resignation. The issue in August was the same as it had been in June. Despite Bethmann's alarm and pique, the council had, in fact, given him a fresh victory, for he had not been overruled, and his power remained intact.

He was able, therefore, to obtain from the Emperor the decisions that he wanted. On the day after the unhappy council, the Chancellor exhibited to the Kaiser the most recent dispatch from Bernstorff, the one warning of imminent rupture. He may also have disclosed a message from the Pope, recommending that Germany come to terms with the United States. Erzberger brought him such a message, but it is not certain exactly when he received it. [62] Meanwhile

[60] Notes by Tirpitz, Aug. 26, 1915, *ibid.*, 406. The source of Bachmann's information is uncertain. It may have been the naval attaché in Washington, or it may, on the other hand, have been Undersecretary Zimmermann, who had swung into the camp of the U-boat enthusiasts: Westarp to Heydebrand, Sept. 1, 1915, *Konservative Politik*, II, 112; Mumm to Hammann, Aug. 31, 1915, Hammann, *Bilder aus der letzten Kaiserzeit*, 121; marginal notes by Zimmermann on Lucius to Jagow, May 22, 1915, German Foreign Ministry Archives (U-boat War). If so, it would help to explain Bethmann's petulant remark to Bachmann after the conference: "even the people on whose understanding and support he ought to have been able to count have left him in the breach." *Politische Dokumente*, II, 407. An alternative explanation is that Bethmann did not yet realize that Müller and Treutler had probably saved him from an adverse ruling by the Kaiser. Still another explanation, of course, is that Bachmann, who was not among his intellectual peers, thought Müller and Treutler had deserted the Chancellor and therefore misinterpreted Bethmann's vexation.

[61] *Politische Dokumente*, II, 407.

[62] Notes by Dr. Schramm on a conversation with Erzberger, Sept. 15, 1915, *ibid.*, 432–433; Erzberger said that he had received the papal message on Aug. 24 and forwarded it to the Chancellor at Pless. Cf. Heydebrand to Westarp, Sept. 10, 1915, *Konservative Politik*, II, 114.

Bethmann invited Bachmann to approve a message to Bernstorff, saying simply "that passenger steamers (liners) will only be sunk after previous warning and rescue of passengers and lives." When Bachmann protested, the Chancellor telegraphed Treutler that the admirals opposed the Kaiser's current orders. Treutler and Müller duly brought this view before the Emperor, in the absence of both Bachmann and Tirpitz, and the Kaiser unhesitatingly issued a new order to the fleet, directing that "henceforward any passenger vessel whatever, not only the large ones, shall only be sunk after warning and safeguarding of passengers." On the following day, again probably at Bethmann's instance, another imperial message ordered that for the time being no U-boats at all should be stationed on the west coast of England, where Atlantic passenger vessels were apt to be found.[63] The Kaiser had consented, in effect, to render the U-boat virtually impotent.

Even though Bethmann had won the Kaiser's decision, he could hardly regard the struggle as finished. The admirals were aware of having fought the Chancellor to a draw in council, and they were not prepared to be defeated again by underhanded means. Bachmann wrote excitedly to the Kaiser, "The U-boat war is now and for the next decade the only weapon with which Your Majesty can effectively menace England and hold her in check. The English must therefore be brought to the realization that Your Majesty will use this weapon unreservedly now and in the future." Tirpitz, more realistically, offered his resignation, writing gravely that the Chancellor evidently attached no value to his services and advice.[64]

Bethmann was able to meet these challenges. Although it was Tirpitz who had offered to resign, it was Bachmann who lost his post. Müller notified him that his behavior had displeased the Kaiser, and Henning von Holtzendorff, a distant relative of Müller's and an admiral known not to be a U-boat fanatic, was gazetted as

<hr />

[63] *Politische Dokumente*, II, 407–409, 411–412; Treutler to Bethmann, Aug. 30, 1915, German Foreign Ministry Archives (U-boat War).

[64] Bachmann to the Kaiser, Aug. 30, 1915, *Politische Dokumente*, II, 413–414; Tirpitz to the Kaiser, Aug. 27, 1915, *ibid.*, 409–410; Müller in *Front wider Bülow*, 191.

his successor. Tirpitz could not be dealt with in the same fashion, for he still retained great popularity and prestige. Erzberger, the Centrist leader, warned the Chancellor, "in no event should there be a 'Tirpitz-crisis.' If Tirpitz goes, then the Chancellor falls too." [65] Bethmann advised the Kaiser to refuse Tirpitz's demission but to reprimand him. The Grand Admiral was directed to keep his post but not in future to interfere in matters that belonged properly either to the political leadership or to the Naval Staff. When Tirpitz then wrote to the Emperor detailing his objections, Wilhelm answered hotly:

America must be prevented from taking part against us as an active enemy. She could provide unlimited money for our foes. . . . As Chief Warlord I had absolutely to prevent this event from occurring. That was wise policy. For that reason I had with a heavy heart to impose *restrictions* in order to achieve that goal. . . . First the *war must be won,* and that end necessitates absolute protection against a new enemy; how that is to be achieved—whether with more or less sacrifice—is immaterial, and *my business.* What I do with my navy is my business *only.*[66]

Although Tirpitz regained his powers by threatening to resign in spite of the imperial command, Bethmann had emerged distinctly stronger than his naval opponents.

Much more troublesome was the evidence of public dissatisfaction. When the Conservatives learned of Bethmann's victory, they almost rose in arms. Reventlow in the *Deutsche Tageszeitung* not only challenged the decisions indirectly by trumpeting the past success of the U-boat campaign, but he went on to declare that a promise to spare passenger ships would constitute a death sentence for submariners. Westarp launched a similar attack in the *Kreuzzeitung.* Knowing that he risked retaliation from the censor, he nevertheless devoted a column to the news of Bernstorff's promise of safety for passenger vessels. "This report," he wrote, "fills us with lively concern and grave thoughts . . . [for] it is one of the most urgent necessities that we use to the full against England every weapon

<hr>

[65] Schramm notes of Sept. 15, *ibid.,* 433; Epstein, "Erzberger," citing material from the Erzberger manuscripts.

[66] *Politische Dokumente,* II; 415–416, 424–428.

that we have in our hand." Nor were the Conservatives alone, for Bassermann and Hirsch of Essen went to the Foreign Ministry to express the alarm and indignation of National Liberals. Although Erzberger, the Centrist, had helped Bethmann during the ministerial crisis, he was said to have declared that his views coincided with the Grand Admiral's.[67] It was all too plain that the Chancellor's policies did not command support in the Reichstag.

Bethmann could not combat this opposition as he could that of the navy. He did employ the power of censorship. Count Mumm, the Foreign Ministry press officer, brought every instance of public criticism to the attention of Major Deutelmoser, the army censor. Though Deutelmoser was hesitant to act in all cases, he did, for example, summon Reventlow and warn him that the *Deutsche Tageszeitung* would be muzzled if it continued to agitate the U-boat issue. Bethmann himself cautioned that further breaches of discipline by the *Kreuzzeitung* might lead to extreme measures on the part of the government. The Chancellor's press officers meanwhile conferred earnestly with friendly journalists, asking them to explain the seriousness of the situation and to help quiet public unrest.[68]

Through these friendly journals, an effort was made to counteract the grumblings of the right. Stories appeared, suggesting that friction between Germany and the United States resulted from British intrigue and intimating that patriots ought not to be taken in by this trickery. Karl Bachem, writing in the Centrist *Kölnische Volkszeitung,* even suggested that the excitement over American munitions exports was enemy-inspired; the actual supply had been grossly exaggerated. It was hinted elsewhere that American help might be forthcoming if friendly relations could only be preserved. The *Kölnische Zeitung* described a pro-German swing among American Catholics. It also reported an offer by Bremen merchants to buy large quantities of American cotton and predicted that the

---

[67] *Deutsche Tageszeitung,* Aug. 25, Aug. 31, 1915; *Kreuzzeitung,* Sept. 3, 1915; Westarp to Heydebrand, Sept. 1, 1915, *Konservative Politik,* II, 112; Schramm notes of Sept. 15, 1915, *Politische Dokumente,* II, 434.

[68] Mumm to Hammann, Aug. 31, 1915, Hammann, *Bilder aus der letzten Kaiserzeit,* 118–121; Heydebrand to Westarp, Sept. 1, 1915, Westarp, *Konservative Politik,* II, 114.

United States government might force shipments through the British blockade. At the same time, these friendly journals sought to reassure the public that no opportunity was being lost to exploit the U-boat weapon. Successes in the Mediterranean were given prominent coverage, and the *Frankfurter Zeitung* declared, in a widely reprinted editorial:

> We cannot be surprised that Count Bernstorff's concessions have created a false opinion of our position abroad. . . . But we must guard against a similar misunderstanding at home. We cannot at present give any indication of the final result of negotiations between Washington and Berlin, but we can at least be sure that the submarine warfare has not come to an end . . . . and . . . . we may confidently assume that the concessions are not entirely on the side of Germany.[69]

This energetic press campaign helped to disguise the extent of opposition, but there is no evidence that it remedied the unpopularity of Bethmann's policy.

In view of the public's uneasiness, the Chancellor was willing to restore any part of the U-boat war that the United States would allow. When Bernstorff's dispatches took on a more cheerful tone, he felt it possible to seek some understanding with the admirals and hence some quieting of the right-wing uproar. The ambassador reported, "a rupture of diplomatic relations appears once more to be indefinitely postponed. . . . If we can prove . . . that after the *Lusitania* incident, orders had been given to attack no passenger ships while negotiations with the United States were going on . . . , all outstanding questions could be solved without difficulty." [70] While Bethmann was arranging to shrink the U-boat war, moreover, the *Hesperian* went down, and the United States neither broke relations nor dispatched an ultimatum. The improved situa-

---

[69] *Berliner Tageblatt*, Sept. 17, 1915; *Frankfurter Zeitung*, Sept. 7, 1915, cited in *Daily Extracts from the Foreign Press*, Sept. 17, 1915; *Kölnische Volkszeitung*, quoted *ibid.*, Sept. 16, 1915; *Kölnische Zeitung*, Aug 27, 1915; *Deutsche Tageszeitung*, Sept. 12, 1915; *Berliner Tageblatt*, Sept. 27, 1915; *Frankfurter Zeitung*, Sept. 20, 1915, quoted in *Berliner Tageblatt*, Sept. 22, 1915.

[70] Bernstorff to Jagow, Aug. 30, 1915 (received Sept. 4, 1915), German Foreign Ministry Archives (General); Bernstorff, *My Three Years in America*, 150–151.

tion had already been reflected in the Bulgarian negotiations, which concluded on September 7 with a military pact. Bethmann found the emergency subsiding.

He felt able to make some gestures toward an accommodation with the navy. He permitted the Naval Staff to take a hand in drafting a note on the *Arabic* case. Since Bernstorff had already been authorized to disclose the earlier orders, there seemed no need for further open concessions. The resultant note, therefore, simply described the circumstances of the *Arabic's* sinking, expressed regret for the lives lost, but denied that the German government had any obligation to pay an indemnity, even if the U-boat commander had been wrong in assuming that the *Arabic* meant to ram him.[71] At the same time, the Chancellor allowed a slight relaxation in orders to submarine commanders. Passenger liners were defined for them as vessels with more than one stack, with speeds above fourteen knots, or with more than one promenade deck; U-boat captains were permitted to assume that other ships carried only freight.[72] By these means the Chancellor temporarily placated the navy and, as he no doubt hoped, produced a calmer mood among the right wing.

His own relief, however, was short-lived. Bernstorff reversed himself, radioing over the fastest channel:

The memorandum on the *Arabic* is not understood here, and in so far as it is understood, is considered to be a manifestation of German bad faith. . . . If we still consider ourselves bound to maintain that the officer concerned in the *Arabic* case was only obeying orders, we can never hope to come to an agreement. . . . Anyway, there is no doubt whatever that a second *Arabic* case is bound to result in war.[73]

Neutral sources meanwhile reported great excitement in the American press.

Bethmann had to revert to the uncompromising position that he

---

[71] Jagow to Gerard, Sept. 8, 1915, *Foreign Relations, Supplement: 1915*, pp. 539–540; Spindler, *Handelskrieg*, II, 284–285.

[72] Order of Sept. 8, 1915, *Politische Dokumente*, II, 428.

[73] Bernstorff to Jagow, Sept. 14, 1915 (received Sept. 15), German Foreign Ministry Archives (General); Bernstorff, *My Three Years in America*, 154–156.

had temporarily deserted. Owing to the changes in the naval command, he did not have to battle through another imperial council. Holtzendorff, the new Naval Staff chief, permitted the Foreign Ministry to concoct a hasty note, canceling the earlier one and offering both an indemnity for the lives lost on the *Arabic* and a reprimand for the U-boat commander. In order to avoid any accident, furthermore, all U-boat operations were suspended, not only on the west coast of England but in the Channel as well, and even boats operating in the North Sea were directed to adhere strictly to the rules of visit and search.[74] The submarine war was suspended altogether.

The decision was, of course, not final. The Chancellor had overcome the admirals, confirmed his own power, replaced Bachmann, and clipped the wings of Tirpitz. But he merely held a temporary grasp on the buttery will of the Kaiser. He depended partly on the support of the army, which he could not hope to hold indefinitely. The issue was bound to arise again even within the imperial government. Right-wing enthusiasm for the U-boat remained undiminished. The executive committee of the Conservative party published a resolution "that amid all the severe problems which the World War has created for the German people, there remains immovably in the forefront the aim which it regards as the most important: *the effort to overpower England with all means at our disposal*." [75] It was apparent that the public pressure would be remorseless until the Chancellor's policy was reversed. Peace between the United States and Germany had been preserved, but only temporarily.

[74] Spindler, *Handelskrieg*, II, 286–287; Jagow to Gerard, Sept. 19, 1915, *Foreign Relations, Supplement: 1915*, pp. 551–552; *Politische Dokumente*, II, 441–442.
[75] Lutz, *Fall of the German Empire*, I, 333–334.

XI

The Tirpitz Crisis

The beginning of 1916 brought a renewal of the U-boat problem. Agitation had not died out after the *Arabic* settlement, but it had at least subsided. Since the winter months were not favorable for U-boat operations, the admirals were willing to wait before reopening the issue, and excitement outside was not only subdued by the censor but also muffled in clamor over other questions, such as war aims, price controls, and emergency revenues. The fleet did quietly resume operations. The coastal command began sinking troop transports in November; one U-boat went out to the English west coast in December. Since Austria consented to bear full responsibility for the *Ancona* and even to hold the offending U-boat on her own naval list, Germany avoided a new controversy with the United States.[1] It was January, 1916, before Bethmann had to resume his struggle with the U-boat enthusiasts.

When the domestic demand revived, it seemed so strong that the Chancellor felt compelled to make a small concession. He approved the sharpened campaign (*verschärfte U-Boot-Krieg*). He was driven to this action by the knowledge that General Falkenhayn was on the verge of deserting him and lining up with Tirpitz. He was also pushed by the mounting agitation of the right-wing press.

[1] *Politische Dokumente,* II, 449–450; Treutler to Jagow, Dec. 12, 1915, German Foreign Ministry Archives (U-boat War); Hohenlohe to Jagow, Dec. 17, 1915, *ibid.*

It is true that the apparent confusion in the United States—the new *Lusitania* demands, the *modus vivendi* proposal, and the Congressional uprising against Wilson—allowed him to relax restraints on the U-boats. But it was primarily the shift in Falkenhayn's view and the revival of public demand that led him to the decision. These events threatened his hold upon the Kaiser and the country, and he had no option but to bend before them.

Falkenhayn's change of heart was readily understandable. Having carried through his Balkan campaign and subdued Serbia, he no longer felt anxious about the route to Constantinople. He had enough troops now to fend off a Dutch attack. Since his earlier hope of separate peace with Russia had faded, he saw the only remaining alternatives for Germany as total victory or total defeat. "We have no choice," he wrote Bethmann, "but are compelled to go on . . . to a good or bitter end whether we wish to or not. The fact is that war is no longer what we used to think it; for all combatants this war has become in the same way a struggle for existence." [2] Adopting this gloomy outlook, he veered toward the admirals' view that victory could be won only by breaking England's will to resist. Not only was it obvious that British money held the enemy alliance together, but also it seemed that Britain's prestige was the chief obstacle to reinforcement of the Central Powers. Enver Pasha, the Turkish leader, told Falkenhayn that only fear of Britain kept the Moslem world quiet, and the General Staff declared that the arrival of British troops and ships at Salonika had prevented Greece from joining in the attack on Serbia.[3] By military light Falkenhayn had every reason to lean toward the admirals' opinion that England was the chief enemy and hence to think more favorably of their U-boat proposals.

The only puzzling element in the change was the innocence that he displayed about the American factor. He had stood staunchly by during the *Lusitania* and *Arabic* debates, while Bethmann spelled out the grim consequences of war with the United States. Yet when Falkenhayn began to plan the campaign for 1916, it was as if he

[2] Falkenhayn to Bethmann, Nov. 28, 1915, Reichsarchiv, *Der Weltkrieg*, X, 1-2.
[3] *Ibid.*, IX, 316, 488-489; *ibid.*, X, 4.

had never read a line or heard a word that the Chancellor had uttered. Treutler wrote to Jagow in December, 1915:

General von Falkenhayn is suddenly taking the standpoint on the American question that America seems to want a rupture, our situation is now different, and he no longer feels so sure that war with America would be insupportable. I answered him that politically the arguments against a rupture were still just the same as they had been earlier. The question has, in fact, become more serious, since close students of the situation advise that the severance of diplomatic relations would now in all probability spell actual war: we must therefore endeavor as long as possible to prevent a break; the entry of America into the war would at the very least strengthen the morale of our enemies in an unwanted degree and thus probably lengthen the war. General von Falkenhayn agreed to the extent of saying that he no longer shrank from a break because of the war but did, however, because of the peace. I hope to have convinced him that it would still be worthwhile to endure certain sacrifices in order to reduce, as much as we can, the likelihood of a war with America.[4]

That Treutler had not succeeded was evidenced when Falkenhayn consulted with the Chancellor on December 30. As Bethmann noted:

General v. Falkenhayn made the remark to me . . . that he could not understand why it was that we did not resume in all severity the U-boat war against England. In response to my remark that a break with America would then be unavoidable, he stated that he could not have run the risk of this break in the late part of the summer, on account of the relations in the Balkans, which at that time were still unsettled, but that now, since we could rely upon Bulgaria, America was no longer in a position to do us injury. We would be able to overcome the disadvantageous commercial results of such a break . . . , and . . . we would also be able to overcome the bad moral effect which this would have on the rest of the neutrals.[5]

It was clear that much of the earlier argument, in and out of imperial councils, had made little impression on the Chief of Staff.

Falkenhayn was slow, nevertheless, in swinging all the way over

[4] Treutler to Jagow, Dec. 12, 1915, *ibid.*, X, 15, note 2.
[5] Memo by Bethmann, Jan. 4, 1916, *Official German Documents*, II, 1116 (I have altered the translation slightly).

to the Tirpitz camp. The Grand Admiral did his best to bring about a complete conversion. On two occasions during the first week of January, he drew Falkenhayn into prolonged discussion of the U-boat's capabilities, and both times he arranged that other admirals should be present to back him up. The Grand Admiral also sent a long and impassioned memorandum to the Chief of Staff and, at the same time, encouraged right-wing leaders in the Reichstag to write, impressing upon the general their desire for an all-out U-boat campaign.[6]

Falkenhayn hesitated to succumb partly because of continued uncertainty about the submarine's real capabilities. Both Tirpitz and the Chief of the Naval Staff swore to him that an unrestricted campaign would force England to make peace by autumn, at the latest. Yet intelligent and well-informed civilians denied this contention flatly. Bethmann and Helfferich declared that the U-boat could not be decisive against England but, by bringing America into the war, could be decisive against Germany.[7] It was while these arguments and counterarguments were being flung at the Chief of Staff that Bethmann declared the submarine to be the *ultima ratio,* whose failure would spell *"finis Germaniae."* [8]

Bewildered by these differing opinions, Falkenhayn adopted for the time being an uncertain and somewhat contradictory position. He told the admirals that he wanted a U-boat war but did not want a break with the United States. He suggested warning neutral ships to stay out of the war zone, ignoring the fact that such a scheme had already failed. When the admirals reminded him of past experience, he retreated into a declaration that the whole issue was one for the Kaiser to decide.[9] Everyone who talked with him during January came away with the impression that he remained confused and undecided.

[6] Tirpitz to Falkenhayn, Jan. 2, 1916, *Politische Dokumente,* II, 450–455; memo by Tirpitz, Jan. 5, 1916, *ibid.,* 456–459; Westarp, *Konservative Politik,* II, 115, 117, 124.

[7] Memo by Bethmann, Jan. 4, 1916, *Official German Documents,* II, 1116–1117.

[8] Memo of a conversation between Bethmann and Holtzendorff, Jan. 8, 1916, Spindler, *Handelskrieg,* III, 75.

[9] Memo by Tirpitz, Jan. 5, 1916, *Politische Dokumente,* II, 457–459.

It had become clear to the Chancellor, nevertheless, that Falkenhayn could no longer be counted on for support against the admirals.
The general might even endorse the Tirpitz policy of unrestricted
warfare, as Admiral Holtzendorff had already done, and the Kaiser
might well decide that he should be guided by the united counsel
of his uniformed advisers rather than by the cautious advice of his
civilian Chancellor. During Bethmann's visits to Supreme Headquarters, indeed, the Emperor seemed deliberately to avoid discussion of the U-boat issue,[10] and he directed the Naval Staff to reconsider "how the U-boat war against England could itself be
carried out ruthlessly while at the same time sparing neutrals as
much as possible." [11] There existed a very real threat that Falkenhayn and the admirals would advocate unrestricted U-boat warfare
and that the Kaiser would follow them.

This danger was enhanced by the growing public agitation on
behalf of a renewed submarine campaign. Since the *Arabic* settlement, the censors had been able to restrict comment on this subject.
Events in January made it difficult to enforce this ban. Publicity
was given to the *Baralong* incident of the preceding August. A
British decoy ship flying an American flag and ostentatiously wearing red, white, and blue markings, the *Baralong* had sunk a German
U-boat that was waiting punctiliously for a prize to disembark its
passengers. The German government had naturally protested, and
when Britain responded the correspondence had to be published.
It provided an opportunity for the *Deutsche Tageszeitung* to renew
its fulminations against the "hideous baseness of our enemy" and
to call for ruthless reprisals. News that the House of Commons was
debating intensified economic warfare permitted the *Kreuzzeitung*
and *Hamburger Nachrichten* to join the *Deutsche Tageszeitung*
in calling for retaliation. Then when the United States suddenly
revived the hoary *Lusitania* case, journals representing the conservative wings of the Progressive and Center parties were also able
to chime in. Georg Bernhard declared in the *Vossische Zeitung*

[10] So Falkenhayn said to Kapt. z. See Wilhelm Widenmann on Feb. 12, 1915,
ibid, 477.
[11] Jan. 15, 1916, *Politische Dokumente,* II, 462.

that Germany had to prosecute a submarine campaign despite the risk of conflict with the United States, and the *Kölnische Volkszeitung* asked, "Were we on the right track in making all those concessions to America?" [12]

The press campaign had its counterpart in the Reichstag. When the censorship came up for debate, a Conservative deputy took occasion to declare, "The way in which America has behaved in respect to neutrality has excited a depth of feeling which cannot be believed, but no expression of this feeling is permitted. . . . No one may say anything as to the cessation of submarine warfare." Gustav Stresemann, a National Liberal leader, asserted that if the censorship were abated, the government would then be able to "realize the indignation of the German people against Mr. Wilson's policy." Nor was feeling confined to the right-wing benches, for a debate on the *Baralong* case indicated that a large majority wanted reprisals of some kind. Even Gustav Noske, a Social Democrat, spoke in this sense, and the lone dissent was registered by a left socialist who had recently refused to approve the new war credits.[13]

It was evident, furthermore, that this agitation was both purposeful and ominous. The Chancellor had grown aware of the right wing's hostility to him personally. As early as October, 1914, the Undersecretary of State in the Chancellery, Arnold Wahnschaffe, had warned Bethmann, "I have the impression that in the great industrial circles and among the extreme Conservatives anything will be tried against your Excellency." In the summer of 1915, the censors had intercepted and given him a telegram from Bassermann to another National Liberal leader, in which the Chancellor was referred to contemptuously as "the long one" and directions were given for mobilizing opposition to him among the South German courts. After Bethmann addressed the Reichstag in August, 1915, he commented to Valentini that his speech had been received by the Conservatives and National Liberals "with a somewhat bitter-

---

[12] *Deutsche Tageszeitung,* Jan. 4, Jan. 15, Jan. 16, Jan. 19, 1916; *Daily Extracts from the Foreign Press,* Jan. 28, Feb. 8, 1916.

[13] *Verhandlungen des Reichstages,* CCCVI (Jan. 15, 1916), pp. 669–675, (Jan. 18, 1916), 719–740.

sweet mien. They have corrupted its meaning." [14] The Chancellor
thus had a sense that the right wing might attempt to mobilize
sentiment for a vote of no confidence.

Nor could he ignore the danger that such a move might succeed.
The Conservatives evidently intended to seek a full-scale debate
on the U-boat. They had raised the question in the budget committee in December and again in January.[15] When excitement rose
over the *Baralong* case, the British debates, and the new *Lusitania*
exchanges, the Chancellor was visited by a delegation which included not only Westarp but also Peter Spahn of the *Zentrum* and
Friedrich von Payer of the Progressive party. This delegation urged
him to approve a U-boat campaign "in accordance with the views
of Tirpitz." [16] When the Chancellor asked Erzberger what he
should do to counteract this campaign, the left Centrist advised
him "to go before the Reichstag, present America's ultimatum [on
the *Lusitania*] as an insult to honor, and at the same time proclaim
a U-boat war. The domestic effect will be magnificent." [17]

This surge in parliamentary and public opinion, coinciding with
Falkenhayn's change of heart, raised for the Chancellor a very
grim outlook. Since the Reichstag adjourned on January 18, not to
reconvene until mid-March, there seemed little immediate danger
of a vote of no confidence. But it might not require a vote to convince the Kaiser that Bethmann no longer enjoyed the trust of the
people. Wilhelm knew that his Chancellor had come to rely on
the support of the left-wing parties, the enemies of the throne.
Quite recently, when he received a memorandum from a Prussian
official, describing the Social Democrats as the chief disruptive force

[14] Westarp, *Konservative Politik*, II, 307; Bethmann to Valentini, Aug. 22, 1915,
Bernhard Schwertfeger, *Kaiser und Kabinettschef: Nach eigenen Aufzeichnungen
und den Briefwechsel des Wirklichen Geheimen Rats Rudolf von Valentini* (Oldenburg, 1931), 228.

[15] Westarp, *Konservative Politik*, II, 115; Hans Peter Hanssen, *Diary of a Dying
Empire* (English translation; Bloomington, Ind., 1955), 124–125.

[16] Note of Jan. 14, 1916, Haussmann, *Schlaglichter*, 56–57; Westarp, *Konservative
Politik*, II, 115.

[17] Note of Feb. 1, 1916, *ibid.*, 116.

in the country, he had jotted in its margin, "fully agreed." This comment had forced Bethmann to prepare a long reply, asserting that the Socialists and Progressives were, in fact, the only true patriots.[18] There existed thus a risk that the Emperor might feel the Chancellor was supported by the wrong people, while Falkenhayn, as a result of his recent success against Serbia, appeared to enjoy heightened prestige among all factions in the country. An open rupture between the Chancellor and the Chief of Staff might lead the Kaiser, ever preoccupied with the security of his throne, to conclude that it was safest to let the civilian fall.

In this situation, Bethmann's only alternatives were to risk all in an open battle with the Chief of Staff or to devise some concession, allowing a partial reopening of the U-boat campaign. If the United States had seemed at the time to be as unyielding as ever, he might have had no choice at all. According to Bernstorff, however, the revival of the *Lusitania* issue was due to the convening of Congress; Wilson wished to appease the chauvinists.[19] In view of subsequent press reports on the pacifist uprising in Congress, the Chancellor could well feel that affairs in America were taking a turn for the better. Lansing's *modus vivendi* proposal then made it seem that the United States meant to reverse her policy of separating German and English questions. Although there is no real evidence of the Chancellor's reaction to events in the United States, it would have been pardonable if he assumed Wilson's firmness to be giving way before domestic pressures and believed, in consequence, that the German government was free to advance the frontier of dispute to a fresh line.

The Chancellor felt able, in any case, to approve the sharpened U-boat war. Even before Lansing's *modus vivendi* proposal, the Chief of the U-boat flotilla in the Mediterranean had urged that

---

[18] Loebell to the Kaiser, Nov. 22, 1915, with marginal comments by the Kaiser, *ibid.*, 282 (from the Chancellery archives); Bethmann to the Kaiser, Dec. 9, 1915, *ibid.*, 283.

[19] Bernstorff to Jagow, Dec. 2, Dec. 7, 1915, German Foreign Ministry Archives (General); Bernstorff, *My Three Years in America*, 182–185.

submarines be allowed to attack armed vessels without warning.[20]
The *Baralong* agitation arose at almost the same moment, and
Undersecretary Zimmermann, who appeared before the Reichstag
to answer questions about the case, uttered a vague promise of
retaliation.[21] The Chief of the Naval Staff therefore hastened to
Pless with the flotilla commander's proposal. The Kaiser took it
under advisement and no doubt consulted Bethmann. Since the
Chancellor felt a campaign against armed vessels would be "proper
and politically unexceptionable," the Naval Staff received notice
that operations could probably begin in early March. The Chancellor, the Foreign Ministry, and the Naval Staff then collaborated
in drawing up a circular to neutral governments, and on February
11, the imperial order went out to the fleet:

Enemy merchant vessels, which are armed with cannon, are to be
treated as warships and to be destroyed by any means.

Commanders must bear in mind that mistakes will lead to rupture
with neutral powers and may proceed with the destruction of a merchant vessel because of its armament only if the armament is recognized.

To permit the necessary warning to neutrals through diplomatic
channels, this order does not go into effect until 29 February.[22]

Menaced by the possible combination of Falkenhayn and the
admirals on the one hand and by Reichstag agitation on the other,
the Chancellor thus made a large concession to the submarine
enthusiasts. The order for sharpened U-boat warfare fell short, it
is true, of an unrestricted campaign. Only armed enemy vessels
were to be attacked. Although the term employed in the order was
"merchant vessel" (*Kauffahrteischiff*) and not the more restrictive
"freighter" (*Frachtdampfer*), it was not clear whether it extended
to armed passenger liners. Neutral vessels, in any case, remained
exempt. In view of the risk of accidents and crises, the fact that the
Chancellor allowed any campaign at all is important. Under constant pressure to accommodate the admirals and their supporters

[20] January 15, 1916, Spindler, *Handelskrieg*, III, 85.
[21] *Verhandlungen des Reichstages*, CCCVI (Jan. 15, 1916), p. 674.
[22] Spindler, *Handelskrieg*, III, 86–87.

in the Reichstag, Bethmann restricted U-boat warfare only at the point where he became fearful of action by the United States. One needs but to examine the background of the sharpened U-boat war to see how futile would have been an American policy of appeasement.

Events of the two months succeeding the proclamation of a sharpened campaign indicate, furthermore, how little chance there was that the German government, once started, could stop short of all-out U-boat warfare. The Chancellor's concession did not appease the advocates of an unrestricted campaign. It merely fired them to fresh exertions. The admirals saw their premises accepted while their plans were rejected, and they attributed this result to fear, doubt, and civilian timidity. The Chancellor's enemies in the Reichstag saw an opportunity to place him in a difficult corner. Having approved a limited campaign, he would now have to explain why half measures were possible when all-out war was not. He no longer had a clear-cut case to argue before simple-minded deputies and citizens. Both to admirals and to parliamentarians, the concession of the sharpened campaign seemed, as in fact it was, an evidence of weakness; they lunged for the jugular vein.

Tirpitz led the assault. He endeavored to mobilize every possible pressure. His son-in-law went to Conservative and National Liberal leaders, asking them to make it evident "that the national parties stand united behind him and withdraw their support from the Chancellor." Tirpitz appears to have supplied the industrialist, Hugo Stinnes, with facts and figures for an expert appeal to the Chancellor. He also solicited the support of the Crown Prince and, indirectly, that of the King of Bavaria. Officers from his ministry meanwhile traveled back and forth over the 240 miles to Pless, spreading the U-boat gospel among the people near the Kaiser.[23]

Tirpitz concentrated, of course, on winning the full support of

---

[23] Note of Feb. 7, 1916, Westarp, *Konservative Politik*, II, 118; *Politische Dokumente*, II, 464–466, 469, 477–479, 483; Victor Naumann, *Dokumente und Argumente* (Berlin, 1928), 110–111.

Falkenhayn. He sent the general eloquent memoranda contending not only that the U-boat could conquer England but that the question of using it was a purely military issue: if the Chief of Staff felt that American intervention would not be militarily disastrous, then he should disregard the weakling counsels of the Chancellor. Tirpitz sent envoys to Pless exclusively for the purpose of reasoning with the Chief of Staff, and he may even have encouraged right-wing leaders to write him in support of an unrestricted U-boat campaign.[24]

When Falkenhayn declared himself in sympathy with Tirpitz, the campaign for unrestricted warfare acquired not only an influential recruit but also a powerful new set of arguments. The general was then directing the mighty offensive against Verdun. Its object was not to break the Allied line but simply to bleed the French of men and supplies and to deprive France of the symbol of her successful resistance in 1914. Even with this limited goal, the offensive made headway only with difficulty. Despite the expenditure of two million shells in a preliminary bombardment, the first three days of attack (February 20–23) gained only two miles of ground. After capturing Douaumont Fort, the initial target, the German armies regrouped under unexpectedly heavy enemy bombardment. It would be of obvious advantage in the next stages of the operation if the flow of British troops and supplies across the Channel could be pinched off, and Falkenhayn was in a position to contend that the lives of German soldiers and the very hope of victory in the west depended on prompt utilization of the U-boat.

Behind this military logic, it is true, there lay some more primitive reasoning. Falkenhayn's exchanges with Treutler and Bethmann had indicated how little impression the subtler points of the U-boat debate had made upon him. When the Chancellor approved a sharpening of the campaign but not a lifting of all restrictions, the distinction escaped the general. He commented in exasperation to one of Tirpitz's envoys, "The diplomats lay everything out to their own taste and then doubt. That is the great difference between

---

[24] *Politische Dokumente*, II, 472–477; Westarp, *Konservative Politik*, II, 118, 124.

a soldier and a diplomat. The soldier is accustomed to acting, while the diplomat cannot bring himself to act, even when the matter has already been decided." [25] Want of subtlety thus played a part in Falkenhayn's advocacy of unrestricted U-boat warfare, but that fact in no way diminished his potential influence over the Kaiser.

After Tirpitz had won Falkenhayn's open support, he ventured to approach the Kaiser. Aware that he had spent most of his credit with the Emperor and that Wilhelm was surrounded by his enemies, he did not press for a decision. Appealing suavely to old comradeship, he sought to appear as a wise and moderate counselor, merely setting before the Kaiser the fact that the navy was virtually united in favor of unrestricted warfare. In his own record of the audience, he notes saying, "I could very well understand that it was difficult for His Majesty to come to a decision, but a decision by him could not be avoided." [26] Tirpitz hoped to bring about a new imperial council where Falkenhayn would speak in behalf of the admirals and Bethmann would stand in solitary opposition to all the Emperor's military advisers.

Holtzendorff was meanwhile seeking the same goal in complete independence of both Tirpitz and Falkenhayn. Despite his initial doubts, he had already made it plain that he favored lifting all limitations on the submarines. "*Only the ruthless conduct* of the U-boat war against English commerce for a period of 6–8 months," he had written Bethmann, "*promises to hold out a prospect of success.*" He notified the Chancellor that he intended to ask the Kaiser's approval of such a campaign, and he appeared at Pless for an audience with the Emperor. Since the Chancellor did not come, this audience was rather a preliminary conference than a decisive council, but Holtzendorff had made it clear that he, too, wished to force a decision by the Crown.[27]

His efforts and those of Tirpitz were abetted independently from outside the narrow circle of the Emperor's ministers and chiefs of

[25] *Politische Dokumente*, II, 474.
[26] Memo of Feb. 23, 1916, *ibid.*, 481–482.
[27] Holtzendorff to Bethmann, Jan. 21, 1916, *ibid.*, 466–468; Spindler, *Handelskrieg*, III, 92–93.

staff. Agitation in the press and also in the Prussian Landtag reached a new pitch of intensity, and right-wing leaders sought to communicate directly with the Kaiser.[28] Officers from the various naval commands seconded the proposals of the Navy Minister and the Chief of the Naval Staff. Reinhold Scheer, the new commander of the High Seas Fleet, for example, gave notice of his complete concurrence with Holtzendorff.[29] But in the contest for control of the Kaiser's will the principal antagonists were, on one side, Tirpitz, Falkenhayn, and Holtzendorff, and on the other, Bethmann and his allies.

The Chancellor stood in a fearful predicament. No less than in January, when forced to approve the sharpened campaign, he was in danger of losing command over the Emperor. The military advisers to the crown stood united, and segments of public opinion appeared to be feverishly anxious for a decision in their favor. It was the impression of the Naval Staff chief, after his meeting with the Kaiser in mid-February, that the imperial decision would almost certainly favor the navy. Holtzendorff was so confident, indeed, that he told Scheer it remained only to set the date for an unrestricted campaign.[30]

Just as Bethmann had earlier been forced to consider modest concessions, he was now compelled to contemplate giving way altogether. He conferred with Tirpitz three times during a week's interval. After Holtzendorff had talked with the Kaiser, Bethmann asked for comments from the Treasury and the Interior Ministry on the feasibility of an unrestricted submarine campaign. He then summoned Holtzendorff to a conference at the Chancellery. Jagow, who remained firmly opposed to any extension of the sharpened campaign, and Zimmermann, who had come to sympathize with the U-boat enthusiasts, were both present. The Chancellor said anxiously that it was necessary "to settle finally the question of the U-boat war, if it is at all possible." [31] It was undoubtedly the

[28] Westarp, *Konservative Politik*, II, 118.
[29] *Politische Dokumente*, II, 483.
[30] *Ibid.*
[31] Spindler, *Handelskrieg*, III, 90–93.

anxiety and uncertainty of Bethmann that made Holtzendorff so sure of an ultimate decision in his favor.

But the circumstances that had permitted Bethmann to accept the sharpened campaign no longer held. On February 16 Lansing had abandoned his *modus vivendi* proposal, stating that the United States still held Germany accountable, even for American citizens traveling on armed ships. Bernstorff warned that the United States was entirely in earnest, and press dispatches from America, though telling of revived pacifist agitation, stressed the evidence of chauvinism in public opinion.[32] These reports indicated that even the sharpened campaign might lead to a rupture. If Bethmann failed to resist the demands of Falkenhayn and the admirals, the unrestricted campaign would almost certainly result in war.

The Chancellor chose to fight the proposal. Ominous reports had come in from Copenhagen and The Hague. The Austrian government had evidenced its fear of any further complications with America. Lansing's repudiation of the *modus vivendi* proposal undoubtedly helped to force Bethmann's decision.[33] It also threatened to handicap him in the forthcoming struggle, for he found it necessary to modify the sharpened campaign even before it began. He summoned Holtzendorff to the Chancellery and induced him to issue a supplementary order, advising U-boat commanders that passenger liners were not to be sunk without warning, even if they were armed.[34] Although the admiral readily consented, no doubt expecting that the Kaiser would shortly issue a directive ending all restrictions, Bethmann had risked having to battle over a minor change instead of over the major issue. But Holtzendorff was too confident and too straightforward to seize this opportunity; Falkenhayn lacked the bureaucratic gift, and Bethmann was to see to it that Tirpitz had no chance to take advantage of the opening.

[32] Bernstorff to Jagow, Feb. 17, 1916, German Foreign Ministry Archives (General); Wolff Bureau report, Feb. 15, 1916, German Foreign Ministry Archives (U-boat War).

[33] Kühlmann to Bethmann, Feb. 8, Feb. 16, Feb. 22, 1916, *ibid.;* Lucius to Jagow, Feb. 28, 1916, *ibid.;* Treutler to Bethmann, Feb. 23, 1916, *ibid.;* memo by Kriege, Feb. 25, 1916, *ibid.*

[34] Spindler, *Handelskrieg,* III, 88; *Politische Dokumente,* II, 485–487, 511.

The contest was to be fought on the broad issue of unrestricted as opposed to sharpened warfare. Holtzendorff and Falkenhayn desired that it should be so, and Bethmann made arrangements for an open encounter before the Emperor. He scheduled no fewer than three days of conferences. On the first day, March 2, he was to present a memorial detailing his own views. On the second day, he was to hold preliminary conferences with his antagonists. On the final day there was to be a formal debate before the throne. Tirpitz was not to be present. The Kaiser did not insist on his presence, and Bethmann and Müller deliberately excluded him. The Chancellor thus disposed at the outset of his most adroit and experienced antagonist, and by allowing three full days of exchanges he provided ample time to employ his persuasive arts upon the Kaiser.

The decision could not be won entirely by maneuver; it had to be taken by argument as well. The Chancellor had to convince the Kaiser of three things: first, that the U-boat was a less decisive weapon than the admirals contended; second, that the *military* damage resulting from an unrestricted campaign would outweigh its *military* benefits; and third, that public opinion would stand by the Kaiser even if he overruled his uniformed advisers. He thus had to contradict the professional estimates of the Naval Staff and the Chief of the General Staff. He also had to neutralize the intensive campaign being conducted against him in the Conservative and National Liberal press and in Center and Progressive journals as well. These were formidable tasks.

In his long memorial to the Kaiser and in the oral argument that he based upon it, Bethmann sought first to prove that unrestricted U-boat warfare would not achieve decisive results over England. Although he had been denied technical information by the Naval Staff, he did have in hand the estimates presented to the Kaiser by both Tirpitz and Holtzendorff.[35] These were markedly vague about the number of U-boats available for an unrestricted

[35] Holtzendorff to Bethmann, Feb. 24, 1916, Spindler, *Handelskrieg,* III, 93–94; Holtzendorff to Bethmann, Jan. 7, 1916, *Official German Documents,* II, 1117–1121; Tirpitz to Bethmann, Feb. 13, 1916, *ibid.,* 1122–1128.

campaign. Tirpitz hinted that approximately one hundred were ready. One of his representatives, appearing before the Bundesrat, gave the figure as fifty-four but asserted that, since an additional 149 were in construction or undergoing sea trials, the true figure was 203.[36] The actual number ready to operate on March 1 appears to have been forty-seven, of which sixteen were older, short-range, lightly armed UA, UB, and UC types.[37] The admirals' unwillingness to state flotilla strengths was understandable, in view of this unimpressive total, but it also rose, no doubt, from the fact that construction time for a U-boat ran to a year or more. Contracts let after the war zone decree of February, 1915, were just beginning to be filled, and the number of first-class boats was to triple before the autumn. The admirals could have advertised this fact, but only at the risk of discouraging Falkenhayn, who wanted help during April and May. Since they chose to hide the figures, Bethmann was able to advise the Kaiser, "In view of the limited number of our U-boats and of their inability to be efficient at night, an absolute cutting off of England is out of the question." [38]

He still had to refute the admirals' contention that unrestricted warfare would cause a critical drop in British tonnage. Their case rested upon an estimate that Britain had eleven to twelve million tons of merchant shipping, that the submarines could destroy between 300,000 and 630,000 tons a month, and that a few months' operations would confront England with the alternatives of surrender or starvation. Bethmann suggested in answer that Britain probably had more tonnage than she admitted. The admirals' estimates, moreover, took no account of construction since the beginning of the war, nor did they reckon with the tonnage that would become Britain's when the U-boat campaign drove the neutrals into the Allied camp. "The calculations of the loss in English cargo space," the Chancellor declared to the Kaiser, ". . . are based on

---

[36] *Politische Dokumente*, II, 635.

[37] I base this estimate on the construction and disposition tables in Spindler's volumes.

[38] Memorial by Bethmann, Feb. 29, 1916, *Official German Documents*, II, 1130–1139.

unstable foundations. And still more uncertain is the estimate of the effect which this shrinkage will have upon England's determination and capacity to fight." Before she would acknowledge her loss of supremacy at sea, he asserted, "she would sacrifice the last man and the last penny."

Meeting the military arguments for unrestricted warfare, Bethmann did not endeavor, as with the naval, to criticize the professional judgments of the army. Instead he undertook to oppose a broad view of Germany's situation to Falkenhayn's narrow view of the relation between the U-boat campaign and the Verdun offensive. The Chancellor restated the military dangers involved in war with the United States: the increase in money and supplies for the enemy, the addition of "a few hundred thousands of volunteers," the drying up of all German imports, and the probability that America would carry Rumania, Holland, and Denmark with her. He also stressed for the Emperor the likely effects on Germany's allies. The Austrian government had strongly advised conciliating the United States, and if this advice were rejected, the Chancellor cautioned:

At the very least, Austria's war spirit will not be heightened. . . . The Turkish Minister, too, has already expressed his earnest solicitude about the possible results of a break with the United States.

These objections apply naturally to Bulgaria as well.

Even the moral effects of the break with the United States upon our allies . . . must not be underestimated. The longer the war lasts, so much clearer does it become that he will win the war who keeps his nerves under best control. History teaches us that in coalition wars which can not be brought to a termination by decisive strokes of the military arm, the end is usually brought about by differences between the allies themselves. It is a dangerous gamble to disregard these differences if one is not assured of success.

In countering the naval and military arguments for unrestricted warfare, Bethmann could only oppose his own opinions to the expert judgments of the Naval and General Staffs. In seeking to neutralize the effect of public opinion upon the Emperor, he had more leverage, for he, Jagow, and Valentini had some control over what the Kaiser read and heard. In early February, the Prussian Conservatives had shown the audacity to propose that the Landtag pass a resolution criticizing the Chancellor. Bethmann and Valentini immediately convinced the Kaiser that this proposal was, in effect, an attack on the throne by the pretended supporters of monarchism. The Conservatives, they contended, were seeking to make the Supreme Warlord accountable to a legislative body, and Wilhelm authorized the publication of a blistering reproof.[39] During the month of February, Bethmann's friends saw to it that the Kaiser read editorials in the *Deutsche Tageszeitung* and the *Kölnische Volkszeitung* demanding unrestricted U-boat warfare and implicitly criticizing the Kaiser's past timidity. They told him that Tirpitz was responsible for these articles, as indeed he partly was.[40] Long before the imperial council convened, the Emperor had been stirred to resentment at the press campaign and led to believe that it was largely artificial. Bethmann could comment in his long memorial that

the morale of Germany is not to be judged merely by the articles of the Pan-German press. The overwhelming preponderance of our enemies has prevented us up to the present time from bringing the war to a triumphant termination. People will ask whether the increase of the number of our enemies could not have been avoided, and the entrance of the United States into the war will have a discouraging and depressing effect in broad circles of the German people.

Having met the principal points of argument by means of this comprehensive memorial, Bethmann was ready for the face-to-face sessions with Falkenhayn and Holtzendorff. The opponents gathered at Charleville on the western front, to which the Kaiser had lately moved his headquarters. The scheduled discussions took place. No new points were raised; the same ground was traversed over and over; the differences between the two factions remained precisely the same. Breakfasts and other hours during the day meanwhile gave Bethmann opportunities to work upon the Kaiser's malleable

[39] Westarp, *Konservative Politik*, II, 119–121; *Norddeutsche Allgemeine Zeitung*, Feb. 13, 1916; see Chapter XII below.
[40] *Politische Dokumente*, II, 488, 491, 498–499.

mind. He led him to agree "that we had far too few U-boats to overcome Great Britain and that he would not permit the 'folly' of
provoking America into a war." [41] Falkenhayn and Holtzendorff
were also talking privately with him, and the final result was by no
means assured. When Bethmann wrote Jagow after the council had
ended, he confessed to being so nervous that he could not hold a
pen steadily.

The decisive moment arrived on the afternoon of March 4, when
Bethmann, Falkenhayn, Holtzendorff, Müller, the Chief of the Military Cabinet, and the Headquarters Commandant gathered in a
crown council.[42] Both Holtzendorff and Falkenhayn presented their
arguments in the strongest possible form. The admiral went so far
as to declare "with great positiveness that in the course of from six
to eight months, England would be forced to sue for peace . . . ; that
as a matter of fact he had overstated the period in question, and that,
according to his personal conviction, all would be up with England
before that time." Falkenhayn, having conferred with the Emperor
in the morning, spoke more tersely but no less emphatically. The
Kaiser, when opening the council, had given strong indication that
he sympathized with the general. Bethmann did not, therefore, seek
to have him reject the unrestricted warfare proposal. As the Chancellor confessed to Jagow, his object was merely "to prevent the situation from reaching a critical stage." As before, he only sought to
prevent the Kaiser from deciding against him. Even to that end, he
found it necessary to play his highest trump—to assert gravely that
if it were decided to risk war with the United States, he would not
be willing to assume the responsibility, that he would, in other words,
resign and allow an internal crisis to follow.

Even though Bethmann made the decision explicitly a question of
the Kaiser's confidence in him, Wilhelm's ruling was ambiguous.
As Holtzendorff noted it:

As Chief of State he has to view a break with America and the siding
of other neutrals with our enemies as very serious. The throne and the

---

[41] Bethmann to Jagow, March 5, 1916, *Official German Documents*, II, 1139–1142.
[42] The two reports of this conference are Bethmann's letter cited above, n. 41,
and Holtzendorff's notes of March 4, 1916, *Politische Dokumente*, II, 503–504.

Empire are, in fact, at stake. On the other hand, the parallel concerns of the Chief Warlord require a military decision in our favor within the space of time allowed by our power of resistance and that of our allies, insofar as these can be reckoned.

Agreement prevails in the judgment that an end of the war by the winter of this year must be sought by all means. Effective prosecution of the U-boat war requires 6–8 months. Therefore on military grounds the conduct *from 1 April on* of an unrestricted U-boat war against England, which alone promises full success, is indispensable. Until then the Chancellor will set in motion all political and diplomatic processes to provide America with a full understanding of our situation, with the object and goal of giving us a free hand. Until then the U-boat war will be carried on as effectively as possible under the orders issued on 1 March.

Bethmann merely recorded that "His Majesty deferred reaching a definite decision." So imprecise was the Kaiser's declaration that Holtzendorff took it to mean a victory for the navy. He notified both the Naval Staff and Admiral Scheer that an unrestricted U-boat campaign would open in April. Bethmann had to tell the admiral tactfully that he was in error; the situation remained unchanged; the sharpened campaign alone would be carried on; in April the Kaiser might be consulted again.[43]

The actual result of the council, of course, was once again to affirm Bethmann's power. Since the Kaiser had not decisively ruled against him, he had, in effect, endorsed whatever Bethmann should do. The pathetic figure on the German throne had given his seasonal performance as a ruler. Until events called him to the stage again, the scepter remained in the hands of the Chancellor.

The proof of Bethmann's triumph came immediately after the crown council. He had taken care to impress upon the Emperor the perfidy of Tirpitz's dealings with the press. As soon as he was safe against an immediate assault on the U-boat issue, he began working to force Tirpitz out of office. At his suggestion, the Kaiser transferred

---

[43] Holtzendorff to Scheer, March 5, 1916, *ibid.,* 504–505; Bethmann to Müller, March 9, 1916, *ibid.,* 505; Bethmann to Treutler, March 31, 1916, German Foreign Ministry Archives (U-boat War).

the press bureau of the Navy Ministry to the Naval Staff. If this action did not lead Tirpitz to resign, Bethmann was ready to create another issue.[44] But the Grand Admiral promptly asked to retire for reasons of health; the Kaiser immediately accepted; Bethmann wrote a farewell letter of two sentences, commenting on Tirpitz's "imperishable services in the construction of the German fleet." [45] The Chancellor had rid the Emperor's councils of an able, powerful, and implacable enemy.

The March crisis had proved that concessions to the U-boat enthusiasts were dangerous. The *Sussex* crisis of April was to demonstrate that concessions were impractical as well. U-boat commanders could not be counted on to observe restrictions. When permitted to operate at all, they committed "accidents" against neutral vessels and lives. Even a restricted war, therefore, endangered the peace between Germany and the United States.

At Charleville Bethmann had stressed his own willingness to carry on the U-boat war as fiercely as the United States would permit. In his memorial he had made a vigorous defense of the sharpened campaign, pointing out that it allowed the sinking of unarmed enemy freighters in the war zone and of armed freighters anywhere. If a campaign thus limited should lead to a break with America, he declared, "it will be a working out of a destiny from which we cannot escape. For we cannot avoid treating as ships of war enemy merchant ships which are provided with orders to attack, and with arms as well, because of the caprice of President Wilson. To give in on this point would not be consonant with our dignity, and would amount to a practical renunciation of the U-boat weapon." In his contemporaneous battle against submarine enthusiasts outside the government, he made similar professions publicly. At a press conference on March 13, for example, he described the sharpened campaign as successful and as promising even greater rewards in the future, and he declared that the government had no intention of abandoning it.[46]

[44] Bethmann to Jagow, March 5, 1916, *Official German Documents*, II, 1142.
[45] *Politische Dokumente*, II, 508–509, 511.
[46] *Official German Documents*, II, 1146–1150.

During March and April, however, the U-boat commanders proved themselves incapable, or unwilling, to observe limitations. The Naval Staff, it is true, encouraged them to recklessness. The orders issued on March 13 were based on a lawyer-like reading of the Chancellor's memorial:

1. *Enemy merchant ships which are found in the war zone are to be destroyed without precaution.*

2. Enemy merchant ships which are found outside the war zone will only be destroyed without precaution if they are *armed*.

3. Enemy *passenger vessels* may not be attacked from under water either in the war zone or outside of it, no matter whether they are armed or not.

4. The order of 11–21–15 to the fleet concerning action against [troop] ships which travel to French ports between Le Havre and Dunkirk remains in effect.[47]

But U-boat commanders were to stretch the Chancellor's concessions still further. When at sea they did not often come upon unguarded steamers. The most active boat in the High Seas Fleet saw only fourteen vessels in twenty-five days at sea.[48] When a captain sighted one, he would scrutinize it through an unsteady and spray-drenched periscope. Since even the newest submarines made less than ten knots surfaced and less than six knots submerged, the opportunity to sink or capture would pass quickly if it came at all. Often the captain had to make a decision before descrying any markings or obtaining any clear idea of the ship's size or character. His natural inclination was to take a chance on exceeding his orders. Especially was this true since he knew beyond doubt that his superiors were contemptuous of the restrictions and willing to overlook his mistakes, if not indeed to commend them.

It should not have been surprising, therefore, when the sharpened campaign brought frequent attacks on neutral ships and on passenger liners. On March 16, the Dutch steamer *Tubantia* went down only thirty miles off the Dutch coast. On the same day, the U-70 torpedoed the *Berwindvale,* a British horse ship westbound from

[47] Spindler, *Handelskrieg,* III, 103.
[48] The U-70, *ibid.,* 107–108.

Ireland, carrying Americans. On the 24th the UB-29 mistook the Channel steamer *Sussex* for a troopship, and the U-43 torpedoed the *Englishman,* also with Americans on board. On March 27 the U-44 took the *Manchester Engineer;* on the 28th the U-70 sank the *Eagle Point,* which it assumed to be armed; Americans were on board these vessels too. Spanish, Norwegian, and other Dutch vessels also went under as mistakes of overzealous submariners.

The result, of course, was tension in the neutral capitals. Despite German assertions that no U-boat had been near the site of the *Tubantia*'s sinking, the Dutch press assumed otherwise; talk of war was rife, and the Dutch parliament convened in secret session to discuss military precautions. From the United States Bernstorff telegraphed, "Situation is looked upon in the White House as beyond hope . . ."; a second *Sussex* incident "would necessarily force the United States into war." Wolff dispatches bore him out. On the evening of April 20 arrived Wilson's long-delayed ultimatum, threatening to sever relations if Germany did not abandon her present methods of conducting submarine warfare.[49]

The Chancellor saw no alternative but to abandon the sharpened campaign altogether. The only questions were, first, how much of a battle the submarine enthusiasts would put up, and second, how much of a public surrender the United States would demand. As soon as the American note came in, he hastened back to Berlin from Charleville. Inviting Gerard to the Chancellery, he asked for a few days' grace, but he made it plain that he wanted to avoid a rupture.[50] Over Easter weekend, April 23–24, he conferred with Holtzendorff, Admiral Eduard von Capelle, the new Navy Minister, and Helfferich, who had recently made a study of the cryptic question of U-boat numbers.[51]

[49] Bernstorff to Jagow, April 11, 1916, *Official German Documents,* II, 971; *Berliner Tageblatt,* April 14, April 15, April 17, 1916; Lansing to Gerard, April 18, 1916, *Foreign Relations, Supplement: 1916,* pp. 232–237; Joseph C. Grew, *Turbulent Era* (2 vols.; New York, 1952), I, 221–222.

[50] Gerard to Lansing, April 24, 1916, *Foreign Relations, Supplement: 1916,* p. 242; Grew, *Turbulent Era,* I, 222.

[51] Helfferich, *Weltkrieg,* II, 341–342. There is an account in Spindler, *Handelskrieg,* III, 143–145, which coincides closely with Helfferich's but which may be based on independent sources.

Neither Holtzendorff nor Capelle made a stiff fight. Both believed in unrestricted warfare; neither had much hope for the sharpened campaign. Helfferich remembers Capelle's saying that the U-boats could accomplish almost as much under the rules of cruiser warfare. The sharpened campaign had, in fact, netted only 155,186 tons during March, and this figure represented an increase of only 60,000 tons over February, when U-boats were strictly following cruiser rules. More than half of the increase, moreover, consisted of neutral tonnage.[52] Capelle could well feel that the whole campaign might be abandoned until new construction had swelled the capabilities of the fleet. Holtzendorff, confronted with unanimity among Chancellor, Treasury Minister, and Navy Minister, yielded gracefully. On April 24 he ordered U-boats henceforward to obey cruiser rules, and Scheer, in pique, withdrew all U-boats from the war zone.[53] The admirals had consented once more, in effect, to suspend the campaign altogether.

There remained for Bethmann the problem of satisfying the United States. He invited Gerard to accompany him to Supreme Headquarters, and he gave the ambassador and his staff almost royal treatment. But he could induce Gerard to accept nothing less than a complete and public surrender of the U-boat campaign. Neither blandishment nor threat availed. As the ambassador's sophisticated assistant noted, "Mr. Gerard was the right man in the right place at this important juncture. He does not mince his words, he speaks with force and directness—which is sometimes the only method of talk that carries weight here—and once he sees an issue clearly he rams it home straight from the shoulder." [54] The ambassador left no doubt as to what the Chancellor had to do.

At Supreme Headquarters Bethmann did run into momentary trouble with Falkenhayn. The general had obviously mistaken, along with Holtzendorff, the result of the imperial council of March 4. Believing an unrestricted U-boat campaign to be in the offing,

---

[52] Tonnage figures and U-boat logs in Spindler, *Handelskrieg,* vol. III.

[53] *Ibid.,* 140–141.

[54] Grew, *Turbulent Era,* I, 240; the visit to Charleville is also described in Gerard, *My Four Years in Germany,* 324–345.

he was thunderstruck when told that, on the contrary, the Chancellor meant to halt submarine operations altogether. He went immediately to the Kaiser, declaring that he would have to forego operations at Verdun if the Chancellor's action were to ensure the French of British supplies. His argument made some impression, for the Kaiser said solemnly to Bethmann, "You have thus the choice between Verdun and America." Sufficiently alarmed so that he telephoned Helfferich, asking him to come to Charleville for moral support, the Chancellor seemed to his American guests "very weary and worn." [55] But Falkenhayn no longer had the power to threaten Bethmann. His prestige had dwindled with each day, as his troops battered hopelessly at *mort homme* and Vaux, gaining no ground, while casualty figures mounted toward 100,000. Even when he threatened to resign, the Kaiser did nothing more than ask him to reconsider, and there was no new domestic crisis.[56]

The Chancellor therefore yielded all of the American demands. He replied to Wilson's ultimatum with the so-called *Sussex* pledge, asserting that U-boats would not sink vessels, either in the war zone or outside of it, without warning and without saving lives. Bethmann thus closed his experiment in concession. The experience had indicated that he would have to prevent any U-boat campaign or else accept war with the United States. Not only did Wilson's firmness preclude any half-measures, but the attitudes of enthusiasts within the government and the behavior of submarine commanders themselves made it impractical for Bethmann to consider any alternatives except all-out war or none.

[55] Helfferich, *Weltkrieg*, II, 343–344; Grew, *Turbulent Era*, I, 230.
[56] Memo by Falkenhayn, Aug. 31, 1916, *Politische Dokumente*, II, 537–538; Falkenhayn to Bethmann, May 4, 1916, *Official German Documents*, II, 1151–1152.

XII

The Chancellor and the Reichstag

The Chancellor's concession of a sharpened U-boat war led not only to crisis within the government but to fierce agitation outside. Even while Bethmann readied himself for the contest at Charleville, he had to fight off a right-wing attack in the Prussian Landtag. No sooner had he returned to Berlin than he met assaults first in the Bundesrat and then in the Reichstag. Although he won all of these engagements, he emerged weakened by them, for he made himself answerable both to the foreign affairs committee of the Bundesrat and to the budget committee of the Reichstag.

The zeal of the U-boat enthusiasts was unconquerable. Bethmann demonstrated in March that he could withstand attack from any flank. He showed that a Reichstag majority could be assembled to support him, even though it might be an artificial majority. In argument, moreover, he smothered his opponents under a weight of hard and unanswerable fact. Yet the agitation did not die. When the Reichstag reassembled in the autumn, Bethmann had to argue the issue all over again, and he did not content his opponents, even though he could call to his own support the immense prestige of the new Supreme Command, Hindenburg and Ludendorff. Among the parties of the right and within broad segments of the German public, the U-boat fever was an incurable disease.

Although the U-boat question was central in German politics during 1916, it was by no means the only issue to divide the right wing from the government. The war aims dispute raged as hotly ✓

as ever. The need for new revenues raised the difficult question of who was to be taxed and how. Rising food costs meanwhile led to contention over price controls. On all these issues the government had to make decisions displeasing to some groups and factions. Neither the right wing's open advocacy of unrestricted U-boat warfare nor the Chancellor's successful resistance can be understood without some reference to these other disputes and to the relations that had developed as a result between the government and the various parties in the Reichstag.

Since the beginning of the war a working alliance had grown up between the Chancellor and the socialists. Before 1914 the Social Democrats had been more or less united in seeking social and constitutional change. An internal split between reformist and revolutionary wings had appeared in theoretical writings and intraparty debates but had been concealed in practice. The doctrine of class solidarity had united the party in apparent hostility to the existing order. In prewar politics this unity had necessarily made it an aim of all Chancellors to maintain an anti-socialist bloc. Bethmann comments in his memoirs that before the war the bourgeois parties "regarded unremitting and remorseless combat against Social Democracy as the principal evidence of zeal on the part of a statesman." [1]

The astonishing wartime alliance between these seemingly natural enemies was partly the result of developments within the Social Democratic party itself. In the emotion of August, 1914, the united party voted for war credits. Although the reformist or moderate wing held control of the party machinery, tactical failures since the election of 1912 had been consistently strengthening those who advocated a revolutionist strategy. The war once again tipped the balance toward the moderates. Many in the rank and file were ready to uphold the Fatherland, even if it meant postponing the socialist millennium. War demand and labor scarcity meanwhile spelled higher wages for labor, and the government's desire for national unity meant new recognition and respectability for the

[1] Bethmann, *Betrachtungen*, I, 34.

party's leaders. It also meant, perhaps incidentally, that the cooperative moderates and trade union leaders could lock their hands once again on the controls. Patriotism and self-interest combined thus to engender in the moderate leaders a willingness to cooperate with the government.[2]

Most difficult and most important among the manifestations of this policy was the refusal to embarrass the Chancellor on the issue of war aims. The party as a whole had a deep-rooted pacifist and anti-imperialist tradition. The moderates had felt compelled to dilute even the first resolution in favor of war credits with a closing appeal for a peace of understanding. The revolutionists naturally wanted the party to go further, to agitate against annexationism as a means of stirring discontent, and to harry the Chancellor for the purpose of weakening public confidence in the existing order. These demands of the revolutionists touched enough sympathy within the party to compel the moderates to hedge. In the autumn of 1915 the party leadership found it necessary to agree that the Chancellor should be questioned publicly about war aims. They refused, however, to ask specific questions about Belgium, Alsace Lorraine, Poland, and the like. In a close vote that foreshadowed the coming secession of some radicals, they prevailed.[3] Scheidemann then blunted the decision still more by having himself designated as party spokesman, going to the Chancellery with an advance text of his speech, and reaching a full agreement with Bethmann on what he was to say and what the Chancellor was to reply.[4]

This cooperation, especially on the war aims issue, was of the utmost importance to the Chancellor. He had been fearful at first

[2] The extensive and contentious literature on the Social Democratic factions is described in Schorske, *German Social Democracy,* 340–346. Schorske's volume is itself, of course, the best treatment of these divisions and their results. See also A. Joseph Berlau, *The German Social Democratic Party, 1914–1921* (Columbia University Studies in History, Economics, and Public Law, No. 557: New York, 1949).

[3] The vote was 58–43, *Vorwärts,* Dec. 1, 1915; see Eugen Präger, *Geschichte der U.S.P.D.: Entstehung und Entwicklung der Unabhängigen Sozialdemokratischen Partei Deutschlands* (Berlin, 1921), 83–85; Gatzke, *Germany's Drive to the West,* 106–109.

[4] Scheidemann, *Der Zusammenbruch,* 30–32; Gatzke, *Germany's Drive to the West,* 70–71.

lest the pacifism and internationalism of the party lead it to resist the war. As he wrote in his memoirs:

> The war and its prosecution could not be put in danger directly except by the lower classes. . . . Class hatred had been too systematically and thoroughly inculcated in the masses for there not to be a fear that in the stress of a long war . . . utopian ideas of international solidarity might grow to oppose the accomplishment of national duty and that, at the same time, a reactionary policy might reawaken old rancors . . . and revive suspicion and animosity toward the State and the governing classes.[5]

Holding such views, Bethmann had, as we have seen, made gestures of appeasement to the socialists during the early days of the war.

The cooperation of the majority Social Democrats surprised and delighted him. In December, 1915, at the time when his staged debate with Scheidemann took place, he addressed to the Emperor a review of party politics. It was an astonishing document to come from the pen of an East Elbian monarchist:

> On the whole the Social Democrats today are serving the Fatherland and cooperating energetically in their fashion. I see this not as a passing war mood but as a situation toward which the best heads in the Social Democracy had quietly aspired before the war. . . . At the beginning of the war it seemed as if violent external events might lead to a new party structure or even to a transformation in party politics. This hope has been fulfilled only by the Social Democrats and Progressives. They have, each in a different way but with the same or much the same result, thrown overboard the largest part of their negative doctrinaire ballast. . . . The *Zentrum,* its nature leading it toward an amphibious existence, has remained what it was. The National Liberals and Conservatives have not thus far seen how to rejuvenate themselves. . . . Mindless and with hearts pumped by the subsidies of labor-hating heavy industry, they go the opposite way and seek their salvation in the same dull demagogic nationalism that adorned their nakedness before the war.[6]

[5] Bethmann, *Betrachtungen,* II, 33–34.
[6] Bethman to the Kaiser, Dec. 9, 1915, Westarp, *Konservative Politik,* II, 283 (from the Chancellery archives).

The attitude of the Social Democrats enabled Bethmann to pursue his "diagonal policy" and attempt to maintain the *Burgfrieden*. The war aims issue was the greatest threat before 1916. Not only the Conservatives and National Liberals but the Center and Progressive parties as well had shown Pan-German leanings, while Social Democrats, minorities in other parties (even including the National Liberals), and many prominent independents had come out just as strongly on the opposite side. Had the Social Democrats been intransigent, the Chancellor would have had no alternative but to face dissolution of the party truce and to carry on the war with the support of either an annexationist or an anti-annexationist coalition. With Scheidemann's cooperation, he was able to remain mysterious ✓ and noncommittal, declaring to the Reichstag:

Gentlemen, it ought not to be said that we are willing to prolong the war a single day without necessity because we wish to conquer this token or that. . . . I cannot say . . . what guarantees the Imperial Government will demand in the Belgian question, or what conditions of power [*Machtgrundlagen*] it deems necessary for this guarantee. But one thing our enemies must say to themselves: the longer they carry on the war against us, and the more embittered they make it, the greater become the guarantees which are necessary for us. . . . Neither in the east nor in the west ought our enemies to have control, from this day forward, of gates for fresh attack.[7]

Scheidemann thus allowed the Chancellor to use words which the annexationist *Kölnische Volkszeitung* could interpret as ensuring the retention of Belgium and Poland and which the anti-annexationists could describe as a plea for the *status quo ante*.[8]

In order to keep the good will of the majority socialists, of course, Bethmann had to veer sometimes from his diagonal line. To retain control of their party, the moderates needed tangible evidence that cooperation was not altogether one-sided. Bethmann felt obliged to promise publicly that after the war the restrictive three-class voting

[7] Thimme, *Bethmann Hollwegs Kriegsreden*, 65–88.
[8] *Daily Extracts from the Foreign Press*, Dec. 22, 1915; *Berliner Tageblatt*, Dec. 10, 1915.

system of Prussia would be reformed.[9] Fixing prices for food, he provided relief for working-class commoners at the expense of the agrarian aristocracy. To pay the mounting costs of the war he asked for direct taxes on large incomes and profits as well as for indirect levies. Although the Chancellor sought to please as many parties as possible, his policies ran increasingly along the left of the middle way.

The result was that while he kept the support of the socialists he lost that of the far right. The National Liberals, as representatives of heavy industry, were antagonized by his profits tax proposals as well as by his U-boat policy and his reticence on annexations. They began quite early to stimulate personal opposition to the Chancellor. Some of the agrarians joined in at once. One of the Anti-Semitic party leaders encouraged Hans, Count von Liebig, to publish a diatribe against the "B-System," which was circulated clandestinely but widely in August, 1915. The Conservative and Free Conservative leadership was more hesitant. As Westarp explains, "For the Conservative party there emerged the sharpest conflict of duties . . . when its convictions on policies that were opposed by the Chancellor and Minister President compelled it to struggle against its Kaiser and King." [10] But price controls injured their basic interests, and the proposed reform of the Prussian suffrage menaced their control of the Landtag, the true source of their power. By the end of 1915, Bethmann's concessions to the left had antagonized even the staunchest monarchists, and almost the entire right wing was united in desiring his overthrow and replacement.

[9] The speech from the throne was actually not an impressive declaration. Bethmann said only "a spirit of mutual understanding and confidence will . . . pervade the manifestations of our public policy and find heartening expression in our Constitution." Westarp, *Konservative Politik*, II, 257. Much stronger was the amplifying statement by the Prussian Minister of the Interior, a known foe of suffrage reform, who explained that the government contemplated large changes after the war, adding, "Among them, I say quite plainly, is an alteration of the legal qualifications for voting for the House of Delegates." *Berliner Tageblatt*, Jan. 26, 1916. It was in response to this that Heydebrand made his Wellingtonian declaration: "The constitution of the Prussian House of Delegates may be described as ideally suited to the needs of the country." *Ibid*.

[10] Westarp, *Konservative Politik*, II, 301.

The U-boat issue as the lever for unseating him was a choice of expediency. The war aims question would have been even better, but Bethmann had already forestalled an annexationist attack. No domestic issue could attract strong support from the Center and Progressive parties. The Conservatives stood alone on the Prussian reform question. The Conservatives and National Liberals did not themselves see eye to eye on tax policies, and the Center and Progressive parties were divided on both taxation and price controls. There remained only U-boat warfare. On that issue alone could the right wing hope to demonstrate that the country lacked confidence in the government.

Submarine warfare represented, of course, a real and burning issue to Conservatives and National Liberals. But it would be a mistake to view their combat for an all-out U-boat campaign as *sui generis*. When National Liberals championed it, they were also implicitly advocating adoption of Pan-German war aims and termination of the war profits tax. Conservatives were contending in addition for repeal of price controls and preservation of the three-class voting system in Prussia. If one remembers these tacit goals of the right-wing parties, it becomes easier to understand the zeal with which they pressed for unrestricted submarine warfare. It also becomes easier to understand the hesitancy which other deputies displayed when summoned to join in an attack on the Chancellor.

The public campaign against the Chancellor opened in February, 1916. The earlier U-boat agitation, frantic though it had been, had disguised itself as advocacy rather than opposition. The new attack, on the other hand, was often directed specifically at the Chancellor. Its object, barely concealed, was to bring about some legislative display of no confidence—in the Prussian Landtag, the imperial Bundesrat, or, as a last alternative, in the Reichstag itself. Although the censorship and the pretenses of the *Burgfrieden* sometimes masked this object, it is not only clear in retrospect, but it was transparent to most observers at the time.

Bassermann was at the head and front of this movement. Despite the relative smallness of his National Liberal delegation, he had usually managed to exercise a disproportionate influence in the Reichstag. Having been, in Prince Bülow's day, probably the most powerful deputy in Germany, he continued to dream of a national-ist bloc which could eventually create a conservative parliamentary monarchy. When he returned early in 1915 from a brief tour of military service, he began at once to feel out the possibilities of an annexationist coalition between his own party, the Conservatives, and the right Center. Bassermann was a jumble of contrasts. He had mediated between left and right wings in his own party. For the sake of strengthening the Reichstag, he had once contemplated coalition with the left, a bloc from Bassermann to Bebel. Yet his personal sympathies seemed to lie with the factions of order, author-ity, and privilege. At thirty-two he had appeared in a tableau, accoutred with long sword and shield, brassarts, and elfin sollerets, representing a fifteenth-century baron. He carried himself with parade-ground stiffness, wore a military moustache, and talked much more of his brief army service than of his extensive law prac-tice in Mannheim. Never enthusiastic about Bethmann and feeling a personal affinity for the right, the shrewd, crafty, and dedicated National Liberal leader was prepared to make war on the U-boat issue as soon as there appeared a chance of building a viable bloc.[11]

✓   It was Bethmann's concession of the sharpened U-boat campaign that brought him the full alliance of the Conservatives. Heydebrand, the Conservative leader, was cautious, not only by temperament, but also because of his party's peculiar dependence upon the un-equal suffrage laws of Prussia. Only in January, 1916, when Beth-mann proclaimed himself in favor of electoral reform did Heyde-brand lose hope of a *rapprochement* with the Chancellor.[12] When

[11] The indispensable work on Bassermann's earlier career is Theodor Eschen-burg's penetrating and sympathetic *Das Kaiserreich am Scheideweg, Bassermann, Bülow und der Block: Nach unveröffentlichen Papieren aus dem Nachlass Ernst Bassermanns* (Berlin, 1929). Karola Bassermann, *Ernst Bassermann: Das Lebensbild eines Parlamentariers aus Deutschlands glücklicher Zeit* (Mannheim, 1919) is sur-prisingly full. A photograph of Bassermann in his medieval costume appears oppo-site p. 22. His attitude in 1915 is indicated on pp. 175–176 and also in Westarp, *Konservative Politik,* II, 308–309.

[12] See Heydebrand to Westarp, Sept. 30, 1915, Westarp, *Konservative Politik,* II, 305–306.

the Chancellor then announced a half-measure in place of all-out submarine warfare, the Conservative leader decided that the moment had come to act. On February 4 he had learned of the plan for a sharpened campaign. On the 5th he had an interview with Jagow. He asked the Foreign Minister if the door were left open for unrestricted warfare, and Jagow answered in the negative. When Heydebrand conferred afterward with Westarp and Baron von Maltzahn, Westarp noted:

Heydebrand was very exercised. . . . We suggested: I should together with Bassermann and Spahn bring about a meeting with the Chancellor for the purpose of declaring . . . that we would fight uncompromisingly against a concession to America and forfeiture of the unrestricted U-boat war. Maltzahn should inform Tirpitz that we now . . . think the moment has possibly come to raise the issue of Bethmann's remaining in office and press it to the full [*die Kabinettsfrage zu stellen und zur äussersten Konsequenz zu treiben*].[13]

Although the Conservative leadership had in effect elected to join a National Liberal movement, circumstances dictated that Conservatives should appear to head it. The Reichstag had adjourned until mid-March. Only the state Landtage were in session, and the obvious place to attack Bethmann was in the Prussian House of Delegates. Heydebrand, "the uncrowned King of Prussia," could virtually dictate to that body. After conferring with its National Liberal, Centrist, and Progressive leaders, most of whom were in sympathy with him anyway, he presented a resolution to the budget committee of the House. It was not only adopted but, over the vehement objections of a government representative, it was published:

That the President of the House be requested to inform the Minister President of the following conclusion arrived at by the committee. The committee would regard it as detrimental to the interests of the country if the attitude of the Government toward America were to result in a restriction of our liberty in waging, at the proper time, an unimpeded and therefore fully effective submarine war against England.[14]

[13] Note of Feb. 5, 1916, *ibid.*, 118–119.
[14] *Ibid.*, 119.

The meaning of this resolution was plain. It called upon the Minister President and Chancellor to reverse his policy. If approved by the Landtag, it would represent either dictation to Bethmann or a vote of no confidence in him by his home parliament.

Although the Chancellor was shocked by this swift and unexpected attack, he retaliated at once. Appearing before the Kaiser, he declared sternly that the Conservatives were challenging the prerogatives of the Emperor. Wilhelm naturally felt outraged at what Bethmann described as unwarrantable intrusion by a mere state legislative body into the imperial preserve of foreign affairs. With the Kaiser's complete support, Bethmann could retort through the columns of the *Norddeutsche Allgemeine Zeitung:*

With regard to the decision by the budget committee of the House of Delegates concerning the negotiations with America and the conduct of the naval war, we wish to observe: It is only natural that the said committee has felt the need of discussing confidentially the various questions relating to the war and to foreign policy which in these serious times occupy the minds of all Germans. The fact that, notwithstanding the emphatic protests of a representative of the government, publicity has been given to these discussions, must create the impression that the committee has sought to exert an influence on these questions of foreign policy and as to employment of certain weapons.

This publication forces us to point out that the conduct of foreign policy and war is the exclusive constitutional prerogative of the German Emperor. Although the supreme military command cannot in any way be subjected to parliamentary influences, the parliamentary discussion of foreign questions is a concern of the Reichstag.

The Chancellor hastened on the following day to elaborate the idea implied in the closing paragraph of this declaration. Again using the *Norddeutsche Allgemeine Zeitung,* he made it plain that he and the Kaiser regarded the action of the Landtag committee as a reproach to the monarch and the Supreme Command.[15]

This counterattack, supported as it obviously was by the King of

[15] Wahnschaffe to Valentini, Feb. 12, 1916, *ibid.* (from the Chancellery archives); *Norddeutsche Allgemeine Zeitung,* Feb. 13, Feb. 14, 1916.

Prussia and German Emperor, routed some of the Conservatives. Despite Heydebrand's confident rejection of the Chancellor's claim, many old monarchists were unnerved by the Chancellor's charge. When Bethmann replied to the President of the House of Delegates and, at the same time, treated the leaders to a forty-five minute discourse on their constitutional responsibilities, the resolution was allowed to die. The committee refused, it is true, to accept the Chancellor's constitutional dictum. It subsequently resolved that the Landtag was within its rights in discussing questions of foreign policy, and, over Jagow's explicit objection, passed the resolution by a vote of twenty-three to five. Only with difficulty was the upper house prevented from enacting a resolution comparable to that originally endorsed by the Delegates' committee. But the opposition was prevented from bringing the issue to an outright vote.[16]

The first essay to unseat the Chancellor had ended in a draw. When Bethmann talked with the Landtag budget committee, he found Conservatives, National Liberals, and Centrists adamant. Heydebrand not only refused to compromise on the issue, but insisted that it was necessary for public opinion to be given a chance to speak. Only hesitancy among his following compelled him to give in and refrain from pressing the question through to a vote of the entire House.[17]

After the skirmish in the Prussian House of Delegates, there was for the moment no other challenge to the Chancellor's authority. Since the Reichstag was not to convene until mid-March, Bethmann's opponents had no outlets for their fury except editorial columns, pamphlets, leaflets, and conversation in the corners of political clubs and the like.

The press campaign of the U-boat enthusiasts was carried on, however, with a bitterness and zeal unmatched in earlier performances. All the points that had been made in the past were rehearsed and vehemently restated. The necessity of striking at England was stressed; the fearful power of the submarine received almost daily advertisement. Right-wing journals returned to describing the

United States as an enemy. The *Kreuzzeitung* declared, for example, that Wilson was virtually an ally of the English and pointed to the revived *Lusitania* issue as proof that he wanted to provoke war, while the *Hamburger Nachrichten* warned its readers that President Wilson saw Germany as "a competitor and a land which must be prevented from becoming a world power." [18] The right-wing press also restated its claim to speak for all patriotic Germans. The right Centrist *Kölnische Volkszeitung* asserted, "In the eyes of the people the submarine is a weapon like any other weapon on land or sea, and as they saw that neither Hindenburg, Mackensen or Falkenhayn worried about what neutrals thought of their campaigns, so they cannot see why the opinion of neutrals should influence the waging of submarine warfare." [19]

The press campaign of February and March wore no disguise of well-intentioned advice; it amounted to open attack on the government. Columns denounced the inadequacy of the sharpened campaign. The *Kreuzzeitung* contended that distinctions between armed and unarmed ships were absurd, that all British vessels should be treated as armed. Reventlow dismissed the sharpened campaign as "not relevant . . . , it constitutes no increase in severity of the submarine war." Right-wing journals leveled personal criticism, moreover, at the people who supported the Chancellor's policy. The *Rheinische-Westfälische Zeitung* commented on the grotesqueness of a monarchical government supported by socialists, democrats, and Poles. The *Kölnische Volkszeitung,* in an editorial reprinted throughout the right-wing press, implied that Bethmann's supporters were chiefly socialists, profiteers, and Jews. It referred to the *Berliner Tageblatt* and *Frankfurter Zeitung,* both of which had Jewish proprietors, as the spokesmen for "small but active groups, which from motives of domestic policy, of pacifist sentimentalism or even of religious persuasion, are opposed to any acquisition of territory by Germany through the war. . . . They are the opponents

[18] *Kreuzzeitung,* Feb. 11, 1916; *Hamburger Nachrichten,* quoted in *Daily Extracts from the Foreign Press,* March 13, 1916.

[19] Feb. 19, 1916, quoted *ibid.,* Feb. 26, 1916.

of Tirpitz, of Falkenhayn, of every strong man, they are against the submarine war, against air raids on England, and look upon the war from the point of view of the Stock Exchange." [20]

The right-wing campaign was also conducted through channels that were more free from the censor's restraints. Innumerable tracts were circulated defending the legality and practicality of submarine warfare. By the end of March, 1916, no fewer than twenty-nine books and articles on the legal question alone had been so widely distributed as to have made their way across the frontier into France.[21] Pamphlets like Liebig's venomous "B-System" had meanwhile been given wider circulation. The *Frankfurter Zeitung* commented stiffly on the large number of illicit brochures and memoranda being found by military authorities.[22]

Bethmann could, of course, reply to this campaign, as he had before, by making use of the censor's powers and of the columns of official and friendly journals. Since the censorship was vested primarily in the General Staff, Falkenhayn's sympathy with the agitation made it harder to curb U-boat propaganda. But Bethmann was able to suspend the *Kölnische Volkszeitung* for one day, and since Centrist organs were usually immune, this example served as a warning to other journals. He was also able, of course, to have his policy justified in the *Berliner Tageblatt,* the *Frankfurter Zeitung,* the *Kölnische Zeitung,* and the Berlin *Lokal-Anzeiger.* The Frankfurt journal asked, for example, "Is it possible or desirable to fight at the present moment against a world—which in this case would be the whole world . . . ?" Pretending to offer an objective statement of the arguments for and against the submarine, the same

---

[20] *Kreuzzeitung,* Feb. 11, 1916; *Deutsche Tageszeitung,* Feb. 24, 1916; *Rheinische-Westfälische Zeitung,* quoted in *Daily Review of the Foreign Press,* April 4, 1916; *Kölnische Volkszeitung,* quoted in *Daily Extracts from the Foreign Press,* Feb. 21, 1916. (For the changes in title of the British War Office press digests, see the Bibliographical Essay, at the end of the book.)

[21] *Résumé de la presse allemande,* no. 32 (La guerre maritime), pp. 63–121, is a summary of this literature.

[22] *Frankfurter Zeitung,* March 17, 1916, quoted in *Daily Extracts from the Foreign Press,* March 24, 1916.

newspaper contrasted the opinions of "naval officers" to those of "statesmen." [23]

The major endeavor of the Chancellor, however, was not to answer but to confuse and divide the opposition. He met their challenges in part by defending the sharpened campaign. The *Norddeutsche Allgemeine Zeitung* and the *Kölnische Zeitung* pretended that the agitation centered on the sharpened campaign, and they replied vigorously to the charge that it would not be carried through.[24] The Chancellor followed the same tactic in his press conference of March 13, declaring:

The U-boat is an effective weapon. The hope of conquering England by means of this weapon is just as enticing a hope to me as it is to any other German. There has been talk about regard for other peoples' feelings, a lack of courage, unnecessary sparing of our enemies. These are representations which are just as stupid as they are injurious. No weapon is cast aside . . . out of sentimentality. This would be a piece of cruelty directed against our own people.[25]

Bethmann and his supporters also sought to split the opposition by raising other issues. The *Berliner Tageblatt* linked the submarine fever with Pan-Germanism, thus hoping to discourage any non-annexationist U-boat advocates. All, including the *Norddeutsche Allgemeine Zeitung,* charged that the Conservatives were primarily interested in blocking reform of the Prussian suffrage. And the *Berliner Tageblatt* responded to the personal accusations of the right wing by implying that the true inciters of the campaign were ambitious politicians, reactionary professors, and profiteering industrialists.[26]

But the isue was not to be fought out merely in public prints.

[23] On the suspension of the *Kölnische Volkszeitung, ibid.,* March 20, 1916; *Frankfurter Zeitung,* Feb. 3, 1916, quoted *ibid.,* Feb. 9, 1916; *Frankfurter Zeitung,* Feb. 25, 1916, quoted *ibid.,* March 3, 1916; cf. *Deutsche Tageszeitung,* Feb. 26, 1916.

[24] *Norddeutsche Allgemeine Zeitung,* Feb. 26, 1916; *Kölnische Zeitung,* Feb. 22, 1916, quoted in *Daily Extracts from the Foreign Press,* Feb. 26, 1916.

[25] Record of press conference, March 13, 1916, *Official German Documents,* II, 1146–1147.

[26] *Berliner Tageblatt,* March 13, March 23, 1916; *Norddeutsche Allgemeine Zeitung,* March 9, 1916.

Although the move in the House of Delegates had been rebuffed, the right-wing leaders had not subsided. Westarp, Bassermann, and two Centrists, Spahn and Adolf Gröber, wrote the Chancellor shortly after the frustration of the Landtag attack. They charged that his policy had prolonged the war for precious months, that the people were dangerously uneasy, and that there was widespread concern over the likelihood that German commercial development after the war would be hindered by a failure to make resolute war on England now.[27] With muted agitation continuing in the Landtag, the ousting of Tirpitz made it inevitable that there should be a new assault upon the Chancellor.

Bethmann's opponents, having failed in the Landtag where they had the best chance of success, turned their thoughts next to the Bundesrat. That body existed largely as a guarantee of states' rights and as a check on possible radicalism in the Reichstag, but it possessed a committee on foreign affairs legally empowered to ask questions of the Chancellor. The committee had met only eighteen times in the forty-five year history of the German Empire, and its functions were, to say the least, vague.[28] But it seemed possible to right-wing leaders that it might interrogate Bethmann and perhaps report to the Bundesrat condemning the Chancellor's submarine policy.

The opposition leaders had some reason for hope. The states represented on the Bundesrat committee were Bavaria, with the permanent chairmanship, Saxony, Württemberg, Baden, and Mecklenburg-Schwerin. The Bavarian and Saxon Landtage had already indicated grave discontent with the Chancellor's tax policies; Württemberg and Baden had both displayed annoyance at plans to partition Alsace-Lorraine between Prussia and Bavaria; Mecklenburg was an agricultural state injured by price control regulations. In Bavaria and Saxony, moreover, there had appeared official criticism of the Chancellor's rebuke to the Prussian Landtag, for the monarchs and diets of these large states were jealous of their independent

[27] Westarp, *Konservative Politik*, II, 126–127.
[28] Deuerlein, *Bundesratsausschuss*, 24–110.

rights. But most important of all, from the standpoint of the right
wing, was the fact that the committee chairman, Count Hertling
of Bavaria, was a friend of Tirpitz and reported to be a supporter
of intensified U-boat warfare.

The right-wing leadership therefore called for a session of the
Bundesrat committee. Conservatives, National Liberals, and Centrists appealed to Hertling through his close friend and adviser,
Victor Naumann. To sweeten the appeal they also told Naumann
confidentially but earnestly that if Bethmann could be unseated,
Hertling should be his successor. Count von Wangenheim, the
director of the Agrarian League, even went to Munich to carry
this message directly. It was talked of so widely, indeed, that Colonel
Hoffmann heard at Hindenburg's headquarters that Hertling had
been picked by the party leaders to replace Bethmann.[29]

Despite the sources of agitation for a meeting of the Bundesrat
committee, Bethman felt obliged to consent. He tried at first to
block it. The Vice Chancellor asserted in the Bundesrat itself that
the foreign affairs committee had no constitutional powers except
to ratify treaties and declare war. The Bavarian government, however, attached great importance to the Bundesrat committee and
insisted that it should be summoned. Bethmann learned in the meantime that he would be supported by the representatives of Mecklenburg and Württemberg, and he gave in to the demand. On February 29, before leaving for the decisive conference at Charleville, he
agreed to a committee meeting early in March.[30]

When the committee convened on March 15, Bethmann was at
his most impressive. He had just succeeded in overcoming Falkenhayn and Holtzendorff. Tirpitz's resignation was announced on the
day that he appeared before the committee. By protesting against the
exaggerated estimate of U-boat numbers given to the full Bundesrat,
moreover, he had at last obtained accurate data on the strength

[29] Naumann to Hertling, March 6, 1916, Naumann, *Dokumente und Argumente,*
110–111; diary entry of March 17, 1916, Max Hoffmann, *War Diaries and Other
Papers* (English translation; 2 vols.; London, 1929), I, 114.
[30] Deuerlein, *Bundesratsausschuss,* 191–193.

of the submarine fleet. Having this new information and having just argued the issues at Charleville, he was well prepared to meet the questions put to him.

He outlined his whole position before the committee. Many of the arguments he used were those which he had employed at Charleville, but he dwelt additionally on the practical objections to unrestricted warfare, and he stated very candidly the domestic political problems that he faced. Speaking as one royalist bureaucrat to others, he explained that his chief task was to appease the lower classes, for they alone could prevent effective prosecution of the war. In achieving this goal, he confessed, it had been necessary to incur the enmity and even hatred of "high-conservative circles," and the U-boat agitation was merely another manifestation of this feeling, disloyally encouraged in this case by the former Navy Minister. So frank was he, and so fully in command of his brief, that even Hertling was converted. The committee voted to issue a statement that "the policy described by the Chancellor has received the complete and confident concurrence of the entire foreign affairs committee." [31]

The Chancellor's victory was complete. Not only did he escape a vote of censure and obtain a vote of confidence, but he won the support of the Bavarian and Saxon governments. When the right wing made its third attack upon him, seeking a vote in the Reichstag, the official journals of the two courts condemned this action and expressed complete support for Bethmann.

This final assault of the right wing was the most publicized but probably the least dangerous of the three. The evidence suggests that it was almost unpremeditated. Westarp, who was privy to most of the plans of both Heydebrand and Bassermann, knew nothing of it until after Tirpitz's ousting, and it seems likely that the Conservative, National Liberal, and right Centrist leaders were stirred into action by the belief that a Reichstag majority might rally around the revered name of the Grand Admiral.

[31] *Ibid.*, 194–195, 284–287.

Bassermann led the attack in this instance. Two days after Tirpitz had received notice of his dismissal, the National Liberal chairman declared in the *Deutsche Stimmen:*

Today there is only one strong desire in every German, the desire
for ruthless war against England, for the rejection of all unjustified
American interference, and for no hesitation over the question whether
a ruthless, resolute waging of war at sea will offend this or that neutral.
On this turns the question whether we can defeat England. Our
Tirpitz assures us of victory if we use the means. No doubt the Reichs-
tag will find the right note of energy. It must clearly declare that the
German people will not let America take away the submarine weapon.
Our existence and might and future depend upon this war. We shall
win it if we use relentlessly all the weapons we possess.[32]

At the moment of the Grand Admiral's announced resignation, the
entire National Liberal, Conservative, and right Center press
warned that it meant abandonment of U-boat warfare. On March
18, the two right-wing parties published resolutions calling in effect
for ruthless use of the submarine weapon.[33]

The purpose of these resolutions was to bring on a debate in the
Reichstag. It was probably not the intention of Bassermann and
Heydebrand to force a vote. With socialists, Progressives, and
national minorities possessing 185 votes, it was most unlikely that
the right wing could obtain a majority. Eleven National Liberals
had declined to endorse their party's stand. Open and fierce debate
on these resolutions could nevertheless display the extent to which
the national parties distrusted the Chancellor, and it could gravely
weaken his standing with the Kaiser. The real issue therefore was
whether the resolutions would be brought to the floor of the Reichstag or merely referred to the budget committee.

The decision was to be made on March 22. With the budget to
be debated, the Seniorenconvent, or senior committee, had the power

---

[32] *Daily Extracts from the Foreign Press,* March 20, 1916; *Résumé de la presse
allemande,* no. 33–1 (March, 1916), pp. 11–12.

[33] *Daily Extracts from the Foreign Press,* March 24, 1916; *Verhandlungen des
Reichstages: Anlagen,* Nos. 231, 232.

to determine whether other matters could be discussed in connection with it. During the four days between publication of the resolutions and the meeting of the Seniorenconvent, therefore, there raged an unbelievably heated campaign in behalf of open debate. Not only did the whole right-wing press appear in unaccustomed guise as champions of the people's right to be heard, but petitions were industriously circulated, especially in Berlin. It was reported that the National Liberals had hired restaurant waiters to obtain signatures from their customers. By the time the Seniorenconvent met, the right wing had done everything it could to force a free debate.[34]

Although this effort had not begun until after Tirpitz's resignation, Bethmann had anticipated an attack in the Reichstag. He had consequently worked to build up a government bloc. To Erzberger, for example, he made a personal appeal contrived almost as carefully as his appeals to the Kaiser and to the Bundesrat committee. Talking with him in late February, Bethmann spelled out the practical objections to unrestricted warfare—the American problem, the probable difficulties with European neutrals, the shortage of U-boats, and the unlikelihood of any real success against England.[35] He endeavored to mobilize a government coalition in the event that the opposition should succeed in bringing the matter to a vote.

He also fought to frustrate debate on the issue. When the Conservative and National Liberal resolutions were brought to the Wolff Bureau for transmission to the press, they were immediately taken to the Chancellery. Bethmann or Wahnschaffe or Hammann then added to them: "The publication of these resolutions could give rise to the unfortunate impression that they were intended to influence the decisions of the Supreme Command. For the prosecution of the war to final victory we need, as at present, complete unity and universal confidence, and the maintenance of that unity

---

[34] *Daily Extracts from the Foreign Press*, March 29, 1916; *Résumé de la presse allemande*, no. 33-1 (March, 1916), pp. 13-19; *Berliner Tageblatt*, March 23, 1916; Bethmann to the Prussian representatives in Munich, Dresden, Stuttgart, Karlsruhe, Oldenburg, and Hamburg, March 19, 1916, German Foreign Ministry Archives (U-boat War); Bethmann to Treutler, March 22, 1916, *ibid.*

[35] *Politische Dokumente*, II, 484.

is the unanimous desire of the entire nation." The whole release was then stamped "Official." Since official statements had to be published in their entirety or not at all, even the *Deutsche Tageszeitung* had to print this attachment.[36]

On the day the resolutions were published, moreover, the Chancellor held a long conference with right-wing leaders, seeking to dissuade them from pressing the issue. He asserted flatly that a more intensified U-boat campaign would bring the United States into the war. When Westarp declared that some stake had to be risked in order to gain the benefits of the submarine weapon, Bethmann exclaimed, "But not the stake of our existence! We should be destroyed like a mad dog!" [37]

It was the Chancellor's parliamentary allies who rescued him. Erzberger had already come to his aid. When the *Zentrum* delegation gathered during the previous week, there had been a movement for a U-boat resolution similar to those of the right-wing parties. Gröber and Spahn, two of the party's three representatives on the budget committee, had been working hand in hand with the Conservatives and the National Liberals. The difficulty that faced proponents of a resolution was the relative absence of sympathy with the broader aims of Bassermann and Heydebrand. As Erzberger interpreted party feeling, there was opposition to any appearance of voting no confidence in Bethmann or of attacking the command rights of the crown. He concluded that the best compromise would be an innocuous resolution. He drafted one that simply declared, "Since the use of the submarine weapon has not yet been regulated by international law, freedom for that use will be preserved in all negotiations with neutrals." Taking this draft to the Chancellery, he obtained Bethmann's approval. Since the right-wing resolutions had already been made known to most of the Reichstag, Bethmann said, he would favor the *Zentrum* delegation's issuing a milder declaration. Armed with this endorsement, Erzberger succeeded in uniting the deputies behind his resolution. Even before the meeting of the Seniorenconvent, therefore, the

[36] See *Daily Extracts from the Foreign Press,* March 29, 1916.
[37] Westarp, *Konservative Politik,* II, 121.

Centrists had partially neutralized the Conservatives and National Liberals, and Erzberger had checked Spahn and Gröber.[38]

On the day of the Seniorenconvent meeting, the Social Democrats dramatically rallied to the Chancellor's support. Mustering all their strength and even inducing the radical minority to cooperate, the majority socialists published a resolution of their own, calling upon the government "not to disregard the just claims of neutrals in a way that might prolong or give a greater scope to the war." Socialists appearing before the Seniorenconvent then threatened, if debate were opened on the U-boat question, to insist on discussing every issue of the war.

The Conservative and National Liberal leaders held out for a time. The sitting of the Reichstag, scheduled for 1:00, was postponed while party leaders consulted their delegations. At 1:45 Bassermann and Heydebrand gave in. The resolutions were all referred to the budget committee, where they were to be debated in secrecy.[39]

Although the first battle had been won, there remained a danger that the budget committee might report a resolution unacceptable to the government. Appearing before the budget committee, therefore, Bethmann displayed as much energy and determination as he had shown at Charleville and at the Bundesrat hearing two weeks earlier. He once again outlined all the arguments against an unrestricted campaign, laying particular stress on the shortage of U-boats. He pointed out, for example, that there were five stations on the west coast of England that would have to be manned if British imports were to be seriously curtailed. Owing to fueling and refitting requirements, a minimum of five boats had to be assigned to each station if one were to be operating at all times. And only seventeen were available for such service. Helfferich also appeared, pointing out to the committee that Germany received food, textiles, and other commodities from neutral sources, nearly

[38] Erzberger to Hertling, March 18, 1916, from the Hertling manuscripts in the Bavarian Bundesarchiv. I am indebted to Prof. Klaus Epstein for lending me his transcript of this letter.

[39] Bethmann to Treutler, March 22, 1916, German Foreign Ministry Archives (U-boat War); *Berliner Tageblatt*, March 23, 1916; *Daily Extracts from the Foreign Press*, March 29, 1916.

all of which she would lose as a result of an unrestricted U-boat campaign. Capelle more or less supported the Chancellor's policy. A tremendous weight of expert testimony was thus thrown against the U-boat advocates.[40]

Within the budget committee, moreover, the Chancellor's partisan allies vigorously supported him. Just as the issue of open debate had made the Conservatives advocates of free speech, so the proposition before the budget committee made the Social Democrats upholders of authority. Scheidemann and Eduard David found themselves contending that it was irresponsible to attack the government, and Scheidemann even reproached right-wing leaders for daring to criticize the military authorities.[41] No less staunchly stood the Progressives, whose entire delegation had resolved on March 24 that the committee should substitute for all the resolutions one merely expressing unlimited confidence in the government. Of the three Progressives on the committee, it was not the Chancellor's friends, Haussmann and Payer, who took the lead; it was instead Ernst Müller-Meiningen, a right-wing Progressive and a Pan-German.[42] The socialist and Progressive deputies stood united in total opposition to the Conservatives and National Liberals.

The Centrists therefore held the deciding votes. Gröber and Spahn evidently continued to strive for a strong resolution. Despite Erzberger's victory in the earlier party conclave, the two right Centrists tried to work out a successful strategy. During every day of the budget committee session, they and the Conservative and National Liberal leaders gathered in Spahn's office.[43] At some point, however, Gröber began to waver. The delegation meeting had disproved earlier rumors of Erzberger's waning strength, and Gröber evidently decided that he could not risk a fight with the dynamic little

[40] Westarp, *Konservative Politik*, II, 122, 138–146; Hanssen, *Diary of a Dying Empire*, 135–141; *Berliner Tageblatt*, March 29, March 30, March 31, 1916; *Daily Review of the Foreign Press*, April 4, 1916; *Résumé de la presse allemande*, no. 33–1 (March, 1916), pp. 19–20.

[41] Westarp, *Konservative Politik*, II, 138, 145.

[42] *Berliner Tageblatt*, March 25, 1916; Westarp, *Konservative Politik*, II, 145.

[43] *Ibid.*, 128–129.

Swabian.[44] Spahn, of course, could not hold out alone. When these Centrists deserted, the Conservatives and National Liberals were beaten. The Conservatives characteristically held out for martyrdom long after the less doctrinaire Bassermann had given up, but they too eventually agreed to accept a compromise.

All the factions, except the minority socialist Georg Lebedour, united on an innocuous formula. For the most part it conformed with the *Zentrum* resolution that Erzberger had drafted and Bethmann had approved. A final clause added by the Social Democrats called upon the government to "preserve freedom in the use of this weapon with due consideration for the rightful interests of neutral states." The compromise, as Bassermann reported, was not intended to express either confidence or lack of confidence in the government; it was designed solely to demonstrate the unity of the nation.[45] But debate on the issue had been forestalled; the Chancellor had apparently won the support of a solid majority in the Reichstag. His public power seemed as secure as his power with the Kaiser.

The results of Bethmann's combat with the right wing were nevertheless far-reaching. Despite his apparent victory, he had been compelled to make concessions. The Landtag resolution had demonstrated the weakness of his hold over Prussia and had consequently increased his dependence on the capricious favor of the Kaiser. Despite the support shown him by the Bundesrat committee, he had admitted in effect that he bore some responsibility toward that body, and in a future crisis he would be answerable to it once again. In the Reichstag Bethmann had won only because he possessed the support of socialists, Progressives, and Centrists. He was thereafter to be at the mercy of the Centrists; they commanded the balance of power. Despite the state of siege and despite the complete confidence shown by the Kaiser, Bethmann had lost his independence

---

[44] For an example of the rumors, see Naumann to Hertling, March 6, 1916, Naumann, *Dokumente und Argumente*, 111.

[45] *Verhandlungen des Reichstages: Anlagen*, no. 255; Bredt, *Der deutsche Reichstag im Weltkrieg*, 65–66; Bethmann to Treutler and Valentini, March 30, 1916, German Foreign Ministry Archives (U-boat War).

of the Reichstag. The fact that the right wing would not abandon its cause thus had twofold importance for the Chancellor. It meant that he would have to fight the same battle over and over, and it also meant that his tenure as Chancellor would be as much at stake in these engagements as in those that took place before the throne.

XIII

The Ebbing of Bethmann's Power

The *Sussex* pledge marked the high point of Bethmann's strength. He had won a decisive victory at Charleville, overcoming the united force of the army and the navy. Secure in the Emperor's confidence, he had met his right-wing opponents and vanquished them first in the Prussian Landtag, then in the Bundesrat, and finally in the Reichstag. He seemed to command an unbeatable coalition of majority socialists, Progressives, and Centrists. To an innocent observer it might have appeared that Bethmann had achieved ascendancy over the Kaiser, the military, and the Reichstag.

This appearance did not last. The opposition soon returned to the attack. While the Reichstag was out of session, the U-boat agitation gained strength, and the inclination of the *Zentrum* came once again to seem doubtful. In the meantime the Supreme Command changed. The artless and impotent Falkenhayn was replaced by the ✓ powerful team of Hindenburg and Ludendorff. When the new masters of the army manifested sympathy with the U-boat enthusiasm, the Chancellor was plunged into confusion. He faced the likelihood of a new imperial debate that would strain his strength beyond its limits. Owing to this danger, moreover, he lost the ability to make a resolute fight against his parliamentary opponents. The result was that by the end of October, 1916, the Chancellor's hold upon the Kaiser had become loose and his control of the Reichstag had slipped away.

After the Reichstag battle of March, 1916, came a temporary restoration of the party truce. Not even the *Sussex* pledge served to revive the storm. Owing to the censorship, it is true, the most intransigent journals were unable to comment at all. But at least one Conservative organ, the *Tägliche Rundschau,* admitted grudgingly that the Chancellor might know what he was doing, and the once violent *Kölnische Volkszeitung* remarked, "If the authorities assembled around the Kaiser . . . believed that this is the only way by which the victory and its aim can be attained, we must all of us bow to such motives for the decision." [1]

Nor did later events provoke the kind of agitation that might have been expected. When the High Seas Fleet emerged victorious from its brush at Jutland with the British Grand Fleet, some journals took occasion to applaud Tirpitz's far-seeing naval policy, but few reverted to the demand for unlimited U-boat war.[2] In early June the Chancellor addressed the Reichstag, declaring that public discussion of the submarine was still undesirable. His opponents indicated dissent only by remaining silent, while the left-wing parties, the Center, and even many National Liberals applauded heartily.[3]

The reasons for this temporary calm were varied. One, obviously, was the fact that the Reichstag was to adjourn for the summer. There were few forums where the Chancellor could be challenged effectively, and it was only prudent for his critics to reserve their thunder. From the end of April until late May, furthermore, many of the opposition leaders were off on a semiofficial trip to Turkey and hence were not on hand to battle the *Sussex* pledge or to exploit the Jutland victory.[4]

A second important reason for the comparative quiet after the March crisis was the apparent firmness of Bethmann's hold upon the Center. Catholic journals which had joined in the earlier U-boat uproar stood staunchly by the Centrist delegation's decision to up-

[1] *Daily Review of the Foreign Press,* May 13, 1916.
[2] *Ibid.,* June 7, June 8, 1916; *Deutsche Tageszeitung,* June 3, 1916.
[3] *Verhandlungen des Reichstages,* CCCVII (June 5, 1916), pp. 1509 ff.
[4] Westarp, *Konservative Politik,* II, 16; K. Bassermann, *Ernst Bassermann,* 178.

hold the Chancellor. When party spokesmen replied to Bethmann's speech of June 5, it was Spahn, the erstwhile U-boat enthusiast, who represented the *Zentrum,* and he declared himself fully satisfied by the explanations given in committee. "We should not have had the present traffic on the Danube," he added, "had our relations with the United States been broken off." [5] So long as the Center maintained this stand, there was little hope of success in a renewed assault on the government.

Most important of all was the general uncertainty resulting from the split in the Social Democratic party. Eighteen members of the Reichstag delegation had voted against the emergency budget of March and, when reprimanded, had formed an independent party. Fifteen other deputies, though not joining the movement, published a manifesto expressing sympathy with the bolters. Although moderates retained a comfortable margin in the Reichstag delegation, the division spread through the party. In Berlin, Brunswick, Nordhausen, Erfurt, Bremen, Essen, and Düsseldorf, local committees supported the minority. Scheidemann's own constituency at Solingen resolved in favor of the bolters and boycotted his speeches. [6]

The spreading of dissension made it seem possible that one of two major changes might occur. The party might adopt a more revolutionary program, hoping to prevent a drift toward the Independents, or it might let all the radicals go and re-form as a moderate party, capable of permanent coalition with the Progressives and either the Center or the National Liberals. In either case, the government would have to look elsewhere than to the left for its necessary support, and either the *Zentrum* or the National Liberal party might be placed in a commanding position. Until the air cleared, it was necessary for both Bassermann and the Centrist leaders to maintain some flexibility.

When it became evident that Scheidemann would not move far either to the left or to the right, opposition leaders reverted to their earlier tactics. The Conservatives had never budged from their

---

[5] *Verhandlungen des Reichstages,* CCCVII (June 6, 1916), pp. 1519–1521.
[6] Präger, *Geschichte der U.S.P.D.,* 94–96; *Daily Review of the Foreign Press,* April 1, April 3, July 5, 1916; *ibid.: Weekly Supplement,* July 14, 1916.

hostility to the Chancellor. In the budget committee and on the floor of the Reichstag, their spokesmen had attacked the *Sussex* pledge and denounced the Chancellor's speech.[7] Gestures by Conservative leaders toward a *rapprochement* with the government had been feeble, to say the least. Count von Zedlitz of the Free Conservatives had spoken in public, mildly applauding the Chancellor's policies, and an envoy from Heydebrand had visited Charleville to discuss "building a bridge" between the party and the Kaiser.[8] But these motions had doubtless been precautions in case the socialist split should bring a realignment of parties, isolating the Conservatives. The far right's distrust of the Chancellor had not abated in any degree.

When Bassermann saw that the government was not to lose its left-wing backing, he resumed his alliance with the Conservatives. During the interval after the independent socialist bolt, most National Liberal gatherings had been characterized by leftist pronouncements. Friedberg, the party leader in Prussia, advocated subordinating foreign policy issues and emphasizing domestic questions. "The great tasks of internal politics," he asserted, "can only be solved in cooperation with parties of the left."[9] The slogan of independence from Heydebrand was taken up in the *Börsenzeitung* and the *Leipziger Tageblatt*. In token of the strength which this movement appeared to gain, even Bassermann's *Magdeburgische Zeitung* played down differences with the government and encouraged hope of collaboration with the left.[10] But the central committee of the party had quietly endorsed the Reichstag delegation's actions and called for resumption of the U-boat agitation at the first opportunity.[11] Bassermann's chief lieutenant, Gustav Stresemann, had visited local organizations, speaking in favor of the Con-

---

[7] Westarp, *Konservative Politik*, II, 130; *Verhandlungen des Reichstages*, CCCVII (May 25, 1916), p. 1261, (May 30, 1916), p. 1314, (June 5, 1916), p. 1533.

[8] Berlin *Post*, quoted in *Daily Review of the Foreign Press*, July 5, 1916; Westarp, *Konservative Politik*, II, 312–313, 328–333; *Kaiser und Kabinettschef*, 231–234.

[9] *Berliner Tageblatt*, May 30, 1916.

[10] *Résumé de la presse allemande*, no. 44–1 (July, 1916), p. 10; *Daily Review of the Foreign Press*, June 12, 1916.

[11] *Daily Review of the Foreign Press*, May 31, 1916.

servative alliance. Before long, local committees in Westphalia, Bavaria, and Hanover had voted down the reformers.[12] Although Bassermann felt obliged to call for some domestic change in order to placate his own left wing, he chose to call for greater parliamentary control of foreign policy—an object which fitted hand in glove with a U-boat demand.[13] It was evident that he and his party were back in the lists of the opposition.

Bassermann and Heydebrand directed their efforts, of course, toward winning the *Zentrum*. It had been the Centrist defection that had frustrated their attack in March. But within the Center party there remained powerful elements to which the Conservative and National Liberal leaders could appeal. Rural Catholics, especially in South Germany, were hostile to the government and opposed to their party's cooperation with socialists and Progressives. Food shortages had led not only to price controls but also to ruthless requisitioning. The result had been to stir latent hostilities between farmers and townspeople. This division had emerged even among the far right, as agrarians began to quarrel with urban Free Conservatives, but it was most marked in the "amphibious" *Zentrum*, where the solitary tie of religion united farmers, laborers, and businessmen.[14]

In South Germany the dissidence of rural Centrists was even more pronounced because of an inborn resentment of Prussian imperial authority. The Bavarian Christian Farmers Union, with 160,000 members, openly opposed Centrist cooperation with the Chancellor and the left.[15] Since the U-boat issue had become the √ symbol of confidence or lack of confidence in the government, it was taken up zealously by this organization, by Centrists in the

[12] Stresemann at Nürnberg, *Berliner Tageblatt*, May 4, 1916; Westphalian committee, *Daily Review of the Foreign Press*, May 6, 1916; Bavarian committee, *ibid.*, May 13, 1916; Hanoverian committee, *Deutsche Tageszeitung*, June 29, 1916.

[13] *National Liberale Korrespondenz* cited in *Daily Review of the Foreign Press: Weekly Supplement*, Sept. 1, 1916.

[14] "The Conflict between Town and Country in Germany," *Daily Review of the Foreign Press*, Sept. 16, 1916; *Résumé de la presse allemande*, no. 46 (La Bavière jusqu'au 1er Septembre 1916), pp. 1–44.

[15] *Résumé da la presse allemande*, no. 46 (La Bavière), pp. 5–6.

Bavarian Landtag, and by the peasants themselves. Victor Naumann tells of a walk in the Bavarian countryside, where he found farmers as convinced and bitter as the U-boat fanatics in the Reichstag.[16]

Nor was this feeling solely a product of peasant emotions. Many Catholics, in cities as well as in the countryside, resented their party's collaboration with the Jews and freethinkers of the socialist and Progressive parties. Some of the clergy joined in criticizing the *Zentrum*'s role in the recent Reichstag sitting. The Jesuit *Stimmen der Zeit* warned against the illusion that Catholics could find common ground with "murderous and incendiary democracy." Cardinal Bettinger in Bavaria rejected a personal plea from Hertling and declined to take any steps toward abating the U-boat agitation. The *Zentrum* was affected by the revived anti-Semitism spreading through all of Germany.[17] During the March crisis, the *Kölnische Volkszeitung* had denounced the Jewish opponents of Tirpitz's policy. By the time of the Reichstag sitting in the autumn, feeling had grown so strong that the entire Reichstag delegation proposed a census of the Jews shirking military duty.[18] Anti-Semitism, rural suffering from the food shortage, the countryman's antipathy toward the city dweller, and South German particularism all offered the Conservatives and National Liberals hope of drawing the *Zentrum* into the opposition camp.

The renewed attack on the Chancellor was first launched in Bavaria. Centrists in the Landtag quickly joined with Conservatives and National Liberals in protesting the government's U-boat policy. It was asserted that Bethmann had sacrificed 500,000 soldiers' lives by his failure to use the submarine against England. Despite efforts by Hertling and his lieutenants to stem the agitation, staid and moderate Centrists were swept into hysteria. The Minister President commented ruefully on the bitterness with which he was being attacked for failing to oppose the Chancellor and Kaiser; his friends

[16] Naumann, *Dokumente und Argumente*, 121.

[17] *Stimmen der Zeit*, quoted in *Vorwärts*, May 15, 1916; Hertling's appeal to Bettinger is detailed in Naumann, *Dokumente und Argumente*, 118–121; on the renewed spread of anti-Semitism see *Daily Review of the Foreign Press*, Nov. 27, 1916, and *Berliner Tageblatt*, Oct. 20, 1916.

[18] *Verhandlungen des Reichstages*, CCCVIII (Nov. 3, 1916), pp. 2038–2040.

were asserting that he must be paralyzed and hence unable to act.[19]

This agitation focused on the Bavarian government. Despite Hertling's open support of Bethmann, the opposition evidently hoped that he might be forced by public opinion into taking a stand against the Chancellor. On July 30 a large meeting of Bavarian leaders was held at Munich, with a number of North German Conservatives and National Liberals appearing to urge action. Count Reventlow was the chief speaker. His address had been censored beforehand, but he punctuated it with long silences, indicating the parts deleted, and these pauses were rewarded with wild applause. During one speech, someone in the audience cried out that the Chancellor should be shot. The man on the platform rejoined that that was too extreme; Bethmann could enjoy a long life, but at Hohenfinow rather than in the Wilhelmstrasse.[20]

After this meeting a delegation called on King Ludwig, petitioning him to ask the Kaiser for an unrestricted U-boat campaign and also to bring about another session of the Bundesrat committee on foreign affairs. Accounts of this meeting vary; some say that Ludwig expressed sympathy, others that he rebuked the petitioners.[21] Hertling had already decided, in any case, that a new meeting of the Bundesrat committee would be desirable. He had warned the Chancellor that feeling in Bavaria ran high and that it had to be counteracted in some fashion. Since the Württemberg government took much the same view, Bethmann had agreed to a new session early in August.[22]

The committee disappointed the opposition, just as it had in March. The U-boat issue was thoroughly canvassed. Both Bethmann and Helfferich explained that the situation had not changed. Only seven large U-boats had been added to the fleet. The danger

[19] Naumann, *Dokumente und Argumente*, 118; *Résumé de la presse allemande*, no. 46 (La Bavière), pp. 4–10.

[20] *Berliner Tageblatt*, Aug. 8, 1916; *Vorwärts*, Aug. 16, 1916; *Magdeburgische Zeitung*, quoted in *Berliner Tageblatt*, Sept. 29, 1916.

[21] *Berliner Tageblatt*, Aug. 7, 1916; *Deutsche Tageszeitung*, Aug. 11, 1916; *Daily Review of the Foreign Press: Weekly Supplement*, Aug. 18, 1916; Deuerlein, *Bundesratsausschuss*, 197; Hanssen, *Diary of a Dying Empire*, 152.

[22] Deuerlein, *Bundesratsausschuss*, 196–197.

of war with America had not diminished. Although Hertling and the Württemberger warned of intense feeling in Munich and Stuttgart, they accepted the Chancellor's explanations unhesitatingly. Once again an official release expressed the committee's full agreement and complete confidence in the government.[23]

Since the opposition had failed again to capture the state governments, its leaders looked naturally to the forthcoming session of the Reichstag. The South German agitation had at least served to redivide the Center. Although the Reichstag was not scheduled to reconvene until late September, Heydebrand and Bassermann chose mid-August to launch their campaign for capture of the whole Centrist delegation. The Conservative leader delivered an address at Frankfurt on August 14.[24] Speaking with unaccustomed moderation, he sought to demonstrate that side issues need not stand in the way of right and Centrist cooperation. He suggested that the Conservatives might be receptive to proposals for reform, even of the Prussian franchise. He seemed open-minded about war aims, saying, for example, "Belgium need not be annexed, but it must be attached to the Empire in the military and economic spheres." It was evident that he meant to reduce the issues between the opposition and the government to one—the U-boat question. On that alone did he speak with fire, declaring, "The authorities give political, not technical, grounds for the limitation of the submarine campaign. It is simply a question whether one is willing to acquiesce in war with America or not.... The view represented by my friends offers the one and only possibility of ending the war, with its unspeakable sacrifices, in victory."

Bassermann followed virtually the same line. Even before Heydebrand spoke, he published in the *Magdeburgische Zeitung* "The Order of the Day," an appeal for concentration on the single object of defeating England. After the Conservative leader's speech, the official *National Liberale Korrespondenz* asserted that the party was at one with the Conservatives on issues of foreign policy. Basser-

---

[23] *Ibid.*, 197–198, 287–292.

[24] Quoted from *Frankfurter Zeitung*, Aug. 15, 1916, in *Daily Review of the Foreign Press: Weekly Supplement*, Aug. 25, 1916.

mann himself underscored this unity in a speech at Stettin on August 19, and the party press began to call loudly for unity among all foes of England, regardless of party.[25] It was obviously Bassermann's intention as well as Heydebrand's to forge a U-boat bloc unhampered by any inner dissensions and to confront the Chancellor with an open show of lack of confidence in his leadership.

The party leaders' declarations were followed by an intense agitation. Nearly all the Conservative and National Liberal press joined in calling for submergence of differences among all elements that desired the U-boat war. Abetting this partisan activity was an effort in the same direction by the Independent Committee for a German Peace. Though formed as an annexationist committee, it adopted almost verbatim the program outlined by Heydebrand. Most of its leading figures, it is true, were themselves National Liberal or Conservative politicians, but it also included representatives of the powerful economic associations, celebrated university professors, and well-known military and naval officers. Its appeals to the Center therefore had a non-partisan flavor.[26]

Agitation by this committee and by partisan organs steadily increased in tempo. The final failure of the Verdun offensive showed an obvious moral, as did the opening of an Allied offensive on the line of the Somme. The unexpected declaration of war by Rumania produced violent editorials. The *Rheinische Westfälische Zeitung,* for example, proclaimed that the Chancellor's submarine policy had been bankrupt; its principal object had been to guarantee food imports from Rumania, and it had failed.[27] And this agitation began to show results, as Centrist organs reprinted this charge or imitated it in their own editorials.[28]

The opposition campaign suffered a temporary check when the Rumanian declaration of war was followed two days later by a change in the German Supreme Command. The team of Hinden-

[25] *Daily Review of the Foreign Press,* Aug. 17, 1916; *ibid.: Weekly Supplement,* Sept. 1, 1916.
[26] *Ibid.; Résumé de la presse allemande,* no. 47–1 (Sept., 1916), pp. 20–21; Gatzke, *Germany's Drive to the West,* 121 ff.
[27] *Daily Review of the Foreign Press,* Sept. 2, 1916.
[28] *Ibid.,* Sept. 9, Sept. 19, 1916.

burg and Ludendorff replaced Falkenhayn. The heroes of the eastern front, who had become popular idols, were now to be associated
with the Chancellor, and the semiofficial press made the most of
the fact. The *Frankfurter Zeitung,* in an editorial that drew wide
notice, declared:

> He who has watched the developments knows that now certain other
> questions have been cleared up, in regard to which it must also be of
> the highest value to the political leader of our Empire to be secure
> and undisturbed. . . .
> Hindenburg has now entered the circle of the few men whom we
> call the imperial leadership *(Reichsleitung).* . . . He, together with the
> Imperial Chancellor and the Kaiser, forms now its head. The circle has
> thus become narrower than it was . . . , and this is good. One may hope,
> indeed one must demand, that in future our Imperial government may
> be spared all doubt as to its strength.[29]

Imitated throughout the semiofficial press, this coupling of Hindenburg and Bethmann caused the opposition, for the moment, to gasp
and sputter. The *Kreuzzeitung* could only retort that use of the
Field Marshal as a shield from criticism would be unconstitutional;
the Chancellor alone bore responsibility for policy, and it would be
he alone whom his critics assailed.[30]

Bethmann made the fullest use of the new Supreme Command's
prestige. The semiofficial press did not cease to sound the argument
that U-boat agitators were enemies of Hindenburg. The *Frankfurter Zeitung* joyfully engaged the *Kreuzzeitung* in debate in
order to keep the point before its readers.[31] Bethmann himself summoned the party leaders to a conference at the Chancellery and told
them firmly that Hindenburg did not believe the time ripe for
opening a submarine campaign.[32]

It is of the utmost significance that these efforts by the Chancellor
produced only a momentary pause in the opposition's campaign.
Hindenburg was by all odds the most popular man in Germany.

[29] *Ibid.,* Sept. 5, 1916.
[30] Quoted in *Berliner Tageblatt,* Sept. 1, 1916.
[31] *Daily Review of the Foreign Press: Weekly Supplement,* Sept. 8, 1916.
[32] Westarp, *Konservative Politik,* II, 131; *Berliner Tageblatt,* Sept. 7, 1916.

Giant wooden sculptures of him had been erected in town squares all over the country. Hundreds of thousands, perhaps millions, had paid the Red Cross for the privilege of pounding devotional nails into these statues. They were treated like icons of a Nordic war god, as Wheeler-Bennett comments, and the marshal himself served as "a figure-head carved upon the prow of the German barque to ward off evil spirits and to bring good fortune." [33] Although he and Ludendorff had not in reality endorsed the Chancellor's policy, this fact was not known to the politicians of the Reichstag. From semiofficial releases and from Bethmann himself, the agitators were given to understand that Hindenburg was at one with Bethmann. Yet they continued, hardly pausing, in their crusade for the submarine.

After only a few days' hesitation, indeed, the campaign gathered even greater momentum. Symptomatic of the Conservative excitement was the fact that Count Reventlow was forbidden by the censors to write or say anything.[34] National Liberal local committees in Pomerania, Thuringia, and Schleswig-Holstein passed resolutions calling upon their party's representatives to demand debate on the U-boat issue.[35] An open letter to Basserman from a prominent member of the Independent Committee for a German Peace called for "rescuing the Fatherland from misdirection by one dangerous man." Allegedly non-partisan meetings meanwhile resolved that the Reichstag should insist on the full use of all weapons against England. One of these was a much publicized gathering in Hamburg, where it was claimed that all the important shipping firms of Germany were represented. Others occurred at Lübeck and Kassel.[36] The excitement among the right-wing parties and among business and industrial circles was in no way tempered by the Hindenburg appointment.

Nor did the change in the Supreme Command check the drift of

[33] John W. Wheeler-Bennett, *Wooden Titan: Hindenburg in Twenty Years of German History, 1914–1934* (New York, 1936), 30–31, 77–78.

[34] *Deutsche Tageszeitung*, Sept. 5, 1916.

[35] *Berliner Tageblatt*, Sept. 4, 1916; *Vorwärts*, Sept. 5, 1916; *Daily Review of the Foreign Press*, Sept. 22, 1916.

[36] *Daily Review of the Foreign Press: Weekly Supplement*, Oct. 6, 1916.

the Center toward the right. The party committee in Bavaria passed a resolution expressing delight at the Field Marshal's appointment and asserting that it now expected the government to use all weapons against England.[37] Centrist leaders in the state adopted completely the tactics of Heydebrand and Bassermann. Addressing the Christian Farmers Union, one of them declared, "We have never belonged to the advocates of annexation. . . . For us there is only one war aim: to win the war by using every weapon." Although it was Bavarians who figured most prominently, Centrists elsewhere identified themselves with the right-wing movement. Those in Kiel joined, for example, with the Free Conservatives, the economic associations, and the Pan-Germans in a resolution favoring all-out U-boat warfare.[38]

The fact that Bethmann was not able to restrain the agitators, even by making the fullest use of Hindenburg's prestige, is indicative of the intensity of feeling against him. Victor Naumann, the shrewd and perceptive Bavarian, had written after the March debates:

The crisis . . . has once more reached a momentary terminus, but Bethmann's victory is only a pyrrhic victory. Only to the circumstance that public opinion must be silent may the Chancellor be thankful that indignation against him does not find open expression. I view this as even more dangerous than public criticism, for with this vent closed, there accumulates in party committees, clubs, and cliques, a rage against him which would be partly relieved if it were possible to speak out; today the manometer stands at 99, and whether this pressure can be contained long without an explosion seems to me very doubtful. The mediating activity of Hertling has succeeded for this moment in making the *Zentrum* stand fast for the Chancellor . . . but the majority is only an artificial one, and the minority knows itself to contain the strongest elements.[39]

The U-boat had ceased to have meaning in itself. It was symbolic

[37] *Vorwärts*, Sept. 9, 1916.

[38] *Münchener Neueste Nachrichten*, Sept. 20, 1916, quoted in *Daily Review of the Foreign Press: Weekly Supplement*, Sept. 29, 1916; *Hamburger Nachrichten*, quoted *ibid.*, Sept. 22, 1916.

[39] Naumann, *Dokumente und Argumente*, 113-114.

of all the suppressed emotion against the Chancellor. Agitation for unrestricted warfare expressed both rightist horror for the government's democratic and socialist support and rightist desire for power. It gave vent to indignation against Bethmann's reticence on war aims. For Prussian Conservatives it provided a means of attacking the threatened new orientation. For peasants it provided a patriotic outlet for discontent with the government's food policies, its centralizing tendencies, and its urban preferences. For South Germans it masked hostility to Prussia and to the Empire. For Protestants and Catholics alike it supplied a vent for anti-Semitism. Most of all, it expressed the widespread uneasiness over the war, its seeming endlessness, and its desperate sacrifices.

It would probably have been impossible for Bethmann to placate his opponents, even by giving in to them on the U-boat issue. An effort by him to demonstrate lack of sentimentality was notably unsuccessful. The submarine enthusiasts had often coupled the Zeppelin with their favorite weapon, asserting that air and underwater attacks on England were both blocked by the Chancellor. Since Bethmann did in fact believe that Zeppelin attacks produced more harm than good, there was truth in this charge. Shortly before the Reichstag meeting, however, the Chancellor obtained a letter from Count Zeppelin, declaring that the air weapon had been used to the fullest extent. He published this letter in the *Norddeutsche Allgemeine Zeitung*.[40] Instead of abating criticism, the letter merely fired it. Right-wing newspapers singled out ambiguities in Zeppelin's phrases and charged that, whatever the present employment of airships, the Chancellor was culpable for having ever restricted their use.[41]

Another indication of implacable opposition to him came in the so-called Valentin-Cossmann affair. Professor Veit Valentin, holding a wartime post as historian in the Foreign Ministry, asserted in the presence of Professor Paul Cossmann of Munich that Tirpitz had falsified the numbers of U-boats available in the spring. When Cossmann reported this statement to Tirpitz, the retired Grand

[40] Sept. 16, 1916.
[41] *Résumé de la presse allemande*, no. 47–1 (Sept., 1916), pp. 13–14.

Admiral immediately published a denial. Bethmann sought to still controversy by explaining that while misleading figures had been given out by an officer of the Navy Ministry, Tirpitz himself had not been at fault. Despite this effort, the right-wing press made the most of the episode. Tirpitz's honor had been stained, editors argued; the Foreign Ministry was a center of "abominable intrigue"; the Chancellor should humble himself before the Grand Admiral and, by all means, rid the government of Valentin and his like. As the *Berliner Tageblatt* admitted, the issue was changed from one between Valentin and Cossmann to one between Bethmann and Tirpitz.[42] If the Chancellor were to give in to the U-boat demand, it was clear, he would face no less bitter criticism for his past policy.

When the Reichstag convened on September 26, the right-wing leadership was more determined than ever to bring about the Chancellor's downfall. The U-boat issue was merely their chosen tool. The fact that success in their campaign would mean war with the United States was one they had faced and accepted. Peace hung in part therefore upon the thread of Bethmann's tenure. If the right wing should secure the support of the Center in its move to unseat the Chancellor, an unrestricted U-boat campaign would probably follow in train, and America's declared policies left little doubt in German minds that war would swiftly ensue.

Bethmann was less able to cope with the opposition than he had been in the spring. For one thing, he was tired and lonely. His wife had died just before the war; his eldest son had been killed in Poland.[43] Nearing sixty, he carried a load of duties that would have taxed a man of thirty. No diplomatic message could be sent, no financial measure devised, no administrative ordinance promulgated, without his careful scrutiny. The Chancellery had ceased to be a quiet and pleasant palace; it had become, as Theodor Wolff observed, more like a seedy boardinghouse.[44] An American visitor

tragic depiction [handwritten marginal note]

---

[42] *Ibid.*, 15–21; *Daily Review of the Foreign Press: Weekly Supplement*, Sept. 29, 1916; *Berliner Tageblatt*, Sept. 22, 1916; *Politische Dokumente*, II, 639–643.

[43] Hammann, *Bilder aus der letzten Kaiserzeit*, 74–75.

[44] Wolff, *Der Marsch durch zwei Jahrzehnte* (Amsterdam, 1936), 142.

noted of an evening at Charleville, "The Chancellor was . . . continually going out of the room and returning for a few moments, only to be called away again."[45] Both at Supreme Headquarters and in Berlin he was surrounded by intrigue and opposition. It is little wonder that he confessed to uneasy nerves and that his friends often found him sad and even morose.

It was not weariness that handicapped him, however, so much as it was the uncertainty which resulted from the change in the Supreme Command. Bethmann had hoped for Hindenburg's appointment. Long before Falkenhayn turned against him on the U-boat issue, the Chancellor had become convinced that a new Chief of Staff was needed. As early as December, 1914, he had begun to hope that Hindenburg might be chosen as a replacement.[46] Though the alignment of Falkenhayn with Tirpitz had strengthened this desire, more important was the failure of Falkenhayn's Verdun strategy. In addition to the frightful losses of the offensive itself, the consequent weakening of the eastern front had permitted the Russian general, Brussilov, to open an attack which tore forty miles into Poland and even penetrated the Hungarian frontier. Falkenhayn's planning seemed to have proved its bankruptcy. The general himself was no longer fit for command: his imagination had played itself out; he had lost all self-confidence, and he no longer believed in victory.[47]

Bethmann, increasingly anxious that the general be replaced, saw Hindenburg as the only possible successor. He hesitated nevertheless to take up the subject with the Kaiser. Although Valentini strongly urged him to recommend a change in the Supreme Command, Bethmann felt timid about encroaching on the imperial preserve of military administration. The Civil Cabinet chief admitted, moreover, that the Emperor was somewhat reluctant to see the Chancellor for fear of being asked to make a decision about Falkenhayn's future. Valentini suggested, characteristically, that Bethmann

[45] Grew, *Turbulent Era*, I, 240.

[46] Reichsarchiv, *Der Weltkrieg*, VI, 415–416, VII, 5–6; Zwehl, *Falkenhayn*, 107–114; Schmidt-Bückeburg, *Das Militärkabinett*, 244.

[47] Reichsarchiv, *Der Weltkrieg*, X, 1–2, 293–324, 411–423, especially pp. 420–421.

propose a crown council on some lesser issue, such as the future of Alsace-Lorraine, and then use the opportunity to raise the larger question.[48]

The Chancellor eventually decided to act. Again it was not the U-boat controversy that stood uppermost in his mind. Although Falkenhayn raised that question again from time to time, Bethmann evidently felt secure against him. It was rather the general's seeming mismanagement of the war that overcame the Chancellor's hesitancy. When Andrassy told him that Austria would collapse if Falkenhayn continued to refuse aid against the Russians, Bethmann telegraphed urgently to Charleville. The Kaiser decided to go immediately to Pless, and the Chancellor met him there, along with Hindenburg and Ludendorff. Although Bethmann now denounced the Chief of Staff openly and earnestly, Wilhelm accepted a compromise. Hindenburg was given command over all the eastern front, while Falkenhayn remained in his post. As Valentini noted, "Falkenhayn's influence over the Kaiser was again fully restored." [49]

It was not until after Rumania declared war that the Chancellor had his way. In the meantime Falkenhayn had not only begun openly to attack Treutler, Jagow, and even Valentini, but he had also threatened to force a new battle over the submarine. With the Allied Somme offensive as a solid pretext, he demanded an unrestricted U-boat campaign in the Channel, to interrupt British troop and supply shipments. Holtzendorff industriously supported him. So, in effect, did Admiral Scheer, whose influence was all the greater by reason of his recent success at Jutland. Capelle seemed to waver.[50] The Chancellor had no choice, therefore, but to schedule a new round of conferences at Supreme Headquarters. These

---

[48] Bethmann to Valentini, June 14, 1916, *Kaiser und Kabinettschef*, 229–230; Bethmann to Valentini, July 10, 1916, *ibid.*, 235–236; Valentini to Bethmann, July 15, 1916, *ibid.*, 238–239.

[49] Memo by Valentini, Feb. 17, 1918, *ibid.*, 136–138; Wheeler-Bennett, *Wooden Titan*, 68–69. The fullest account of the change in the Supreme Command is in Reichsarchiv, *Der Weltkrieg*, X, 634–645.

[50] *Ibid.*, XI, 443–444; Holtzendorff to Bethmann, July 7, 1916, German Foreign Ministry Archives (U-boat War); Bethmann to Müller, Aug. 7, 1916, *ibid.*; Grünau to Bethmann, Aug. 8, 1916, *ibid.*; Holtzendorff to Bethmann, Aug. 15, 1916, *ibid.*; Grünau to Bethmann, Aug. 28, 1916, *ibid.*

sessions were scheduled to begin on the 30th of August. On the 27th Rumania declared war.

This event sealed Falkenhayn's fate. The Cabinet chiefs advised the Kaiser with one voice that Hindenburg would have to be called. Valentini telephoned Bethmann, and the Chancellor hurried to Pless. Even before his arrival, the Kaiser had reached his decision. The Rumanian action had upset Wilhelm's delicate nervous balance; he had cried out that the war was lost and that there remained no choice but to make peace. It also scarred his pride, for Falkenhayn had assured him it would not happen, and he had cheerfully repeated the prophecy as his own. Without consulting Falkenhayn, therefore, he summoned Hindenburg to Supreme Headquarters. This by-passing of the Chief of Staff was in itself an act which could be answered only by resignation, but the Emperor additionally notified Falkenhayn of his intention to change the Supreme Command. The general tendered his resignation and immediately departed for Berlin. On the morning of August 29 the Kaiser, Bethmann, Ludendorff, and a number of others gathered in the castle. It was agreed that Hindenburg should become Chief of Staff and Ludendorff First Quartermaster General, sharing the responsibility of the Supreme Command equally with the Field Marshal.[51]

Although the U-boat issue had played only a small part in Bethmann's determination to bring about this change, it is evident that he expected the support of Hindenburg and Ludendorff against the fanatics. He had kept up a regular correspondence with the Field Marshal, and Hindenburg seemed to understand his views much better than Falkenhayn had.[52] Having openly worked for the change in the Supreme Command, moreover, he had reason to feel that Hindenburg and Ludendorff were in his debt. As Valentini commented, "We congratulated ourselves not least for the assurance that now the heretofore untenable relation-

[51] *Kaiser und Kabinettschef*, 139–140; Wheeler-Bennett, *Wooden Titan*, 71–74; Reichsarchiv, *Der Weltkrieg*, XI, 1–2; Colonel M. Bauer, *Der grosse Krieg in Feld und Heimat: Erinnerungen und Betrachtungen* (Tübingen, 1922), 123–124.

[52] These letters are in the German Foreign Ministry Archives (Secret); see also Reichsarchiv, *Der Weltkrieg*, VI, 415–416, and Schmidt-Bückeburg, *Das Militär-kabinett*, 244.

ship between the Supreme Command and the political leadership
would give way to trust and cooperation. How could anything else
be envisioned in view of the intimate and trustful relationship that
had grown up between Hindenburg and Bethmann during the
recent difficult time and especially in view of the energetic intervention of Bethmann with the Kaiser on behalf of the appointment
of Hindenburg!" [53]

Expecting the support of the generals, Bethmann went ahead confidently with the arrangements for a conference on the submarine
question. Even though the new Supreme Command would have
been in office only two days, the debate with the admirals was to
occur on August 31. On the 29th, while the generals were still set-
tling into their new quarters, he held his first private meeting with
them to explain the issues. In the meantime he evidently authorized
Hammann to have the friendly press advertise the Supreme Command's support of his policies, and he indicated that the Reichstag
might be summoned ahead of time so that the opposition's agitation
could be firmly put to rest.[54]

His hopes were shattered. Instead of expressing their complete
trust in his judgment, the generals indicated strong sympathy with
the navy. "We would shout with joy if we could begin the U-boat
war immediately . . . ," Hindenburg said at the full-scale conference
on the 31st. The Rumanian intervention placed a momentary strain
on the army's resources, they admitted, and it would be dangerous
if Denmark and the Netherlands declared war in the near future.
As soon as the Balkan situation had cleared, however, there would
be no further need to fear these small neutrals. After a decisive
campaign against Rumania, Ludendorff asserted, "I shall be obliged
to advise that the U-boat war be carried on." [55] The potentialities
of the United States evidently held even less terror for them than
for Falkenhayn. Instead of being able to count on the generals for

[53] *Kaiser und Kabinettschef*, 140.

[54] Bethmann to Jagow, Aug. 29, 1916, German Foreign Ministry Archives (U-
boat War); Mumm to Montgelas, Aug. 29, 1916, *ibid.*; *Berliner Tageblatt*, Aug. 31,
1916; *Official German Documents*, II, 1158–1159.

[55] Minutes of a conference of Aug. 31, 1916, *Official German Documents*, II,
1154–1163.

support against the admirals and the Reichstag, the Chancellor had
to recognize, on the contrary, that they might at any moment become champions of the submarine.

This fact not only foreshadowed a new and far more uncertain
contest for control of the Kaiser, but it seriously complicated the
forthcoming struggle in the Reichstag. In view of Hindenburg's
immense popularity, Bethmann could not fight him as he had
fought Falkenhayn. If the Kaiser were faced with a choice between
the Chief of Staff and the Chancellor, he would almost certainly
let the Chancellor go. Bethmann could prevent his own defeat, if
at all, only by deceit and artifice, of the kind he had used when it
seemed that Tirpitz was indispensable. He would have to pretend
sympathy with the generals' objectives, and he could not do so if
he had taken an uncompromising stand in public against the submarine. He had no choice but to equivocate.

At the same time he could not seem to yield to the U-boat enthusiasts. Not only would it gain him nothing, as the Zeppelin letters
and the Valentin-Cossmann affair had proved, but it would likely
lose him the indispensable support of the left. Scheidemann did,
after all, have to hold the loyalties of Social Democrats who sympathized with the Independents, and one of his tactics was to lay
great stress on the party's rejection of submarine warfare. It was
the clearest proof, he declared at a party conference in September,
of the majority's profound desire for peace.[56] The Progressives, too,
felt obliged to stand fast, for it was the U-boat issue chiefly that
restrained those in the party who preferred National Liberals to
socialists. If the Chancellor should suddenly abandon the stand that
he had taken in the spring, it might be impossible for Social Democrats and Progressives to continue supporting him on other issues.
The *Zentrum* would undoubtedly swing over to the right, and
Bethmann would be at the mercy of his enemies.

The opening of the Reichstag therefore found Bethmann standing
on slippery ground. He faced the possibility of a new battle within
imperial councils. To be ready for that contest, he had to preserve
the utmost flexibility for himself. Such power as he could throw

[56] *Vorwärts*, Sept. 27, 1916; Präger, *Geschichte der U.S.P.D.*, 109–110.

into the scales against Hindenburg and Ludendorff depended, however, upon his continued control of the Reichstag, for it was that alone which might cause the Kaiser to regard him as indispensable. He had to see to it that his parliamentary opponents did not triumph, either by bringing about a vote of no confidence or by forcing a debate that would demonstrate the extent to which he was mistrusted. Yet he could not offer to his own supporters the kind of confident leadership that he had given them in the spring. He was compelled to depend upon the parties themselves and to hope that the Social Democrats and Progressives, unaided, could hold the backing of the Center.

When the Reichstag reconvened, the Chancellor deliberately steered an evasive course. Addressing the deputies, he declared:

The German statesman who would hesitate to use . . . every available weapon that would really shorten the war ought to be hanged. Gentlemen, I desire you to realize from these words the degree of disgust and contempt that I feel for the assertion that . . . for some dark reasons that fear the light of day, all means that are in any way useful are not employed against every enemy to the fullest possible extent.[57]

He seemed to be yielding to his enemies. In reality, of course, he was seeking only to withdraw himself from the approaching struggle, so that his left-wing allies might bear the burden of fighting against the U-boat. There is no record, unfortunately, of his pre-session conferences with parliamentary leaders, but it does appear that he made clear his own desire to avoid any open debate. The Social Democrats, Progressives, and Centrists cooperated, at any rate, in shifting discussion of the Chancellor's speech to the budget committee. It was announced that the Seniorenconvent had agreed to suspend sittings for a few days while the committee heard secret testimony and debate on the issues that might later be discussed in plenum.[58]

During the budget committee sittings, Bethmann preserved his pretense of neutrality. He did, it is true, restate his earlier objections

[57] *Verhandlungen des Reichstages,* CCCVIII (Sept. 28, 1916), p. 1693.
[58] *Berliner Tageblatt,* Sept. 29, 1916.

and repeat that the submarine fleet was not large enough to under-take a successful campaign. But he tempered these declarations with an admission that U-boats could do considerable damage to British commerce and that prospects were better than they had been in the spring.[59] So ambivalent did he seem that his Progressive allies became alarmed. Haussmann thought him indecisive and perhaps in danger of capitulating to the fanatics.[60]

Bethmann threw the burden of resisting the U-boat demand onto Helfferich. In his weariness and solitude, he had begun to shift more and more responsibility to the energetic young economist, whom he had recently promoted to the Vice Chancellorship. He assigned him the task of arguing the government's case, and Helfferich, who loved the spotlight, allowed himself to be used as the Chancellor's stalking horse. Saying that he was no convinced foe of the submarine, Helfferich admitted that some advantage might come from an unrestricted campaign. He laid out in impressive detail, however, the naval and economic arguments against it, pointing out the relatively small proportion of British tonnage that could be sunk, the gains in manpower as well as money and supplies that would come to the Allies from American intervention, and the critical loss to Germany of food and other imports from neighboring neutrals. He concluded by declaring: "We must bear in mind: if the card of ruthless U-boat war is played, and it doesn't win, then we are lost. Then we are lost for a century." [61]

Despite the Chancellor's apparent vacillation, this statement by Helfferich seemed to rally the government coalition. Newspapers reported that it had made a profound effect upon listeners.[62] The Social Democratic spokesman declared himself unalterably opposed to a U-boat campaign and warned of a proletarian revolution if the right wing persisted in its demand.[63] The Progressives stood with equal firmness. After a twenty-hour caucus, they resolved to

[59] Westarp, *Konservative Politik*, II, 132; Hanssen, *Diary of a Dying Empire*, 146–147.

[60] Haussmann, *Schlaglichter*, 63–64.

[61] His speech is summarized in his own *Der Weltkrieg*, II, 384–390.

[62] *Berliner Tageblatt*, Oct. 5, Oct. 6, 1916.

[63] Westarp, *Konservative Politik*, II, 132.

reject any compromise.[64] It seemed for the moment, moreover, as if the *Zentrum* would also hold fast.

The Center was, of course, the critical and uncertain factor. There were powerful elements within the party who wanted to break with the government, but there were others whose interests would be best served by continued collaboration with the left. Catholic labor unions were conscious of the similarity between their objectives and those of the majority socialists. The *Arbeiter* and the *Holzarbeiter,* two of their journals, had strongly opposed the anti-Bethmann movement within the *Zentrum.*[65] Urban Centrist leaders were aware that a combination between their party and the right would be, in effect, an agrarian coalition, which would subordinate the desires of consumers to those of producers. Outside of South Germany and the Rhineland, moreover, many local Catholic parties were not strong enough to work safely with the right. The Centrists in Prussia, for example, could serve Catholic interests only by combining with other enemies of the dominant Conservatives. Labor spokesmen and many urban and provincial leaders resisted the rightist movement within their party.

At the opening of the budget committee sessions, it had seemed as if these elements were firmly in control. Urban and labor journals had presented an impressively solid front in criticizing the actions of the party in Bavaria. Not only had several local committees passed resolutions upholding the government, but the leader in the Rhineland, where the clerical party held majorities, had also joined in.[66] At a central committee meeting held just before the convening of the Reichstag, these groups had joined in forcing through a resolution which read: "We lend no support to those who wish to overthrow the Chancellor . . . because he is supposed not to be thoroughgoing enough in the matter of the submarine war."[67]

During the course of the committee's meetings, however, the

[64] Haussmann, *Schlaglichter,* 63.
[65] *Daily Review of the Foreign Press,* Sept. 19, Oct. 13, 1916.
[66] Julius Bachem in *Düsseldorfer Tageblatt,* quoted *ibid.,* Oct. 12, 1916.
[67] *Berliner Tageblatt,* Oct. 7, 1916.

Centrists began to waver. On October 5, Erzberger delivered a magnificent speech against the U-boat faction. Everyone wanted to use all weapons to the full, he said, but Germans had to recognize that they could no longer hope for triumph over all their enemies; they had to divide the Allies and make peace first with one then with another. "With that in mind, I ask my colleagues who underestimate America's war strength: How will you make peace with America?" He seemed to stand fast with the socialists and Progressives.[68] Immediately afterward, however, there seems to have been a decisive meeting of the *Zentrum* leaders. Gröber, Spahn, and probably others, refused to remain in a Bethmann-ite coalition. They proposed that the party offer to support the Supreme Command rather than the Chancellor. Erzberger, conscious of the strong feeling in Bavaria and the Rhineland, evidently saw that he could not hold out. He reasoned, in any case, that the Chancellor could not but follow the generals. As he wrote to Hertling, "If Hindenburg should decide in favor of a ruthless U-boat war, in my opinion no Chancellor, no matter who he might be, could take a different position."[69] On October 6 Gröber rose in the budget committee, declaring it to be his party's position that Hindenburg should have the final decision. Erzberger acquiesced by silence. Naval officers in the committee room grinned in triumph.[70]

On the following day, October 7, the entire *Zentrum* contingent united on a resolution saying:

For the political decision concerning the conduct of the war the Chancellor alone is responsible to the Reichstag. The decision of the Chancellor will have to be supported basically by the conclusion of the Supreme Command. If the decision is against the conduct of a ruthless U-boat war, then the Chancellor may be sure of the agreement of the Reichstag.

The coalition of March, 1916, had fragmented.

Bethmann became alarmed. He had already written to Hinden-

[68] Hanssen, *Diary of a Dying Empire*, 150.
[69] Erzberger to Hertling, Oct. 8, 1916, from the Hertling manuscripts (transcript by Prof. Klaus Epstein); cf. Willy Bongard, *Die Zentrumsresolution von 7. Oktober 1916* (Cologne, 1937).
[70] Hanssen, *Diary of a Dying Empire*, 155–156.

burg, asking if he could not use the Field Marshal's authority for a statement that the U-boat war was at the moment both impractical and undesirable. Even though Hindenburg refused, on the ground that the Supreme Command should not be drawn into partisan debates, Bethmann hinted broadly to the committee that any resolution at all would be offensive to the Field Marshal. He proposed that at most the committee should reaffirm its resolution of the previous March.[71] His own effort to use the prestige of the Supreme Command merely confirmed the Centrists in their stand.

The budget committee therefore reported out the *Zentrum* resolution. The Conservatives had opposed it, saying that they would not accept a decision against the U-boat, even if it were endorsed by Hindenburg and Ludendorff. The Social Democrats also resisted, arguing that the resolution in fact made the Supreme Command responsible for a political decision.[72] But neither the National Liberals nor the Progressives could hold out, since neither could afford a break with the Center. It was understood that the Centrists should bring their resolution to the floor of the Reichstag, but it was agreed by a twenty-four to four vote (the three Conservatives and the Independent Social Democrat opposing) that there should be no open debate.[73] On October 11 the *Zentrum* resolution was quietly read to the Reichstag.

The Chancellor could no longer claim to speak in imperial councils as the representative of a Reichstag majority. The Center resolution had indicated that body's confidence in Hindenburg. The opposition, moreover, remained both united and strong. At the end of October, Haussmann commented that the *Fronde* was hardier than he would ever have believed possible.[74] Most important of all, the Chancellor had detached himself from the socialists by failing to give leadership against the opposition. When the Reichstag adjourned at the end of October, Scheidemann wrote in *Vorwärts* that

[71] Bethmann to Hindenburg, Oct. 5, 1916, Westarp, *Konservative Politik*, II, 132; Bethmann to Wahnschaffe, Oct. 10, 1916, *ibid.*, 133.

[72] *Ibid.*, 134.

[73] Bassermann's report, *Verhandlungen des Reichstages*, CCCVIII (Oct. 11, 1916), p. 1704.

[74] Haussmann, *Schlaglichter*, 71.

the government was isolated. It could not govern because there was no party upon whose support it could count. The reputation of the Social Democrats as the government party was false, he declared; "if they had ever been such, they would have ceased to be on 28 October," when the Reichstag was prorogued without having passed a single constructive act.[75]

The Chancellor stood in an almost impossible position. Not only could he no longer count on a majority, but his opponents were henceforth to have a permanent forum, for the Reichstag had agreed to change the budget committee (*Haushaltsausschuss*) into a chief committee (*Hauptausschuss*) and keep it in permanent session.[76] Subject to constant and weakly opposed attack from his parliamentary foes, he faced the probability of a contest over the U-boat question between himself and the Supreme Command.

There remained little hope of preventing an early decision for unrestricted submarine war. Aside from the dim chance that the Chancellor might outmaneuver the slow-witted Field Marshal and his assertive, egotistic associate, there seemed only two faint possibilities of averting an American declaration of war. One lay in the increasing friction between the United States and Britain. Bethmann had long hoped that restraint on his part might allow the latent conflict between English and American interests to come to the surface. In that case the United States might be unable to act against Germany. The other and more promising possibility was of a successful mediation action by Wilson which would bring the entire war to an end. Bethmann began energetically to promote mediation almost as soon as he recognized the mood of the new Supreme Command. Since neither of these last-ditch hopes was realized, it may not be too much to say that the peace between Germany and the United States was lost in the interval between the *Sussex* pledge and the *Zentrum* resolution. After October, 1916, efforts to prevent war were efforts to check a downhill plunge.

[75] *Vorwärts*, Oct. 31, 1916.
[76] *Verhandlungen des Reichstages*, CCCVIII (Oct. 27, 1916), pp. 1864–1866.

PART IV

The Faltering of Anglo-American Friendship

XIV

England: The End of Conciliation

During the first six months of the war, the British government had been sparing in its interference with American trade and rights. Grey had insisted that it was more important to keep the friendship of the United States than to blockade Germany, and he had imposed his views upon the Cabinet. The early policy of conciliating the United States had resulted partly from Grey's own prestige, partly from the patriotic unity that permitted the Cabinet to guide the country, and partly from the preoccupation of the navy with other tasks. By the spring of 1915 all these conditions had begun to change. As a result, the British government progressively intensified its economic war. By 1916 the Cabinet had ceased almost altogether to display any concern for either the interests or the feelings of the United States.

A demand for intensified economic war arose in the spring of 1915. By that time even the hardiest optimists had ceased to expect an early peace. The war in France had become a bloody stalemate. The Russian steamroller had been stopped. The German High Seas Fleet showed no signs of venturing forth for a decisive engagement. With the oceans at last cleared of German raiders, the navy was free to apply economic pressures to the enemy. A force of twenty-four new converted cruisers was soon to be available for patrolling the North Sea, and smaller craft in plenty could guard the Channel and the Downs. Blockade was a traditional weapon of Britain. In view of the fact that other measures were failing to bring decisive results, there was every argument for imposing a blockade on Germany. The only consideration weighing against such a policy was the desirability of avoiding offense to neutrals.

The Admiralty naturally stressed the importance of using naval weapons to the full. Sir John Fisher, the First Sea Lord, complained to journalists of Grey's hypersensitivity to foreign opinion. As early as January 18, 1915, he lunched with the editor of the London *Times* and vented his dissatisfaction with the Foreign Secretary. Not long afterward he held a similar conversation with Lord Riddell, proprietor of the *News of the World*.[1] Although Fisher was so erratic that inferences about him are unsafe, it seems probable that he had already pressed this case upon the First Lord and perhaps also upon the Cabinet. If so, he must have found his civil superiors unresponsive and decided to appeal to the press for support.

When the Germans issued their first submarine decree, the civilians swung toward Fisher's view. Churchill joined the First Sea Lord in asking the Cabinet to approve a wider economic war. Within two weeks of the German proclamation, he had also risen in the House of Commons to promise that the government would soon begin to interfere with enemy imports of food and to restrict all neutral commerce with Germany. A declaration would soon be made, he pledged, "which will have the effect for the first time of applying the full force of naval pressure to the enemy." Although the Cabinet had not yet approved any specific new measures, Grey took the precaution of consulting the French about the timing and content of a new order-in-council.[2]

Newspapers meanwhile demanded that the government fulfill Churchill's promise. The Tory *Morning Post* and *Daily Mail* spoke harshly of the government for not having acted sooner. Although moderate Liberal and Conservative journals were less critical of

[1] John Evelyn Wrench, *Geoffrey Dawson and Our Times* (London, 1955), 118; *Lord Riddell's War Diary*, 58.
[2] *Parliamentary Debates: Commons*, 5th Series, LIX (Feb. 15, 1915), p. 714; Poincaré, *Au service de la France*, VI, 66; the French had already suggested an all-out blockade: Siney, *Allied Blockade*, 64.

the past, they did express delight at Churchill's speech. When the United States promptly proposed that England ease the blockade in return for Germany's abandoning the U-boat, the entire press opposed any such arrangement. "Our policy is settled," said the London *Daily News,* widely regarded as the authentic voice of Liberalism. The *Daily Express,* which spoke for the Conservative leader, Bonar Law, dismissed the proposal as ridiculous.[3]

Since the Admiralty's demand was so evidently supported by public opinion, the Cabinet promptly yielded to it. On February 10, Churchill had offered a draft proclamation, ordering the seizure of all cargoes presumed to be bound for Germany. During the following week, after Churchill made his promise to the House of Commons, debate in the Cabinet was renewed. Asquith reported to the King:

Mr. Churchill and the majority of the Cabinet were strong for the seizure of all cargoes with presumed German destination. The Prime Minister, Sir Edward Grey, and Lord Crewe urged very strongly the importance of not alienating and embittering neutral and particularly American opinion; the proposed reprisals being obviously more injurious to neutral commerce and interests than the more or less illusory German threat.[4]

By February 18 it had been agreed that some step would be taken without delay. The French government was so notified, and Grey gently hinted as much to Page.[5] Although the American compromise proposal caused a brief postponement, the government was ready by March 1 to announce its intention "to detain and take into port ships carrying goods of presumed enemy destination, ownership, or origin."[6]

By order-in-council, a virtual blockade was proclaimed. For legal reasons, the term "blockade" was avoided, but the practical effect ✓

[3] Rappaport, *British Press,* 31; Willis, *England's Holy War,* 199; *Saturday Review,* CXIX (Jan. 16, 1915), 54–55.

[4] Churchill, *World Crisis,* II, 284; Spender and Asquith, *Asquith,* II, 130–131.

[5] Poincaré, *Au service de la France,* VI, 73; *Foreign Relations, Supplement: 1915,* pp. 118–119.

[6] *Ibid.,* 128; *Parliamentary Debates: Commons,* 5th Series, LXX (March 1, 1915), p. 600; Bell, *Englische Hungerblockade,* 220–223.

of the order was to close nearly all water entrances to Germany. Banned trade included, of course, that in foodstuffs and cotton, the two articles which the United States still shipped in quantity to the Central Powers.

Despite this decree, the awakened criticism of the government did not die out. The Tory *Morning Post* and *Daily Mail* continued to upbraid the Liberal Cabinet for having acted so late and also to demand more stringent measures. The *Daily Express,* acting for Bonar Law, also joined in the attack. Underlying this Tory and Conservative demand was a dissent from the premise of Grey's earlier policy. The same journals that took up the cry for a stiffer economic war were those that had reproached the American government for being taken in by the German *Dacia* plot. They expressed pique at the compromise proposal, resentment at America's stated reservations about the order-in-council, and criticism of Wilson's failure to follow up his strict accountability note to Germany. The Foreign Office had officially warned the press not to attack the United States, but the appeal for a stronger blockade was attended nevertheless by a rising strain of anti-Americanism. As the *Nation* pointed out, those who called for a more inflexible blockade were also saying "to hell with the neutrals." [7]

The government, of course, had its defenders. The *Chronicle, Pall Mall Gazette,* and *Westminster Gazette,* as well as the Liberal weeklies, answered the Tories by commenting on the importance of preserving American good will. But, as Irene Cooper Willis has pointed out, they also felt compelled to defend the government by declaring that it had left nothing undone in the way of applying economic pressure to the enemy. News from the battlefronts was so uniformly discouraging that Liberals could counteract criticism only by contending that victory was coming through undramatic and unpublicized measures, such as the relentless application of naval power. "It is easy to forget the magnitude of that influence," said the *Daily News,* "because its greatest achievements are as silent

[7] Rappaport, *British Press,* 24–25, 29–33, 62–64; *Literary Digest,* L (April 3, 1915), 742; *Saturday Review,* CXIX (March 20, 1915), 297; Strachey, *St. Loe Strachey,* 236; *Nation,* XVII (July 24, 1915), pp. 531–533.

as they are crushing. . . . It makes Germany a nation . . . doomed by the mere flux of time." [8] Although Liberal journals defended Grey's premises, they also committed themselves to support of an all-out economic war.

Partly because of the order-in-council and partly because of this Liberal attitude, the blockade issue played a minor part in criticism of the government. During the spring of 1915 dissatisfaction with Asquith's government found expression in attacks upon Churchill. His confident statements about sea power were contrasted with such events as the escape of two German cruisers into the Black Sea, the submarine sinkings in the Channel, and the costly battle at Coronel. Discontent also found voice in the questioning of the Cabinet's efficiency in stockpiling munitions, its wisdom in continuing to rely on voluntary enlistments for the manning of the army, and its judgment in hinting that the liquor trade might be brought under government ownership. Complaints against its tender-hearted blockade policy did appear in newspaper editorials and in private speeches in the House of Commons, but they were minor noises in the rising clamor of opposition.

It was, in any case, a general dissatisfaction with the government, and not protest on a specific issue, that led to the Cabinet crisis of May, 1915. Two distressing events coincided. One was the sudden and somewhat harebrained decision of Fisher to resign as First Sea Lord. Annoyed by Churchill's single-handed management of the Admiralty, Fisher lost his patience altogether when an important dispatch went out without his approval. Writing a curt note of resignation, Fisher vanished from London, and not even a personal recall from the King could locate him. Hard upon this unusual incident followed a dispatch from the *Times* correspondent in France, reporting on the authority of Field Marshal French that the British army faced a woeful shortage of ammunition. The Conservative leaders had already warned Asquith that they would force a debate on the question of Fisher's resignation. The *Times*'s dramatic revelation ensured that any debate would be bitter and diffi-

---

[8] Willis, *England's Holy War*, 195–196, 203; *Literary Digest*, L (Feb. 27, 1915), 418, (March 13, 1915), 540, (April 17, 1915), 866.

cult. The Prime Minister decided, therefore, to avert a breach in the nation's unity by forming a coalition government.[9]

The new government was decidedly less well equipped than its predecessor to resist extremist demands. Grey's feeling about the importance of American friendship was shared, it is true, by several members of the new Cabinet. He himself remained as Foreign Secretary. Asquith continued to be Prime Minister, and Crewe was Lord President of the Council. Two of the new Conservative ministers, Arthur Balfour and Lord Lansdowne, had been early promoters of Anglo-American friendship. But the Cabinet also had in its ranks Austen Chamberlain, Walter Long, Lord Curzon, and Sir Edward Carson, all of whom were stout Tories. Whenever a question of blockade policy came before the Cabinet, their voices were undoubtedly raised against concessions to neutral opinion. Since they possessed the power to dissolve the coalition and form an opposition in the House, their views could not be ignored.

When a new demand arose in the press for intensified economic war, it pressed heavily upon the Cabinet. Tory newspapers began to insist that cotton be placed on the contraband list. Shipments directly to Germany were already being halted under the order-in-council, but large quantities were still reported to be slipping through neutral European ports. The *Daily Mail* opened an intensive campaign to compel the addition of cotton to the contraband list. An announcement that the government had not yet done so was inset daily in the middle of a page in the *Mail*. A typical editorial was that of July 23, 1915, declaring, "Every bale of cotton which reaches Germany means either an Allied cripple or a corpse." The *Morning Post* and such Tory weeklies as the *English Review* and the *Saturday Review* joined in the crusade. So did the London *Times,* the more moderate organ of the *Mail*'s proprietor, Lord Northcliffe, and so eventually did the newspapers that were thought to represent the Conservative leadership—the *Daily Express* for Bonar Law, the Birmingham *Post* for Austen Chamberlain, and

[9] Spender and Asquith, *Asquith,* II, 164–169; Churchill, *World Crisis,* II, 364–397; Blake, *Bonar Law,* 241–247; Lord Beaverbrook, *Politicians and the War, 1914–1916* (2 vols.; London, 1928–1932), I, 100–119.

the London *Daily Telegraph* and Edinburgh *Scotsman* for Arthur Balfour. It seemed as if a powerful combination of Tory and Conservative opinion insisted upon the reversal of Grey's earlier concession to the United States.[10]

The Liberal press, consistent with its defense of the government, raised only feeble resistance. The *Daily News,* for example, still answered criticism of Asquith by insisting that he used sea power undramatically but to the full. "The pressure of sea power," said an editorial of July 31, "though slow to make itself felt, has a deadly and cumulative certainty that is the more irresistible because its operations are so subtle and incalculable." Liberal journals could only counsel the government to meet the Tory demand but to avoid injury to the United States by buying up American cotton. They did not call for taking issue with the opposition on the question of preserving American friendship.[11]

The government, stoutly attacked and weakly defended, succumbed quickly. The Tories in the Cabinet no doubt put forward the demand that Tory newspapers were making outside. If the editorial columns of the *Daily Express,* the *Daily Telegraph,* and the Edinburgh *Scotsman* are any index to the views of the men whose fortunes they promoted, this demand was upheld by the Conservative members of the government. And the Liberals resisted it only by tactics of delay. Grey had gone to Fallodon for two months to rest his failing eyes. Crewe, who managed the Foreign Office for him, was no longer apprehensive of American reprisals. The Russian ambassador, who talked with Crewe in early July, reported to St. Petersburg:

Crewe believed it would be very difficult for the United States to assume an attitude entirely hostile to England, for the better element in American public opinion would not accept such a departure from tradition. There remains the difficulty of the conflict between the trade

[10] Rappaport, *British Press,* 68–69; London *Morning Post,* May 15, May 17, May 20, June 1, June 5, June 13, June 29, July 4, July 11, July 14, July 18, July 31, 1915; London *Times,* July 17, July 21, July 23, July 24, Aug. 11, 1915; *Saturday Review,* CXX (July 10, 1915), 40, (July 24, 1915), 82, (July 31, 1915), 101–102, (Aug. 14, 1915), 149–150.

[11] Willis, *England's Holy War,* 196; Rappaport, *British Press,* 68.

of neutrals and the impossibility of actually and effectively permitting the provisioning of Germany. He holds this question to be neither insoluble nor urgent.[12]

Lloyd George seems to have felt that America was so securely bound to Britain by economic ties that no concessions to her were necessary. Asquith had no choice but to concede the demand made by Tories and Conservatives.

The decision was nevertheless taken slowly. The President of the Board of Trade confessed in the House of Commons that cotton was still reaching Germany in spite of the order-in-council. Asquith admitted that the government was considering some action. Not until after Grey's return to London in mid-summer, however, was any final decision reached. Grey appears to have toyed with alternative schemes, such as coupling a cotton proclamation with a new order-in-council which would establish a legal blockade. Several weeks were allowed, moreover, for informal negotiations with Americans, which resulted in a promise that Britain would buy enough cotton to maintain a price in the United States of ten cents a pound. Only when notified that this arrangement was acceptable to Wilson did the government announce that cotton had been declared contraband.[13] The delay indicated the extent to which Grey could still impose his views, even upon the coalition government. The action itself displayed, on the other hand, the Cabinet's fundamental inability to resist a demand for tightened economic war, even at the expense of some American good will.

After the cotton decision, the blockade ceased for a time to be a political issue. The *Daily Mail*, it is true, greeted the proclamation by declaring, "The Foreign Office has at last confessed to the Cotton Crime. After . . . shuffling on the subject for months, after attacking

[12] Benckendorff to Sazonov, July 1, 1915, *Mezhdunarodnye Otnosheniya*, Series Three, VIII, no. 223.

[13] *Parliamentary Debates: Commons*, 5th Series, LXXII (June 10, 1915), pp. 424–425; Arthur S. Link, "The Cotton Crisis, the South, and Anglo-American Diplomacy, 1914–1915," J. C. Sitterson (ed.), *Studies in Southern History in Memory of Albert Ray Newsome, 1894–1951* (Chapel Hill, N.C., 1957), 136–138; Siney, *Allied Blockade*, 128–129.

the Press, and particularly the *Daily Mail,* it has, 13 months too late, declared Cotton Contraband." [14] But the Tory press turned almost at once to other grievances. The demand for conscription, which Curzon and Carson and Long were advancing in the Cabinet, was taken up as the chief appeal of right-wing newspapers. The government was also criticized for the failure of the Dardanelles offensive. In the autumn, when Bulgaria joined the Central Powers and Serbia was overwhelmed, Tory and Conservative journals alike opened an intensive attack on Grey and the Foreign Office.

Within the House of Commons, meanwhile, there began to crystallize a formidable opposition, eager to exploit any issue that might undermine the Prime Minister. The public leader was Sir Edward Carson, who resigned from the Cabinet in October, protesting the failure to aid Serbia, but the private directorate was a small group of politicians and newspaper editors who began to meet on Monday evenings, usually at Lord Milner's mansion. Known as the "ginger" faction, this group appealed broadly for more energetic prosecution of the war. It commanded the support of the Tory press and also of the London *Times* and the London *Observer,* whose directors were members of its inner council. According to the *Times,* it controlled 150 votes in the House of Commons.[15]

The existence of this opposition had special importance because of the divisions that had arisen in the Cabinet. The Dardanelles issue demonstrated Lloyd George's willingness to range himself with the Conservatives and Tories. He, Bonar Law, Austen Chamberlain, and Carson formed a solid bloc in demanding that troops be withdrawn from the Dardanelles and sent instead to Salonika, where they might be of help to the Serbs. The conscription issue hardened the antagonism between Lloyd George and his Liberal

[14] Aug. 21, 1915, Willis, *England's Holy War,* 218.
[15] Edward Marjoribanks and Ian Colvin, *The Life of Lord Carson* (3 vols.; London, 1932–1936), III, 126; Wrench, *Dawson and Our Times,* 127; Stephen Gwynn (ed.), *The Anvil of War: Letters between F. S. Oliver and His Brother, 1914–1918* (London, 1936), 25; L. S. Amery, *My Political Life* (2 vols.; London, 1953), II, 81–82; London *Times,* March 4, 1916.

colleagues, for he allied not only with the moderate Conservatives but also with such hard-shell Tories as Walter Long and Lord Curzon. Although Lloyd George continued to profess loyalty to Asquith, he also developed a close though clandestine relation with the Tory, Lord Milner, and subsequently joined in the Monday evening sessions of Carson's informal committee.[16]

The result was to give the "ginger" group greater influence than it would have possessed, even if it had controlled the government. Conservatives in the Cabinet had to advocate policies at least partially satisfactory to Carson. If he took issue with the party leaders, charging them with weakness or irresoluteness, he could at the very least split the party and deprive Bonar Law, Chamberlain, and Long of half their influence. Liberals in the Cabinet, on the other hand, had to compromise with Lloyd George, for he was reputed to command 100 votes within the party.[17] If he resigned and ranged himself with Carson, the Liberal leadership would have lost all claim to represent a majority. The alternative to compromise with Carson and Lloyd George was the calling of a general election, an event which both Asquith and Bonar Law regarded as unthinkable. By the beginning of 1916, it was virtually impossible for the Cabinet to stand staunchly against any demand of the "ginger" group.

Grey had meanwhile lost nearly all of his earlier influence within the government. He had been on the losing side in both the Dardanelles dispute and the conscription controversy. When the decision was made to veer from voluntary enlistments toward conscription, he offered to resign, giving as his reason the persistent public attacks upon himself, his friends, and his office. He, the Chancellor of the Exchequer, and the President of the Board of Trade were to leave in a body. But Asquith dissuaded them all with the plea that he would have to "reconsider his own position" if his oldest and best friends should desert him.[18] It does not appear that

---

[16] Blake, *Bonar Law*, Chapters XVII, XVIII; Earl of Ronaldshay, *The Life of Lord Curzon* (3 vols.; London, n.d.), III, 135–137; Wrench, *Dawson and Our Times*, 122–123.

[17] London *Times*, May 31, 1915.

[18] Trevelyan, *Grey of Fallodon*, 370.

the Cabinet itself yielded at all to their views. Since the anti-conscriptionists in the House proved able to muster only 37 votes, it became evident that while Grey and his friends could create a disturbance by resigning, they could not imperil the government.[19]

The Foreign Secretary's inability to maintain his American policy against assault from the "ginger" group was demonstrated early in 1916. The Tory press had kept up a running attack on the weakness of the blockade. In September, 1915, for example, the *Morning Post* had declared of Grey: "It is not his duty to encourage Christmas trade in New York and Philadelphia. England will not allow the Foreign Office to interfere with the affairs of the Admiralty. . . . It is Grey's personal character alone which has hitherto saved him from the consequences of a diplomacy which was anything but brilliant. . . . Let him touch the Fleet and nothing in the world can save him." [20] Carson announced the "ginger" group's opposition to the Foreign Secretary's blockade policy in a letter written in December. "It is only by using every ounce of power and advantage which our naval supremacy gives us," he declared, "that we can successfully bring the war to a conclusion in the shortest time, and I believe the nation would greatly resent any relaxation on any ground of the principles of blockade." [21]

Grey was prepared to fight for the principle of seeking to preserve American good will. He circulated a White Paper which defended the economic war as it had been thus far conducted:

It is already successful to a degree which good judges both here and in Germany thought absolutely impossible, and its efficiency is growing day by day. It is right to add that these results have been obtained without any serious friction with any neutral Government. . . . There is a great danger when dealing with international questions in concentrating attention exclusively on one point in them, even if that point be as vital as is undoubtedly the blockade of Germany.[22]

[19] *Journals of the House of Commons*, CLXX (Jan. 19, 1916), p. 340; London *Times*, Jan. 20, Jan. 21, 1916; London *Morning Post*, Jan. 21, 1916.

[20] Sept. 1, 1915.

[21] Colvin, *Carson*, III, 129.

[22] "Statement of the Measures adopted to Intercept the Sea-Borne Commerce of Germany," Cd. 8145.

But the navy was not prepared to accept this reasoning. Admiral Jellicoe wrote hotly to the Lords of the Admiralty asserting that Germany was still obtaining essential imports in large quantities. "It seems evident," he declared, "that we are not using to the full the weapon that could materially shorten the war." Although Grey defended himself, he seems not to have raised the issue in Cabinet.[23]

It was carried instead to the public and the House of Commons. The "ginger" group and the Tory press launched an all-out attack on the Foreign Secretary's conduct of the blockade. The *Morning Post* published statistics, evidently obtained from naval sources, on the leakage of strategic materials to Germany. Leading articles there and in the *Daily Mail* spelled out the implication of these figures: the Foreign Office was allowing legalism or sentimentality to override military necessity. Writers for Tory magazines turned a neat point by contending that Britain should be at least as ruthless as the Union had been during the Civil War. While the *Times* did not fulminate like the *Morning Post* and *Daily Mail,* it suggested that there might be merit in the right-wing argument. Certain Conservative organs followed the same moderate line, and so did important Liberal journals which had attached themselves to the cause of Lloyd George.[24] The effects of this agitation were displayed in mass meetings, called to protest the weakness of the blockade. Picketers paraded by the Houses of Parliament carrying placards for "More Push and Go." Liberal members of the Commons rose to ask the Foreign Secretary "how much longer our Navy is to be crippled by the Foreign Office, the war prolonged, and many more thousands of our men sacrificed?"[25] It was evident that the call for stiffened economic warfare had wide appeal.

The government sought not to meet these attacks but to neutral-

[23] Guichard, *Blocus naval,* 53–54.
[24] *Literary Digest,* LII (Feb. 19, 1916), 428–429; Rappaport, *British Press,* 77–78; London *Morning Post,* Jan. 19, Jan. 20, Jan. 27, Jan. 28, Jan. 31, 1916; London *Times,* Jan. 21, Feb. 21, 1916.
[25] London *Times,* Feb. 5, Feb. 12, 1916; *Parliamentary Debates: Commons,* 5th Series, LXXVIII (Jan. 20, 1916), 582, (Jan. 26, 1916), 1279–1295; Viscount Sandhurst, *From Day to Day, 1916–1921* (London, 1929), 24, 31.

ize them. When Grey defended himself on the floor of the House, he stressed the success which had been achieved, and he denied that any material concessions had been made to neutrals. Asquith meanwhile held a press conference in which he presented the same arguments in even more vigorous form. The government did not undertake to defend the importance of preserving American good will.[26]

The Cabinet, indeed, made concessions to the public demand. Grey resigned responsibility for economic warfare. A new Ministry of Blockade was created under the direction of Lord Robert Cecil. Although Cecil had served as Grey's Undersecretary, he was an advocate of uncompromising economic warfare, and he chose as his own Undersecretary in the new Ministry Eyre Crowe, who had long been urging more resolute measures, who was scornful of the pro-Americans in the Foreign Office, and who was intimate with the editorial board of the *Morning Post*.[27] An example of the spirit which animated the new Ministry was an exchange in the House in April, 1916. A member of the "ginger" group asked Cecil if more items could not be added to the contraband list. The Minister replied that some certainly could and that he intended to publish a new and larger list without delay.[28] From that time forward the government gave the "ginger" group little opportunity to revive the blockade issue.

The new Ministry applied every screw to neutral trade. Not only did Cecil lengthen the contraband lists, but he abolished every lingering distinction between absolute and conditional contraband. He had himself been a resolute foe of the Declaration of London when Grey brought it forward in 1909.[29] Almost as soon as he took office, he set about to end all pretense that wartime measures were merely "modifications and additions" to the Declaration. He met

[26] *Parliamentary Debates: Commons*, 5th Series, LXXVIII (Jan. 26, 1916), 1315–1327; *Lord Riddell's War Diary*, 150–151.

[27] Lloyd George, *War Memoirs*, II, 123–124; Gwynn, *Spring-Rice*, II, 317–318; Hale, *Publicity and Diplomacy*, 286.

[28] *Parliamentary Debates: Commons*, LXXXI (April 5, 1916), 1198–1199.

[29] Guichard, *Blocus naval*, 60.

some resistance in France, but he soon won abandonment of the conditional contraband category, and by mid-summer he had persuaded the ally to void the Declaration.[30]

Other measures were adopted. Rationing was extended. The Allies had begun in 1915 to limit the imports of neutrals neighboring Germany, using prewar figures as indexes of the quantities that these nations actually needed. Eyre Crowe had been a chief advocate of this device, and the new Ministry of Blockade extended its application.[31] An interallied rationing committee was set up to coordinate English and French restrictions. The new Ministry also made greater use of the weapon of blacklist. From the beginning of the war the British and French governments had been circulating confidential lists of neutral firms that had traded with the enemy.[32] Cecil insisted that these lists be consolidated and published so that all Allied merchants could be prevented from dealing with blacklisted concerns and so that Allied vessels could refuse to carry their products.[33] The new Ministry additionally began to issue white lists of firms that had agreed not to traffic with the Germans. Provisioners in British overseas ports were instructed to deny bunker coal to shipowners who declined to meet the requirements of this white list.[34] Practically no measure of economic war that intelligence could devise was left unused by Cecil and his ministry.

In thus intensifying the economic war, Cecil was almost ostentatiously unregardful of American interests and feelings. Since the United States had so ardently defended the Declaration of London in 1914, he must have recognized that the total abandonment of it would irritate American lawyers. He must also have seen that adding American firms to the blacklist would offend the United States government. He could have endeavored to avoid trouble by keeping American concerns on a confidential list, as was done with Swiss firms, but he chose instead to publish a blacklist that included

---

[30] *Ibid.*, 59–62; Cochin, *Organisations de blocus*, 20–22; Siney, *Allied Blockade*, 181–185.

[31] *Ibid.*, chapters V and VII, *passim.*

[32] *Ibid.*, 144–145.

[33] Cochin, *Organisations de blocus*, 21–22; *Diary of Lord Bertie*, II, 9–10.

[34] Guichard, *Blocus naval*, 72–74; Siney, *Allied Blockade*, 162–164.

eighty-five American names.[35] While the Foreign Office sought slowly to cajole the American government out of its resulting anger, Cecil gave an interview to a reporter, declaring the blacklist to be not only perfectly proper but a weapon which Britain intended to use on a larger scale.[36] It would have been very difficult for any critic to substantiate a charge that the Ministry of Blockade was hypersensitive to American opinion. And there is no evidence that the Ministry was checked in any way by other departments of the government. The Chief of the Imperial General Staff commented ruefully that the actions of the navy were never questioned by the Cabinet.[37]

It is evident that by the end of 1916 the forces in Britain working for the preservation of Anglo-American harmony had grown very weak. During 1914 Grey had been able to control the Cabinet, and the Cabinet in turn had been free to balance the interest of preserving Anglo-American friendship against the interest of conducting an economic war. By 1916 Grey's influence had almost evaporated, and the Cabinet had become a plaything of public opinion, yielding lest resistance cause its own centrifugal pressures to explode.

No one can say, of course, what the action of the government might have been had the United States demanded modification of the blockade. Powerful segments of public and parliamentary opinion would undoubtedly have pressed the government to defy the demand. Despite efforts by the censors to keep anti-Americanism out of the press, the columns of Liberal and Conservative, as well as Tory, journals had increasingly displayed a bias against the United States.[38] At the beginning of 1917, the editor of the London

[35] *Foreign Relations, Supplement: 1916*, pp. 423–424; Cochin, *Organisations de blocus*, 102–105; Siney, *Allied Blockade*, 146.

[36] London *Times*, Oct. 6, 1916; *Foreign Relations, Supplement: 1916*, p. 454.

[37] Repington, *The First World War*, I, 392–393.

[38] Rappaport, *British Press*, especially 126–127; a good example is provided by the contrast between two articles both entitled "The American Point of View" in the *Saturday Review*, CXX (Nov. 13, 1915), 462–464, and CXXI (Feb. 12, 1916), 149–150. Both attempt to explain America's rationale, but the latter is much more astringent and unsympathetic.

Times wrote to his American correspondent: "Personally I believe that nothing would be so popular here as a real anti-American outburst and the sacking, let us say, of poor old Page's house. . . . In my judgment it is a real and very rare example of the *restraining* influence of the press." [39] Had the government elected to conciliate the United States, there might have been a public outcry comparable to that aroused in Germany by Bethmann's U-boat policy. Britain's Prime Minister might have had no easier time than Germany's Chancellor in pursuing a sane course.

Had the British government been faced with a choice between defying or placating the United States, it is not at all certain that its decision would have gone against defiance. Grey remained as Foreign Secretary until the end of 1916. He would have battled for a conciliatory policy. It seems probable that certain Liberals and elder Conservatives would have supported him; so probably would Asquith. But Grey and all his potential allies, including the Prime Minister, were minor figures. The two most powerful members of the Cabinet were Lloyd George and Bonar Law. As the latter's biographer has pointed out, Asquith had become little more than an umpire between these two. He retained his title only because they could not unite.[40] And it is far from certain that Lloyd George and Bonar Law would not have favored a defiant rather than a conciliatory policy.

It would have required dramatic action by Wilson to make either fear a war with America. Ever since the *Lusitania* incident, it had been assumed that the United States was morally allied with the Entente.[41] The growing anti-Americanism of the public was partly due to Wilson's continued inaction and to his maintenance of an appearance of neutrality. The *American Press Résumés* submitted periodically to the Cabinet did warn, it is true, of American vexation with the blockade, but they also advised confidently that this vexa-

[39] Wrench, *Dawson and Our Times*, 147.

[40] Blake, *Bonar Law*, 322.

[41] See, for example, London *Times*, May 10, 1915; Rappaport, *British Press*, *passim*.

tion was not apt to take practical form. The public, the press, and the government in the United States, the *Résumés* said complacently, recognized the country's economic dependence on the Allies.[42] Spring-Rice confirmed this estimate, and so did Americans who were friendly with members of the government. Since these Americans were by and large ardently pro-Ally Republicans, they told their English acquaintances that Wilson's neutrality was not popular at home, that the President would not dare to go against the pro-Ally feeling of the American public by taking any real action against Britain, and that Wilson himself was spineless and effete. Discriminating Englishmen recognized the bias of these informants, but the general impression remained that a determined American stand against Britain was almost out of the question.[43] Lloyd George and Bonar Law undoubtedly took this view.

There remained, of course, the possibility of economic reprisals by Wilson. He could conceivably embargo shipments of munitions. The Cabinet had been warned repeatedly of the strong pacifist and neutralist movement for such an embargo. The President could also block shipments of other supplies, such as food and gasoline. Or he could deny credit to the Allies. Had Lloyd George and Bonar Law been confronted with the choice between placating or defying the United States, they would have had to take account of these possibilities.

By the end of 1916, however, they no longer had reason to be terrified by them. The arms embargo movement had been a source of real concern during 1915, when the Allies suffered a critical shortage of shells and explosives. Kitchener had been sufficiently worried that even after the *Lusitania* incident he transferred some munitions orders to Canada.[44] Lloyd George, as Minister of Munitions, had concentrated on building factories in the United King-

---

[42] *American Press Résumé*, Jan. 28, Feb. 5, Aug. 5, 1916, Peterson, *Propaganda for War*, 175–176, 193.

[43] Repington, *The First World War*, I, 309–310; *Diary of Lord Bertie*, II, 12, 43–44; Sandhurst, *From Day to Day*, 10–11.

[44] Spender and Asquith, *Asquith*, II, 90.

dom. Seventy-three had gone up during 1915 alone, and by the end of 1916 these plants and those of the Commonwealth were capable of meeting nearly all Allied requirements.[45] An American embargo could be inconvenient but not disastrous.

Embargoes on other supplies could be more damaging. The Allies faced a critical shortage of food for 1917. But at the end of 1916 the United Kingdom had four months' supplies in its warehouses, and the Cabinet was already on the verge of drastic legislation, converting idle land to agricultural purposes. An American embargo on wheat could cause temporary suffering—a turnip winter like Germany's—but not calamity. Embargoes on other supplies, except gasoline, could be of actual advantage. The Cabinet was already concerned about the amount of shipping engaged in the North Atlantic trade, and Lord Curzon was advocating stringent import restrictions in order to free tonnage. The chief obstacle to such action was the probability of public discontent, and if Wilson imposed embargoes he would simply free the Cabinet from an onerous responsibility.[46] Gasoline, which was in critically short supply, was a different matter, but, on the whole, Lloyd George and Bonar Law had little reason for fearing such embargoes as Wilson might impose.

There remained the possibility of credit restrictions. The Allies had already borrowed nearly two billion dollars in the United States. At the end of 1916, representatives of the Treasury were endeavoring to arrange for further loans to be secured not by collateral but merely by the credit of the British government. The importance of these negotiations to Lloyd George was reflected in a memorandum which he drafted in the autumn of 1916, saying: "Our dependence upon America is growing for food, raw material and munitions. We are rapidly exhausting the securities negotiable in America. . . . The problem of finance is the problem of victory." From these often

---

[45] Lloyd George, *War Memoirs*, II, 17–109; Christopher Addison, *Four and a Half Years: A Personal Diary from June 1914 to January 1919* (2 vols.; London, 1934), I, 203.

[46] Lloyd George, *War Memoirs*, II, 371–378; Ronaldshay, *Curzon*, III, 138–141; Viscount Long of Wraxhall, *Memories* (London, 1923), 257.

quoted sentences it might be inferred that a threat of financial reprisals would have forced Lloyd George to favor a policy of conciliation.[47]

Such a conclusion is not necessarily justified. The document from which these lines are taken was a draft of a memorandum to be handed the French representatives at the Chantilly conference of November 15–16, 1916. Its object was to persuade the ally that the proper strategy for 1917 was concentration of forces in the Balkans, where a dramatic victory might be won. The argument which Lloyd George put forward was that American bankers were reluctant to finance a stalemated war. "If victory shone upon our banners our difficulties would disappear," he wished to declare. "Success means credit; financiers never hesitate to lend to a prosperous concern: but business which is lumbering along amidst great difficulties and which is making no headway in spite of enormous expenditures will find the banks gradually closing their books against it." The meaning of his final sentence was "The problem of finance is the problem of victory . . . [in the field in 1917] not debatable victory, but unchallengeable victory; not victory won here countered by disaster there." Lloyd George knew, moreover, that the French Ministry of Finance was gravely concerned about American credits. He may have been appealing to the ally's fears rather than stating his own. The position taken even by his timid and pessimistic colleague, the President of the Board of Trade, was that whatever America did, Britain would still be able to command unlimited credit elsewhere.[48] The evidence suggests, in other words, that the possibility of financial reprisals by the United States need not have terrified the dominant members of the Cabinet any more than the possibility of other economic sanctions.

Since the United States did not make demands upon Britain or issue threats comparable to those provoked by the submarine war, the Cabinet's probable reactions must remain surmises. It is possible to say that the state of public opinion, the domestic political situation, the estimates of American attitudes, and the economic posi-

[47] Lloyd George, *War Memoirs*, II, 340.
[48] Repington, *First World War*, I, 431.

tion of Britain were not favorable to a conciliatory policy. Circumstances changed, of course, in the winter of 1916–1917. A *rapprochement* between Lloyd George and Bonar Law at last brought down the Asquith government. Lloyd George became Prime Minister; Carson took office as First Lord of the Admiralty; Lord Milner and Lord Curzon became members of the inner Cabinet. The "ginger" group thus acquired a moderating sense of responsibility. The opening by Germany of an unrestricted U-boat campaign meanwhile multiplied the economic difficulties of the Allies. After January, 1917, conditions perhaps ceased to favor an intransigent policy.

From the spring of 1915 to the spring of 1917, however, the preservation of tranquillity in Anglo-American relations had turned largely upon the policies of the United States. Britain had gradually ceased to do anything toward avoiding irritation or injury to American interests. The reaction of the British government to a demand that it lighten the economic war was problematical. The absence of friction resulted from the fact that the United States did not make such a demand and did not reinforce its complaints with threats of retaliation.

XV

Wilson and the Blockade

Despite Britain's shift away from conciliation, the United States only gradually took a resolute stand against the blockade. Six months were allowed to elapse before the order-in-council of March, 1915, was challenged. The cotton proclamation produced only a momentary crisis. It was summer of 1916 before consideration was given to pressing and threatening Britain as Germany had been pressed and threatened earlier. In the submarine controversy the sequence from denunciation to demand to threat took only fourteen weeks. In the blockade dispute it required more than a year and a half.

The United States was remarkably slow in responding to the blockade decree of March, 1915. Wilson's initial response was not a protest but merely a note asserting his expectation that Britain would not violate the traditional principles of international law. Lansing advocated something stronger, so that America's legal position would be made clear from the outset. He suggested that Britain might even appreciate such action, remembering that she herself would probably be neutral in future wars. He did not have in mind a genuine protest. As he explained, *"The declaration of neutral rights will amount to a reservation rather than cause a relaxation in the enforcement of the Order in Council."* [1] But Wilson would not approve even such mild action as Lansing proposed.

[1] Memo by Lansing, March 24, 1915, *Lansing Papers,* I, 290.

"We are face to face with *something they are going to do,*" he commented, "and they are going to do it no matter what representations we make." [2]

Even though Britain's blockade violated international law, as Americans interpreted it, it was six months before any further formal action was taken. The Department of State made representations about individual cases, sometimes using relatively strong language. Lansing warned that if Britain did not mend her ways she would have to expect an open protest. "The course pursued by Great Britain has produced widespread irritation and dissatisfaction through this country," he cabled Page, "and unless some radical change is made, the situation will become so serious politically that it will be difficult, if not impossible, to find a solution." House meanwhile sent more tactful warnings to Grey and other acquaintances in England.[3] The possibilities of informal arrangements with the British were thus explored to the fullest possible extent.

This method yielded some results. In individual cases it was often possible to obtain some satisfaction for aggrieved shippers or exporters. When it was announced confidentially that cotton would be placed on the contraband list, House and two of his friends negotiated an arrangement for British purchases to stabilize the price at ten cents a pound. Since the order-in-council of March had already affected the cotton trade, the result of this agreement was to improve the situation of American growers and exporters. Certainly it was far more effective than the formal protest that both Wilson and Lansing had thought of when the news first arrived.[4] But arrangements of this kind could only be palliative, for the blockade necessarily resulted in a serious curtailment of American trade with neutral Europe.

In late October the United States openly declared her opposition to the principles of the blockade. A note of protest had first been

[2] Wilson to Bryan, March 24, 1915, *ibid.,* 288–289.
[3] *Foreign Relations, Supplement: 1915,* pp. 473–474; *Intimate Papers,* II, 56–57, 60–62, 63–64; House to Grey, April 12, 1915, House Papers.
[4] Baker, *Wilson,* V, 369–370, 377–378; *Lansing Papers,* I, 301–302; Lansing to Wilson, Aug. 7, 1915, Wilson Papers; Link, "The Cotton Crisis, The South, and Anglo-American Diplomacy, 1914–1915," *loc. cit.,* 136–138.

worked out in July.[5] After the *Arabic* crisis cleared, the note was put in final form. Wilson added a few flourishes, and it was dispatched on October 21.[6] Though phrased so politely and technically as to make dull headlines, it amounted to a categorical denunciation of the Allied economic war. It insisted, in effect, that Britain did wrong in conducting search in port instead of at sea and in detaining neutral cargoes without clear proof of enemy destination. It asserted that the decisions of British prize courts could not be binding upon Americans. As Grey commented, "if we admitted all its contentions, it would be tantamount to admitting that, under modern conditions, we could not prevent Germany from trading, at any rate through neutral ports, as freely in time of war as in time of peace. . . . I am convinced that the real question is . . . whether we are to do what we are doing or nothing at all." [7]

This note resembled the strict accountability note to Germany. It made a strong case against the blockade, but it did not demand that Britain give up her practices. Nor did it suggest any measures of retaliation that the United States might employ if Britain remained obdurate. It was a statement of attitude and not of policy.

The President continued to rely upon the method of private negotiation, hoping that Britain would voluntarily mend her conduct. He retained some of his earlier feeling that Anglo-American differences were not matters of principle. When no real improvement occurred after the note of protest, he came to suspect that the diplomatic machinery was at fault. He concluded that Spring-Rice was incompetent and that Page was not representing the American viewpoint with sufficient vigor. Since House had already been discussing with him the possibility of a new peace mission, he decided to send the colonel to London at once. Although the President was keenly interested in the mediation scheme, he sped the colonel on his journey chiefly because of his dissatisfaction with Britain. "His reasoning," House noted, "is that Great Britain is so inadequately

[5] Diary, July 15, 1915, Anderson Papers.

[6] *Foreign Relations, Supplement: 1915*, pp. 578–601; 763.72112/1861, State Department Archives.

[7] Grey to House, Nov. 11, 1915, *Intimate Papers*, II, 79–80.

represented here that it is essential that we get in better communication with them. . . . He is evidently not satisfied with existing conditions, particularly in regard to our relations with the Allies, and he thinks I may materially strengthen our position by this trip." [8]

The result of House's mission was merely to demonstrate that informal negotiation could no longer bridge the differences between America and Britain. The colonel employed all the arguments that had once seemed effective. He explained that only interference with American trade stood in the way of complete harmony between the two governments, and he asked his English friends if any interest could be of as much moment as the friendship of the United States. He found Grey as sympathetic as ever. The Foreign Secretary said to him, indeed, that he would be willing to give up the blockade altogether if it were necessary to keep America's friendship, even though the result might be England's defeat. But the colonel quickly sensed that Grey was no longer a dominating figure and that the new powers in the Cabinet did not share Grey's views. Lloyd George showed no disposition to compromise. The issues between London and Washington, he said, would dissolve only when peace was restored or when the United States intervened. [9]

Since House's mission failed to achieve any modification of the blockade, the United States was left in an embarrassing position. With the war evidently to continue for months if not years, the government had but three broad alternatives. It could abandon its earlier stand and acquiesce in Britain's alterations of international law. It could continue to uphold the law but agree to defer all settlements until the end of the war, which would have the same practical effect. Or it could demand that Britain change her ways and threaten reprisals if she failed to do so.

Wilson ultimately chose the middle course. He did in fact acquiesce in the blockade. Although the Department of State continued to make representations about specific cases, the President accepted

[8] Diary, Dec. 15, 1915, House Papers.
[9] *Intimate Papers*, II, 112–134; diary, Jan. 8, 1916, House Papers.

the limitation of American trade with neutral Europe. He complained bitterly of Britain's conduct, but he adhered to the principle that he had worked out when first confronted with simultaneous threats from the submarine and the blockade. As he summarized it in September, 1916, when accepting renomination for the Presidency: "property rights can be vindicated by claims for damages when the war is over, and no modern nation can decline to arbitrate such claims; but the fundamental rights of humanity cannot be. The loss of life is irreparable." [10] To the orders-in-council abandoning the Declaration of London, extending the contraband list, and ending the distinction between absolute and conditional contraband, the United States replied curtly, reserving her rights and promising future legislation.[11]

Though Wilson had decided not to press economic issues, he was not prepared to suffer British injuries against American prestige or, in his favorite term, her honor. The blacklist did relatively little damage to business, but the President saw the inclusion of American firms as an insult. In outrage he wrote to House that he might ask Congress for power to forbid loans and embargo exports. With these weapons in hand he might be able to compel Britain's respect.[12] The colonel urged him to be cautious. He might notify the British government that he was considering such action, House suggested, without actually moving to obtain the power. But Wilson no longer trusted pure negotiation. The colonel himself had come to the conclusion that the United States could influence Britain only by brandishing a club, and the President could not help reaching a similar conclusion.

Wilson decided to move a short step in the direction of a firmer policy. Working with Polk, the Counselor of the State Department, he swiftly prepared a sharp note of protest. Lansing, who had not been well, was resting at his home in Watertown, New York. House,

[10] *Public Papers*, IV, 282.
[11] *Foreign Relations, Supplement: 1916*, pp. 362, 446–447.
[12] Wilson to House, July 23, 1916, Baker, *Wilson*, VI, 312; *Intimate Papers*, II, 314–315.

who never could bear the Washington summer, was secluded at Sunapee, New Hampshire. Polk, the President's nearest adviser, was himself convinced that the time had come to stand up to the British. The note which he prepared under the President's general direction was, as a result, very strong indeed. It did not contain an explicit threat, but it came very near to doing so. Calling attention, "in the gravest terms, to the many serious consequences to neutral rights and neutral relations . . . ," the note declared, "It is manifestly out of the question that the Government of the United States should acquiesce in such methods or applications of punishment to its citizens." [13]

Wilson also elected to warn the British that he might invoke economic sanctions if they failed to mend their behavior. He had been troubled all along by uncertainty about what action he could take against the Allies. As he had confessed to Bernstorff, he could not hint at war, if only because nobody would believe him.[14] When working out the blacklist note, he discussed with Polk the possibility of obtaining power to limit imports and exports. When Lansing returned to Washington, the President obtained suggestions for appropriate legislation. He then put the matter in the hands of the Postmaster General, and by early September the law had been enacted. The President obtained discretionary power to ban imports and to deny clearance for vessels.[15] Although the scope of his authority was uncertain, it was clear that if he chose he could stop the importation of any and all goods from the Allied states, deny clearance to ships that refused to carry goods for blacklisted firms, or in effect embargo the export of munitions or any other products by refusing clearance to vessels carrying such cargoes. Under these acts

[13] Diary, July 26, 1916, Private Papers of Frank L. Polk, Yale University Library; 763.72112/2757-2758, State Department Archives; *Foreign Relations, Supplement: 1916*, pp. 421-422.

[14] Bernstorff to Jagow, July 13, 1916, German Foreign Ministry Archives (General); Bernstorff, *My Three Years in America*, 238.

[15] Diary, July 26, 1916, Polk Papers; Lansing to Wilson, Aug. 26, 1916, 763.72112/2898, State Department Archives; desk diary, Lansing Papers; Polk to Lansing, July 28, 1916, *ibid.*; United States, *Statutes at Large*, XXXIX, pp. 798, 800; New York *Times*, Sept. 9, Sept. 10, 1916.

the President had the power to threaten the Allies with reprisals short of war.

He made cautious use of his new ability to threaten sanctions.
In discussing the blacklist with the British ambassador, Polk did
warn of possible reprisals.[16] After the retaliatory legislation had
been passed, however, Wilson would not allow the State Department to make threats. Lansing proposed an informal warning. It
would be possible, he suggested, to write the American embassy in
London, stating that the President would have no choice but to
make use of his retaliatory powers if the British failed to make
concessions. The chargé d'affaires could simply leave a copy of
this message at the Foreign Office. It would not be an official note
but simply a private warning. Even so, the President rejected the
proposal. Such a message "might change the whole face of our
foreign relations," he observed. "Therefore I think it would be most
unwise." [17]

Wilson confined himself to sly and noncommittal warnings.
Walter Page had been recalled for consultations. When Wilson
finally talked with him, he asked the ambassador to tell the British
government that he would make no use of his new powers until
after the Presidential election. "But he hinted," Page noted, "that
if there were continued provocation afterward . . . he would." Wilson felt that he had "left nothing to be desired in the way of ex-
plicitness or firmness of tone." [18] Page, he felt sure, would warn the
British government, and he asked House to write Grey, adding
emphasis to the message that Page would bring.[19] But he did not
render any kind of ultimatum. He did not stake the dignity of the
United States upon a demand which Britain would then have the
option of accepting or rejecting.

He postponed any action at all while the Presidential campaign
was at its height. Confessing publicly that it would be "practically
impossible for the present Administration to handle any critical

[16] *Foreign Relations, Supplement: 1916*, pp. 411–412.
[17] *Lansing Papers*, I, 314–319.
[18] Hendrick, *Page*, II, 186; *Lansing Papers*, I, 319.
[19] Wilson to House, Oct. 10, 1916, House Papers.

matter concerning our foreign relations," he advised Lansing to confine the work of the State Department to routine matters, since political considerations might exert an unconscious influence on any action taken before election day.[20] In the meanwhile the British government had time to make concessions which would free the President from any need to move toward demands and threats.

Britain failed to make use of this opportunity. Grey did promise to whittle down the number of American firms on the blacklist. Page reported that the British government thought its publication to have been a mistake, but there were no further indications of a disposition toward concession.[21] Answering complaints about the bunkering agreements, indeed, Cecil suggested that the best arrangement would be for American ships to coal at other than British ports in the West Indies.[22] These indications of intransigence did nothing to reduce the President's vexation.

His advisers cautioned him against any precipitate action. Lansing, who had returned to duty in August, was apprehensive lest the President bring on an Anglo-American crisis. He jotted in his diary during September:

Nothing in our controversies with Great Britain must be brought to a head. We must keep on exchanging notes because if we do not we will have to take radical measures. . . . Nothing . . . can move me from my fixed purpose to remain on friendly terms with Great Britain.

The real danger, the one which I fear, is that the President's resentment at British invasions of our rights will continue to increase. It is already very bitter and he even discusses bringing that Government "to book". . . .

I only hope that the President will adopt the true policy which is "Join the Allies as soon as possible and crush the German Autocrats." If he takes drastic measures against Great Britain, he will never be forgiven. . . .

As to my own position, I will never sign an ultimatum to Great Britain.[23]

[20] Address at Shadow Lawn, Sept. 30, 1916, *Public Papers*, IV, 330; *Lansing Papers*, I, 319; Baker, *Wilson*, VI, 353.
[21] *Foreign Relations, Supplement: 1916*, pp. 455–456, 484.
[22] *Ibid.*, 480.
[23] Entry dated September, 1916, Lansing Papers.

House, whose views were not unlike the Secretary's, was equally alarmed. Returning to Washington after the election, he found the President's temper so high as to need some neutralization. He noted in his diary that he, Polk, and Lansing would have to "keep in close touch ... until the skies are clear. We must do team-work and keep our wits about us. We not only have foreign countries to deal with, but the President must be guided. ... His tendency to offend the Allies ... is likely to lead us into trouble with them. If we are to have war, let it be with Germany by all means."[24] Both he and the Secretary of State worked on Wilson in order to prevent his rushing into a crisis.

Although neither Lansing nor House could curb the President's anger, Wilson moved nevertheless with shrewdness and caution. Even after the election had been safely won and he had recovered from the exertions of the campaign, he still made no open threat against Britain. The Secretary of Commerce had advised him that the retaliatory powers, if invoked, could hurt the United States more than the Allies.[25] If imports from Britain and France were blocked, these nations could in turn restrict exports to America, and since the British Commonwealth was the sole source of many essential items, the American economy might be seriously damaged as a result. If the President denied clearance to ships, he would merely reduce the amount of tonnage available for America's own export trade. If he embargoed the export of munitions, he would deprive Americans of an annual quarter billion dollars' worth of business without appreciably injuring the Allies, for they had taken the precaution of building emergency plants and stores. If he embargoed wheat, which the Allies did need desperately, he would depress the domestic price and raise an outcry among the nation's entire farm population. "We can attack their commerce," he concluded, "but our own commerce will unavoidably suffer in consequence even more than it has suffered from the restrictions placed on it by the countries at war."

[24] Diary, Nov. 17, 1916, House Papers.
[25] Redfield to Lansing, Oct. 23, 1916, *Foreign Relations, Supplement: 1916,* pp. 466–478.

The course that Wilson chose, in any case, was not to threaten economic reprisals but to create difficulties for the British. He discussed with Polk the possibility of restricting the export of gasoline.[26] The action could be taken inoffensively, on the ground that there was a domestic shortage. He also talked over with the Counselor the possibility of tightening credit. The British, foreseeing a need to spend ten million dollars a day in the United States, had begun to seek long-term loans, secured only by the credit of the government. The President's financial advisers were already alarmed at the possible inflationary effect of such loans, and Wilson saw in this situation an opportunity for effective diplomatic action. When the Federal Reserve Board drafted a circular, warning banks against overcommitting their resources, the President asked that the statement be toughened. It would, he wrote, be "very embarrassing to have banks invest in this kind of security, if there should be any change in our foreign policy." [27] Loans against short-term renewable treasury notes were, in effect, prohibited, and the Allies were presented with the necessity for putting up collateral or else begging the American government to compromise. It was obvious that they could obtain financial concessions in Washington only by meeting some of the objections to their methods of economic warfare. Without having to risk the prestige or the interests of the United States, the President had placed himself in a position to press the British government for concessions.

Despite Wilson's anger, therefore, his policy did not yet involve risks. He had forcefully denounced the blacklists, but he had issued no ultimata. He remained in full command of the situation. Decisions taken in London could vex him, but they could not drive him to action until he himself had drawn a line and demanded that the British either stay behind it or defy him. It is not inconceivable that the President might eventually have come to such a stand. But that point was still far off when the German government proclaimed unrestricted submarine warfare and thus foreclosed controversy between the United States and Britain.

[26] Diary, July 26, 1916, Polk Papers.
[27] Baker, *Wilson*, VI, 377.

It is manifest that the President's slowness in defining a policy toward Great Britain was largely attributable to the troubled state of German-American relations. Before the submarine decree of February, 1915, he had shown little hesitation in insisting that Britain respect the commercial interests of the United States. After the first exchanges with Berlin, he was more than cautious in dealing with the British. It was not coincidence that his formal protest against the blockade was delayed until after the *Arabic* settlement or that his stiffening attitude followed the *Sussex* pledge.

The danger of war with Germany made it inexpedient to challenge the Allies. As Wilson explained to a complaining Senator during the summer of 1915, "it would be nothing less than folly to press our neutral claims both against Germany and against Great Britain at one and the same time and so to make our situation more nearly impossible." [28] Wilson could not afford, like Madison, to risk conflict with both sets of belligerents. Nor, as he had once explained to Bryan, could he afford to make it easier for the Germans to reject his demands by encouraging them to think that he was in just such a predicament.[29] Simple considerations of security and of diplomatic tactics compelled him to defer a contest with Britain until he had won or lost in his conflict with Germany.

In the President's conscience, moreover, the submarine issue overshadowed the blockade question. The distinction between loss of life and loss of property seemed to him both sharp and clear. He once commented in exasperation, "The German Foreign Office goes over the same ground . . . and always misses the essential point involved, that England's violation of neutral rights is different from Germany's violation of the rights of humanity." [30] So strongly did he feel this difference that he did not abandon it, even after the *Sussex* pledge. His complaint against the blacklist and the bunkering agreements was that they went beyond violations of neutral rights. They were, he implied, violations of national sovereignty. In his acceptance speech of September, 1916, after saying that the

[28] *Ibid.*, V, 266–267.
[29] *Lansing Papers*, I, 411.
[30] *Ibid.*, 421.

loss of life was irreparable, he added: "Neither can direct violations of a nation's sovereignty await vindication in suits for damages. The nation that violates these essential rights must expect to be checked and called to account by direct challenge and resistance." While the submarine war remained an immediate threat, he regarded Britain's legal and moral offenses as comparatively venial.

Even after the *Sussex* pledge, tension in German-American relations continued to exert both a practical and an emotional effect upon American policy toward Britain. Bethmann had warned, after all, that if the United States did not compel some relaxation in the Allied economic war, Germany would have to resume her liberty of action. The American embassy in Berlin faithfully reported the continuing U-boat agitation, and the President's advisers frequently reminded him that German policy might change at any time.

In the autumn of 1916, when Wilson was becoming increasingly vexed at Britain's intensified war, the German danger became more acute. Just as the election campaign drew to a close, sinkings by German submarines commenced once again. In the week preceding the election, reports reached the Department of State concerning the *Rowanmore*, the *Marina*, the *Rievaulx Abbey*, the *Strathtay*, the *Antwerpian*, and the *Arabia*.[31] All of these vessels were sunk in accordance with the rules of cruiser warfare, but all of them had Americans on board. Coupled with reports from Berlin of excitement in the Reichstag, accounts of these sinkings were enough to revive fears of a renewed U-boat campaign in repudiation of the *Sussex* pledge. Just when Wilson became free once again to develop his policy toward the blockade, it once again became inexpedient for him to risk serious controversy with the Allies.

Nor was it any less important for the President to maintain a firm and menacing opposition to a renewed submarine campaign. The value of the trade which would be menaced by such a campaign exceeded three billion dollars in 1916. Prosperity had truly arrived. Later estimates showed that per capita income had risen by an astonishing 25 per cent between January 1, 1916, and January 1,

[31] *Foreign Relations, Supplement: 1916*, pp. 298–299, 308–309.

1917, and much of this rise seemed attributable to expanded trade with the Allies. In Missouri, for example, the St. Louis and Kansas City newspapers described the state's flourishing condition as a result of British and French orders for boots, railroad cars, canned meat, beer, flour, and horses. Foreign trade, as the President himself said, had ceased to seem marginal for America; it had become essential.[32] The economic interests which a German submarine campaign would menace had grown in importance rather than declined.

As a result of the apparent diplomatic victory in the *Sussex* case, the prestige of the United States was more than ever bound up in holding the Germans to their pledge. It had contributed to an increasing sense of national power and pride, which was of course encouraged and exploited by campaign orators. When Wilson accepted renomination he not only restated the principles he had defended against Germany but went on to declare, "We are to play a leading part in the world drama whether we wish it or not. We shall lend, not borrow; act for ourselves, not imitate or follow; organize and initiate, not peep about merely to see where we may get in." Speaking earlier, he had defended preparedness by saying, "mankind is going to know that when America speaks she means what she says."[33] To yield before a fresh challenge from Germany would mean even deeper humiliation than the administration had feared in 1915, and a serious conflict with the Allies would have made it much more difficult for the President to hold his ground.

Even while submarines were inactive, moreover, Germany continued to give the President reasons for doubting both the wisdom and the justice of pressing his grievances against the British. House had been contending all along that Germany would be an enemy of the United States if she emerged victorious over the Allies. During 1916 two new long-range submarines turned up in American waters. The *Deutschland* came in August, carrying mail and cargo. The U-53 arrived in October and sank several Allied vessels not far off the American coast. Although these events provided little

[32] Crighton, *Missouri and the World War*, 41–61; Address at Baltimore, Sept. 25, 1916, *Public Papers*, IV, 311–323.

[33] *Public Papers*, IV, 289; Address at West Point, June 13, 1916, *ibid.*, 202–203.

ground for immediate fear, they did suggest that the time might not be far off when Germany would be capable of waging a naval war in the western Atlantic. Gerard warned meanwhile that Germany contemplated fighting the United States through Mexico, and Lansing advised the President in the autumn that German submarines had secretly been visiting in Mexican waters.[34] It was freely predicted, furthermore, that Germany would ally herself after the war with Russia and Japan in a combination against the United States. Although rumor and speculation of this sort could hardly be controlling in the determination of American policy, long-range considerations of security undoubtedly exercised some restraint over the President's wrath against the enemies of Germany.

Of greater immediate importance probably was the fact that Germany's disregard of morality still appeared to outweigh that of the Allies. For Wilson, it is true, the Allies lost much of their moral luster during 1916. In addition to blacklists and bunkering agreements, the British erred, from Wilson's viewpoint, when they chose to execute Sir Roger Casement and others who attempted, as German agents, to stir a revolution in Ireland. They also placed obstacles in the way of the Belgian relief program, fearing that supplies might be diverted to Germany, and they blocked altogether the President's efforts to encourage a similar program for Poland. Most important of all, they demonstrated an unwillingness to consider any peace short of total victory. But the worst offenses of the Allies were still overshadowed by the Turkish massacres of Armenians and by the German policy of impressing French and Belgian civilians into forced labor. Reports of wholesale deportations from Belgium reached the United States just as the election campaign drew to a close and Wilson became free to consider his future policy toward the Allies. In 1915 he could feel pure outrage against Germany because the Allies still seemed comparatively upright. In 1916 he could feel anger toward Britain, but, with Germany seeming no better, he could not muster his old moral fervor.

The German problem, in all its aspects, necessarily slowed the

---

[34] *Foreign Relations, Supplement: 1916*, p. 264; *Lansing Papers*, I, 224–225, 690.

development of Anglo-American friction. Whenever Bethmann was in full command of German policy, the tension between the United States and Britain increased. Since Lloyd George and his associates were doing little or nothing to ease this tension, it slackened when German actions were such as to distract attention from the Allied economic war. Had Bethmann secured power and held it for a long period of time, it is conceivable that the United States and Britain might have edged so near to a conflict as to reduce the danger of war between the United States and Germany. As it was, however, the German-American tension provided the surest guarantee of Anglo-American peace.

The slowness of the United States in accepting the British challenge was also due, of course, to a recognition of the nation's economic interests and to the peculiarities of public attitudes toward the Allies. The fact that American prosperity was due partly to Allied purchases was so evident that it was almost universally acknowledged. Although there was intense public demand for resistance to the blockade and the blacklist, antagonism toward Britain was always undermined by a recognition of the economic dangers involved in conflict with her and by a sense of partnership in opposition to Germany. In resisting Britain, the administration was afflicted by practical doubts which did not enter into the formulation of policy toward Germany. Nor was it subject to quite the same domestic pressures that affected its decisions concerning the submarine.

It was perfectly evident that the United States had more to lose than to gain by opposing the blockade. Even Bryan had been impressed with the fact that America's trade with Germany was so small as to be hardly worth protesting for.[35] While it was true that America's potential export trade with the European neutrals was being reduced by the blockade, it was also true that America's exports to them far exceeded any prewar levels. Trade with Sweden

[35] Bryan to Wilson, Jan. 12, 1915, Bryan-Wilson Correspondence, State Department Archives.

had quadrupled; trade with Norway has increased sixfold. Even the highest calculations of potential trade with the Central Powers and the neutrals paled by comparison with the three billion dollars' worth of goods bought by the Allies in 1916. The economic interest of the United States was plainly served by acquiescing in the Allied economic war rather than by resisting it.

Considerations of national honor and pride did to some extent offset these considerations of interest. When the blockade was proclaimed in March, 1915, newspapers of all shades demanded a protest. The gamut ran from the chauvinistic New York *Tribune* to the near pacifist New York *Evening Post* and from the business-minded New York *Journal of Commerce* to the demagogic Hearst press.[36] Although this demand was obscured by the outrage against Germany's submarine campaign, it revived, even during the *Lusitania* crisis.[37] During the summer lull in submarine activity, the outcry against England seemed to rise in full vigor. Shortly before the *Arabic* crisis, the President wrote House that representations against the blockade would soon have to be made: "Our public opinion clearly demands it." [38] In the interval before the sharpened U-boat campaign began, Wilson was apprehensive lest Congress try to force his hand by enacting an arms embargo. His concern found reflection in his instructions to House: "The errand upon which you are primarily bound you understand as fully as I do, and the demand in the Senate for further, immediate, and imperative pressure on England and her allies makes the necessity for it the more pressing." [39]

After the *Sussex* settlement, of course, feeling against Britain found virtually free rein. Tumulty clipped editorials from four strongly pro-Ally newspapers, all calling for strong action against England. Senator Paul O. Husting of Wisconsin, who was a pronounced nationalist and who had loyally supported the President's German policy, wrote Wilson cautioning him that the public now

---

[36] *Literary Digest*, L (March 13, 1915), 529–530, (March 27, 1915), 650.
[37] *Ibid.*, LI (July 10, 1915), 45–47.
[38] July 27, 1915, Baker, *Wilson*, V, 369.
[39] Wilson to House, Dec. 24, 1915, House Papers.

demanded the pressing of claims against Britain.[40] In the summer meetings of Congress there was much discussion of retaliation against the blockade and the blacklist, and administration leaders feared a movement to make the reprisal legislation mandatory instead of permissive. In November, 1916, Wilson asked House to tell Grey that feeling against Britain was "as hot . . . as it was at first against Germany and likely to grow hotter still." [41] There could be no doubt of public sentiment against Britain's maritime policy.

The principle of combating Britain, moreover, had a wide appeal. German-Americans were, of course, enthusiastic advocates of action against England. A number of Irish-Americans joined in.[42] Fervent Irish nationalists, like the leaders of the Clan-na-Gael, had called from the beginning of the war for American aid to Germany. Some who did not belong to extremist factions had drifted into a neutralist position. Some 2,300 delegates of the "Irish Race in America" had gathered in New York in the spring of 1916 to endorse the principles of the Gore-McLemore resolutions and to call for impartial defense of American rights. The Casement execution brought still more recruits. One of the many memorial meetings for the Easter martyrs was addressed by Bainbridge Colby, the New Yorker who was to figure in bringing Progressive votes to Wilson. Although not all the Irish joined in clamor for action against Britain, those who did formed a solid complement to the German-Americans and those Jews who were pro-German because they were anti-Russian.

The appeal naturally ran much more broadly. Pacifists and neutralists favored action against Britain as second-best to inaction against all belligerents. Senator Stone had talked anxiously with Lansing. As the Secretary wrote Wilson:

He clearly indicated . . . that he thought that we were bearing too severely upon the Teutonic Allies and were not pressing Great Britain

[40] Tumulty to Lansing, May 18, 1916, Lansing Papers; Husting to Wilson, May 16, 1916, Wilson Papers.

[41] Wilson to House, Nov. 24, 1916, House Papers.

[42] Carl Wittke, *The Irish in America* (Baton Rouge, La., 1956), 276–282; Blum, *Tumulty and the Wilson Era*, 105–109.

as strongly as we should in insisting upon observance of our trade rights. When I suggested that loss of life seemed to me to require more drastic treatment than loss of property, he replied that they both involved *rights*. . . . [H]e then referred to German babies dying because Great Britain would not allow us to send them condensed milk.[43]

Similar sentiments were expressed by agrarian spokesmen. When cotton prices were at their lowest point, the Georgia legislature resolved that the President should "induce or compel Great Britain to withdraw her illegal blockade of neutral ports." Granger organizations in the South and Midwest passed similar resolves.[44] Bryan and other veteran silver Democrats were almost as ardent in championing resistance to the blockade as in calling for retreat before the German challenge.

The idea of defending American rights against Britain appealed also, of course, to nationalism. Tumulty warned that after the *Sussex* settlement Republican campaigners would charge Wilson with having failed to uphold American independence against Britain.[45] Hughes justified this prediction at least to the extent of cautiously denouncing the blacklist: "No American who is exercising only American rights shall be put on any blacklist by any foreign nations." Ardent Republican newspapers meanwhile criticized Wilson's leniency in resisting the blockade and the blacklist, even though many were themselves emphatically pro-Ally.[46]

The anti-British temper in the United States was nevertheless of a different order from anti-German feeling. Newspaper comment on the blockade rarely descended to recommendations for specific means of combating it. As Sir Gilbert Parker assured the British Cabinet in the spring of 1916, the American press "generally does not discuss the steps which the Administration might take against England. Where it does so it usually suggests a protest now, and

---

[43] Dec. 21, 1915, *Lansing Papers*, I, 221.

[44] *Literary Digest*, LI (July 10, 1915), 45–46; Link, "The Cotton Crisis, The South, and Anglo-American Diplomacy, 1914–1915," *loc. cit.*, 133–135.

[45] Tumulty to Lansing, May 18, 1916, Lansing Papers.

[46] New York *Times*, Oct. 10, 1916; Syrett, "Business Press and American Neutrality," *loc. cit.*, 220–221; Cummins, *Indiana Public Opinion*, 200–201.

a claim for indemnity after the war." [47] The one device widely championed was, of course, the arms embargo, and much of the agitation for that measure was pacifist, neutralist, or pro-German. Hardly any nationalist would associate himself with the "hyphenates" who had taken the lead in that movement, and some pacifists and neutralists were reluctant to do so. Bryan, for example, continued to hold that an arms embargo would be unneutral. [48] The feeling against Britain failed to form itself into a demand for specific action.

One reason for the amorphous state of public opinion was the widespread recognition of the relation between prosperity and Allied buying. Some journals were candid enough to admit that they hoped Anglo-American controversy would remain verbal rather than practical. The New York *Journal of Commerce,* for example, was a business organ which frequently criticized Britain's maritime war, yet its editorial page once declared, "We profit by helping the Allies . . . through our trade, and we can afford to sacrifice something even of our rights in not hindering them." [49] The Chicago *Tribune* often fulminated against the blockade, yet it opposed the arms embargo movement. In the winter of 1915 its editor described the embargo as threatening "consequences so grave and far-reaching that neither the President nor Congress would care to assume the responsibility involved, unless compelled by a far more exigent need than any which has appeared thus far." [50]

The awareness of economic interest penetrated to the county and precinct level. During the spring and summer of 1915, when the blockade was forcing down the price of cotton, the Southern states were reportedly up in arms. Senator John Sharp Williams of Mississippi, though himself ardently pro-British, reported to the President that no Southern politician could afford to be other than a lion-baiter. [51] When the British cotton proclamation was followed by

---

[47] *American Press Résumé,* Feb. 5, 1916, Peterson, *Propaganda for War,* 82.

[48] Bryan to [?] Weisman, Aug. 27, 1915, Bryan Papers.

[49] *Literary Digest,* LI (Nov. 20, 1915), 1139–1140; Syrett, "Business Press and American Neutrality," *loc. cit.,* 220–221.

[50] *Literary Digest,* LI (Nov. 20, 1915), 1141.

[51] June 29, 1915, Wilson Papers.

purchases that stabilized the crop's price, much of this feeling lightened. A Southern correspondent reported to the British War Propaganda Bureau in November, 1915, "England is the South's best customer, and its sympathies naturally lie with its customers." [52] In the Midwest, where there was reportedly such strong neutralist and pacifist sentiment, there was also pronounced opposition to any practical steps that might endanger American trade with Britain. John Clark Crighton, in his absorbing study of the Missouri press, tells of rural newspapers that attacked Lansing's *modus vivendi* proposal because it might result in a reduction of the British shipping available for America's export trade. The Paris *Mercury* pointed out that the English vessels carried Missouri grain, meat, mules, and horses; the Joplin *News-Herald* commented that British bottoms carried Jasper County's zinc products.[53] The economic concerns of the United States were as much local as national and there was hence a profound and widespread disinclination to translate feeling against Britain into action.

Resentment against Britain was, moreover, a feeling rather than a movement. The German-Americans and the Irish nationalists who were prepared to advocate action could not gather a following. The passion against Germany and the disclosures of German sabotage and espionage activity had isolated the German-Americans.[54] They were cut off even from the agrarian pacifists, in the first place because they were erroneously regarded as a Republican bloc and, in the second place, because they were in large number Catholics and hence anathema to Protestant farmers. When nationalists attacked the "hyphenates," neutralists and pacifists stood complacently by. The Irish who joined the Germans were, of course, also thrown into this classification. It was to an Irish leader that Wilson addressed his famous campaign telegram: "I would feel deeply morti-

---

[52] *American Press Résumé*, Nov. 5, 1915, Peterson, *Propaganda for War*, 80; Link, "The Cotton Crisis, The South, and Anglo-American Diplomacy, 1914–1915," *loc. cit.*, 137–138.

[53] *Missouri and the World War*, 103–104; Cummins, *Indiana Public Opinion*, 200–201.

[54] Wittke, *German-Americans and the World War*, 83–111; Child, *German-Americans in Politics*, 85–153.

fied to have you or anybody like you vote for me. Since you have access to many disloyal Americans and I have not I will ask you to convey this message to them." Neither the Germans nor the Irish could lead an anti-British movement, and other groups who might have done so were necessarily reluctant even to cooperate with them.[55]

Nor could the anti-British feeling be marshaled against the administration by groups who opposed it for other reasons. Businessmen, who were antagonistic toward Wilson's domestic policies would not, as a group, join such a movement. Harold Syrett, in surveying the business press, found very few commercial organs that were prepared to speak out strongly against Britain.[56] The rich and well-born, though they left few editorials behind as proof, appear to have been predominantly pro-Ally and to have felt relatively little concern about the blockade. Such, at any rate, were the impressions gathered by European ambassadors who traveled the social circuits of Washington, Philadelphia, New York, Newport, and Boston. Since the Republican party was necessarily linked to both the business community and to high society, its leaders would have suffered great inner turmoil before crusading against Wilson's leniency toward the blockade. Taft, who was more nearly a neutralist than most eminent Republicans, does not seem to have favored the issue. Root thought the administration to have gone too far in attacking Britain as it was, and Lodge held this view even more strongly. Hughes, as the party's candidate, reproached Wilson's policy toward England only when he was near large German or Irish constituencies. Since many Progressives remained loyal to Theodore Roosevelt, who was an open champion of the Allies, there was little or no framework for a partisan challenge to Wilson's policy toward the blockade.

The considerations that affected American policy toward Britain

---

[55] Wilson to Jeremiah O'Leary, Sept. 29, 1916, Baker, *Wilson*, VI, 290; Wittke, *Irish in America*, 279–282; G. M. Stephenson, "The Attitude of Swedish-Americans toward the World War," Mississippi Valley Historical Association *Proceedings*, vol. X, part 1 (1918), 79 ff.

[56] "Business Press and American Neutrality," *loc. cit.*, 220–221.

were thus quite different from those which affected policy toward Germany. While the economic interests of the United States were gravely imperiled by the submarine threat, they were not seriously injured by the blockade, and the nation stood to lose rather than to gain by pressing for changes in Allied policy. If the President failed to maintain an appearance of firmness against Germany, he might well jeopardize his domestic leadership; Republicans and Progressives could unite in seizing command of nationalist feeling. If he failed to stand up to Britain, he would face at most the disorganized opposition of national minorities, pacifists, and neutralists. He had overcome such opposition in the Gore-McLemore battle, and he was infinitely stronger at the end of 1916 by reason of his unexpected re-election. To yield before Germany, furthermore, would cost Wilson whatever moral influence he might have over the Allies. It was not equally clear that he could gain moral influence over Germany by standing firm against Britain. Quite apart from the persistent tension in German-American relations, therefore, there were powerful domestic forces in the United States slowing down the growth of Anglo-American friction. Despite the policies of the British Cabinet, peace between the United States and Britain remained relatively secure. Grey had safeguarded that peace during the dangerous early months of the war. The German government, the exchanges, the American public, and the American government protected it thereafter.

XVI

Wilson's Threats of Mediation

In naval gunfire calculations, the unpredictable elements are grouped as the *j* factor, irreverently termed the "Jesus factor." In British-American and German-American relations alike, the *j* factor was Wilson's ambition to mediate. His desire for peace had threatened the success of Grey's conciliatory policy. Germany could conceivably have played upon this ambition to offset Anglo-American cultural and economic ties. Bethmann's failure to do so, coupled with House's achievement in persuading Wilson that a satisfactory peace could only come through Anglo-American cooperation, made the President's hopes a force preserving accord with England.

Throughout the year of submarine crises, Colonel House remained the chief prompter and agent of the President's mediation ambition. The failure of his first wartime mission to Europe had not ended the President's confidence in him. House had advised, after all, that the groundwork for a new peace effort would have to be laid slowly. The submarine issue had intervened to make war seem more likely than peace, and the German-American tension seemed meanwhile to confirm the colonel's premises—that real cooperation with Germany was impossible, that it was of the first importance to prevent any breach between the United States and the Allies, and that mediation could only result from an invitation by the Allied governments. These remained the premises of America's peace policy down to the spring of 1916.

During the winter of 1915–1916, however, these assumptions were tested and found inadequate. House devised an ingenious plan for inducing the Allies to request mediation. Wilson approved the colonel's scheme. House revisited Europe and actually concluded an informal agreement with Grey. By the time House returned to America, Wilson had discovered the strength of neutralist and pacifist opinion. The *Sussex* crisis soon revealed the nearness of war, and Cecil's management of the blockade made it impossible for Wilson much longer to maintain silence about Britain's economic war. When the Allied governments refused to invite mediation, even upon the terms arranged by House, the President realized that peace would not come through Anglo-American cooperation. He concluded that it would be necessary to exert pressure on all the belligerents and even to cooperate with the Germans, if they showed an inclination to ask for mediation.

When House visited Europe in the spring of 1915, before the *Lusitania* crisis, he found little to encourage Wilson's hopes. Both the Allies and the Germans seemed bent on continuing the war until their enemies had been overwhelmed. The British and French governments might call upon Wilson to accept Germany's surrender for them or ask him to mediate if they faced total defeat. In House's view, of course, either moment would be too late. If the President were to help in bringing permanent peace, he would have to act before the balance of power had been permanently overthrown. The problem was, as it had been earlier, to create an opportunity for mediation before either side had won and to do so without alienating the Allies.

During the summer of the *Lusitania* crisis, House applied his intelligence to this exacting problem. He had found persuasion alone to be useless. Characteristically, his thoughts turned toward compulsion. The glimmering of an idea appeared in a remark that he made casually, when prompting Wilson to build up the army and the navy. If the armed forces had been expanded earlier, he commented, "by now we would have been in a position almost to enforce peace." [1] Subsequently he elaborated this notion. If the

[1] House to Wilson, July 14, 1915, *Intimate Papers*, II, 19.

United States were to demand peace, threatening to use her military power against the side that refused, he suggested to Wilson, she might be able to frighten the belligerents into negotiating. To his surprise, the President seemed interested.[2]

Heartened by Wilson's receptiveness, House proceeded to work out a complex and risky scheme. As he outlined it for the President, the first step would be to undertake close and confidential negotiations with the British and French. They would have to be convinced that the American concept of a just and lasting peace was the same as theirs. But once persuaded, he believed, they would agree to Wilson's demanding peace negotiations and threatening to make war on the party that refused. The Allies, after some hesitation, could assent to a conference with the enemy. "[I]f the Central Powers accepted," House explained, "we would then have accomplished a masterstroke in diplomacy. If the Central Powers refused to acquiesce, we could then push our insistence to a point where diplomatic relations would first be broken off, and later the whole force of our Government, and perhaps the force of every neutral—might be brought against them." [3]

This extraordinary scheme is susceptible of many interpretations. Fond students of American neutrality have been shocked by it and have tended to assume that House's ulterior object was to trick Wilson into declaring war. Certainly House did speak of the plan in his diary as one which would "practically . . . ensure victory to the Allies." While he was perfecting it, he encouraged Lansing to cut America's relations with the Central Powers to a "single thread." [4] Europeans, on the other hand, have mostly taken the view that House meant to trick the Allies into making peace. In disclosing the plan to Grey, he was less than candid. Although he had actually worked it out in detail with Wilson, he presented it to the Foreign Secretary as a proposal in the interest of the Allies which he would make to the President if Grey thought it worthwhile.[5]

[2] Diary, Sept. 22, 1915, House Papers.
[3] Diary, Oct. 8, 1915, *ibid.; Intimate Papers*, II, 85.
[4] Diary, Nov. 25, 1915, *Intimate Papers*, II, 98; diary, Nov. 28, 1915, House Papers.
[5] House to Grey, Oct. 17, 1915, House Papers.

When talking with Allied representatives, moreover, he indicated that the chances of Germany's accepting were practically nil, and he laid stress on the term, "intervention," speaking only sparingly of mediation. Yet his diary entries show that, as a result of conversations with Bernstorff, he was actually optimistic about the chances of Germany's accepting a peace demand.[6] It is possible, in other words, to regard House's plan as the work of a warmonger or of a sly peacemonger.

Neither of these simplified judgments does credit to the colonel's complicated genius. There can be no question that he actually wanted peace. Even those who view him as a warmonger concede that he would have been pleased if both sides had accepted Wilson's mediation. His primary concern was to work for this end without alienating the Allies. Realizing that tactless peace proposals by the President could only create bad feeling, he felt that the British and French governments would have to be lured into accepting mediation. Only by promising armed intervention in the event the peace effort failed, he believed, could they be led to welcome action by Wilson. His plan offered the one and only hope, therefore, of a mediation move that would not endanger Anglo-American friendship.

But the offer of military action would not, in House's scheme, be a mere trick. He was prepared to advocate armed intervention if the peace effort failed. As he saw it, the United States and Germany already stood on the edge of war because of the submarine issue. He believed, indeed, that he had to struggle against Lansing in order to prevent war over the long-dormant *Lusitania* issue. He urged cutting relations with the Central Powers to a single thread so that the Germans could be made to realize the danger of any resumption of U-boat warfare. If sufficiently impressed, he thought, they would delay fresh provocation at least until the Balkan situation had cleared.[7] But war was, in any case, only a matter of time. The essence of his plan is misunderstood if it is not realized that he regarded war with Germany as inevitable.

[6] Diary, Dec. 16, Dec. 22, 1915, *ibid.; Intimate Papers,* II, 106–107.
[7] Diary, Nov. 27, Nov. 28, 1915, House Papers.

What he proposed was a desperate attempt to prevent war by restoring general peace. If this effort failed, as was probable, the United States would nevertheless have raised its issues with Germany to a higher level. The American government would enter the war not merely to exact revenge for submarine atrocities but to achieve a just and lasting peace. The political objects of American intervention would have been made clear at the outset, and the United States would be fighting not to overthrow the balance of power but to rescue it. His plan offered a distant chance of bringing peace. The United States could gamble on this chance without at the same time risking its friendly relations with the Allies. War, if it came, would have positive objects.

Some elements of this plan were attractive to Wilson. House thought at first that the President had endorsed it completely. "I was pleased," he noted in his diary, "to find the President cordially acquiescing in my views regarding intervention in Europe, and that it was only a question as to when and how it should be done. I now have the matter in my own hands, and it will probably be left to my judgment as to when and how to act." [8] The President approved entirely of House's reaching a secret agreement with the Allies about peace terms, so that they would accept his mediation offer when it was made. He also approved of luring them into acceptance with the hope of armed intervention by the United States. He was well aware of the extraordinary and politically dangerous character of House's plan. When the colonel drafted a letter to Grey, sketching the proposal, Wilson edited it carefully and returned it to the colonel. He did not sign his covering letters, for fear they might miscarry.[9] But Wilson did not, as before, give the colonel carte blanche.

The President had reservations about the final part of House's scheme. He was not so convinced as House that war with Germany was inevitable. Although he was ready to tempt the Allies with a hope of intervention, he would not promise to go to war if Germany refused to make peace. Editing the colonel's letter to Grey, he added

[8] Diary, Oct. 14, 1915, *ibid.*
[9] Diary, Oct. 19, 1915, *ibid.*

the word "probably" in the sentence, "If the Central Powers were
. . . obdurate, it would [probably] be necessary for us to join the
Allies and force the issue." As he explained to House, "I do not
want to make it inevitable quite, that we should take part to force
terms on Germany, because the exact circumstances of such a crisis
are impossible to determine."[10] The President may have thought
that, if the plan came to fruition and the Germans refused peace,
he could break relations. At the time he believed that severance of
relations would not necessarily mean war.[11] He may have been
prepared, as Arthur Link suggests, to exert moral rather than physi-
cal force upon the Central Powers. In his instructions to House,
he wrote, "If either party to the present war will let us say to the
other that they are willing to discuss peace . . . , it will clearly be
our duty to use our utmost moral force to oblige the other to
parley."[12]

The spring of 1916 saw the high point of the effort to bring peace
through Anglo-American cooperation. House arrived in London
on January 5, 1916. He spent some time feeling out the ground
before proceeding to Berlin and Paris. Talking with officials and
journalists, he quickly realized that conditions had changed in the
eight months since his previous visit. Grey not only was weaker but
was in real danger of losing his post. The likelihood of Britain's
moderating her economic war had become remote, and future friction was almost certain. The colonel, who had felt theretofore that
his plan might be developed slowly, changed his mind. He began
to think it urgent that an agreement be reached whereby Wilson
could safely demand peace.[13]

After traveling to Berlin, House felt even more strongly that his
plan should be carried out quickly. He found little to encourage a
hope that Germany would accept a peace bid. Bethmann spoke of

---

[10] Wilson to House, Oct. 18, 1915, Baker, *Wilson*, VI, 128.

[11] See Wilson to Lansing, Dec. 29, 1915, *Lansing Papers*, I, 508–509.

[12] Wilson to House, Dec. 24, 1915, Baker, *Wilson*, VI, 138; Link, *Wilson and the
Progressive Era*, 199.

[13] *Intimate Papers*, II, 117–134; diary, Jan. 6, Jan. 8, Jan. 10, Jan. 12, Jan. 14,
Jan. 15, Jan. 19, 1916, House Papers.

terms which the Allies certainly would not accept. He mentioned guarantees in Belgium and Poland and compensation for the surrender of occupied territory in France. The strongest impression received by the colonel, however, was not of the Chancellor's intransigence but of his weakness. Seeing evidence of the U-boat fervor, House concluded that it would not be long before Bethman was overwhelmed and an unrestricted submarine campaign launched. Even though the German government showed little disposition to make peace, House had reason to feel that prompt mediation offered the only chance of avoiding war or, if war were inevitable, of making it something purer than a war of revenge.[14]

Returning to London by way of Paris, House was preoccupied with this sense of urgency. His English friends had expressed doubt of his plan on the ground that the French were resolutely opposed to any peace short of victory. House unquestionably thought it imperative that he obtain France's consent to his plan. For this reason he was less than candid when speaking with Aristide Briand, the French Premier, and with Jules Cambon, the chief of the Foreign Ministry. He stressed Wilson's sympathy with the Allies and his desire to intervene. According to his own diary entry, *"In the event the Allies are successful during the next few months I promised that the President would not intervene. In the event they were losing ground, I promised the President would intervene."* He also recorded in his diary, "I again told them that the lower the fortunes of the Allies ebbed, the closer the United States would stand by them."[15] Reading Cambon's memorandum of this conversation, House later objected to the Frenchman's use of almost identical language. He "reported me as saying that no matter how low the fortunes of France got, when they said the word we would intervene." House noted, "I asked Grey to be certain to correct this impression in their minds, because . . . if the Allies put off calling for our assistance to a time when our intervention cannot serve them, then we will not make the attempt."[16] The explanation of this

[14] House to Wilson, Jan. 30, 1916, Wilson Papers.
[15] Diary, Feb. 7, 1916, House Papers.
[16] Diary, Feb. 17, 1916, *Intimate Papers,* II, 194.

apparent inconsistency lies undoubtedly in the colonel's knowledge of the impending Verdun offensive. Expecting the French to be shaken by Falkenhayn's massive onslaught, he wanted them to believe that Wilson would be acting to save them in their hour of peril.

His one object in Paris was to lure the French into agreeing to a peace bid. Convinced that Germany would soon force a war, he was desperately eager that Wilson should first have a chance to transform the issues. As he wrote to the President, explaining his pledge to the French government, "It is impossible for any unprejudiced person to believe that it would be wise for America to take part in the war unless it comes about by intervention based upon the highest human motives." [17] Since he now felt sure that Germany would reject a peace demand, he was not wholly dishonest in his affirmations to the French. He expected the demand to result in armed intervention. But he was willing to go to great lengths to induce the French government to invite such intervention "upon the highest human motives."

Returning to London, he was still impelled by the same sense of urgency. He found British officials divided about peace terms. Rather than delay matters, he abandoned the idea of obtaining agreement upon the general terms of disarmament and restoration of the *status quo ante*. He indicated a willingness to see France regain Alsace and Lorraine and Germany stripped of her Polish lands. His one reservation was that Germany might be compensated elsewhere. Anxious to arrange for mediation before the German government launched its new U-boat campaign, he agreed that Wilson should spell out no conditions whatever but merely call for a conference. He promised that the President would insist upon terms "not unfavorable to the Allies." [18]

The tension rising out of the sharpened U-boat campaign not only increased House's sense of urgency but also made his task in London more difficult. Lloyd George said that if Wilson wanted

[17] House to Wilson, Feb. 9, 1916, *ibid.*, 164.
[18] *Ibid.*, 169–197; diary, Feb. 10, Feb. 11, Feb. 14, Feb. 17, Feb. 22, Feb. 23, 1916, House Papers; Grey, *Twenty-five Years*, II, 126–128.

to intervene, he ought to break with Germany over the *Lusitania* case or, if not that, over "another such issue that was alive and burning." Grey advanced the same view. House believed that he overcame these arguments by contending, "If once in, in my opinion, we would have to remain until all sides were exhausted, or a decisive defeat had been brought about."[19] The colonel evidently expected that English statesmen, in their cooler moments, would see the restoration of a balance of power as an interest of both America and Britain. As he had done in Paris, however, he laid emphasis less upon the possibility of a negotiated peace than on the probability of armed intervention.

He succeeded in reaching an agreement with Grey. The extraordinary document which he and the Foreign Secretary initialed on February 22, 1916, provided, in Grey's words:

Colonel House told me that President Wilson was ready, on hearing from France and England that the moment was opportune, to propose that a Conference should be summoned to put an end to the war. Should the Allies accept this proposal, and should Germany refuse it, the United States would probably enter the war against Germany.

Colonel House expressed the opinion that, if such a Conference met, it would secure peace on terms not unfavourable to the Allies; and, if it failed to secure peace, the United States would leave the Conference as a belligerent on the side of the Allies, if Germany was unreasonable.[20]

The one provision conspicuously missing from this agreement was a specification of the time when Wilson's intervention should be invited. House had pressed Grey to set a date, but the Foreign Secretary had pleaded the necessity of discussing the question with the Cabinet and with the Allies. He had expressed such fear of French reaction, indeed, that House agreed to send him regular offers. When Grey judged the time appropriate, he could simply refer the current offer to Paris as if it came from the United States and not from the British government. Both Grey and Asquith seemed, House judged, to be ready for prompt action. Lloyd George appeared more doubtful. But House departed for America on Feb-

[19] Diary, Feb. 11, 1916, House Papers.
[20] *Intimate Papers*, II, 201–202; Grey, *Twenty-five Years*, II, 127–128.

ruary 25 hopeful that a request for mediation would soon arrive in Washington.[21]

He and the President then waited for a summons from London. Wilson approved almost everything the colonel had done. He made one change in the agreement with Grey, providing that if the conference failed, "the United States would *probably* leave the Conference as a belligerent on the side of the Allies." With this one modification, he authorized House to inform Grey that insofar as he could speak for the future action of the United States, he agreed to the memorandum which House and Grey had drawn up. Informing the Foreign Secretary of the President's decision, House declared, "If the situation continues as now, and if Congress does not restrict him, everything will go through as planned. . . . It is now squarely up to you to make the next move." [22]

In the weeks just preceding the *Sussex* sinking, House was optimistic. The resignation of Tirpitz seemed a favorable omen. After talking with Bernstorff, House revised the opinions he had brought back from Europe. "If we can get the Allies to give the word," he wrote in his diary, "I believe Germany will acquiesce." [23] A letter from Balfour meanwhile encouraged him to believe that a request might soon come from London. "Unless . . . I am making a mistake," wrote the Conservative elder statesman, "it will not be very long before I have again the pleasure of meeting you." Answered House, "I eagerly await the summons." [24]

The *Sussex* incident greatly increased the eagerness of both House and Wilson. Believing that the President had to respond with an ultimatum and that war was probable, House felt all his earlier sense of urgency reawaken. He saw slipping away the last chance to ensure that America's power would be used for a just peace and not merely for revenge. The President, desperately eager to escape from war, saw in mediation the brightest alternative. He person-

[21] Diary, Feb. 10, Feb. 14, 1916, House Papers; House to Wilson, Feb. 10, Feb. 11, Feb. 15, 1916, *ibid.*

[22] House to Grey, March 10, 1916, *Intimate Papers*, II, 220–221.

[23] Diary, March 12, 1916, *ibid.*, 224.

[24] Balfour to House, March 2, 1916, *ibid.*, 270–271; House to Balfour, March 24, 1916, House Papers.

ally composed a message which House was to cable to Grey, suggesting that Britain consult her allies and act at once to request an American peace demand. Otherwise a break with Germany over the submarine seemed inevitable, and "if this country should once become a belligerent, the war would undoubtedly be prolonged." House followed up this cablegram with a letter, offering further explanation. "The President and I both think," he wrote, "if we are once in the war it will lengthen it indefinitely. . . . We have another reason . . . and that is we are not so sure of the support of the American people on the submarine issue, while we are confident that they would respond to the higher and nobler issue of stopping the war." [25] The colonel thus sought to warn the British that if they wanted American help, they had best seek it by inviting mediation.

Despite these appeals and warnings, the Allies did not respond. House received a chilling letter from Grey, stating that he and Asquith were departing for Paris, but "We all feel that we cannot at this moment take the initiative in asking the French to consider a conference." Jusserand, the French ambassador, meanwhile advised the colonel that his plan was impractical and that the United States ought to go to war over the *Sussex* case. Grey eventually gave the same advice. [26]

When the submarine crisis ended satisfactorily, the President and the colonel did not cease to hope for an invitation from the Allies. House suggested writing Grey again, warning him of increasing public pressure on the President both to move for peace and to protest the blockade. Wilson heartily approved. House was instructed to tell Grey that the hint of peace in the German *Sussex* note made it imperative that he act soon and that "the sympathy of this country is apt to be alienated from Great Britain in a very significant degree in the immediate future." [27]

[25] *Intimate Papers*, II, 230–231; House to Grey, April 7, 1916, House Papers.
[26] Grey to House, March 24, 1916, *Intimate Papers*, II, 273–274; diary, March 30, 1916, House Papers; Grey to House, April 7, 1916, *Intimate Papers*, II, 275–276.
[27] House to Wilson, May 7, 1916, House Papers; Wilson to House, May 8, 1916, *ibid.;* House to Grey, May 11, 1916, *Intimate Papers*, II, 279–280.

When even this appeal met rebuff, the President decided to prod the Allies by means of a public speech. Hoping against hope that they might still invoke the agreement with House, Wilson wrote the colonel, asking what he would say in the President's place if he "were seeking to make the proposal as nearly what you deem Grey and his colleagues to have agreed upon in principle as it is possible to make it when concretely formulated as a proposal?" [28]

The occasion that the President used was an address to the League to Enforce Peace. Having obtained a draft from House, he followed it very closely.[29] He outlined the broad conditions which Grey had accepted, and he also called implicitly for the specific terms embodied in the House-Grey memorandum. "[E]very people has a right," he declared, "to choose the sovereignty under which they shall live." Although self-determination was a Liberal principle, which Wilson heartily accepted, it is reasonable to assume that he expected the Allies to sense its applicability to Alsace-Lorraine and to the Polish parts of Germany. "[T]he small states of the world," Wilson went on, "have a right to enjoy the same respect for their sovereignty and for their territorial integrity that great and powerful nations expect and insist upon." The reference to Belgium in these words could not have been clearer. And the President's third principle read, "the world has a right to be free from every disturbance of its peace that has its origin in aggression and disregard of the rights of peoples and nations." These words formed an eloquent paraphrase of Grey's often repeated condition, "an end to militarism forever." Wilson's speech was an appeal to the Allies to act upon the understanding between Grey and House.

It contained additional bait. Its best remembered passage called for "an universal association of nations." Wilson's subsequent enthusiasm for the League of Nations is usually dated from this declaration, and there can, of course, be no doubt that he had in fact become convinced of the desirability of some postwar international organization. But his main purpose in introducing this note into his speech was to prompt the Allies to invite mediation. House had

[28] May 18, 1916, House Papers.
[29] See *Intimate Papers*, II, 337–338; *Public Papers*, IV, 184–188.

reported Grey as feeling keenly that a postwar league, with the United States as a member, was indispensable for the preservation of peace. When Wilson asked House to help him with the speech, he asked the colonel if he should not come out for some form of international tribunal. "The only inducement we can hold out to the Allies," he observed, "is one which will actually remove the menace of Militarism."[30] The entire speech was so constructed as to draw the Allies into negotiation on the basis of the House-Grey understanding.

When nothing came of this public appeal, Wilson lost hope of bringing peace by cooperating with the Allies. The English seized upon the minor assertion that the United States was not concerned with the causes or objects of the war. While Grey wrote that he had read the speech in the light of his conversations with House and therefore welcomed it, he observed that the general reaction was unfavorable. Page described to House the common view that Wilson didn't "in the least understand the war and . . . that he was speaking only to the gallery filled with peace cranks."[31] The President concluded that the British were no longer capable of cooperating with him. He had already written angrily to House about a proposed message to Grey:

It is deeply discouraging to think what the effect will be upon the minds of the men who will confer about it. They have been blindly stupid in the policy they have pursued on the seas, and must now take the consequences. They would not in any case have been able, even if willing, to be even handed with us in the trade rivalries which must inevitably follow the war.[32]

The President had ceased all of a sudden to regard Anglo-American cooperation as a prerequisite for mediation. He had concluded that the Allies were no more eager than the Germans to make peace. He had come, moreover, to be almost as suspicious of Britain's future intentions as of Germany's. The President's ambition to

[30] Wilson to House, May 18, 1916, House Papers.
[31] Grey to House, May 29, 1916, *ibid.;* Page to House, May 30, 1916, *Intimate Papers,* II, 301–302.
[32] May 18, 1916, House Papers.

mediate had ceased to form a bond between Britain and the United States.

Wilson had not by any means given up his ambition. The desire to be a peacemaker was too deeply rooted in his own conscience and ambition. Owing to the constant risk of war with Germany, he was more eager than ever for a peace that would end his anxieties. He was certainly aware that evidence of his desire to mediate, like evidence of his resistance to Britain, salved mistrust of his firm policy toward Germany. It was almost the case that Wilson would have had to contemplate further peace efforts even if his heart had been set, like Lansing's, against any result except the defeat of the Central Powers.

Having found House's plan a failure, he was left with little alternative except to revert to the tactics earlier proposed by Bryan. If he could not obtain the acceptance of his good offices by means of secret and even compromising negotiations, he could only apply publicly to the belligerents, asking that they make peace or, as Bryan once suggested, that they merely state their terms. He would have to do so, moreover, without any prior arrangements with either side. As he wrote to House, "it will be up to us to judge for ourselves when the time has arrived for us to make an imperative suggestion. I mean a suggestion which they will have no choice but to heed, because the opinion of the non-official world and the desire of all peoples will be behind it." [33]

Such a seemingly innocent and helpful course, once pressed upon Wilson by Bryan, was in fact pregnant with the most ominous possibilities. Bryan had never reflected upon the possible consequences of a peace demand. As a Christian pacifist, he could face national humiliation with equanimity. Wilson's pacifism, on the other hand, was only vestigial. He had to give serious thought to the risks involved in appealing independently for peace negotiations. Such an effort might result in total failure; all the belligerents could reject his proposal out of hand. As House warned, the consequence might

[33] June 22, 1916, *ibid.*

be fatal to Wilson's own prestige and influence.[34] Although the President could not be wholly unconcerned about anything that affected his own stature, this possibility was the least of the dangers that he might create.

Far more frightening was the chance that one side would welcome his offer and the other reject it. It was this contingency for which House's plan had provided. Even after the failure of his arrangement with Grey, the colonel continued to insist that no peace proposal should be made until the Allies had first agreed not to refuse it. Both House and Lansing pointed out to Wilson the risk he would otherwise run. The Secretary wrote to him in December, 1916:

[S]uppose that the unacceptable answer comes from the belligerents whom we could least afford to see defeated on account of our national interest and on account of the future domination of the principles of liberty and democracy in the world—then what? Would we not be forced into an even worse state than that in which we are now? I think that we must consider the possibility of such a situation resulting.[35]

The President's keen intelligence, now concentrated on foreign affairs, cannot have overlooked this risk. If the Germans cooperated with him and the Allies balked, he would have to choose between withdrawing his offer or pressing the Allies to accept. The former course would demonstrate conclusively that he was incapable of taking action against the British and French; it would rob him of all power to rebuke them for violations of American rights and also, probably, of all power to influence the Germans. It would, in other words, be infinitely costly in terms of prestige. To press the Allies, on the other hand, could lead to serious friction. The idea of a public peace appeal, toward which Wilson's thoughts turned after the collapse of House's arrangements, involved almost as much risk to the peace of the United States as had the colonel's plan, and it entailed considerably more peril to America's interests and prestige.

There is evidence that Wilson wrestled with the question of

[34] House to Wilson, Nov. 30, 1916, Wilson Papers.
[35] Lansing to Wilson, Dec. 10, 1916, *ibid.*

whether, for the sake of peace, he would be willing to line up with the Germans and chance a conflict with the Allies. Angry at Britain's maritime policies, he could at times entertain such a thought. He shocked Walter Page by saying that if Germany proposed an armistice looking toward peace he would gladly support her, even though the Allies opposed it.[36] Once when House warned that a peace demand might lead to war with the British, Wilson retorted that they would not dare to fight and, if they did, "they could do this country no serious hurt."[37] His caution and deliberation showed, nevertheless, his realization of the grave consequences short of war that his action might bring.

During all the summer and autumn of 1916, he made no gesture at all. Even though he spoke often in public while campaigning for re-election, he mentioned his desire for peace less often than had been his custom during the earlier part of the war. Any appeal made before November 7 might seem an electioneering maneuver, and this thought was enough to confirm his instinct for delay.[38] In any case, the situation was too fluid to encourage action. It was never impossible that the Germans would break through at Verdun or the French on the Somme. Rumania's entry into the war and the consequent struggle in the Balkans added fresh uncertainties. So did the growing inner turmoil in Russia. And the President was not pressed, as he had been earlier, by a day-to-day fear of impending crisis with Germany.

By mid-November the excuses for inaction were mostly gone. Wilson had been re-elected; the offensives on the western front had come to naught; the triumph of Germany over Rumania was virtually certain. The submarine peril had revived, and the German government had given explicit warning of unrestricted warfare if peace were not soon restored. The President had received a communication from the Kaiser, warning that a mediation effort should be made promptly: "the German Government foresees the time at which it will be forced to regain the freedom of action that it has

[36] Diary, n.d., Page Papers; Hendrick, *Page,* II, 186.
[37] Diary, Nov. 14, 1916, House Papers.
[38] Bernstorff to Jagow, Oct. 14, 1916, *Official German Documents,* II, 987–988.

reserved to itself . . . and thus the President's steps may be jeopardized." [39] As Wilson said to House, "the submarine situation would not permit of delay and it was worth while to try mediation before breaking off with Germany." [40] Apart from the pressures created by omens of a revived U-boat campaign, the President had also to be concerned about the approaching session of Congress. He had been putting off pacifist solicitations by saying that he was giving "constant and most anxious thought" to mediation.[41] He could not long continue without provoking reproach.

He was still troubled by the necessity of avoiding a flat rejection by the Allies. Russian, French, and British leaders had all given voice recently to intransigence. The most publicized declaration was Lloyd George's to an American journalist. Calling for a fight "to the finish—to a knockout," he asserted, "neutrals of the highest purposes . . . must know that there can be no outside interference at this stage." To prevent the British government from answering a peace proposal with similar truculence, Wilson thought of sending House to Europe again. Even though the colonel could not be commissioned to arrange a prior agreement, he could at least be on hand when the offer arrived, and the Cabinet would have the benefit of his soothing advice. When House demurred, saying that he would go but that he would prefer Hades, the President gave up the idea.[42] The colonel suggested as an alternative that the earlier understanding with Grey be revived. He proposed cabling Lloyd George, the new Prime Minister, inviting a preliminary agreement on peace terms. Despite Wilson's eagerness to prevent a hostile reaction by the British, he was not willing to relive the disappointments of the previous spring. He wrote House that mediation could not be "such as we were proposing when you were last on the other side of the water. . . . We cannot go back to those old plans. We must shape new ones." [43]

[39] Oct. 9, 1916, *ibid.*, 987.

[40] Diary, Nov. 14, 1916, *Intimate Papers*, II, 301–302.

[41] E.g., Wilson to S. J. Blum, Oct. 9, 1916, Wilson Papers.

[42] Diary, Nov. 14, 1916, House Papers.

[43] House to Wilson, Dec. 6, Dec. 7, 1916, *ibid.;* Wilson to House, Dec. 8, 1916, *ibid.*

Still doubt lingered. Even though Wilson no longer depended on House as he once had, he respected the colonel's judgment, and House was determinedly opposed to an unsolicited peace offer. Lansing could barely disguise his own marked distaste not only for mediation but for a negotiated peace of any kind. Dispatches from Europe, news reports, and conversations with informed travelers gave the President a confused impression. On the one hand stood advice from Page and from friendly Englishmen who visited House. They declared that England would bitterly resent a peace proposal and predicted that the Allied governments would give it short shrift. On the other hand, the President received reports of war weariness dragging on the morale of all the belligerents.[44] The Cabinet changes that brought Lloyd George to the premiership in England and strengthened Briand in France made the outcome of a peace offer all the more uncertain. Since dispatches from Berlin caused less apprehension of a renewed U-boat campaign, the President had every reason to remain, for the moment, quiet and watchful.

He seized upon the German deportations of Belgian civilians as a reason for delay. In addition to genuine perturbation about what Lansing described as "a system of slavery which has not been practiced . . . by civilized nations within modern times," Wilson undoubtedly saw the issue as an obstacle to peace negotiations.[45] The Allies had often enough reproached him for protesting their maritime practices while leaving unprotested the invasion of Belgium and the atrocities reported by Lord Bryce's committee. They might retort that they could not negotiate with the enslavers of Belgian civilians. If he had already protested these acts, he could win some praise in France and England and hence improve the climate for a peace offer. By calling for an end to the deportations and making compliance a prerequisite to mediation, moreover, he could test the willingness of the Germans to cooperate with him. He directed Lansing to make such an appeal and, for the moment, he put aside

---

[44] *Foreign Relations, Supplement: 1916*, p. 57; *Intimate Papers*, II, 390–393; Baker, *Wilson*, VI, 355–356, 369–370.

[45] *Lansing Papers*, I, 43; see Link, *Wilson and the Progressive Era*, 257.

his peace appeal.[46] The excuse was real enough, but it reflected Wilson's own natural reluctance to take the perilous step toward which he was moving. It indicated his continuing uncertainty about risking a *rapprochement* with Germany.

While he still procrastinated, the German government made its own peace bid. Bethmann addressed the Allies through various neutral capitals, proposing that they agree at once to send representatives to a conference about peace terms. When Wilson received the message that he was to transmit to the Allied capitals, he was in effect challenged to align himself with the Germans or to remain silent. Even though he confessed that he welcomed the German note, as an evidence of one side's readiness to talk peace, he still hesitated.[47] Unable to delay forwarding the unexpected German note, he attached to it a covering message, stating that he intended to make representations of his own in the near future but that he deferred doing so lest they be interpreted as a mere complement to the German proposal.[48] He still shrank from any appearance of cooperation with the Central Powers.

Within a matter of days, nevertheless, he felt obliged to act. He had drafted a note some weeks earlier and discussed it in detail with House. Even before the German message arrived, he had sent a nearly final draft to the State Department for Lansing's criticism and comment.[49] Except for a few final embellishments it was ready for transmission, and the covering letter which Wilson attached to the German communication indicated that he had almost made up his mind to issue an appeal. What finally decided him was partly the mounting evidence that he could exert some influence over the Allies. House wrote that an unofficial British envoy, Sir William Wiseman, had come to visit him and talked very encouragingly about prospects for peace.[50] Wilson had meanwhile decided upon

[46] Wilson to Lansing, Nov. 26, 1916, Baker, *Wilson*, VI, 343–344.

[47] *Ibid.*, 393–394.

[48] *Foreign Relations, Supplement: 1916*, pp. 94–95; drafts in file of Dec. 14, 1916, Wilson Papers.

[49] Baker, *Wilson*, VI, 380–388.

[50] House to Wilson, Dec. 17, 1916, *Intimate Papers*, II, 401.

the measures that would restrict Allied credit, and English responses to the public announcement had seemed, perhaps erroneously, to indicate that he was in a position to exert a powerful influence on British policy. The President must have felt renewed confidence that the Allies would not defy him. From London and Paris dispatches, he must also have grown alarmed lest they reject the German proposal so forcibly as to close the door on any future tender by himself. He wrote House, at any rate, that he had had to act quickly "for fear the governments of the Entente might in the meantime so have committed themselves against peace as to make the situation even more hopeless than it had been." [51]

The President's original intention had been to pronounce a bold demand for peace. The first draft of his note had called for either parleys or statements of terms. It had contained an almost explicit warning that the United States might have to throw her strength on the side that yielded to this demand.[52] Such, at any rate, was the unmistakable implication of the words:

The world can still only conjecture what definitive results, what actual interchanges of guarantees, what political readjustments or changes, what stage or degree of military success even, would bring [the war] . . . to an end. If any other nation now neutral should be drawn in, it would know only that it was drawn in by some force it could not resist, because it had been hurt and saw no remedy but to risk still greater, it might be even irreparable, injury, in order to make the weight in the one scale or the other decisive; and even as a participant it would not know how far the scales must tip before the end would come or what was being weighed in the balance.

Coupled with this threat was to have been an explicit promise that the United States would put all her resources behind a postwar league of nations. Wilson hoped thus to offer the Allies the same guarantee of future peace that he had offered them in the spring.

His final note was much more cautious.[53] Some of Wilson's

[51] Wilson to House, Dec. 19, 1916, House Papers.
[52] Baker, *Wilson*, VI, 382.
[53] *Foreign Relations, Supplement: 1916*, pp. 97–99.

earlier draft came out under Colonel House's criticism. Some of it was excised at the suggestion of Lansing. Some words were removed lest they seem to echo the German proposal. Wilson withdrew the suggestion of parleys, for example, and asked only for statements of terms. The threat of ultimate action by the United States was whittled down to a suggestive but ambiguous sentence. The President thus reduced to a bare minimum the risk involved in his proposal. But he had still created an opportunity for the Germans to throw themselves into his arms, saying that they welcomed any peace consistent with his note and with the principles he had outlined before the League to Enforce Peace. He also made it possible for the Allies to say to him, as Lloyd George had said to the world, that they did not desire any neutral to "butt in." Despite its cautious wording, the peace note of December 18, 1916, was the most dangerous document that Wilson had approved since the House-Grey memorandum and the *Sussex* ultimatum.

The peril which it involved was manifested almost at once. German officials were reported to be pleased by the President's actions. British reactions, on the other hand, were almost uniformly sour. Lloyd George proceeded to answer the German note in a vehement speech to the House of Commons in which he pointedly quoted Abraham Lincoln, " 'We accepted this war for an object—a worthy object—and the war will end when that object is attained. Under God, I hope it will never end until that time.' " Page described "a deep feeling of disappointment and . . . even of anger" coursing through all segments of British opinion except for a small group of pacifists. Wiseman and Plunkett communicated similar views to House, and so did Lord Bryce, one of America's best friends in England.[54] To make matters worse, Lansing tactlessly expressed to newspaper reporters the threat that Wilson had deliberately minimized in his note. The Secretary of State said, "we are draw-

---

[54] *Parliamentary Debates: Commons*, 5th Series, LXXXVIII (Dec. 19, 1916), p. 1334; Page to Lansing, Dec. 22, 1916, *Foreign Relations, Supplement: 1916*, pp. 108–109; *Intimate Papers*, II, 407–408; House to Wilson, Jan. 7, 1917, Wilson Papers.

ing near to the verge of war ourselves, and, therefore, we are entitled to know exactly what each belligerent seeks, in order that we may regulate our conduct in the future." [55]

Wilson was compelled, as a result, to modify his proposal almost as soon as he had made it. He sent Lansing a cold command to retract his words and say that no change in the policy of neutrality was contemplated.[56] Acting upon a suggestion providentially made by Bernstorff, he also directed the Secretary to send out a postscript to the peace offer. The belligerents were invited to reply confidentially instead of openly to the President's request for statements of war aims.[57] The original note had suggested this possibility. The reason for turning it into an admonition was undoubtedly the President's fear that the various war leaders might feel it necessary in open answers to meet the moods of their "ginger" benches.

Considering all the grave potentialities hidden in Wilson's appeal, the actual results were anticlimactic. The Germans did not seize their opportunity. Their official reply, indeed, was unencouraging. The German government hoped for direct exchanges of views with the Allies, it asserted; neutral powers might take part in the great work of preventing future wars but not in ending the present conflict.[58] This answer was made publicly instead of privately. So was the joint reply of the Allies, delivered only two weeks after their defiant answer to the German proposal. By comparison, however, the Allied reply was both friendly and candid. It stated terms, and these terms were not unlike those which had been endorsed in the House-Grey memorandum: evacuation of occupied territories, liberation of national minorities, autonomy for Poland, the return of Alsace-Lorraine, reparations, and a postwar league of nations. In a covering letter, Balfour, the new British Foreign Secretary, explained gently that the Allies did not believe suitable terms could

---

[55] Lansing, *War Memoirs*, 186–187.

[56] Wilson to Lansing, Dec. 21, 1916, Baker, *Wilson*, VI, 405.

[57] Circular note, Dec. 24, 1916, *Foreign Relations, Supplement: 1916*, p. 112; draft in Wilson Papers.

[58] Gerard to Lansing, Dec. 26, 1916, *Foreign Relations, Supplement: 1916*, pp. 117–118.

be achieved except through victory.[59] But they had responded, nevertheless, exactly as the President desired. The peace move had neither driven a wedge between the United States and the Allies nor altered the relations between the United States and Germany.

Wilson now felt able to press his peace proposal with the utmost vigor. House, who had disapproved of the December note, returned to the President's side. As soon as the Germans declined to state terms, the colonel's fears evaporated. He suggested that the President utter a statement summarizing the general peace terms that he thought desirable.[60] The colonel still thought that American and British interests would both be served if the Germans agreed, in effect, to a restoration of the *status quo ante*. Foreseeing a new submarine crisis that would inevitably result in war, he also wanted Wilson to seize this last opportunity for stating the political conditions of America's armed intervention. The President accepted the colonel's suggestions with enthusiasm. Even before receiving the Allied reply to his note, he sketched out a list of terms which almost coincided with those the Allies were to demand. After reading it and attendant reports from London and Paris, he felt confident of being able to arrange a peace. "If Germany really wants peace," he wrote House, "she can get it, and get it soon." He instructed the colonel to tell Bernstorff "that with something reasonable to suggest . . . I can bring things about." [61]

The President seemed to be in much the same position as he had believed himself to be in the preceding spring. He and the Allies seemed in substantial agreement on terms. The clue to peace, he believed, lay in Berlin.

His public summary of peace conditions, the celebrated "Peace without Victory" speech to the Senate, was addressed almost exclusively to Germany. He began by asserting that the Allies had stated terms while the Germans had not. Attempting to counter the often repeated objection that he could not be an impartial mediator, he

[59] Sharp to Lansing, Jan. 10, 1917, *Foreign Relations, Supplement One: 1917*, pp. 6–9; Balfour to Spring-Rice, Jan. 13, 1917, *ibid.*, 17–21.
[60] House to Wilson, Dec. 27, 1916, House Papers.
[61] Baker, *Wilson*, VI, 414–415; Wilson to House, Jan. 24, 1917, *ibid.*, 440.

declared that the United States would have no share in defining the articles of peace. But he offered conditions for mediation which were plainly designed to attract the Germans: naval disarmament, freedom of the seas, independence (rather than autonomy) for Poland, and a "just settlement of vexed questions of territory or of racial and national allegiance." The measure of his confidence in the cooperation of the Allies was the fact that he slurred over in generalities all the conditions that they had fixed, stressed those which were sure to be least well received in London, Paris, and St. Petersburg, and called, against the vehement objections of Page, for a "peace without victory." [62]

[Wilson presented the German government with yet another opportunity to attempt a *rapprochement*. Owing to his own acceptance of the Allied terms, a meeting of minds had become unlikely but not impossible. As it was, however, the German government seemed to slap away his outstretched hand. Bernstorff delivered a confidential summary of the conditions which Germany *"would have been willing"* to accept if the Allies had agreed to negotiate directly.[63] These terms included the retention of Alsace-Lorraine, annexations in the east, strategic and economic improvements in the French boundary, the conditional restoration of Belgian colonial gains, and reparations for Germany. None of these terms was pleasing to Wilson.] Not only were they unsatisfactory, but they appeared at exactly the same moment that Germany announced her new U-boat campaign.

The President's early willingness to align himself with the Allies in pursuit of peace had helped to preserve tranquillity in Anglo-American relations. His later willingness to align himself with either side had not, in the long run, assisted in preserving peace with Germany.

[62] *Public Papers*, IV, 407–414; Hendrick, *Page*, III, 317–318.
[63] *Official German Documents*, II, 1048–1050.

XVII

The Peace Dream and

Anglo-American Friendship

Wilson's threats of mediation presented the Allies with both challenges and opportunities. His first feelers in 1914 had imperiled the accord that Grey worked so hard to preserve. House's influence on Wilson, added to Grey's skill in diplomacy, had averted the danger. With House's second effort, however, the British were presented with a great opportunity. Under the colonel's plan they could at the very least have forced an issue between the United States and Germany. They might have succeeded in obtaining America's armed intervention in the spring or summer of 1916. They might even have secured a conqueror's peace without having to spend the billions of dollars and thousands of lives that wasted away against the German lines. This opportunity was wasted, and the President's subsequent peace appeal in December, 1916, presented anew the danger of a moral breach between Britain and the United States.

With the paucity of evidence available, it is almost impossible to state how the British government arrived at its decision to reject the House proposal. Writing retrospectively, Grey explained simply, "At present there was no use to be made of it. We believed and the French believed, that defeat of the German armies was the only sure overthrow of Prussian militarism. . . . We all felt that we could take no initiative in the American direction." Stressing in retrospect the very point he had raised with House, Grey also wrote later of the difficulties involved in broaching the question to the French. To mention the colonel's proposal to them might appear an indication of Britain's desire to get out of the war. Not to mention it, on the other hand, could result ultimately in reproaches for having failed to follow it up. And Grey wrote, "If we ignored President Wilson's offer, the Allies might forfeit his sympathy, and for that we alone should be held responsible, if the French had not known of what had passed between House and ourselves." Raising these issues before the War Council, he found his principal colleagues opposed to inviting French comment. So Grey merely notified Briand of it, without making any recommendation.[1]

Writing later, Lloyd George offered a somewhat different version of the decision. According to his recollection, the Cabinet's leaders had been enthusiastic up to the time when Wilson approved the House-Grey memorandum. The President's addition of the word, "probably," soured Grey, who then took the view "that this completely changed the character of the proposal, and, therefore, he did not think it worthwhile to communicate the purport of the negotiations to the Allies." Blaming the failure of the House plan on the timidity of Wilson and Grey, Lloyd George lamented that otherwise the world would have been "saved a whole year of ruin, havoc, and destruction."[2]

While Lloyd George's recollections may contain elements of truth, it is hard to believe that the War Council made a complete turnabout when it received Wilson's amendment to the House-Grey understanding. The members of the Council were Asquith, Lloyd George, Balfour, Chancellor of the Exchequer Reginald McKenna, and the taciturn Kitchener. Both Lloyd George and Balfour were at the time determined that the war should be prosecuted until Germany was "thoroughly beaten."[3] Kitchener had no thought of a

[1] Grey, *Twenty-five Years*, II, 128–129, 132.
[2] Lloyd George, *War Memoirs*, II, 137–140.
[3] *Diary of Lord Bertie*, I, 336–337.

negotiated peace. Asquith had taken his stand publicly in favor of carrying on the war until success had been achieved, and Grey supported him in this view.[4] Although McKenna was by nature a pessimist, he had not yet come to favor a negotiated peace. It seems probable that the Council would, in any case, have been dubious about taking a step that might have miscarried and resulted in a peace without victory.

For the government to have invited mediation, even if sure it would fail, would have been politically dangerous. The "ginger" group was even more opposed to conciliating neutral mediation ambitions than to conciliating their trade interests. The *Morning Post* argued that the war was a fight to the death and advised that the government politely answer any neutral by saying that the British people "are determined, at whatever cost, to win." [5] Although a small but active group of pacifists and Labourites persisted in agitating for a negotiated peace, Liberal and Conservative spokesmen were not far from the Tories in their insistence on thoroughgoing victory. The Liberal *Westminster Gazette* opposed neutral interference almost as vehemently as the *Morning Post,* and the Liberal *Chronicle* called for reducing Germany to second-rate status and dismembering Austria and Turkey.[6] Grey was probably not exaggerating when he told House that mobs would break his windows if it were rumored that he was discussing peace.[7]

Two considerations might nevertheless have inclined the Cabinet to act on the House-Grey understanding. One would have been pressure from the Allies. Grey continually warned of the danger that France or Russia might negotiate a separate peace. The Germans were willing to offer any one of them favorable terms, he believed, and Britain had to bend every effort to prevent their accepting. The Cabinet could not urge them to use neutral good

[4] London *Times,* April 11, 1916; *Parliamentary Debates: Commons,* 5th Series, LXXXII (May 24, 1916), pp. 2198–2202.

[5] London *Morning Post,* Feb. 9, April 22, June 17, 1916.

[6] *Current Opinion,* LX (Jan., 1916), 12, LXI (July, 1916), 7–8; Forster, *Failures of Peace,* 31-34; Sir Arthur Willert, *The Road to Safety: A Study in Anglo-American Relations* (London, 1952), 41.

[7] Diary, Feb. 11, 1916, House Papers.

offices when they were probably able to obtain better terms independently. On the other hand, it could not refuse to go along if one of the allies should indicate a desire to invite neutral mediation.[8]

Neither Russia nor France, however, expressed the slightest interest in acting on House's offer. The Russian government, it is true, was never fully told of it. The Tsar's ambassador in Paris reported:

> Cambon advised me of the following details of the conversations he and Briand held with . . . Colonel House. . . . House, alluding to America's profound sympathy for the Allied states, and particularly for France, let it be understood that if the said Powers desired to propose peace on terms satisfactory to themselves and, at the same time, just, the U.S.A. is ready to support such a proposal. He was answered that so long as Germany continues to consider herself a victor, there could be neither peace arrangements nor discussions. House then declared that from his trip to Berlin he brought away the conviction that Germany intends in the near future to stiffen her methods of conducting maritime war with submarines and mines, and that this will inevitably lead to a collision with the U.S.A. House remarked that controversy over the *Lusitania* should preferably end amicably, for at the present moment the U.S.A. is not prepared for war; but this condition may quickly change, in his opinion highly satisfactorily, so that the affair will end after all in the intervention of the U.S.A. on the side of the Allies.[9]

Through London the Russian government learned even less. If Grey was the one who informed Benckendorff of House's visit, he did not in this instance display his customary candor. Benckendorff reported to St. Petersburg that House

> has advised that the President, while personally sympathetic toward the Allies, cannot adopt any attitude except the most benevolent neutrality, an attitude that might in certain circumstances, however, provoke conflict with Germany. House declared, at the same time, that American public opinion was favorable to the Allies, but distinctly

---

[8] Memo by Grey, Feb. 18, 1916, Trevelyan, *Grey of Fallodon*, 360–361.

[9] Isvolski to Sazonov, Feb. 9, 1916, *Mezhdunarodnye Otnosheniya*, Series Three, X, no. 169.

pacific. . . . House has . . . affirmed that he did not carry to Berlin any message connected with mediation or with peace.[10]

Instead of inviting Russian comment on the American mediation proposal, the French and British governments encouraged their ally to expect armed intervention by the United States. Since Russia did not take it upon herself to suggest the use of American good offices, the British government encountered no pressure from St. Petersburg to act upon the House proposals.

The French actually discouraged any action. When Grey gave notice of his understanding with the colonel, the French government either ignored the information or advised rejection of the plan. Grey reported to House that Briand simply made no comment. Bertie heard, on the other hand, that Cambon had received Grey's report and "laughed it to scorn." [11] Although Cambon's disclosures to the Russians were undoubtedly framed with an eye to reactions in St. Petersburg, they also reflected his own impressions of House's remarks. Bertie was given to believe, at any rate, that House had simply said "that the war will be long, that the Allies will win in the end, and that in a year's time America will be with us." [12] Briand was reported to be overconfident of America's ultimate intervention.[13] In any case, the French government showed no interest in mediation by anyone. The principal condition that might have led to action on the House-Grey understanding was therefore absent.

The only other consideration that might have prompted action would have been expectation of America's armed intervention. The Cabinet by and large was eager to have the United States as an ally. Grey reasoned that with America's alliance Britain would no longer need to temper her economic war, and she could be confident of ultimate victory. Kitchener believed American contributions in supplies and manpower would be of great help to the

---

[10] Feb. 21, 1916, *ibid.*, no. 233.

[11] Grey to House, March 24, 1916, *Intimate Papers*, II, 273–274; *Diary of Lord Bertie*, I, 311.

[12] *Ibid.*, 301, 311-312.

[13] Letter of April 26, 1916, Henri Cambon (ed.), *Paul Cambon: Correspondance, 1870–1924* (3 vols.; Paris, 1940), III, 103.

Allies. Although Lloyd George felt some concern about a possible interruption in supplies resulting from an American rearmament effort, he was perhaps impressed by confidential reports that United States army planners envisioned an expeditionary force of half a million men. When recommending to House that the United States go to war over the *Sussex* case, Balfour cabled, "The Cabinet unanimously believe your intervention would be immensely helpful and probably decisive." [14]

It should not be thought, however, that Englishmen were unanimous in this desire. Benckendorff reported to St. Petersburg that there was opposition to American intervention as well as eagerness for it. Spring-Rice was one of the opponents. He believed the diversion of supplies for a build-up of an American army would imperil the Allies.[15] Another brand of opponent was the high Tory or traditionalist, like Bertie, who feared Wilson's influence on the peace settlement.[16] Very few people in either group, it is true, believed that Britain should actively block armed intervention by the United States. But there could well have been a strong minority protest against the purchase of American aid through the acceptance of Wilsonian peace conditions. In view of the government's precarious hold upon the people and the Commons, this current of Tory feeling formed a barrier to action under the House-Grey understanding unless it promised to lead almost immediately to an American alliance.

In these circumstances Wilson's addition of the word "probably" may in fact have been the conclusive deterrent. Lloyd George was the dominant member of the War Council. If he had been convinced that House's plan offered a sure method of bringing America into the war, he might have pressed his colleagues to act. If the President's amendment confirmed his suspicion that Wilson would

[14] Benckendorff to Sazonov, May 13, 1915, *Mezhdunarodnye Otnosheniya,* Series Three, VII, no. 750; *Lord Riddell's War Diary,* 85–86; diary, April 20, 1916, House Papers.

[15] Benckendorff to Sazonov, May 13, 1915, *Mezhdunarodnye Otnosheniya,* Series Three, VII, no. 750; Military Attaché, Washington, to War Ministry, June 8, 1915, *ibid.,* VIII, no. 82.

[16] E.g., *Diary of Lord Bertie,* I, 163.

not go to war, it ensured that he would resist any proposal to invite mediation, and his attitude was decisive.

In any event, Britain did not exploit her opportunity to force an issue between the United States and Germany. Nor did she exploit the President's ambition, as Grey had done earlier, to reinforce the slackening guarantees of Anglo-American accord.

The President's independent peace move presented a direct threat to Anglo-American tranquillity. By the time Wilson had made his appeal, the British government had carefully considered the question of negotiating with Germany, and the Cabinet had conclusively decided against any discussion of peace. Conversations with the Allies had led to an even clearer recognition of their opposition to any neutral mediation effort. The dying months of the Asquith government had seen the power of the intransigents increase and the opposition to peace talk spread more widely among all factions in British political life.

Debate on the issue of negotiating peace had arisen during the summer of 1916. It may have been stimulated by Bethmann's reference to peace in the closing paragraphs of his *Sussex* pledge. It may have been prompted by rumors stemming from Bern and Madrid. Or it may have been due to the dismissal of Sazonov, with attendant fears that the re-formed Russian government might negotiate a separate peace. Whatever the stimulus, the Prime Minister asked that the Foreign Office, the General Staff, and perhaps other agencies prepare memoranda on the terms that would form a satisfactory peace in the event of victory or of stalemate.[17]

Answers flowed in upon the Cabinet. Two high Foreign Office officials prepared a detailed summary of the territorial and other conditions that might ensure lasting peace.[18] These conditions, they concluded, could be attained only by defeating Germany. Any terms predicated on a stalemate would be in the nature of truce terms, sure to be followed by renewed war in which the German position

---

[17] Lloyd George, *War Memoirs*, II, 264; Lloyd George, *The Truth about the Peace Treaties* (2 vols.; London, 1938), I, 31.

[18] *Ibid.*, 31–50.

would be more advantageous than at present. The Chief of the Imperial General Staff seconded this conclusion.[19] Although he contended that it was to Britain's interest for Germany to remain strong after the war, he felt that a reasonable balance of power could be established only if terms were dictated. Britain should not even accept an armistice unless Germany agreed to evacuate all occupied territory, return all Allied prisoners, and surrender a portion of her fleet.

Since rumors of enemy peace offers, neutral mediation efforts, and separate peace negotiations by Russia all proved unfounded, the debate proceeded at a leisurely pace. Some five weeks after the Chief of Staff had rendered his advice, Lord Balfour circulated a memorandum resembling the one that had come from the Foreign Office.[20] Lasting peace could be ensured, he argued, only if Germany were limited in future in the number of men and the amount of money available to her. Her frontiers had to be shrunk, in other words, and this contraction could only occur if terms were dictated by the Allies. Memoranda from other members of the government dealt with the reparations and indemnities that would have to be extracted from the enemy. Exchanges with the French meanwhile produced unmistakable evidence of that ally's determination to strip Germany of all lands west of the Rhine—a goal that could be achieved only through complete military victory.[21]

Even as Cabinet memoranda and diplomatic correspondence disclosed the rational arguments against a negotiated peace, the public opposition to peace without victory was revealed in naked clarity. Lloyd George issued his declaration in favor of "a fight to a knockout." He apologized to Grey, saying that he thought it necessary to warn Wilson off a renewed mediation attempt, and he gave the same explanation to Liberal journalists.[22] But it is hard to believe that his manifesto was unconnected with a recent editorial in

[19] Memo by Robertson, Aug. 31, 1916, Lloyd George, *War Memoirs*, II, 264–272.

[20] Oct. 4, 1916, *ibid.*, 300–305.

[21] Asquith, *Memories and Reflections*, II, 166–168; Suarez, *Briand*, IV, 129–130.

[22] Lloyd George, *War Memoirs*, II, 282–285; J. L. Hammond, *C. P. Scott of the Manchester Guardian* (London, 1934), 201.

the Tory *Morning Post*. After Kitchener's accidental death on June 5, Lloyd George had succeeded to the War Ministry, partly through hearty backing from the *Morning Post* and other "ginger" journals. As an advocate of concentration in the Balkans, he had come into conflict with what Viscount Esher called "the narrow Calvinistic doctrine . . . that salvation can only be found between Dunkerque and the Vosges." [23] His differences with the General Staff had aroused mistrust among his erstwhile Tory supporters. By seizing the lead against the rumored peace faction of the Cabinet, he allayed their doubts. The *Morning Post* and the "Young Conservatives" in the House rallied to his standard.[24]

The general reception of his "knock-out blow" declaration indicated the intensity of feeling against negotiating with the Germans. The *Daily Mail,* of course, rattled its applause. But so, more significantly, did the *Daily Express,* which usually spoke for Bonar Law, and the Birmingham *Post,* which was thought to reflect the views of Austen Chamberlain and the Midland Conservatives.[25] Nor did any important segment of the Liberal press dissent. The weathervane *Daily News* took occasion to editorialize on the spirit of rededication in which England approached her third winter of war. The left-Liberal Manchester *Guardian* expressed mild reservations, but its editor was one of Lloyd George's staunch supporters, and he was contented by the explanation that it had been necessary to fend off a German-inspired mediation effort on the part of Wilson.[26] So evident was the public mood and so threatening the Tory-guided rumors of division in the Cabinet that both Asquith and Grey felt obliged to reassure the country. The Prime Minister told the House that he would accept no "patched-up, precarious, and dishonouring compromise, masquerading under the name of Peace." Grey pledged, "It is our determination . . . to continue the war till we

---

[23] London *Morning Post*, Sept. 23, 1916; *Lord Riddell's War Diary*, 212; Oliver, Viscount Esher (ed.), *The Captains and the Kings Depart: Journal and Letters of Reginald, Viscount Esher* (2 vols.; New York, 1930), II, 70.

[24] London *Morning Post*, Sept. 30, 1916; London *Times*, Oct. 1, 1916.

[25] Rappaport, *British Press*, 115–116.

[26] Willis, *England's Holy War*, 234–235; Rappaport, *British Press*, 116; Hammond, *Scott of the Guardian*, 201.

have made it certain that the Allies in common shall have achieved the success which must, and ought to be theirs." [27] The government had decided, almost involuntarily, to refuse proposals of peace or mediation.

Subsequent debate within the Cabinet had an academic quality. Lord Lansdowne's well-known memorandum of November 13, 1916, was a call for reflection and reconsideration.[28] Profoundly troubled by an awareness that the social order could not survive another year or more of war, the Marquis declared, "it is . . . our duty to consider . . . what our plight, and the plight of the civilized world, will be . . . . [and] we ought not . . . to discourage any movement, no matter where originating, in favour of an interchange of views as to the possibility of a settlement." Despite the opinions that had emerged during the earlier debate and despite the evident mood of public opinion, Lansdowne's views found support. The President of the Board of Trade was pessimistic about the shipping situation if the war continued. The President of the Board of Agriculture had made a gloomy forecast of future food shortages if peace were not made soon.[29]

The Cabinet did not swerve from its earlier resolution. Cecil and Grey took the trouble to reply to Lansdowne. Cecil commented that present negotiations could only yield the *status quo ante,* which would be "disastrous." Grey observed neutrally that the issue really lay with the military and naval authorities. If they believed either complete success or a material improvement of the situation to be foreseeable, then it was "premature to make peace." The Chief of Staff expressed confidence in the future and, as he paraphrased himself, declared that peace could be considered only by "cowards, cranks, and philosophers." [30] The earlier involuntary

[27] *Parliamentary Debates: Commons,* 5th Series, LXXXVI (Oct. 11, 1916), p. 103; London *Times,* Oct. 24, 1916.
[28] Asquith, *Memories and Reflections,* II, 165–174.
[29] *Ibid.,* 166–167.
[30] Memo by Cecil, Nov. 27, 1916, *ibid.,* 175–177; memo by Grey, Nov. 27, 1916, Trevelyan, *Grey of Fallodon,* 366–367; Callwell, *Field Marshal Sir Henry Wilson,* I, 299.

decision against accepting a peace proposal was thus reaffirmed shortly before Wilson made his bold gesture of December, 1916.

When Wilson delivered his appeal, conditions favored a stern refusal by the British government. Grey had felt that Lloyd George's knock-out blow declaration closed the door to any future cooperation with Wilson.[31] He was still prepared, as he advised Spring-Rice, to counsel that the Allies return a friendly answer to any open plea by the President.[32] But the stern attitude of most politicians was unmistakable. The German proposal, coming only a few days before Wilson's, had resulted in a new display of public feeling. The Liberal *Chronicle, Westminster Gazette,* and Manchester *Guardian* declared no less earnestly than the Tory papers that the final destruction of Prussian militarism was the only assurance of lasting peace.[33] The German offer had also led Britain's allies to make uncompromising declarations. When the Germans themselves replied to Wilson, indicating that they desired no neutral interference, the British government could very easily have made a similar rejoinder.

That it did not was almost a result of chance. Two weeks before Wilson's note arrived, Lloyd George had become Prime Minister. Although he still depended on the "ginger" group, he now needed a broader political base. Commanding only half of the Liberal party, he would be at the mercy of his Tory collaborators if he could not obtain additional support from among moderate Conservatives on the one hand and radicals and Labourites on the other. He could not secure this wider backing unless he retreated from the militancy that had brought him to office. He proceeded, therefore, to break openly with Lord Northcliffe, the Tory press baron who had been instrumental in his rise to power. He also solicited actively the cooperation of the Labour party. In order to obtain it he had to declare his willingness to negotiate peace if either the enemy or a neutral put forward reasonable proposals.

[31] Grey to Lloyd George, Sept. 29, 1916, Lloyd George, *War Memoirs,* II, 282.
[32] Nov. 26, 1916, Trevelyan, *Grey of Fallodon,* 368.
[33] Forster, *Failures of Peace,* 51.

"Surely no one imagined that we wanted to go on with the War and have our sons killed," said the author of the knock-out doctrine.[34]

By answering Wilson in a conciliatory manner, Lloyd George could improve his uncertain hold over moderate Conservatives, who sympathized with Lansdowne, and over his Labour allies. Having just risen to office on the shoulders of Carson and the Tories, he was for the moment safe against their wrath. It is paradoxical but true that Lloyd George was able, was almost compelled, to answer Wilson more softly than Asquith and Grey could have.

Lloyd George's inner Cabinet, which he, Bonar Law, and a Labour representative dominated, decided almost at once to make a conciliatory reply to Wilson. The French suggested a vague and evasive joint note, but this proposal was rejected. Cecil and Balfour, the new Foreign Secretary, were directed to draft "explicit and candid" replies.[35] After a conference with French representatives, a compromise text was drawn up by an officer of the French Foreign Ministry. It conformed roughly to Balfour's draft, specifying the terms required for Belgium, Poland, Serbia, Rumania, Italy, and Turkey. The clause relating to Alsace-Lorraine was ingeniously phrased. It called for the restoration by Germany of territories conquered in the past. Not until much later was it to be learned by the outside world that France, having in mind further gains on the Rhine, meant "the past" to include eleven centuries.[36] The final note, in any event, seemed explicit and candid. Approved by the other allies in late December, it was delivered to Wilson on January 10, 1917.[37] As we have seen, it succeeded in the aim of restoring Wilson's confidence in the Entente.

Lloyd George might have found it more troublesome to answer Wilson's "peace without victory" speech. His government was six weeks old. It had already begun to be attacked by the Northcliffe press, and members of the "ginger" faction had resumed their efforts

[34] Lloyd George, *War Memoirs*, III, 20.
[35] *Ibid.*, 60–61.
[36] *Ibid.*, 61–63; Briand to Cambon, Jan. 12, 1917, Suarez, *Briand*, IV, 129–130.
[37] *Foreign Relations, Supplement One: 1917*, pp. 6–9.

to unseat moderates in the Conservative party. Knowing from naval intelligence, however, that a new German submarine campaign was at hand, the Prime Minister felt no urgency about answering Wilson's new appeal.[38] Wiseman was permitted to encourage the President.[39] When the expected U-boat declaration came and Wilson severed relations with Germany, the problem disappeared. Lloyd George and the Cabinet began to discuss financial and military arrangements for America's entry into the war.

The time span between Wilson's peace appeal and the German submarine proclamation was so short that the whole affair may have been inconsequential. It is conceivable that an uncompromising retort by Britain might have pushed Wilson into a decision on his policy toward the blockade. It might have altered his disposition toward Germany. Even though these possibilities were remote, the British government chose to fend them off by answering in conciliatory form. The Asquith Cabinet had been unable and unwilling to seize the earlier opportunities offered by Wilson's mediation hopes. As a matter of chance rather than of policy, Lloyd George's government evaded the dangers implicit in the President's unrepentant ambition.

[38] Hendrick, *Page,* III, 335.
[39] House to Wilson, Jan. 20, Jan. 26, 1917, Wilson Papers.

PART V

The End of Diplomacy

XVIII

Germany: Peace or War

The four weeks from December 12, 1916, to January 9, 1917, brought the tragic climax to Bethmann's long struggle for peace with America. He offered to end the war. Had he succeeded, the German-American issue would have dissolved. Had he even been able to link his own peace hopes with Wilson's, he might have loosened the knots in German-American relations. But his peace effort failed not only to close the war but even to prevent a break with the United States. It was overtaken by a decision in favor of unrestricted U-boat war.

Bethmann had at first ignored Wilson's ambition to mediate. He had deliberately passed up the first opportunities to cooperate with the President. Only when the *Lusitania* and *Arabic* controversies brought the danger of war did he realize the use that might be made of Wilson's dream. Until the crises passed, of course, he had no chance to exploit this knowledge. Hopefully seeking to detach Russia from her allies, moreover, he had to be circumspect in discussing peace with western states. Not until the winter of 1915–1916 did it become practical for him to hint at possibilities of German cooperation with the President.

He did not at first encourage Wilson. He merely sought not to dishearten him. Talking with one of Ambassador Gerard's close friends, for example, he said nothing about mediation, but he did take pains to outline his own seemingly modest and reasonable aims. All that Germany wanted in Belgium, he said, was security against future attack.[1] When he learned that Wilson's ambassador in Turkey was discussing mediation, he had Jagow outline Germany's policy for the guidance of the German ambassador in Constantinople: "Even though we could hardly desire the United States as a mediator, owing to her unfriendly disposition, still in view of the precarious negotiations about the *Lusitania* and the *Ancona* it would be useful if a contrary *belief* could be aroused in Wilson, for we could thus reduce the danger of America's . . . actively going over to our enemies."[2] The Chancellor had lost none of his distaste for actual mediation by Wilson. He had simply seen that it was imprudent to dampen the President's hopes.

When House visited Berlin in late January, 1916, the Chancellor could have tried deceitfully to promise eventual cooperation with the President. In view of the impending sharpened U-boat campaign, it might have seemed a shrewd tactic to confuse Wilson's emotions. According to Bernstorff's reports, furthermore, the President's current ambitions were not especially dangerous for Germany. Wilson did not have in mind participating in a peace conference, the ambassador had advised; he merely wanted to call for negotiations, stipulating that the powers should put an end to "militarism" and "navalism" and secure "freedom of the seas."[3] Since Bernstorff reported House to be somewhat pro-German, Bethmann could have jollied the colonel along by seeming to talk seriously of mediation prospects. Jagow and Zimmermann actually pursued this tack, even though Zimmermann promised an acquaintance that if Wilson really mediated he would hang himself from his office window.[4] But Bethmann was almost as reticent as he had been during the colonel's earlier visit.

His failure to exploit the opportunity can hardly be ascribed to innate love of truth and horror of duplicity. The Chancellor could

[1] Memo by Bethmann, Oct. 1, 1915, German Foreign Ministry Archives (Secret Mediation).

[2] Jagow to Wangenheim, Dec. 19, 1915, *ibid.*

[3] Bernstorff to Jagow, Nov. 13, 1915 (rcd. Dec. 17, 1915), *ibid.*

[4] Lutz, *Fall of the German Empire*, I, 393–394; diary, Jan. 28, Jan. 29, 1916, House Papers.

not say anything to House without taking account of what might happen if the colonel were indiscreet. If he encouraged House, he would undoubtedly be asked for a statement of war aims, and any statement satisfactory to the colonel would be offensive to the annexationists in the Reichstag. December, 1915, had seen the high point of annexationist fever among the German parties, and Bethmann had barely prevented opposition forces from rallying an annexationist bloc against him. He could not chance the leakage of any statement. Nor could he even allow it to be rumored that he was receptive to American mediation. Erzberger had written the Foreign Ministry about the news releases welcoming House to Berlin. They implied, he protested, that Germany wanted America's help.[5] Bethmann could not risk alienating this powerful Centrist and others of his parliamentary allies. Even though he had recognized Wilson's ambition, he could not afford to play upon it.

He gave only the faintest comfort to House. He talked with him only once. Already engaged in the struggle that preceded the Tirpitz crisis, he devoted himself chiefly to justifying the impending sharpened U-boat campaign. Speaking briefly of mediation prospects, he did try to do two things. He sought first to convince House that Wilson could improve his chances of mediating by either taking a stronger stand against the blockade or a more lenient stand against the U-boat. Bethmann's second object was to indicate cautiously that German peace conditions would not be unreasonable. Though arguing that Germany had the upper hand, he suggested that she might be willing to settle for guarantees against future attack through Belgium and Poland and for the payment of an indemnity by France. He could say no more, and he left House with the impression that he was befuddled and that peace prospects were very dim.[6] Although the Chancellor evidently sought not to discourage the colonel, he was able to do little toward building a hope of German-American cooperation.

[5] Erzberger to Montgelas, Jan. 21, 1916, German Foreign Ministry Archives (Secret Mediation).
[6] Memo by Bethmann, Jan. 28, 1916, *Official German Documents*, II, 1281-1283; diary, Jan. 28, 1916, House Papers.

After the crises of March and April, 1916, Bethmann's own attitude toward American mediation changed. That he began actively to stimulate Wilson's ambition was partly due, it is true, to the desperate situation that resulted from the *Sussex* incident. Seeking to postpone a break until he could arrange the necessary concessions, he called in Gerard and told him earnestly that if the crisis could be overcome Wilson would be given a chance to mediate.[7] He also had Jagow cable House, "If President Wilson is desirous of peace his wishes are in full accord with the desires of Germany, which entertains the hope that German-American relations can be so moulded as to make possible cooperation in the bringing about of peace." [8] But Bethmann was not altogether insincere in holding out this hope.

He no longer needed to be so fearful of talking about peace. In the previous year it had seemed as if all the national parties, from the Conservatives around to the Progressives, might league together in an annexationist bloc. The spring of 1916 saw this danger lifting. The U-boat issue, the Prussian franchise question, and the taxation problem had driven the Center and Progressive parties away from the right. The socialist split had created a possibility of left-center combinations, and the continued insistence of majority Social Democrats upon a peace of understanding necessitated some drift away from annexationism on the part of their would-be allies. Astute politicians had come to recognize, moreover, that the stalemated war was making the Pan-German program of world conquest increasingly absurd. They also sensed a spreading weariness among the public. Significant of the domestic change since the previous winter was Erzberger's moderation of the Pan-German program that he had advocated early in the war. During April, 1916, he collaborated with Bethmann's adjutants, Wahnschaffe and Hammann, in setting up the National Committee for a German Peace, an organization designed to combat Pan-German agitation.[9] Significant also

---

[7] Gerard to Lansing, April 25, 1916, *Foreign Relations, Supplement: 1916*, pp. 243–244.

[8] Jagow to Bernstorff, April 11, 1916, *Official German Documents*, II, 971.

[9] Gatzke, *Germany's Drive to the West*, 132–137; Westarp, *Konservative Politik*, II, 185–186.

was the visible breach among National Liberals who openly differed over whether the party should continue to demand annexation of Belgium.[10] The Chancellor did not, for various reasons, feel it possible to assume leadership of a peace movement. He still felt compelled to speak ambiguously about war aims and to give occasional encouragement to annexationists. But he did feel free, as he had not during the first year and a half of war, to consider steps toward opening peace negotiations.

His attitude toward possible mediation by Wilson had also undergone a change. After proclaiming in the *Sussex* pledge his "readiness to make peace on a basis safeguarding Germany's vital interests," he explained very confidentially to the German ambassadors in Denmark, Sweden, the Netherlands, and Switzerland that his note would place Wilson

once again in a very doubtful position, since he can only advance the interests of his Presidential candidacy if he exerts strong pressure for peace upon England. He still need not step forward immediately as a mediator, which at least at the moment would hardly be consistent with his hitherto very partisan attitude. . . .

Certainly a peace intervention by Wilson at the present moment would raise opposition among us for many reasons. That Wilson's pressure for peace on England would have success *immediately* is, however, not to be expected. And once a short time has passed, the antagonism will subside. The desire for peace among us is still very great and our economic difficulties will become catastrophic if the harvest should fail. If we are once of the conviction that the U-boat war cannot defeat England, then we must grasp by the forelock any opportunity to make peace.[11]

Bethmann still had no desire for Wilson's presence at the peace table. Jagow instructed Bernstorff that if the President's plans assumed "concrete form," it would be the ambassador's duty to block them.[12] As Bethmann put it later, he opposed *mediation* by the President but favored an eventual *peace move* by him.

[10] *Daily Extracts from the Foreign Press*, March 11, 1916; *Daily Review of the Foreign Press*, April 18, May 1, May 13, May 31, 1916.
[11] May 5, 1916, German Foreign Ministry Archives (Secret Mediation).
[12] June 7, 1916, *Official German Documents*, II, 976–978.

Even though he had thus modified his attitude toward Wilson, he still had no wish for an early move by the President. As he had confided to the ambassadors in Copenhagen, Stockholm, The Hague, and Bern, the effects of the *Sussex* crisis would first have to wear off.[13] So long as active military operations continued on all fronts, it was almost necessary to await their results. Much depended, too, on the size of the harvest. If it were bad, the Chancellor might have to sue for terms. If it were good, his position would be all the stronger in a peace conference over which brooded the threat of endless hostilities. In addition, the Chancellor had to reach some preliminary agreements with Austria. The Polish question needed to be settled, he had long recognized, before the Central Powers could sit down with their enemies, and it was August, 1916, before he could drag agreement from his dilatory ally.[14] Although Bethmann had decided at the time of the *Sussex* crisis that he might someday seek Wilson's cooperation in a peace move, it was late summer before he could even give further thought to this idea.

As it happened, this moment coincided with the revival of the U-boat menace. August was the month when the Chancellor failed to unseat Falkenhayn, when the Naval Staff resumed its pleas for a submarine campaign, and when the Bavarian Centrists openly joined the opposition. When Bethmann received a letter from Bernstorff asking for fresh instructions, he decided to give Wilson strong encouragement. Bernstorff assured him once again that Wilson had no thought of taking part in the peace negotiations. The President wanted only a postwar conference, the ambassador advised, in which the major powers could agree on disarmament and freedom of the seas:

He only wants to play the peacemaker; he wants to earn the name of having brought the belligerents to the point of negotiating with one

---

[13] Memo by Bethmann, May 5, 1916, German Foreign Ministry Archives (Secret Mediation).

[14] Bethmann to Falkenhayn, Aug. 4, 1915, *ibid.*; Erich Ludendorff, *Urkunden der Obersten Heeresleitung über ihre Tätigkeit 1916/1918* (Berlin, 1922), 298–300.

another. In view of the feeling on this side, it is quite presumable that such a result would assure his reelection. I am therefore convinced that the President will make an appeal for peace in the course of a few weeks, provided the futility of the offensive of our enemies shall have manifested itself at that time. Mr. Wilson would then say to the English that he was forced, as a matter of domestic politics, to very definitely oppose the blockade, in case the point of peace negotiations had not been reached.[15]

Assured thus that Wilson's aim was to make a peace move and not to mediate, Bethmann replied that he would welcome action by the President. He troubled, nevertheless, to make it quite clear that he did not mean mediation, that he would not state terms in advance, and that the President's own aims would have to be achieved through a separate postwar conference.[16] Bethmann was no longer insincere in encouraging a peace move by Wilson, but it was still his policy to meet with refusal any American attempt at mediation. This policy was to remain unaltered throughout the winter of 1916.

The relation between Bethmann's encouragement of Wilson and his own peace offer of December 12 is not easily untangled. For a long time it was common in the United States, England, and even Germany, to regard the peace offer as a mere preliminary to the subsequent declaration of unrestricted submarine war—an effort to disarm Wilson by playing upon his hope of peace. In France the view persists that Bethmann's offer was a ruse of a different kind. Karl, the new Emperor of Austria-Hungary, was related to the house of Bourbon. Through a Bourbon prince he intimated his interest in a separate peace with the French. Bethmann's peace offer, it is charged, was intended to frustrate these negotiations, to break the new Emperor's hopes, and to permit continuation of a German war of conquest.[17] Neither of these cynical explanations takes just account of the predicament in which the German Chancellor stood at the end of 1916.

Bethmann's decision to offer peace can only be understood as an

[15] July 13, 1916 (rcd. Aug. 16, 1916), *Official German Documents*, II, 979–981.
[16] Aug. 18, 1916, *ibid.*, 981–982.
[17] Suarez, *Briand*, IV, 74 ff.

act of despair. Not that he assumed Germany to be beaten; he knew the military and economic plight of the Allies to be no better than that of the Central Powers. What made him desperate was an expectation that Germany's situation would get no better, that the Austrian and Turkish allies were losing heart, and that the German government, over which he was fast losing control, would eventually commit suicide with the U-boat weapon. It was not in order to prepare the way for a submarine decision that Bethmann offered to make peace; it was to prevent that decision.

The Chancellor must also have been prompted, of course, by a recognition of his own weakening power. The new Supreme Command was gradually substituting its authority for his. The *Zentrum* resolution had demonstrated that the Chancellor no longer commanded the Reichstag. If peace negotiations were to begin, however, his words would once again become weightier than Hindenburg's, not only with the Kaiser but with the Reichstag as well. The U-boat bloc would break up. On the issue of moderate as opposed to annexationist terms, it seemed as if he could reunite his left and center support. The socialist peace manifesto, letters to the Chancellor from Progressive deputies, and editorials in the Centrist *Germania* foreshadowed the peace resolution majority of the succeeding year.[18] The opening of peace negotiations must have seemed to Bethmann the sole means of saving Germany from her own madness and of rescuing himself and the imperial constitution that he symbolized.

The form which the peace offer took was largely due, it is true, to the situation in Austria. Bethmann decided in August to invite an eventual peace move by Wilson. It is difficult to believe that this decision was not influenced by a conversation held in July with Julius, Count Andrassy, the Hungarian Minister President, on which Bethmann reported: "Andrassy is very despondent. Men, materiel running out. Confidence in the army broken. Teschen is a swamp. . . . Victory we can no longer reach for; catastrophe is

[18] *Daily Review of the Foreign Press,* Aug. 17, Aug. 26, Sept. 1, Sept. 6, 1916; Haussmann, *Schlaglichter,* 72–74.

almost certain. Should we not promptly bestir ourselves for peace?"[19] Though Bethmann's intentions in approaching Wilson can only be inferred, it seems safe to say that he expected the President to call for negotiations among the belligerents and that he planned to respond by hurriedly communicating with Vienna, proposing that the Central Powers accept. In view of Austria's condition, she could not refuse. After acceding to Wilson's plea, the Chancellor would only have to wait until the President had compelled the Allies to do likewise.

If this was Bethmann's plan, he began to act upon it almost as soon as Hindenburg and Ludendorff became his associates. The intervention of Rumania had made it seem unlikely that Germany's military situation would improve before the end of the year. Reports from the food controller indicated a harvest large enough to permit continued war but not to promise a comfortable winter.[20] Most important of all, the new Supreme Command had indicated in the first conference at Pless that they would ultimately vote for a U-boat campaign. The Chancellor therefore dispatched an immediate cablegram to Bernstorff telling the ambassador that he hoped "to conclude peace before winter" and asking how he could stir the President into prompt action.[21]

When Bernstorff reported Wilson's unwillingness to act before the election, Bethmann decided to press the President. He asked the Kaiser's consent for a message to Washington, warning that a new U-boat campaign was likely and asking that Wilson move for peace in order to prevent it. As soon as Wilhelm agreed, a long and urgent dispatch went off to Bernstorff.[22] Jagow meanwhile gave the message to Gerard. Since the ambassador's wife was leaving for a vacation in America, the Foreign Minister urged Gerard

[19] Bethmann to Jagow, July 23, 1916, German Foreign Ministry Archives (Peace Negotiations).

[20] Batocki to Bethmann, Sept. 1, Sept. 30, 1916, German Foreign Ministry Archives (Secret).

[21] Sept. 2, 1916, *Official German Documents*, II, 983.

[22] Bethmann to Bernstorff, Sept. 25, 1916, *ibid.*, 984–986; Bethmann to the Kaiser, Sept. 23, 1916, Ludendorff, *Urkunden*, 305–306.

to accompany her so that he could impress on Wilson the necessity for a prompt move.[23] Although Gerard was at best an unreliable instrument of communication, even he understood that Wilson was supposed to do nothing more than call for direct negotiations between the belligerents and that the German government planned to answer only "in general terms." [24]

From the middle of October on, however, Bethmann found it necessary to adapt his tactics to the wishes of Austria. Baron Stephan Burian, the Austrian Foreign Minister, had already indicated that he desired the Central Powers' peace offer to be independent of any action by neutrals. He had also made no secret of his opposition to a U-boat campaign by Germany if it were likely to result in American intervention.[25] Bethmann had explained his overtures to Wilson as results of the heightened submarine agitation and the consequent possibility of a new campaign. When Burian arrived in Berlin on October 18, it became necessary for the Chancellor to discuss in detail the prospects for peace.

Although Burian wanted peace as much as Bethmann, he did not see eye to eye with him about the method of opening negotiations. He was eager, in the first place, to obtain personal credit for a peace offer. The eighty-six-year-old Franz Joseph had taken the throne of Austria-Hungary during the revolution of 1848. Although a creature of extraordinary stamina, he was visibly failing. His heir, the Archduke Karl, was an unknown quantity, although it was well understood that he resented the Germans and probably desired to make peace with his French kinsmen. If Burian and the other ministers of Franz Joseph were to remain in power when the Archduke succeeded, they needed to demonstrate their own independence of Germany and inclination for peace.

Burian's differences with Bethmann were chiefly two. The Austrian was anxious, in the first place, for an agreement upon the terms that should be demanded of the Entente. As the weaker

[23] Memo by Jagow, Sept. 25, 1916, German Foreign Ministry Archives (Secret Mediation); Gerard, *My Four Years in Germany*, 346.
[24] Gerard to Lansing, Sept. 25, 1916, *Foreign Relations, Supplement: 1916*, p. 55.
[25] Memo by Bethmann, April 25, 1916, German Foreign Ministry Archives (Peace Negotiations); Bethmann to Jagow, July 23, 1916, *ibid.*

power, Austria would otherwise find her aims subordinated to Germany's. Bethmann, on the other hand, wanted to maintain the utmost flexibility. As he explained to Hindenburg, he foresaw several months of negotiation, during which the fighting would continue. The delegates of the Central Powers would be equipped at the outset with a list of maximum but not of minimum demands A continually changing military situation, as well as the pull and haul of negotiation, would reveal what could be obtained. There should be no *sine qua non* of peace.[26] In taking this view, Bethmann was undoubtedly influenced by the bitter public divisions over war aims and by unwillingness to discuss this difficult subject with the Supreme Command.

The second major difference turned on the question of method. Burian wanted the Central Powers to compose a message and send it through neutral capitals to the Allies. This message should, he felt, state the conditions upon which Germany and Austria were able to agree and invite face-to-face negotiations. It should be dispatched at some distant date, when the Central Powers were once again victorious on all fronts, especially those in Italy and the Balkans. Bethmann, for obvious reasons, was altogether opposed to any declaration of terms before the conference actually assembled. Desiring to evade responsibility for the peace offer rather than to obtain credit for it, he also preferred the method of acting in response to an American proposal. Most important of all, he wanted the offer to be made as soon as possible. Since Franz Joseph had not yet come down with the attack of bronchitis that was soon to kill him, Burian felt less sense of urgency. Bethmann, who saw his power ebbing day by day, could not be so patient.

The principal result of these differences was that Bethmann had to work out a set of specific peace terms. Since it was the Austrian's aim to commit Germany insofar as possible to his own kingdom's objectives, Bethmann had to meet him with an equally ambitious list of German conditions. Burian proposed, among other things, to annex substantial parts of Serbia and Rumania and segments of the Italian and Russian frontiers, to make Montenegro a protec-

[26] Bethmann to Hindenburg, Jan. 4, 1917, *Official German Documents*, II, 1097.

torate, and to enlarge Bulgaria.[27] If Bethmann failed to counter-balance these demands with some of his own, he would face the prospect of sitting down at the peace table as a bargainer for the dual monarchy. He felt that, at the very least, the Austrian terms should be offset by German claims for annexations in Courland and Lithuania and on the French frontier, indemnities from France, independence for Poland, and return of the German colonies.[28] Since he continued to oppose any irrevocable proclamation of terms, he undoubtedly viewed these demands as little more than balance weights against the conditions set by Burian.

To negotiate an abstract and academic set of terms with the Austrian Foreign Minister unfortunately required that Bethmann consult the Supreme Command. He had evidently gone behind their backs to obtain the Kaiser's approval of his peace plan. It was not until late September, at any rate, that Hindenburg and Ludendorff learned of the overtures to Wilson.[29] Apprised of Bethmann's pro-posed prompter to Wilson, they insisted that the message to Bern-storff should begin with a declaration that the Central Powers remained confident of ultimate victory, doubting only whether it could be achieved during 1916.[30] The Chancellor had so engaged the Kaiser's sympathies that the generals could not block the Chancel-lor's plans. Wilhelm had become so eager for peace, indeed, that when a Reichstag delegation mentioned the word he burst into tears.[31] He had personally composed a message for Gerard to de-liver to Wilson, urging a prompt appeal. The intensity of his feel-ing was displayed in a letter to Bethmann saying, "To make an effort for peace is a moral act which is necessary to free the world —the neutrals as well—from all their oppressive burdens. Such an act is appropriate for a monarch who has a soul and who feels him-

[27] Memo by Bethmann, Oct. 18, 1916, *ibid.*, 1053–1056. Much the best account of Austro-German relations in connection with the peace appeal is in Richard Fester, *Die Politik Kaiser Karls und der Wendepunkt des Weltkrieges* (Munich, 1925).

[28] Bethmann to Hindenburg, Nov. 4, 1916, *Official German Documents*, II, 1059–1060.

[29] Reichsarchiv, *Der Weltkrieg*, XI, 447.

[30] Hindenburg and Ludendorff to the Kaiser, Sept. 24, 1916, *ibid.*, 448–449.

[31] Haussmann, *Schlaglichter*, 66.

self responsible to God and who has a feeling for his people and the enemy's, who is unshaken by the probable misunderstanding of his action but who has the will to liberate the world from its sorrows." [32] With the Kaiser in such a mood, the generals had not been able to obstruct the Chancellor. Since Ludendorff was in a frenzy, moreover, to obtain a law permitting labor drafts, he had been temporarily at Bethmann's mercy, and he had agreed to a peace effort on condition only that the national service law be passed first and the military situation be advantageous. [33]

When Burian compelled Bethmann to draw up a list of war aims, the Chancellor had no choice but to consult again with the Supreme Command. The generals insisted upon more extensive annexations, both east and west, and they also called for indemnities or economic concessions from France, Russia, and England. With regard to the critical Belgian issue, where Bethmann was inclined to set no meaningful conditions whatever, the generals demanded specific guarantees. As they summarized for a Conservative leader, "Belgium we must secure as flank cover: Liége and hinterland, which is not much, for us, but additionally the right of garrisoning, railroads, Antwerp as a German port, no Belgian army." They demanded, furthermore, that one abstract condition be translated into fact. The German governor in Warsaw had reported that he could recruit several hundred thousand native troops if Polish independence were proclaimed. The Supreme Command therefore insisted on military grounds that a Polish kingdom be established at once, and Bethmann reluctantly agreed, issuing the proclamation on November 5. [34] The peace conditions set by the Supreme Command were in the main acceptable to the Chancellor, since he still regarded them as nothing more than bargaining terms. But the result had been to neutralize the Chancellor's earlier maneuver and to give the generals an equal share with him in the preparation of the peace offer.

[32] Oct. 31, 1916, Bethmann, *Betrachtungen*, II, 152, note 1.
[33] Hindenburg to Bethmann, Nov. 6, 1916, *Official German Documents*, II, 1061-1062.
[34] Westarp, *Konservative Politik*, II, 62–64; Ludendorff, *Urkunden*, 300.

The negotiations with Austria and with the Supreme Command also led to considerable delay. Had Wilson made his move, it is true, Bethmann might have been able to force an immediate response by the Central Powers. Since the President remained silent, the slow negotiations with Burian continued, and a set of theoretical conditions was finally agreed upon.[35] The Chancellor meanwhile had to fulfill his promise to obtain a national service act from the Reichstag. In this matter, it is true, he moved with deliberate slowness. Ludendorff's eagerness for this law gave Bethmann his one hold over the Supreme Command. Whether these various delays were irksome to Bethmann or not is a moot question. It had been his original plan to act in apparent cooperation with Wilson. Under his arrangement with Burian, the Central Powers were to make a voluntary offer, merely asking neutrals to recommend it to the enemy. Bethmann seems to have been uncertain which plan was the more likely to succeed. He felt, in any case, that "the psychological moment" should not be allowed to pass.[36]

By late November he had decided to act as soon as possible, whether Wilson moved or not. The factors that influenced that decision were many and complex. Of first importance was the situation in Austria. On November 21 Franz Joseph died and Karl became Emperor. Burian of course abandoned his earlier insistence on delay.[37] The moment for action could not come too soon for him. More important in its influence on Bethmann was the realization that Kaiser Karl might sue for a separate peace. The German ambassador in Vienna had recently died, and the chargé d'affaires was not in a position to predict the Emperor's policy. If Karl actually were to put out feelers, Bethmann must have reasoned, the Entente would be very unlikely to act upon his own proposal. Karl's succession to the throne therefore made it imperative that the Central Powers act. Through the Foreign Ministry, Bethmann sent a final appeal to Wilson, warning him that time was running out.[38]

[35] Bethmann to Wedel, Nov. 23, 1916, *Official German Documents*, II, 1065–1068.

[36] Bethmann to Hindenburg, Nov. 27, 1916, *ibid.*, 1068–1069.

[37] Wedel to Zimmermann, Dec. 3, 1916, *ibid.*, 1070–1071.

[38] Zimmermann to Bernstorff, Nov. 26, 1916, *ibid.*, 994–995.

While conditions in Austria hurried the Chancellor, military events set a time limit upon his action. In early November one German army succeeded in penetrating the mountain barrier and deploying onto the plains east of Bucharest. On November 23 another force crossed the Danube. Capture of the capital was only a matter of time. The triumph over Rumania would supply the victory needed to prevent its being said that the Central Powers were suing for peace in a moment of defeat. More important, it would release almost 100,000 men for service elsewhere. Once Hindenburg and Ludendorff had this manpower to protect the Dutch and Danish frontiers, they were certain to reopen the U-boat issue. If they were given time to redeploy these troops, moreover, they might seek to postpone the peace move indefinitely, hoping for some success in the field. While the Austrian problem created a powerful sense of urgency, the Chancellor's relations with the Supreme Command made it impossible for him to delay much beyond the date when Bucharest's capture became imminent.

A minor factor in Bethmann's decision may have been the state of parliamentary and public opinion. He had cautiously and fretfully disclosed the possibility of peace negotiations to the state governments, the Reichstag budget committee, and in veiled form to the public. The response had been favorable to a degree that could not have been anticipated. The Bundesrat committee on foreign affairs gave Bethmann the warmest encouragement.[39] When he addressed the Reichstag committee, he provoked a debate on war aims which indicated the continuance of bitter divisions. He had done no more in his speech than hint at the possibility of Germany's entering a postwar league of nations. When it was published, nevertheless, socialist and Progressive organs commented hopefully on the possibility of negotiating peace. The key Centrist organ, *Germania,* indicated agreement. Public feeling was suggested by the 900,000 signatures obtained for the socialist peace petition. It appeared also in the defensive attitude taken by certain annexationist journals like the *Kreuzzeitung* and the *Vossische*

[39] Deuerlein, *Bundesratsausschuss,* 199, 292–293.

Zeitung.[40] The outlines of the later peace resolution majority were becoming increasingly distinct. Bethmann may have come, like Burian, to want credit for sponsoring a peace appeal. It may have been a sense of the public mood that caused him to write Hindenburg on November 27 saying that he was unsure whether it was better to wait for Wilson's move or to anticipate him.[41] When he decided not to wait, at any rate, he showed no regret.

He reached this decision during the last week in November, immediately after Karl's accession and Mackensen's crossing of the Danube. Notifying the Supreme Command, he pointed out that the national service law would probably be passed by November 30 or December 1. He proposed to act as soon as the Rumanian campaign reached its climax.[42] By December 9 a fixed date had been set. Bethmann summoned the Reichstag to convene on December 12, giving no indication of the reason for this extraordinary call. On the eleventh he met with a group of party leaders and confidentially informed them of his intention. On the twelfth he went before the Reichstag to proclaim the willingness of the Central Powers to enter immediate negotiations with their enemies. His note through neutral capitals was dispatched the same day.[43]

When Wilson's anticlimactic appeal arrived a week later, Bethmann had no choice but to answer as he did. He had, in the first place, made his position perfectly clear. Only Bernstorff's eagerness to bring about cooperation with Wilson had prevented the President from knowing in advance that Germany would not state terms. In view of Austrian attitudes, he could not easily change his stand. Burian wanted Wilson to have as little connection as possible with the Central Powers' bid. One reason that he had given for urging haste, indeed, had been the danger of Wilson's acting first,

[40] Westarp, *Konservative Politik,* II, 62, 177; *Daily Review of the Foreign Press,* Nov. 3, Nov. 18, Nov. 23, 1916.

[41] *Official German Documents,* II, 1068–1069.

[42] *Ibid.*

[43] *Ibid.,* 1071–1073; *Norddeutsche Allgemeine Zeitung,* Dec. 9, 1916; Westarp, *Konservative Politik,* II, 74–76; *Verhandlungen des Reichstages,* CCCVIII (Dec. 12, 1916), 2331–2332; Department of State, *Diplomatic Correspondence with Belligerent Governments* (European War No. 4), 305–306.

and the Chancellor would have had the utmost difficulty in overcoming his ally's distaste for American good offices.[44] In view of
domestic conditions, Bethmann could not afford to meet Wilson's
appeal for a statement of terms. Annexationists had shown skepticism about his peace offer. Zimmermann had sought to disarm
some of them by pleading that the Chancellor's move had been
necessary to anticipate intervention by Wilson.[45] Reception of the
American note by the party press was on the whole unenthusiastic,
with the right Centrist *Kölnische Volkszeitung* denouncing it more
violently even than Conservative and National Liberal journals.[46]
Some of the Chancellor's potential left-center support might break
away if he seemed to cede the initiative to Wilson. Most important
of all, the Supreme Command had precipitated a fresh U-boat debate, and the Chancellor could not at the moment afford to ask
permission from Hindenburg and Ludendorff to conciliate Wilson's
mediation ambitions.

To answer the President with anything except noncommittal
thanks would require reformulation of war aims. Those agreed
upon earlier would be certain to outrage Wilson rather than to satisfy him. Since that time, moreover, the Supreme Command had
given wholehearted endorsement to a set of naval conditions that
would have been still more obnoxious to the President, for they
included annexation by Germany of Valona, the Faroes, the Azores,
Dakar and its hinterland, Portuguese Timor, and Tahiti.[47] Bethmann might have deferred answering the President, but he undoubtedly hoped, by replying quickly, to demonstrate his real
eagerness for negotiations with the Entente. He chose therefore to
notify the Supreme Command through Zimmermann, "In order
to prevent any meddling on the part of President Wilson in peace
negotiations, we have decided to answer his note in such a way as

[44] Wedel to Zimmermann, Dec. 5, 1916, *Official German Documents*, II, 1070–
1071.
    [45] Westarp, *Konservative Politik*, II, 75.
    [46] *Daily Review of the Foreign Press: Enemy Press Supplement*, Dec. 21, Dec. 28,
1916.
    [47] Holtzendorff to Bethmann, Dec. 24, 1916, German Foreign Ministry Archives
(Peace Negotiations).

to reflect the spirit of our peace move, but to make it perfectly clear that it is our desire to deal directly with our enemies." [48]

It is doubtful, of course, whether either the timing of Bethmann's offer or the character of his reply to Wilson actually had any effect on the course of events. Had the President acted first and suggested parleys, as was initially intended, the Chancellor would have seemed to move at America's request. The Allies were willing, however, to state their terms. The question of German war aims would inevitably have arisen, and only time could have brought Wilson around to the view that conditions were unimportant, that only negotiations mattered. Only time, if anything, could have persuaded the Allies. But time was precisely what was lacking. Barely four weeks after the Chancellor's peace offer, his whole house lay about him. The decision for unrestricted submarine war had been irrevocably taken.

Even while the Chancellor awaited responses to his appeal, the decisive moment for German-American relations arrived. The Supreme Command, which had been threatening to do so for months, resolved in favor of unrestricted U-boat war. The Chancellor, having lost control of the Reichstag, also lost command over the Kaiser. He found himself unable to resist.

A test with the Supreme Command had been impending ever since Hindenburg and Ludendorff succeeded Falkenhayn. At their very first conference, it will be remembered, the generals had dismayed Bethmann by declaring that as soon as the military situation altered they would have to resort to a U-boat campaign. Bethmann's uneasiness at this declaration had been reflected two days later when he made his first genuine solicitation of an American peace move.

The likelihood of an early option for the U-boat by the Supreme Command had appeared at the time when the peace move was first decided upon. When Bethmann secured the Kaiser's approval of an overture through Bernstorff, he suggested warning mildly of a possible necessity for resuming submarine warfare. It

[48] Zimmermann to Lersner, Dec. 24, 1916, *Official German Documents*, II, 1087–1088.

was Ludendorff who insisted that the message should begin with a ringing affirmation of confidence in victory and that it should say, "the Imperial fleet promises that swift success will follow the unrestricted participation of an increased number of U-boats. . . . For this reason, the Supreme Command must take the unrestricted U-boat war into consideration in the course of their calculations, in order to relieve the situation at the Somme front." Ludendorff had desired, indeed, that the message declare unequivocally, "we must regain the freedom of action which we reserved for ourselves" in the *Sussex* pledge.[49] Not only did the First Quartermaster General betray the trend of his own thought, but he sought perhaps to entrap the Chancellor into a commitment.

When Bethmann was struggling against the U-boat advocates in the Reichstag, he received a serious fright. Admiral von Holtzendorff wrote him on October 1 that the Supreme Command had decided to open an unrestricted campaign on October 18.[50] Bethmann had just emerged from budget committee sessions where he had asserted that the army opposed immediate use of the underwater weapon. Holtzendorff's message threatened to put him in a ridiculous position. It also shocked him to the fibers. As he immediately telegraphed to Hindenburg, "I cannot conceive of a final decision being taken on this question and of my being merely informed thereof by the Chief of the Naval Staff." He took the trouble to point out that there were abiding political objections to such a move, and he also observed that a decision was impossible until the peace effort had been tried.[51] Although Bethmann promised to supply the field marshal with an exhaustive memorandum on the subject, Hindenburg cut him off. He had merely discussed the possibility, he explained, and he fully understood the Chancellor's responsibility. According to the Foreign Ministry representative at Supreme Headquarters, Hindenburg and Ludendorff were both extremely apologetic:

[49] Hindenburg and Ludendorff to the Kaiser, Sept. 24, 1916, Reichsarchiv, *Der Weltkrieg*, XI, 448–449.
[50] German Foreign Ministry Archives (U-boat War).
[51] *Official German Documents*, II, 1168–1169.

Both gentlemen expressed themselves repeatedly to the effect that the loyal cooperation now existing with your Excellency can not be allowed to be disturbed by any lack of harmony, and that nothing was further from their intention than to carry on a separate policy behind your Excellency's back, or in any way to intermeddle with political matters; that the more numerous the material differences of opinion, the more frankly must opinions be exchanged, but that they had no use for a game of hide and seek.[52]

The representative himself indicated sophisticated skepticism at these professions. In any case, Bethmann had received both a fright and a warning.

For some time after this encounter, the generals actually seemed to be cooperating loyally. When the public agitation for a U-boat campaign continued, Hindenburg lent a hand to the Chancellor. So it seemed, at any rate, from accounts of a meeting held on October 14 by the Pan-German Independent Committee for a German Peace.[53] After several committee members had spoken out for intensified agitation, an industrialist from Leverkunen arose. He was, he said, an official representative of the field marshal, and he brought a message calling upon the committee, for purely military reasons, to cease its efforts on behalf of U-boat warfare. The meeting dissolved into chaos. When Conservative deputies called at Supreme Headquarters, moreover, the generals gave them little encouragement. They said candidly what they had said to Bethmann: as soon as the military situation permitted, they would favor opening a submarine campaign. A Progressive deputy who also visited Headquarters came away with the impression that the generals were working comfortably with the Chancellor.[54]

All the while, of course, the inevitable division between Bethmann and Ludendorff was widening. The Naval Staff conducted a careful campaign to persuade the generals that Bethmann was wrong in his estimates of probable neutral reactions. Reports from the naval attachés in Sweden and Denmark were brought to them.

[52] Grünau to Bethmann, Oct. 2, 1916 (two messages), *ibid.*, 1170–1171.
[53] Erzberger to Jagow, Oct. 18, 1916, German Foreign Ministry Archives (U-boat War); *Daily Review of the Foreign Press,* Oct. 26, 1916.
[54] Westarp, *Konservative Politik,* II, 134–135; Haussmann, *Schlaglichter,* 76.

Contradicting information from the Foreign Ministry, these reports expressed certainty that neither the northern neutrals nor the Netherlands would go to war over the U-boat. Extensive and impressive printed memoranda, circulated by the Naval Staff, meanwhile offered evidence to back up the prediction that England could be starved into submission within six months.[55] Nor were naval officers the only ones seeking to turn the generals' minds. Conservative politicians did not visit Supreme Headquarters just to learn Ludendorff's opinions; they also came to preach. When Valentini returned from a long vacation, he recorded the impression that Falkenhayn holdovers had been at work on Hindenburg and Ludendorff, trying to alienate them from the Chancellor.[56]

But it needs no sinister influence to explain Ludendorff's growing antagonism toward Bethmann. The fact that the Chancellor competed for power was enough. In Ludendorff's memoirs there recurs the phrase, "I could not work with" so and so. The individual named is invariably someone who did not agree with the general. It must be admitted, of course, that Ludendorff had some provocation for seizing power from all his rivals. When he came to the Supreme Command, the government was virtually without plans. Since the collapse of the Schlieffen scheme, the army's strategy had been a matter of almost pure improvisation. The Chancellor had not mustered the full resources of the country. Ludendorff believed, accurately as it turned out, that industry, finance, and labor could be marshaled for a much greater effort. He recognized his own ability to do what others could not. But he could only "work with" the dull, phlegmatic, and pliable field marshal. He could never for long abide a man of independent will, and his struggle with Bethmann was almost foredestined.

Before the decisive contest occurred, Ludendorff made one unsuccessful attack. Despite his own later testimony that he was

[55] Holtzendorff to Hindenburg, Sept. 16, 1916, German Foreign Ministry Archives (U-boat War); report by Naval Attaché, Stockholm, Sept. 26, 1916, *ibid.;* report by Naval Attaché, Copenhagen, Oct. 12, 1916, *ibid.;* Holtzendorff to Hindenburg, Dec. 17, Dec. 19, Dec. 22, Dec. 28, 1916, *ibid.*
[56] *Kaiser und Kabinettschef,* 141–143.

"secretly pleased" by the Chancellor's peace plan, the evidence is almost indisputable that he resisted it. In approving the message to Bernstorff, which he could not block, he raised the touchy question of a U-boat decision. He endorsed the subsequent plan for an Austro-German peace offer, which the Kaiser had already enthusiastically accepted, but he conditioned his approval upon prompt passage of a national service law. It was when Bethmann proposed actually to make the offer that he stepped in with a challenge.

The encounter occurred on December 8. Bethmann had earlier indicated that he would be ready to act by the ninth. He had asked the Supreme Command to prophesy when Bucharest would fall, so that he could time his proposal accordingly. The Kaiser evidently pressed Hindenburg to comply, and the field marshal predicted a triumph by December 6 or 7. It actually occurred on the sixth, but on that evening, Bethmann was notified, Ludendorff still withheld his approval of the peace offer. The general requested that the Chancellor speak with him at Pless.[57]

Between the 8th and the 10th of December, Ludendorff suffered a partial defeat. He sent Hindenburg to a conference with the Kaiser on the eighth, equipped with a list of conditions for the Supreme Command's approval of the peace move. The field marshal first reported on the success in Rumania and sketched the Supreme Command's basic war plan for 1917: redeployment of troops for a determined offense in the spring and "the submarine war to be loosed in full force against England." Hindenburg then informed the Kaiser that he could approve of the peace offer only if:

1. Operations on land and the U-boat war on the ocean can be carried on without any further hindrance;
2. An army order is issued announcing this;
3. And the political branch believes that it can bring about the kind of peace that Germany needs.

The field marshal defined the first condition as meaning an unrestricted submarine campaign by the end of January.[58]

[57] Memo by Bartenwerffer, Dec. 6, 1916, Reichsarchiv, *Der Weltkrieg*, XI, 453.
[58] *Ibid.;* memo by Hindenburg, Dec. 8, 1916, Ludendorff, *Urkunden*, 310.

Bethmann did not have a chance to interpose his objections until the following day. Meeting the generals in an audience before the Kaiser, he protested that they had already agreed to the peace move and allowed him to make arrangements with the other Central Powers. Their original conditions had been met, and their present demands were inconsistent with their earlier undertaking to the Kaiser. He objected strenuously, however, only to the submarine warfare proposal. Military operations would of course be continued, he observed, if the peace offer were refused; an encouraging order to the army could not be objected to; the term, "the kind of a peace that Germany needs," was impossible of definition.[59] Although the Kaiser directed that the Chancellor should proceed with the peace proposal, Bethmann had nevertheless lost some ground. He had been put on the defensive. He had been forced to ratify the Supreme Command's joint responsibility with him for the definition of peace terms. He had also felt obliged to concede that in the event his offer was rejected he would be willing to approve a new U-boat campaign against armed merchant vessels. This possibility had lately been discussed between the navy and the Foreign Ministry, but Bethmann had avoided committing himself.[60] Even though he had now yielded this potentially dangerous point, he had nevertheless triumphed in his insistence that the question of unrestricted U-boat war would have to be decided at a later time.

As soon as the peace offer had been made, Ludendorff returned to the attack. He left the conference at Pless to visit the Somme front. There he became even more convinced that it was necessary to cut off the enemy's supplies across the Channel. He may also have regarded the evident lack of enthusiasm on the part of German troops as a partial result of the peace proposal itself. Seizing upon almost the first excuse, at any rate, he telegraphed Berlin that the Chancellor's effort had failed.[61] The evidence that he cited was

[59] Memo by Bethmann, n.d., *Official German Documents*, II, 1072–1073.
[60] Holtzendorff to Bethmann, Nov. 26, Dec. 5, 1916, German Foreign Ministry Archives (U-boat War).
[61] Reichsarchiv, *Der Weltkrieg*, XI, 165; Ludendorff to Bethmann, Dec. 20, 1916, *Official German Documents*, II, 1199.

Lloyd George's preliminary speech to the House of Commons, the one quoting Lincoln against peace without victory. "Since Lloyd George has rejected our peace proposal . . . ," he declared, "I am of the opinion that . . . the U-boat war should now be launched with the greatest vigor." Although the Chancellor protested that his note had not even been answered as yet, Ludendorff would not retreat. He threatened a cabinet crisis, declaring "that the Field Marshal would no longer be able to shoulder the responsibility of the campaign in case the government should not agree." [62]

There resulted a direct clash between the Chancellor and the Supreme Command. The question, Bethmann wrote to Hindenburg, is one "of foreign policy for which I have to bear the sole responsibility, a responsibility which is constitutional and can not be delegated." The Chancellor promised, it is true, to take full account of the Supreme Command's views. He volunteered to approve a campaign against armed merchant vessels as soon as the Allies formally answered his peace note, and he offered to discuss the issue of unrestricted warfare "as soon as our peace move has been brought to a definite conclusion as the result of the answer which the Entente will make." [63] But Ludendorff would not be put off. Over Hindenburg's signature the Chancellor was warned that the majority of the German people regarded the Supreme Command as sharing responsibility. If their views were rejected, the generals would have to announce their disagreement publicly.[64]

Bethmann hurried to Pless on December 29 for a confrontation with the generals. Judging from his past tactics and from the sparse evidence available, it can be inferred that he hoped to outmaneuver the generals. The question of a limited campaign, directed only against armed vessels, had been under discussion since the previous October. Bethmann had approved it in principle but insisted that no order be issued until the peace proposal bore fruit and until the

[62] Zimmermann to Lersner, Dec. 21, 1916, *ibid.*, 1199–1200; Lersner to Zimmermann, Dec. 22, 1916, *ibid.*, 1200–1201.

[63] Bethmann to Lersner, Dec. 23, 1916, *ibid.*, 1202–1203.

[64] Lersner to Zimmermann, Dec. 26, 1916, *ibid.*, 1204–1205.

American government had been prepared for it.[65] It appears that he hoped to draw the generals into debate on the narrower issue of postponing the limited campaign. In view of the complexity of the question and of the Kaiser's enthusiasm for peace, he might win a tactical victory such as he had won earlier against Tirpitz and Bachmann.

Prepared for a genuine duel, he had brought with him the bluff, good-humored Zimmermann. In response to suggestions from Ludendorff, Bethmann had recently removed Jagow and put Zimmermann in his place. He had reason to assume that the new Foreign Minister could exert some influence on the generals. He also brought with him Helfferich, whose sharp tongue and precise mind had proved useful in earlier debates. To buttress his arguments he had already sent the generals dispatches from Holland and America testifying to the unrelieved danger of war.[66]

Instead of a battle on the limited issue that he had chosen, Bethmann found himself involved in a series of even lesser skirmishes. The first turned on the presence of Helfferich. The field marshal sent a cavalry officer to meet Bethmann at the railroad station and tell him that the Chancellor and Foreign Minister would be welcome but that Helfferich's presence was not desired. As soon as he could, Bethmann protested to Hindenburg that Helfferich was Vice Chancellor and that, in any case, it was his business whom he chose to accompany him. For the field marshal to have given him such a message through a young officer, he complained, was as if he had dispatched a junior civil servant to say that he would see Hindenburg but not in the presence of the War Minister. Aside from this personal matter, the Chancellor found himself also meeting charges from Ludendorff that he had allowed his censors to pass articles identifying the views of the Supreme Command with his own,

---

[65] Holtzendorff to Zimmermann, Dec. 22, Dec. 28, 1916, German Foreign Ministry Archives (U-boat War); Bethmann to Lersner, Dec. 26, 1916, *Official German Documents*, II, 1205.

[66] Helfferich, *Weltkrieg*, II, 396–397; Bethmann to Lersner, Dec. 28, 1916, German Foreign Ministry Archives (U-boat War).

that "they" wished in Berlin to sow division between the two chiefs of the Supreme Command, and that the Chancellor "sought to restrain the field marshal from a decision about the U-boat war."

The conference, as a result, became pointless. Bethmann denied knowledge of the questionable news items. He offered to punish the "infamous slanderers" if Ludendorff could identify his anonymous "they." With regard to the U-boat matter, he had no choice but to set forth his views fully:

Never have I sought . . . to restrain the Supreme Command. It is not now possible . . . for them independently to command a ruthless U-boat war. First we have to take back the promises we have made to America. That is a political act, for which constitutionally I alone bear responsibility. . . . Since the retraction of our promises could mean war with America, my responsibility in the question is a fateful one. Obviously the opinion of the Supreme Command would have the greatest weight with me, and it is my strongest hope to bring about complete understanding between us. Should that, contrary to my hopes, prove impossible, then a combined audience before the Kaiser will have to decide.

When he attempted to draw the generals into debate on the issues of a limited campaign, they declined to argue. They accepted his contentions but asserted that the real question still remained. Instead of discussing it, they turned to other matters. Despite the sharp telegrams recently interchanged, the generals seemed not to want to debate the submarine problem. Bethmann returned to Berlin encouraged but somewhat puzzled.[67]

Barely a week later he found himself challenged once again. In that short time his position had materially weakened. The Allied answer to his peace note had been published. The Kaiser had angrily declared that Germany now needed to fight on, that Belgium would have to be annexed, and that there could be no understanding with France.[68] The Emperor was no longer to be held in check by warnings against endangering the peace move. Nor could the Chancellor any longer command a peace bloc in the Reichstag. Even the majority socialists admitted in their newspapers that the

---

[67] Bethmann to Valentini, Dec. 31, 1916, *Kaiser und Kabinettschef*, 241–245.
[68] Grünau to Bethmann, Jan. 2, 1917, *Official German Documents*, II, 1091.

Allied reply killed all chances of immediate negotiations. Progressive journals meanwhile sidled toward advocacy of a U-boat campaign, and Progressive deputies were heard declaring that the people would never forgive the government if it failed to use all weapons to the full.[69] Just as the Chancellor saw his grip loosening over both the Kaiser and the country, he received from Hindenburg a terse telegram declaring, "the military situation is such that unrestricted U-boat warfare can begin on the 1st of February and for that very reason should begin."[70]

Bethmann hurried once again to Pless. The decisive audience before the Kaiser was scheduled to occur on the evening of January 9. He had less than thirty hours in which to prepare for it. Although he talked earnestly with Zimmermann and Helfferich before leaving Berlin, neither could accompany him. Helfferich did sit up all night, however, preparing an exhaustive memorandum which the Chancellor would receive by telegraph.[71] At Pless Bethmann found himself in for a lonely struggle. Müller evidently offered him no help, saying simply that the Kaiser's mind was already made up.[72] Although Valentini still resolutely opposed a U-boat campaign, he was confined to his bed. The Chancellor did arrange that the final audience should be held in the chambers of the Civil Cabinet chief.[73] But he first had to meet Hindenburg and Ludendorff alone.

He spent the entire morning debating with the generals. There is no record of the arguments he employed, but they cannot have been much different from those he had advanced again and again. If he commented on the danger of drawing Holland and Denmark into the war, the generals replied that they were ready. The western front had been reinforced, and three cavalry brigades stood on the Danish frontier. The key problem was, of course, the United States. Bethmann still felt that a U-boat campaign would unquestionably bring America into the war and that her intervention

[69] *Daily Review of the Foreign Press: Enemy Press Supplement,* Jan. 11, Jan. 18, 1917; Naumann, *Dokumente und Argumente,* 208–209.

[70] Jan. 8, 1917, *Official German Documents,* II, 1205.

[71] Helfferich, *Weltkrieg,* II, 405–406.

[72] *Ibid.,* 409.

[73] *Kaiser und Kabinettschef,* 144.

THE END OF DIPLOMACY

would mean, at the very least, an interminable prolongation of hostilities. But Hindenburg had said to Holtzendorff on the previous day, "We are counting on the possibility of war with the United States, and have made all preparations to meet it. Things can not be worse than they are now."[74] Ludendorff was to explain a few days later to the Austrian chief of staff that he did not believe the United States could supply more shipping or war materiel to the Allies, that money was of no importance, and that American contributions of manpower would be slow in arriving.[75] Since Ludendorff was already convinced that he could not "work with" Bethmann, it is doubtful that he made any concessions at all.[76] The Chancellor returned to Valentini's room at 1 o'clock grey and exhausted.[77]

He realized that the issue was decided. Holtzendorff had prepared the Kaiser on the previous day. Müller would not stand out against the Supreme Command. When the Chancellor and the generals assembled before the throne in the evening, as Valentini has described:

Everyone stood around a large table, on which the Kaiser, pale and excited, leaned his hand. Holtzendorff spoke first, and, from the standpoint of the navy, both well and above all in confidence of victory. England will lie on the ground in at most six months, before a single American has set foot on the continent; the American danger does not disturb him at all. Hindenburg spoke very briefly, observing only that from the measure a reduction in American munitions exports had to be expected. Bethmann finally, with a visible inner excitement, set forth once again the reasons that had led him in the past to cast an opposing vote against a U-boat war beyond the limits of cruiser warfare, namely concern about the prompt entry of America into the ranks of our enemies, with all the ensuing consequences, but he closed by saying that in view of the recently altered stand of the Supreme Command and the categorical declarations of the admirals as to the success of the measure, he wished to withdraw his opposition. The Kaiser fol-

[74] Protocols of a session of Jan. 8, 1917, *Official German Documents*, II, 1317–1319.
[75] Hindenburg to Hötzendorff, Jan. 15, 1917, Reichsarchiv, *Der Weltkrieg*, XI, 467.
[76] *Official German Documents*, II, 1318–1319; *Kaiser und Kabinettschef*, 147–149.
[77] *Ibid.*, 145–146.

lowed his statements with every sign of impatience and opposition and declared in closing that the unrestricted U-boat war was therefore decided.[78]

The decision was final. Bethmann could have resigned, hoping to force a crisis in the Reichstag. Valentini urged him to do so, and the socialist leaders later regretted that he had not. But the *Zentrum* would probably not have supported him; its resolution of the previous October at least indicated that it would not. Bethmann evidently felt that an open fight would be futile and that it was better to save the *Burgfrieden*. He may have hoped to retrieve his power, perhaps even to reverse the Kaiser's decision. But the generals, as he soon learned, were determined to get rid of him. They were waiting only for a likely candidate and a favorable moment, and the Emperor remained in their spell. The Chancellor's power had gone; his fall in July, 1917, was an anticlimax. His long struggle to prevent Germany's ruin had ended at Pless on January 9.

[78] *Ibid.*

XIX

The Last Crisis

When Wilson learned of the new German submarine campaign, he had no reason to believe that Germany had made a final choice between war and peace. Twice in 1915 and once in 1916 the German government had seemed to challenge the United States, only to back down before the President's patient firmness. The new announcement was more abrupt than the proclamations of 1915 and 1916—submarine operations were to begin immediately. It was also more thoroughgoing. But it could still be read as a mere test of America's toughness.

The President's immediate problem was to manifest his unyielding opposition to the U-boat. The obvious course was to break relations with Germany. Such had been the threat in the *Sussex* ultimatum, and House and Lansing counseled Wilson against doing anything less. Both argued that America's prestige could not be maintained if the President merely sent a new note of protest. Lansing laid so much stress on this point that his words deserve quotation:

I said that if we failed to act I did not think we could hold up our heads as a great nation and that our voice in the future would be treated with contempt by both the Allies and Germany. . . . I felt that the greatness of the part which a nation plays in the world depends largely upon its character and the high regard of other nations; that I felt that to permit Germany to do this abominable thing without firmly following out to the letter what we had proclaimed to the world we would do, would be to lose our character as a great power and the esteem of all nations; and that to be considered a "bluffer" was an impossible position for a nation which cherished self-respect.[1]

The President did not at once accept his advisers' opinions. Lansing, who had already said that severance of relations would mean war, spoke as if a break would be a mere preliminary to hostilities, but Wilson did not entirely trust his Secretary of State, and he was not ready to accept war as a foregone conclusion.[2]

He did decide that he had to break relations. Nothing less seemed apt to make an impression in Berlin. If a note were sent instead, it would have to contain an ultimatum even stronger than that implicit in the *Sussex* note, and a threat might be more risky than a mere break in relations. Wilson discussed with House the possibility of deferring the break until an actual sinking occurred, but the colonel strongly advised prompt action. "If we waited for the overt act," House noted in his diary, "they would believe we had accepted their ultimatum. I had in mind, too, the effect it would have on the Allies. We would not be nearly so advantageously situated if we waited, as if we acted promptly."[3] The President reluctantly agreed and deferred the break only until he could give prior notice to Senator Stone. On February 3 he went before Congress to announce the severance of relations.

Through most of February, 1917, Wilson held to his policy of patient firmness. He did not underrate the force of the new challenge. The Germans seemed to be behaving, he commented, like madmen.[4] Nor did he exaggerate his chances. When House and Lansing foretold failure, he did not dispute. So long as the faintest hope remained, however, he had to continue his earlier policy.

He made every effort to convince the Germans of his resoluteness. When giving public notice of the break in relations, he used menacing language. "[I]f American ships and American lives should in

---

[1] Memo by Lansing, Feb. 4, 1917, Lansing, *War Memoirs*, 213.
[2] Diary, Jan. 2, Jan. 11, 1917, House Papers.
[3] Diary, Feb. 1, 1917, *Intimate Papers*, II, 439.
[4] *Ibid.*, 440.

fact be sacrificed . . . ," he declared, "I shall take the liberty of coming again before the Congress, to ask that authority be given me to use any means that may be necessary for the protection of our seamen and our people." [5] Of America's principles he asserted, "These are the bases of peace, not war. God grant we may not be challenged to defend them." When the suggestion reached him through neutral channels that the United States and Germany negotiate while the submarine campaign continued, he refused point-blank. The precondition of any resumption of relations, he let it be known, was a return to the *Sussex* pledge of the preceding spring.[6]

He insisted, at the same time, on remaining as patient as ever. Lansing favored proclaiming Germany an international outlaw.[7] Various members of the cabinet urged the defensive arming of American merchant vessels. But Wilson declined all such advice. Although he recognized the need for military precautions, he warned the Secretary of War to give "no basis . . . for opinion abroad that we are mobilizing." [8] So long as there remained any chance of diplomatic success, he risked no provocative move.

He did use every kind of diplomatic pressure. Inviting other neutrals to join in breaking relations, he sought to show Germany how world opinion disapproved of her act. He also hoped undoubtedly that she would see the immensity of the dangers that she ran. Polk conferred with the Swiss minister, and House talked with the representative of the Netherlands.[9] Although Wilson had told Congress that he took it for granted other neutrals would join him, China was the only one to do so. The Swiss government begged off on the ground of its vulnerable situation. The Dutch minister commented that European neutrals had been trying for two years to obtain Wilson's cooperation. Since he had not helped them,

[5] *Public Papers*, IV, 422–426.
[6] *Foreign Relations, Supplement One: 1917*, pp. 126, 129.
[7] *Lansing Papers*, I, 591–592.
[8] Baker, *Wilson*, VI, 460–461.
[9] *Foreign Relations, Supplement One: 1917*, pp. 139–141; House to Wilson, Feb. 10, 1917, *Intimate Papers*, II, 445–446; Wilson to House, Feb. 12, 1917, House Papers.

they were not prepared to rescue him.[10] The President's effort to show the Germans that they were alienating all neutrals was unsuccessful.

He could seek to impress them with the danger of alienating the United States alone. House, who understood Wilson's purposes, used every channel to convey "some idea of the potential force of this country from a military, financial, and industrial viewpoint."[11] Wilson meanwhile allowed the Germans to be warned gently of the loss to be suffered if Belgian relief stopped.[12] What he wanted to do, of course, was not to provoke the Germans but to bring them to a realization of the stakes with which they were gambling.

He sought also to bring pressure of another kind upon Germany. Reports from the American embassy in Vienna had given a picture of near despair. Although Austria joined her ally in proclaiming unrestricted submarine warfare, Count Czernin appealed to the United States to continue her efforts for a peace with "no victors and no vanquished."[13] The President elected not to break relations with Austria or with Bulgaria and Turkey. There existed a possibility of inducing Germany's allies to bring her to her senses or alternatively of frightening Germany with the prospect of a break-up in her own coalition.

The President sought, indeed, to pry the Central Powers apart. He directed Lansing to cable London, asking permission to offer Austria a separate peace with a promise that her territory would remain intact.[14] Even though this scheme was at variance with principles which Wilson had already uttered, it held much promise. Austria might be emboldened to press for German conciliation of the United States. Or she might compel her ally to resume discus-

[10] *Foreign Relations, Supplement One: 1917*, pp. 116, 118, 123–124, 126–127, 130, 143; House to Wilson, Feb. 10, 1917, *Intimate Papers*, II, 445.

[11] *Ibid.*, 446.

[12] Lansing to Whitlock, Feb. 4, Feb. 15, 1917, *Foreign Relations, Supplement One: 1917*, pp. 632–633, 639–640.

[13] Penfield to Lansing, Feb. 4, 1917, *ibid.*, 113; Lansing to Wilson, Feb. 10, 1917, Wilson Papers.

[14] Lansing to Page, Feb. 8, 1917, *Foreign Relations, Supplement One: 1917*, pp. 40–41.

sion of a general peace. In that case Wilson was prepared to offer Germany terms even more enticing than those outlined in the "peace without victory" message. "Four Bases of Peace," sketched by the President in early February, included equality of economic opportunity and naval disarmament.[15] Another possibility was, of course, that Austria might actually be detached from America's prospective enemies. Since Lloyd George delayed his answer, no offer was made until after Wilson had lost nearly all hope of bringing the Germans to reason. The President asked Czernin to consider a separate peace and not to discuss it with Germany.[16] At the outset, however, he must have considered the offer a tactic that might bring victory in the submarine controversy.

Among the conceivable devices by which the President could press or lure the Germans into concession, only one was not used. Wilson could have demonstrated his willingness to act against the Allies if only Germany would first abandon the U-boat. He had held out such a hope during earlier crises. Despite his own continuing anger at the blockade and the blacklist, he did not do so in February, 1917. The only gesture in that direction was a curt note protesting a British decree that made part of the North Sea a defensive zone.[17] In refraining from any other challenge to the Allies, Wilson may have been sidestepping criticism from Anglophiles whose support he would need if Germany failed to give in. He may have held in mind the possibility that he might soon need cooperation from the Allied governments themselves. Or he may simply have recognized that having failed to press the Allies when U-boats were quiet he was not likely to impress the Germans with action at this stage. With this one exception, Wilson employed every pressure and enticement consistent with his basic policy. Although his chief effort failed when the European neutrals declined to join him, he was in no position to compel their cooperation. The quickness and adroitness of his tactics contrasted with his slow-

[15] *Lansing Papers*, I, 19–20.
[16] Lansing to Penfield, Feb. 22, 1917, *Foreign Relations, Supplement One: 1917*, pp. 57–58.
[17] Lansing to Spring-Rice, Feb. 19, 1917, *ibid.*, 519–520.

ness and awkwardness in 1915. He had become a much more accomplished diplomatist. But his adversary was no longer the same. Diplomacy was of no avail against Ludendorff.

By the end of February Wilson had seen that patient firmness would no longer work. In earlier crises the German government had quickly shown a conciliatory disposition. Now there was no such sign. Swiss intermediaries reported Berlin willing to negotiate, it is true, but not to modify the U-boat campaign.[18] Dispatches to the Department of State meanwhile told of frequent torpedoings. No American vessel happened to be sunk without warning, but submarine commanders were said to be ignoring neutral flags, and two Norwegian ships were among those destroyed.[19] It appeared to be pure chance that no American citizens were among the dead. The occurrence of some critical incident was almost certain.

Three weeks after the break, moreover, Wilson received evidence that Germany anticipated war. The proof was Zimmermann's telegram to Eckhardt, proposing a German-Mexican-Japanese alliance in case of war. Intercepted by British naval intelligence more than a month before, its disclosure to Page had been delayed until the method could be concealed from the Germans.[20] Page lost no time in cabling Wilson. The President thus had before him a document of unquestionable authenticity, indicating that Germany preferred war to abandonment of the U-boat campaign.

His principal advisers had already urged active measures of resistance. At the first cabinet discussion of breaking relations, several members had suggested arming American merchantmen. The President had agreed to let the State Department tell shipowners that they could arm, but he refused to supply guns and ammunition.[21] McAdoo and others became increasingly insistent that he

[18] Memo by Ritter, Feb. 11, 1917, *ibid.*, 126; memo by Lansing, Feb. 21, 1917, *ibid.*, 139–141.

[19] *Ibid.*, 112, 114–115, 122–123, 125–126, 129–131, 133–135, 138–139, 141–146, 149.

[20] Page to Lansing, Feb. 24, 1917, *ibid.*, 147–148; Samuel R. Spencer, Jr., *Decision for War, 1917* (Rindge, N.H., 1953), 55–69.

[21] Diary, Feb. 4, 1917, Lansing Papers; Houston, *Eight Years with Wilson's Cabinet*, I, 230–231; F. D. Roosevelt to Daniels, Feb. 10, 1917, Wilson Papers.

change his decision. The Secretary of the Treasury argued that American vessels were staying in port out of fear. The result was not only injury to the American economy but indirect aid to Germany: the United States was in effect cooperating in the German blockade. At a cabinet meeting on February 23, McAdoo and those who sympathized with him became so demanding as to anger Wilson. He accused them of trying to push the country into war. One of the members referred to the session subsequently as "one of the most animated . . . that I suppose has ever been held under this or any other President." [22]

Not long after this meeting, Wilson decided partially to follow McAdoo's advice. He does not seem to have been so concerned as the Treasury Secretary over the timidity of American shippers. He believed that constitutionally he possessed the power to supply merchantmen with defensive armament.[23] Yet he chose not to do so on his own authority. Instead he took the slower method of addressing Congress, asking for a gratuitous grant of power and for a suitable appropriation. He delivered this request on February 26, three days after the turbulent cabinet session and two days after he learned of the Zimmermann note.

One obvious reason for addressing Congress instead of acting was, of course, to test sentiment. The election campaign of 1916 had displayed the firm hold of pacifism and neutralism on large segments of the public. Against Wilson's will and wishes, "He kept us out of war" had become the Democrats' most potent slogan. [24] Toward the end of the campaign, the President commented to House, "I do not believe the American people would wish to go to war no matter how many Americans were lost at sea." He said much the same thing again early in 1917.[25] Press summaries and comments by politicians indicated that a sharp change had occurred

---

[22] Houston, *Eight Years with Wilson's Cabinet*, I, 233–237; *Letters of Franklin K. Lane*, 233–241.

[23] Address to Congress, Feb. 26, 1917, *Public Papers*, IV, 430.

[24] See Baker, *Wilson*, VI, chapter VII, *passim*.

[25] Diary, Nov. 2, 1916, Jan. 4, 1917, House Papers.

when Germany announced unrestricted warfare.[26] The Senate's 78–5 approval of the severance of relations bore out this judgment. But Wilson undoubtedly remembered expert estimates proved wrong both by the Gore-McLemore resolutions and by the pacifist outbursts of the 1916 campaign. One good reason for asking Congress to authorize the arming of merchantmen was, as Wilson openly confessed, "to feel that the authority and the power of the Congress are behind me in whatever it may become necessary for me to do." [27]

[In addition to testing pacifist and neutralist strength, the appeal to Congress also served to frustrate the chauvinists.] Hardly had the Senate endorsed the break in relations before Roosevelt and his friends began to demand further steps.[28] On February 23 the New York *Times* revealed that Lodge and other Republicans meant to block essential bills so that Wilson would have to call the new Congress into early session. Some members were reported complaisant, feeling that the diplomatic situation made it desirable for the House to sit anyway. By obtaining the existing Congress' sanction not only to arm ships but also "to employ any other instrumentalities or methods that may be necessary . . . to protect our ships and our people," Wilson could counter the strongest arguments for a special session. He could hope thus to block jingo pressures from Congress.

Even so, it seems unlikely that Wilson was solely concerned with domestic opinion. His message to Congress was addressed to Germany as well as to America. Without actually taking a provocative step, he was making it clear that he would not permit Germany to win by default. At the same time, with passionate earnestness he asked the Germans to realize that he did not want war or even armed neutrality. In guarded language he even implied a possible

[26] *Literary Digest*, LIV (Feb. 10, 1917), 321, (March 10, 1917), 605–607; Crighton, *Missouri and the World War*, 162–163; Cummins, *Indiana Public Opinion*, 240 ff.; Syrett, "Business Press and American Neutrality," *loc. cit.*, 223–224; Blum, *Tumulty and the Wilson Era*, 130–131.

[27] *Public Papers*, IV, 430.

[28] *Literary Digest*, LIV (Feb. 17, 1917), 386–387.

willingness to negotiate the whole submarine issue afresh. He was not so much concerned with American commerce and travel, he asserted, as with "those great principles of compassion and of protection which mankind has sought to throw about human lives, the lives of noncombatants, the lives of men who are peacefully at work keeping the industrial processes of the world quick and vital, the lives of women and children and of those who supply the labour which ministers to their sustenance." [29] His message to Congress of February 26, 1917, embodied the last adaptation of patient firmness. Intended to display the unity and resoluteness of America, it was meant as a final appeal to Germany to turn back.

As such it was a total failure. The House approved a resolution 403–13. The Senate indicated that it would have followed suit by something like 75–12.[30] Although some neutralists approved of armed neutrality as a desperate substitute for war, these ballots reinforced the advice of Tumulty and others that the country would follow wherever the President led.[31] A determined filibuster by pacifists in the Senate prevented this sentiment from materializing as legislation. It also frustrated the President's hope of avoiding a special session. Most important of all, it denied him that clear demonstration of national unity which he hoped might bring the Germans to their senses. The importance which he attached to such a demonstration appeared in his angry comment upon the filibuster: "A little group of willful men, representing no opinion but their own, have *rendered the great Government of the United States helpless and contemptible.*" [32]

On March 4 Wilson entered his second term. During part of early March he secluded himself in the White House, much as he had in the anguished interval after the sinking of the *Lusitania*. The policy contrived at that time had broken down. The President had to review once again the alternative of surrendering before the German challenge. The option earlier had been to risk war. The

[29] *Public Papers*, IV, 432.
[30] *Congressional Record*, 64 Cong., 2 sess., pp. 4692, 4988–4989.
[31] Blum, *Tumulty and the Wilson Era*, 130–131; New York *Times*, March 5, 1917.
[32] *Public Papers*, IV, 435 (italics mine).

option now was war itself. Between March 7 and March 19 he wrestled with this choice. In the end he emerged, satisfied that the right and rational course was war.

Too little attention has been given to the address with which Wilson opened his second term. His biographers have passed it by. Yet it is the one document showing his state of mind on the eve of deciding for war, and its stresses are revealing. In it Wilson observed sadly that the United States had reached a point from which there was no turning back: "matters lying outside our own life as a nation and over which we had no control, . . . despite our wish to keep free of them, have drawn us more and more irresistibly into their own current and influence." The United States, he declared, had to be concerned with the peace that followed the war. The one hope of preserving a world in which America's peculiar values could thrive lay in a settlement that averted future wars, and such a peace could be achieved only if the United States exerted the influence to which her power and virtue entitled her. The President asserted, in other words, that a policy which sacrificed America's prestige and moral reputation would mortgage the welfare and happiness of generations yet to come.

In this same address Wilson laid heavy stress on the need for national unity. Some of it might be dismissed as rhetorical imitation, following the fashions of Jefferson and Lincoln. But its closing paragraphs cannot be read as mere flourishes. Wilson pleaded with his hearers to understand:

[I]t is imperative that we should stand together. We are being forged into a new unity amidst the fires that now blaze throughout the world. In their ardent heat we shall, in God's providence, let us hope, be purged of faction and division, purified of the errant humors of party and private interest, and shall stand forth in the days to come with a new dignity of national pride and spirit. . . . The thing I shall count upon, the thing without which neither counsel nor action will avail, is the unity of America—an America united in feeling, in purpose, in its vision of duty, of opportunity, and of service. . . . The shadows that now lie dark upon our path will soon be dispelled and we shall walk with the light all about us if we be but true to ourselves

—to ourselves as we have wished to be known in the counsels of the world and in the thought of all those who love liberty and justice and the right exalted.

If Wilson spoke candidly as well as feelingly, then he entered his days in the wilderness sure of two things: first, that the prestige of the United States had to be maintained; second, that it was his duty as President to unify the people.[33]

No one knows or can know what went through Wilson's mind in those decisive days of March. He talked revealingly to no one. Such letters as he wrote were formal or perfunctory. During much of the time his superb analytical powers undoubtedly sought every possible alternative. He had by this time acquired considerable knowledge and experience in international politics. Few emotional attachments remained to blur the precision of his thought. Over a period of more than two years he had canvassed the subject of German-American relations with a wide range of advisers, especially with his shrewd and perceptive friend, House. It is true that he could not foresee what actually was to happen in 1919 and after. Nor could he foretell Brest-Litovsk, the offensives of 1918, and the expeditionary force of two million men. Otherwise, it can be assumed, he reviewed every consideration that any analyst has been able to imagine in restrospect.

The one clear alternative was that which Wilson had rejected before. He could surrender, asserting that American property losses would be the subjects of postwar claims. He could ask legislation in the spirit of the Gore and McLemore resolutions to prevent the loss of American life. There was no longer a compelling economic reason for resisting the German blockade. America had become so prosperous that she could afford to lose part of her trade with the Allies. The unrestricted submarine campaign had seemed thus far to be relatively ineffective. Statistics published at the beginning of March indicated only slight increases in Allied tonnage losses.[34]

Nor was it evident that acquiescence would injure the visible

[33] *Public Papers*, V, 1–5.
[34] New York *Times*, March 1, 1917.

security interests of the United States. Despite the Zimmermann
note and other warnings of German activity in Latin America,
Wilson had not retracted his earlier assertion to House that no
European power offered an immediate menace to the United States.
A relatively long period of recovery would be necessary for Germany, he had said, even if she triumphed in Europe. And he had
little or no reason to suspect that Germany would win, even if the
United States tolerated the U-boat blockade. Page warned him, it
is true, that the Allies were on their last legs, but Wilson had long
made allowance for Page's excitable temper. Other reports from
London, Paris, and even St. Petersburg exhaled confidence.[35] No
longer regarding the Allies as upholders of law and civilization,
Wilson had said time and again that America's interest lay in a
peace without victory. There was no reason for him to believe in
March, 1917, that this interest precluded acquiescence in the recent
German decree.

[What did make it impossible was the fact that it would sacrifice
America's prestige and moral influence.] At the outset of the submarine controversy it had seemed apparent that America would
not live up to her potential if she allowed her citizens to be denied
the free right of travel. Partly to demonstrate that the United States
was a power entitled to respect and deserving of influence, Wilson
had taken the cautious gamble of resisting indiscriminate U-boat
warfare. Each subsequent diplomatic victory had committed America's prestige more deeply. [The submarine issue had also become
the symbol of Wilson's willingness to stand up for the rule of law,
for international justice, and, as he termed it, for the rights of
humanity. If he now retreated he would, in effect, prove America
incapable of exercising influence compatible with her population,
resources, and ideals.] He would demonstrate her Pharisaism, her
inability to endure martyrdom for what she believed right. In view
of his conviction that her own future turned upon her ability to
prevent a recurrence of war, he simply could not accept the pacifist
alternative.

[35] *Literary Digest*, LIV (March 3, 1917), 539–541.

Acquiescence was not, of course, the only alternative. Another was armed neutrality. American ships could be provided with guns. They could defend themselves against U-boats. The United States would thus be upholding her principles while waging only a very limited war. Professor Carlton J. H. Hayes of Columbia University had prepared a long and compelling memorandum outlining the virtues of this course. It would make clear that the United States opposed only Germany's illegal and immoral method of warfare. It would allow America to escape military involvement on the continent and leave her unentangled in the intricacies of Allied ambitions and European power rivalries. The President had read this memorandum before asking Congress for power to arm merchantmen.[36] From his address at that time and from other comments, it is evident that this alternative had some attraction for him. While it is comparatively simple to infer his reasons for rejecting pacifism, it is rather harder to sense the rationale that led him away from limited belligerency.

One consideration undoubtedly was the practical difficulty of devising a suitable policy. The Navy Department sketched for him the alternative methods of carrying out an armed neutrality.[37] One was for American ships to acknowledge the legal right of U-boats to conduct visit and search but to resist unlawful attacks. A second was for them to treat German submarines as hostile craft when encountered inside the war zone. A third was to treat U-boats as hostile craft wherever met and to attack them on sight. Each course presented obvious difficulties. One invited torpedoings; the second risked them; the third was not very different from a state of war.

Armed neutrality in any form involved a further danger of blurring the issues. American merchantmen might err in sinking submarines. Especially if the United States were to follow the third of the navy's three forms of armed neutrality, American captains were likely to act in excess of zeal. The result might easily be an American *Baralong* case, which the Germans might employ as a moral pretext for war. Armed neutrality would, in any case, allow Ger-

---

[36] N.d., Wilson Papers, enclosed in Wilson to Lansing Feb. 10, 1917, *ibid.*
[37] Daniels to Wilson, March 9, 1917, *Lansing Papers,* I, 618–621.

many to choose her own time and occasion for opening hostilities.

Even so, Wilson could still have elected the alternative. He had always shown a disposition to postpone crises. It would not have been out of character for him to adopt a policy that threw the choice of peace or war back upon Berlin. The keys to his final decision probably lay first of all in his complete mistrust of Germany, secondly in his emphatic desire to preserve domestic unity, and thirdly in his conception of America's probable war effort.

He could no longer expect Germany to be deterred from any action by fear of war with the United States. Responses to the pressures applied during early February had indicated total indifference. Not only had Zimmermann asserted that there was no turning back, but a semiofficial newspaper (the Berlin *Lokal-Anzeiger*), quoted in the United States, had declared, "As to the neutrals—we can no longer be bothered by their opinions." [38] In his message to Congress asking authority to arm ships, Wilson had referred to uncompromising statements by German officials and by the German press. The Zimmermann telegram itself had indicated no more than that Germany anticipated war. Wilson was more shocked apparently by the method of its dispatch.[39] Zimmermann had sent the message to Bernstorff for forwarding, using State Department cable lines which had been opened for the sake of peace discussions. Coupled with Zimmermann's insouciant admission that the telegram was genuine, this revelation seemed to demonstrate that Germany no longer saw any advantage in keeping the peace. The *coup de grâce* for any lingering hope came in Bethmann Hollweg's address to the Reichstag, delivered on the day after Wilson requested power to arm merchantmen. According to the State Department's report of this speech, Bethmann spoke of America's "subjection to English power and control"; he declared that the severance of relations was meant neither to protect freedom of the seas nor to promote peace but only to help "starve Germany and increase bloodshed"; he ended by asserting, "now that our sincere desire to promote peace has met with nothing but ridicule at hands of our enemies there is no longer

[38] *Literary Digest*, LIV (Feb. 17, 1917), 394.
[39] Lansing diary, March 4, 1917, Lansing, *War Memoirs*, 226–231.

any retreat for us—nothing but 'Forward.' " [40] It appeared from Wilson's perspective as if there were no longer a moderate party in Berlin. Whether the United States declared war or simply proclaimed an armed neutrality, Germany was likely in either case to treat her as an all-out enemy.

In view of this probability, Wilson undoubtedly foresaw difficulty in maintaining a mere armed neutrality. At the moment it seemed as if most of the country approved such a course. Many neutralists and some pacifists reluctantly accepted armed neutrality as an alternative to war. But chauvinism was visibly on the rise. The Zimmermann telegram and the sinking of the Cunard liner *Laconia,* with three Americans among the lost, had created a spreading excitement. The *Literary Digest* reported newspapers all over the country to be joining in a clamor for war.[41] The pacifists who filibustered against armed neutrality were widely denounced as traitors, and Tumulty advised the President that these passions were not likely to cool.[42] The President could also see, of course, the latent strength of pacifism. Bryan had thrown all his enormous energy into an outcry against war. Pacifist and socialist groups across the land joined him.[43] But these forces remained for the moment inchoate and disorganized. The Zimmermann telegram and the *Laconia* sinking had shaken them. It was foreseeable, nevertheless, that a long period of armed neutrality would allow pacifists to regroup. Wilson had reason to believe that German agents were seeking to organize and finance them. Another intercepted German dispatch told of $50,000 to be spent in this cause.[44] Future incidents would meanwhile strengthen and embitter the chauvinists. Other *Laconias* were certain to sink. Even as Wilson sat meditating in the White House, five American ships went down.[45] Other disclosures

[40] Langhorne to Lansing, Feb. 28, 1917, *Foreign Relations, Supplement One: 1917,* pp. 153–155.

[41] LIV (March 10, 1917), 605–607.

[42] *Ibid.* (March 24, 1917), 803; Tumulty to Wilson, March 8, 1917, Blum, *Tumulty and the Wilson Era,* 130–131.

[43] Link, *Wilson and the Progressive Era,* 275.

[44] McAdoo, *Crowded Years,* 367.

[45] *Algonquin, City of Memphis, Healdton, Vigilancia, Illinois: Foreign Relations, Supplement One: 1917,* pp. 174, 177, 180–183.

like the Zimmermann telegram were also probable. There were suspicions, for example, of German activity in troubled Cuba.[46] Armed neutrality was likely therefore to divide the country into irreconcilable groups.

From Wilson's standpoint such a division was dangerous to all his objects. He sought national unity for its own sake. He also sought it in order that the United States might influence the peace settlement. If the extremist factions grew, with erstwhile neutralists and nationalists swinging toward either pacifism or chauvinism, the inner strength of America would weaken. As it was, moreover, the extremist leaders differed with Wilson over the conditions of lasting peace. The winter had seen a queer alliance between pacifists like Bryan and Borah and chauvinists like Roosevelt and Lodge. They had joined in attacking the proposed League of Nations.[47] If their respective followings should grow as a result of armed neutrality, the President might find it impossible either to exert significant influence over Europe's peacemakers or even to guide them by his own ideals.

If Wilson had foreseen the AEF of 1918 and the casualties of Chateau-Thierry and the Meuse-Argonne, he might still have chosen armed neutrality as a course that at least postponed full-scale war. His decision to reject this alternative probably grew in part out of a reasonable, if mistaken, estimate of what war would require. No statement by an Allied leader had indicated pressing requirements for manpower. Field Marshal Sir Douglas Haig had recently said, indeed, that he needed only ammunition and rolling stock to achieve victory in 1917. His prediction of early triumph had been reaffirmed by General Brussilov, and the Russian revolution, so far from seeming to spell withdrawal from the war, was interpreted as an event which would strengthen her against Germany.[48] The President knew, of course, of the War Department's plan for an expeditionary force, and when the Allies subsequently asked for men he readily complied. But 500,000 was the limit set by army planners, and most

---

[46] Wilson to Lansing, Feb. 6, 1917, *Lansing Papers*, I, 594.

[47] See Baker, *Wilson*, VI, 417–418.

[48] *Literary Digest*, LIV (March 3, 1917), 541; New York *Times*, March 18, 1917.

of these were to be regular troops or volunteers. The draft, for which Wilson called in his war message, was to replace these men at home stations.[49] He need not have been inwardly shaken by the thought of sending into the trenches men who went there willingly. He evidently conceived of America's war effort as designed primarily to reinforce the Allies with arms, supplies, money, and naval craft.[50]

The relatively small difference that he saw between armed neutrality and war was vividly indicated in a letter written after he had decided on war. It was written, indeed, after he had composed his stirring message to Congress. Answering a Progressive who advocated armed neutrality, Wilson asserted, "To defend our right on the seas, we must fight submarines. . . . Apparently, to make even the measures of defense legitimate we must obtain the status of belligerents." [51] [Expecting America to fight mainly with her factories and ships, Wilson chose war in preference to armed neutrality.]

This is not to say that the President found the choice easy. No matter how little American blood appeared in his imaginations, war remained horrible to him. He had never ceased to express disgust for its barbarity and for the passions it aroused. He was well aware that divisions into extremist factions would be avoided only at the price of uniting the country in animal hatred of a foreign enemy. He was not at all sure that American institutions and ideals could emerge unscarred.[52] He was simply more sure that they could not survive if the end of the war did not spell the end of all wars. The same dream of peace that had entered into all his diplomacy finally led him paradoxically to a decision for war.

On March 19 he emerged from his solitude, still anxious and troubled but apparently satisfied that the alternatives of acquiescence and armed neutrality were impossible. He talked with Lansing.[53] On March 20 he conferred with the cabinet. No one had any alter-

[49] Frederick Palmer, *Newton D. Baker: America at War* (2 vols.; New York, 1931), I, 184; Baker to Wilson, March 19, April 13, 1917, Wilson Papers.

[50] Note the emphases in his war message: *Public Papers*, V, 6–17.

[51] Wilson to Matthew Hale, March 31, 1917, Wilson Papers.

[52] Baker, *Wilson*, VI, 505–507.

[53] Diary, March 20, 1917, Lansing Papers; Lansing to Wilson, March 20, 1917, Lansing, *War Memoirs*, 234–236.

native to suggest. The neutralist members who had theretofore resisted were now themselves sure that war was the only course. The Attorney General and the Secretary of Labor seconded the arguments for it. When the President asked the Postmaster General to speak, Burleson said quietly: "We are at war. I am in favour of calling Congress at the earliest possible moment." The Secretary of the Navy, who remained a close friend of Bryan's, was the last to agree.[54] The cabinet was one. On the following day the President summoned Congress to meet on April 2. He began issuing directives preparatory for war. When Congress assembled, he asked for a declaration, saying:

We are glad . . . to fight thus for the ultimate peace of the world and for the liberation of its people. . . . The world must be made safe for democracy. Its peace must be planted upon the tested foundations of political liberty . . . [W]e shall fight . . . for a universal dominion of right by such a concert of free peoples as shall bring peace and safety to all nations and make the world itself at last free.[55]

Peace between Britain and the United States had been saved. It had been potentially in jeopardy, if at all, during the early months of the war. At that time there had been no German-American dispute to reinsure it. The American government had been preoccupied with saving the country from economic depression, and the men who made American policy had been unusually ingenuous and doctrinaire. Had the British government then flagrantly disregarded American interests or ideals, it could well have generated tension which not even German recklessness could have relieved.

It is clear that this danger was averted in part by the prudent and skillful diplomacy of Sir Edward Grey. It was he who worked out compromises that avoided offense to America while still safeguarding Britain's future capacity to interrupt German trade. It was he, most importantly, who prevented cotton from going onto the con-

---

[54] Diary, March 20, 1917, Lansing Papers; diary, March 20, 1917, Daniels Papers; Houston, *Eight Years with Wilson's Cabinet*, I, 241–244. It is clear from Lansing's account that the Russian revolution played little if any part in the President's decision. See George F. Kennan, *Russia Leaves the War* (Princeton, 1956), 14–16.
[55] *Public Papers*, V, 6–17.

traband list in the autumn of 1914. But even these concrete acts owed something to conditions beyond his or anyone's control. Grey was able to moderate British policy because he possessed a momentary hold upon the Cabinet, the House of Commons, and the public, because few people were able to foresee the long years ahead, and because the fleet was temporarily preoccupied.

The preservation of Anglo-American peace resulted in the long run from forces of even more remote origin. It was possible for Grey to effect compromises largely because Britain and the United States shared a community of beliefs. English and American diplomatists spoke the same language, even when using moral abstractions that neither party could define. It is true that Grey maneuvered with great skill to draw the teeth of Wilson's mediation schemes, but he owed his successes chiefly to the similarity of English and American ideals. The differences he disguised were, in any case, minor. The peace between America and England stood upon a common heritage. It also rested on foundations of mutual trust which had been built up in the Oregon and *Alabama* negotiations, in the secretary-ships of Hay, Root, Balfour, and Lansdowne, in the intermarriages of families, the interchange of books and travelers, and the interplay of English and American reform movements. Grave as were the threats to accord, the forces that made for its preservation were stronger.

After German-American tension developed, the peace between America and Britain was relatively secure. It held despite the triumphs of factions in England that did not prize it. It survived even though considerable elements of the American public were willing, even eager, to risk trouble with Britain. The Anglophobes in America, it is true, were disunited and incapable of pressing a program on the President, and the tradition of Anglo-American friendship exerted some effect upon even the most visceral of the "ginger" group in England. Relations between the two countries could nevertheless have been much sorer if Grey had not continued to exercise a waning influence in the Cabinet and, equally importantly, if Wilson had not been restrained by the hope of bringing general peace through cooperation with England. Tension could have developed if the President, after losing this hope, had not acted with such patience and prudence. But it is a moot question whether Britain and the United States were ever in danger of serious friction after the spring of 1915. The real guarantee of their peace, regrettably, was the trouble between Germany and America.

What Germany and the United States lacked was precisely the underpinning of mutual comprehension and trust that allowed Britain and America to adjust their differences. Not only extremists but even moderates lacked understanding of one another. When Wilson spoke of "lasting peace," he thought of the ages. Most of his countrymen, bred in the Liberal consensus that Louis Hartz has described, understood what he meant. So did most Englishmen. When Bethmann called for *"dauernden Frieden,"* on the other hand, he had in mind a settlement fixing the balance of power for a generation. Despite Kant's famous essay, few Germans shared the Liberal dream of eternal peace. Other words like "rights" and "militarism" posed similar problems. German-American negotiations were always troubled by differences in meaning, intention, and outlook.

In the background of their misunderstandings stood a heritage of unpleasant memories, distorted perhaps but nonetheless vivid. Americans recalled Admiral Diederichs at Manila Bay, Wilhelm's instructions to Waldersee during the Boxer affair ("give no quarter, spare nobody, make no prisoners. . . . Be terrible as Attila's huns."), the frustrated Danish West Indies purchase, the Venezuela crisis, the *Panther,* Agadir, Zabern, and Bethmann's "scrap of paper" interview. Germans, on the other hand, remembered America's discriminatory tariffs, instances of firms that had dumped shoddy goods and infected meat, the seeming hypocrisy of the Monroe Doctrine and the Open Door, Roosevelt's desertion of Wilhelm at Algeçiras, America's cooperation with Germany's enemies at the Hague and London conferences, her missionary zeal in promoting Liberal principles, and Wilson's insistence on the right to sell munitions to the Allies. While mutual misunderstanding and mistrust did not make it impossible for Germany and America to adjust their differences, they did make the task harder.

This heritage of misunderstanding makes it all the more extra-

ordinary that men in Berlin and Washington should have been able
for so long to preserve the peace. Bethmann's achievement lay, it is
true, in seeing what in retrospect is obvious: if America entered the
war Germany was bound to be defeated. But this truth was not
apparent to most Germans, even to those who supported the Chancellor. Bethmann was not a great statesman. He was an accomplished courtier and a shrewd politician. At a conference table with
Grey, Lloyd George, Wilson, and House, he would not have stood
out. He was simply wiser than most of his associates, and he used
his arts with remarkable effectiveness. Peace between Germany and
America was largely preserved by his prudence and skill. It was lost
when his power lapsed.

To credit Bethmann with the chief role in keeping peace between
America and Germany is not, of course, to deny Wilson's share.
The President's patience in 1915 and 1916 undoubtedly owed something to inertia and timidity and something to divisions in American public opinion. Pacifism and neutralism were powerful forces,
even at the end. It is arguable, indeed, that Wilson had little choice
except to be both firm and patient. But others would conceivably
have done otherwise. House, though an extraordinarily imaginative
diplomatist, favored abandoning patience in the *Arabic* and *Sussex*
crises. He might have denied Bethmann the time that was always
necessary to win a favorable decision from the Kaiser. House might
have forced a war when America's aims could still be attained by
diplomacy. Bryan, who was in some ways the purest idealist in
American politics, would have abandoned firmness. Had his policy
been adopted, the U-boats would never have been restrained. America would have suffered a series of injuries and humiliations. While
Bryan could have borne them gladly, the public would likely have
sent a chauvinist to the White House in 1916. Wilson's mixed firmness and patience offered the only hope in the long run of keeping
the peace, and he held to that policy with persistence, foresight, and
courage.

It is hard, indeed, to find fault with Wilson's statesmanship. Retro-
spective analysts have contended that he was unrealistic. He should,
it is suggested, have thrown America into the war in order to pre-

vent German victory, preserve Anglo-American control of the seas, and overturn authoritarian and militarist ideologies. But this criticism supposes that Wilson should have acted against a German menace that might never have materialized. Although the President's dreams could look to the eternal future, his diplomacy conformed to Bismarck's rule: it assumed any contingency more than six months away to be out of calculation. Dealing with both Britain and Germany, Wilson concerned himself with the immediate interests of his country. America's security was not threatened in the predictable future. Her economic power and her prestige were in danger. His policy fended off present threats.

His moralism found expression in his quest for world peace. Since peace without victory would have resulted in recreating a balance of power, it has been argued that Wilson was here a *Realpolitiker*. House, who did believe in the balance of power, was so much the manager of Wilson's mediation efforts that his views and the President's mingled. Where Wilson's own ideas emerge with distinctness, the balance-of-power concept is subsidiary. His declaration of war was itself evidence of his belief that eternal peace could be secured even if victory created a power vacuum. He sought lasting peace for its own sake. Since it offered the only sure escape from the dilemmas of his wartime relations with Britain and Germany, it did have its practical side. But the House-Grey understanding and the peace offer of December, 1916, as well as the declaration of war, all indicated his willingness to risk immediate interests for the sake of his dream. If this was realism, it was a sublime realism.

The struggle for peace ended in war. Reviewing its history, one has a sense that it could not have ended otherwise. Bethmann, Grey, and even Wilson were continually pitted against men of less wisdom and compassion. The sufferings and frenzies of endless war inevitably strengthened Lloyd George and Carson, Tirpitz, Bassermann, and Ludendorff. There was no way out. Triumph for the immoderates was only a matter of time. Grey nevertheless saw his hope fulfilled. America and Britain did not become enemies. Bethmann and Wilson kept the peace for more than two years. Despite its tragic ending, the struggle was heroic.

Bibliographical Essay

GREAT BRITAIN

Documents and Official Histories
Memoirs and Biographies
Newspapers
Studies: Economic warfare and diplomacy; Domestic politics; Background

GERMANY

Archives, Documents, and Official Histories
Memoirs and Biographies
Newspapers
Studies: General; Submarine warfare; Diplomacy and domestic politics

UNITED STATES

Archives and Documents
Manuscripts, Collections, Memoirs, and Biographies
Newspapers
Studies: General; Neutrality; Public opinion

GREAT BRITAIN

Documents and Official Histories

There is a shortage of diplomatic documents for the war years. G. P. Gooch and H. W. V. Temperley, *British Documents on the Origins of the War, 1898-1914* (14 vols.; London, 1925-1938), stop with the declarations of 1914. E. L. Woodward, *Documents on British Foreign Policy, 1919–1939* (in progress), takes up with the peace conference. A handful of wartime dispatches from the Foreign Office files appears in Viscount Grey of Fallodon, *Twenty-five Years, 1892-1916* (2 vols.; London, 1925). A few more, taken from the Grey papers, appear in G. M. Trevelyan, *Grey of Fallodon* (New York, 1937). Rather more extensive are the selections from the papers of the British ambassador in Washington in Stephen Gwynn (ed.), *The Letters and Friendships of Sir Cecil Spring-Rice* (2 vols.; Boston, 1929). These volumes include a number of exchanges between Spring-Rice and Grey. Some extremely important Cabinet papers are reproduced in David Lloyd George, *War Memoirs, 1914-1918* (6 vols.; London, 1933-1937) and *The Truth about the Peace Treaties* (2 vols.; London, 1938). One or two others appear in the biography of Grey's successor, Blanche E. C. Dugdale, *Arthur James Balfour* (2 vols.; London, 1936). Some documents from the Admiralty archives are in Winston S. Churchill, *The World Crisis, 1911–1918* (5 vols.; New York, 1923–1929).

There is considerable material from the War Office files in Historical Section, Committee of Imperial Defence, *History of the Great War, based on Official Documents*. The various *Military Operations* series include documentary appendices. The *Naval Operations* series is less rewarding, for the authors used archival materials but chose to quote nothing that had not already appeared in print. There is also a confidential official history which, if published, might be very useful indeed. One volume of it was somehow pirated by the Germans during World War II and printed in translation: Archibald C. Bell, *Die englische Hungerblockade im Weltkrieg, 1914-1915* (Essen, 1943).

Some light is shed on British diplomacy by the records of her allies. Of first importance are the extracts from the Russian archives appearing in Historical Commission, Central Executive Committee of the U.S.S.R., *Mezhdunarodnye Otnosheniya v Epokhu Imperializma* (Series Three: 1914–1917) (10 vols. to date; Moscow, 1930—). Extending to the end of March, 1916, this series is very full, including what appears to be the bulk of dispatches from the Russian ambassadors in London and Paris, certain intercepted correspondence of the British Embassy in St. Petersburg, some intercepted enemy and neutral traffic, and selected communications from the Russian ambassador and the military attaché in Washington. There is a German translation of eight volumes, reaching to October, 1915: Otto Hoetzsch (ed.), *Die internationalen Beziehungen im Zeitalter des Imperialismus* (Berlin, 1931—). There is still more Russian correspondence in separate volumes dealing chiefly with Near Eastern questions, but they reveal hardly anything about British policy toward the United States. A few relevant items do appear in the additional correspondence of the Russian ambassador in Paris: F. Stieve (ed.), *Iswolski im Weltkrieg* (Berlin, 1926). (How Dr. Stieve came by these files has never been explained.) Some material on economic relations between the Allies and the United States appears in the Russian records of the financial conferences of 1915 and 1916, printed in *Krasnyi Arkhiv,* IV, 50–81.

French records, on the other hand, are as sparse as British. A limited amount of material from the diplomatic files is printed in Albert Pingaud, *Histoire diplomatique de la France pendant la grande guerre* (2 vols.; Paris, 1938), and there is a relatively barren collection of letters from the French ambassador in London: Henri Cambon (ed.), *Paul Cambon: Correspondance, 1870–1924* (3 vols.; Paris, 1940). The French President cites a few unpublished communications in his journals: Raymond Poincaré, *Au service de la France* (9 vols.; Paris, 1925–1932), and Georges Suarez in his biography of the French Foreign Minister, *Briand: son oeuvre et sa vie* (6 vols.; Paris, 1938–1952), employed some manuscript materials. France's official military history, *Les Armées françaises dans la Grande Guerre* (68 vols.; Paris, 1923–1939), is almost entirely documentary and, of course, is immensely full, but it has relatively little material that bears on diplomacy. Official volumes on naval history are almost wholly uninformative, with the single exception of Lt. Louis Guichard, *Histoire du blocus naval (1914–1918)* (Paris, 1929), of which there is an unsatisfactory English translation, *The Naval Blockade* (London, 1930). The unofficial volume by former officers of the Ministry of Blockade, Denys Cochin (ed.), *Les organisations de blocus en France pendant la guerre (1914–1918)* (Paris, 1926), is actually more rewarding. From the Italian side certain documents are beginning to appear, but *I Documenti Diplomatici Italiani,* Fifth Series: 1914–1918 (1 vol. in progress; Rome, 1954—), extends, at this writing, only to October 16, 1914. A few dispatches from the Italian ambassador in Washington appear in the small commemorative volume, Justus (Dolores Macchi di Cellere), *V. Macchi di Cellere, all' Ambasciata di Washington* (Florence, 1920).

On parliament the chief source is, of course, the *Parliamentary Debates.*

Memoirs and Biographies

A certain amount of information is obtainable from the diaries, memoirs, and private letters of British diplomats. Gwynn's *Spring-Rice* contains much useful personal correspondence. Of equal value is the diary kept by the British ambassador in Paris, *The Diary of Lord Bertie of Thame, 1914–1918* (2 vols.; London, 1924), edited by Lady Algernon Gordon Lennox. Some letters of one of the key men in the Foreign Office appear in Edgar T. S. Dugdale, *Maurice de Bunsen* (London, 1934). Sir George Buchanan, *My Mission to Russia and Other Diplomatic Memories* (London, 1923), is concentrated almost exclusively on Russian affairs. The autobiographies of the ambassadors in Rome and Stockholm, Sir James Rennell Rodd, *Social and Diplomatic Memories* (London, 1925), and Sir Esmé Howard, *Theatre of Life* (2 vols.; London, 1935), are principally valuable as indicating the difficulties which the Foreign Office met in other neutral capitals. The manuscripts of Sir William Wiseman, chief of British intelligence in the United States, are deposited in the E. M. House collection in the Yale University Library, and some use is made of them in Arthur Willert, *The Road to Safety: A Study in Anglo-American Relations* (London, 1952). Since Wiseman reached America only in late 1916, the manuscripts are principally useful for the war years.

For the study of policy as distinguished from diplomacy, one has to rely primarily on the autobiographies and biographies of men in and around the Cabinet. The Prime Minister's own memoirs, Lord Oxford and Asquith, *Memories and Reflections* (2 vols.; London, 1928), are supplemented by a massive, dogged, but on the whole disappointing authorized biography: J. A. Spender and Cyril Asquith, *Lord Oxford and Asquith* (2 vols.; London, 1932). Grey's *Twenty-five Years* is of the first importance, and it is only complemented by Trevelyan's *Grey of Fallodon*. Churchill's *World Crisis* is, as someone remarked, an autobiography disguised as the history of the world. It is very useful for the first year of the war, when Churchill was still a member of the Cabinet. Lloyd George's *War Memoirs* is of paramount importance for 1915–1917. Not much is added by the various biographies of him, although one, Thomas Jones, *Lloyd George* (Cambridge, Mass., and London, 1951), is by a close associate, and two others, Frank Owen, *Tempestuous Journey: Lloyd George, His Life and Times* (London, 1954), and Malcolm Thomson, *David Lloyd George: the Official Biography* (London, n.d.), are by men who had access to unpublished papers. Nor is much on the work of the Cabinet to be obtained from the memoirs and biographies of others in it. This statement extends even to Robert Blake, *The Unknown Prime Minister: The Life and Times of Andrew Bonar Law* (London, 1955). Though a superb biography, it contains relatively little about issues of foreign policy. Other works are Sir George Arthur, *Life of Lord Kitchener* (3 vols.; London, 1920), Dugdale's *Balfour,* Lord Newton, *Lord Lansdowne* (London, 1929), Viscount Long of Wraxhall, *Memories* (London, 1923), Sir Charles Petrie, *Walter Long and His Times* (London, 1936) and *The Life and Letters of the Right Hon. Sir Austen Chamberlain* (2 vols.; London, 1940), Chamberlain's own *Down the Years* (London, 1935), and the Earl of Ronaldshay, *The Life of Lord Curzon* (3 vols.; London, n.d.). Edward Marjoribanks and Ian Colvin, *The Life of Lord Carson* (3 vols.; London, 1932–1936), tells more about Carson in opposition than about Carson in the Cabinet. One simply has to piece together fragments from these various sources.

The same is true of memoirs and the like from men on the fringes of the Cabinet. Among the most valuable are those of military and naval men. Viscount Fisher of Kilverstone, *Memories and Records* (2 vols.; London, 1920), contains jottings from the onetime First Sea Lord. Viscount Jellicoe of Scapa, *The Grand Fleet, 1914–1916* (London, 1919) and *The Crisis of the Naval War* (London, 1920), are by the Commander of the Grand Fleet. Two other works of importance are W. S. Chalmers, *The Life and Letters of David Beatty, Admiral of the Fleet* (London, 1951), and Arthur J. Marder, *Portrait of an Admiral: The Life and Papers of Sir Herbert Richmond* (Cambridge, Mass., 1952). C. E. Callwell (ed.), *Field Marshal Sir Henry Wilson: His Life and Diaries* (2 vols.; London, 1927), reproduces the candid and acidulous records of the army's foremost soldier-politician. Sir William Robertson, *From Private to Field Marshal* (London, 1921) and *Soldiers and Statesmen, 1914–1919* (2 vols.; London, 1926), are by the Chief of the Imperial General Staff. Robert Blake (ed.), *The Private Papers 1914–1919: Being Selections from the Private Diary and Correspondence of Field Marshal the Earl Haig of Bemersyde* (London, 1952), is a collection of great importance for the military politics of the period.

From ministerial subordinates there are only Christopher Addison, *Four and a Half Years: A Personal Diary from June 1914 to January 1919* (2 vols.; London, 1934) and *Politics from Within, 1911–1918* (2 vols.; London, 1924), by a man who served under Lloyd George in the Ministry of Munitions.

From the court circle, on the other hand, there are several useful works: Reginald, Viscount Esher, *The Journals of Viscount Esher* (4 vols.; London, 1934–1938), and Oliver, Viscount Esher (ed.), *The Captains and the Kings Depart: Journals and Letters of Reginald, Viscount Esher* (2 vols.; London, 1930), Sir Almeric Fitzroy, *Memories* (2 vols.; London, 1925), and Viscount Sandhurst, *From Day to Day, 1916–1921* (London, 1921). These volumes are particularly valuable because blockade decrees had to pass through the archaic machinery of the Privy Council. Sir Harold Nicolson, *George V* (London, 1954), is, of course, brilliantly written, but it contains only fragments.

Of as much value as the personal writings of officials are the records of leading journalists. Lord Beaverbrook, *Politicians and the War, 1914–1916* (2 vols.; London, 1928), by the publisher of the *Daily Express,* sees things very much from the point of view of Bonar Law. Charles à Court Repington, *The First World War, 1914–1918* (2 vols.; London, 1920), by the famous military correspondent of the *Times,* has much on War Office views. John Evelyn Wrench, *Geoffrey Dawson and Our Times* (London, 1955), is an intimate biography of the Thunderer's editor. It includes, among other things, some of Dawson's correspondence with Arthur Willert, the *Times* correspondent in Washington. *Lord Riddell's War Diary, 1914–1918* (London, 1933) contains many records of conversations with Lloyd George. J. L. Hammond, *C. P. Scott of the Manchester Guardian* (London, 1934), tells of another of Lloyd George's newspaper supporters. Amy Strachey, *St. Loe Strachey: His Life and His Paper* (London, 1930), is about the influential editor of the *Specator.*

Of some interest for wartime party politics are the Labourite T. P. Conwell-Evans, *Foreign Policy from a Back Bench* (London, 1932), taken from the papers of Lord Noel Buxton, and the Tory *The Anvil of War: Letters between F. S. Oliver and His Brother* (London, 1936), edited by Stephen Gwynn.

Newspapers

It is needless to mention individual newspapers except to say that the London *Times* is the best source of fact, the London *Morning Post* the weathervane for Toryism, and the London *Daily News* that for orthodox Liberalism. Much detail on proprietorship and partisan affiliations can be found in Max Grünbeck, *Die Presse Grossbritanniens* (2 vols.; Leipzig, 1936), with historical background in Oron J. Hale, *Publicity and Diplomacy, with Special Reference to England and Germany,*

1890–1914 (New York, 1940). A work of exceptional utility is Armin Rappaport, *The British Press and Wilsonian Neutrality, 1914–1917* (Stanford, 1951). It covers all the major dailies and magazines. Extracts from the *Daily News,* accompanied by penetrating commentary, appear in Irene Cooper Willis, *England's Holy War* (New York, 1928). The London *Times, The History of the TIMES: the 150th Anniversary and Beyond, 1912–1948* (2 vols.; London, 1952), is more than a study of the newspaper. It is one of the most important works on the period, and it reproduces some correspondence from members of the *Times* staff, as well as some material from the Milner manuscripts. It supersedes all writing on Northcliffe for the war period.

Studies

ECONOMIC WARFARE AND DIPLOMACY. Of writing on British policy during the war there is relatively little. Margret Boveri, *Sir Edward Grey und das Foreign Office* (Berlin, 1933), analyzes relations between the Foreign Secretary and his subordinates by careful scrutiny of the prewar documents. Some light is shed on the complex of Allied diplomatic problems by C. Jay Smith, Jr., *The Russian Struggle for Power, 1914–1917: A Study of Russian Foreign Policy during the First World War* (New York, 1956). On the war aims debate disappointingly little appears in the Inaugural-Dissertation, at once contentious and pedestrian, of Friederike Recktenwald, *Kriegsziele und öffentliche Meinung Englands 1914/16* (Stuttgart, 1929). More appears in the relatively brief passages on Britain in Kent Forster, *The Failures of Peace: The Search for a Negotiated Peace during the First World War* (Philadelphia, 1941). Forster also illumines the French attitude toward mediation, thus complementing Ebba Dahlin, *French and German Public Opinion on Declared War Aims* (Palo Alto, Calif., 1933) Rudolf Stadelmann, "Friedensversuche im ersten Jahre des Weltkriegs," *Historische Zeitschrift,* CLVI (1937), 485–545, argues that Grey, abetted by Bethmann, prevented peace negotiations in 1914–1915 in order to conserve his political power at home.

On economic warfare much the best work is Marion C. Siney, *The Allied Blockade of Germany, 1914–1916* (Ann Arbor, Mich., 1957), the first of a projected two volumes, but there is still utility, especially for naval detail, in the older works: Maurice Parmelee, *Blockade and Sea Power* (New York, 1924), Montague W. P. Consett and O. H. Daniel, *The Triumph of Unarmed Forces, 1914–1918* (New York,

1923), E. Keble Chatterton, *The Big Blockade* (London, 1932), and relevant parts of R. G. Albion and J. B. Pope, *Sea Lanes in Wartime* (Boston, 1942).

DOMESTIC POLITICS. The best studies are Blake's *Bonar Law* and *The History of the TIMES*. The second rank is occupied by the biographies of Carson, Asquith, and Lloyd George. On special topics two valuable works are Henry R. Winkler, *The League of Nations Movement in Great Britain, 1914–1919* (New Brunswick, N.J., 1952), and Gerda Richards Crosby, *Disarmament and Peace in British Politics, 1914–1919* (Cambridge, Mass., 1957). Illuminating on the mechanics of the left opposition is William P. Maddox, *Foreign Relations in British Labour Politics* (Cambridge, Mass., 1934). A suggestive but not particularly helpful social analysis of the leadership group appears in W. L. Guttsman, "Aristocracy and the Middle Class in the British Political Elite, 1886–1916," *British Journal of Sociology,* V (1954), 12–32.

BACKGROUND. Six works are indispensable: E. L. Woodward, *Great Britain and the German Navy* (London, 1934), Richard H. Heindel, *The American Impact on Great Britain, 1898–1914* (Philadelphia, 1940), Henry Pelling, *America and the British Left: From Bright to Bevan* (New York, 1957), H. C. Allen, *Great Britain and the United States* (New York, 1955), R. C. K. Ensor, *England, 1870–1914* (Oxford, 1936), and above all, Elie Halévy, *A History of the English People: Epilogue* (2 vols.; London, 1934).

GERMANY

Archives, Documents, and Official Histories

The situation with regard to German documents is much happier than with regard to British. Much of the correspondence between Berlin and Washington as well as many important intragovernmental communications of 1916–1917 appear as annexes to Germany, National Assembly, *Stenographische Berichte über die öffentlichen Verhandlungen des Untersuchungsausschusses, 2. Unterausschuss* (Berlin, 1920), under the title, *Aktenstücke zur Friedensaktion Wilsons.* The whole collection, including the oral testimony of Bethmann, Zimmermann, Helfferich, Bernstorff, and others, was translated by the Carnegie Foundation and published as *Official German Documents Relating to the World War* (2 vols.; New York, 1920). Additional documents and testimony appear in volumes from other committees, especially *Die Ursachen des*

Deutschen Zusammenbruches, Zweite Abteilung: Der innere Zu-sammenbruch (12 vols.; Berlin, 1925–1929).

Extensive extracts from the files of the Naval Staff appear in Arno Spindler, *Der Handelskrieg mit U-Booten* (3 vols.; Berlin, 1932–1934), which is part of Eberhard von Mantey (ed.), *Der Krieg zur See herausgegeben vom Marine-archiv.* Documents from the Navy Ministry files appear in Alfred von Tirpitz, *Politische Dokumente* (2 vols.; Berlin, 1926). Volume II, subtitled *Deutschlands Ohnmachtspolitik im Weltkrieg,* is absolutely indispensable. Some material from General Staff files has been printed in Reichsarchiv und Reichskriegsministerium, *Der Weltkrieg, 1914 bis 1918, bearbeitet und herausgegeben von der Kriegsgeschichtlichen Forschungsanstalt des Heeres: Die militärischen Operationen zu Lande* (15 vols. in progress; Berlin, 1925—). A few military documents not printed elsewhere are in Ludendorff's *Urkunden der Oberste Heeresleitung über ihre Tätigkeit 1916/18* (Berlin, 1922).

In addition to these extensive printed documents, the Foreign Ministry archives for the war period are available on microfilm in the National Archives. The files are in various series, all arranged chronologically. Those which were most useful for this work were:

1. General File, which includes all routine correspondence received by the Foreign Ministry, even some classified as *streng vertraulich, geheim,* and *ganz geheim.* This file includes much of Bernstorff's correspondence from Washington for 1914–1915. Thereafter most of the ambassador's traffic went into more exclusive series.

2. Outbreak and Mediation, a small series containing mostly documents that date before August 4, 1914, but also including some material on early mediation proposals.

3. Secret Mediation, a file of great importance that includes all confidential traffic relating to neutral mediation efforts.

4. Secret, a brief but important file containing mostly communications between the Foreign Ministry and the General Staff.

5. GHQ-Amerika, key documents on the breach of 1917, all of which are published in the *Aktenstücke zur Friedensaktion Wilsons,* but which are here in draft form.

6. Peace Negotiations, a file given over before 1917 to intragovernmental memoranda on war aims. For its contents after December, 1916, see Klaus Epstein, "The Development of German-Austrian War Aims in the Spring of 1917," *Journal of Central European Affairs,* XVII (1957), 24–47.

7. U-boat War, a file included in the St. Anthony Collection. It contains much important correspondence between the Foreign Ministry and Supreme Headquarters, not all of which is printed in Tirpitz's *Politische Dokumente* or in the *Aktenstücke zur Friedensaktion Wilsons.*

On the Reichstag, the principal source is, of course, the *Stenographische Berichte der Verhandlungen des deutschen Reichstages* (Berlin, 1871 *et seq.*). Kuno, Count Westarp, *Konservative Politik im letzten Jahrzehnt des Kaiserreiches* (2 vols.; Berlin, 1935), contains many extracts from the protocols of the Reichstag budget committee, which, since the destruction of the Reichstag Library, are now unobtainable. It also includes documents from the Chancellery archives, and it must be ranked with Tirpitz's *Politische Dokumente* and the *Aktenstücke zur Friedensaktion Wilsons* as one of the three most important printed sources on the German side.

Memoirs and Biographies

In addition to the documents there are some very important autobiographies. The Kaiser's *Ereignisse und Gestalten an den Jahren 1878–1918* (Berlin, 1922), translated as *The Kaiser's Memoirs* (New York, 1922), is almost totally valueless, as are most of the biographies and studies of him. The best, probably, is Joachim von Kürenberg, *War alles falsch?* (Basel, 1940), translated as *The Kaiser* (London, 1954). Erich Eyck, *Das persönliche Regiment Wilhelms II: Politische Geschichte des deutschen Kaiserreiches von 1890 bis 1914* (Zürich, 1948), is a general political history.

While Bethmann Hollweg's *Betrachtungen zum Weltkriege* (2 vols.; Berlin, 1919) supplies little information, it is singularly revealing of the man himself. Only the first volume, going up to the outbreak of war, is translated (London, 1920). The Chancellor's speeches are collected in Friedrich Thimme (ed.), *Bethmann Hollwegs Kriegsreden* (Stuttgart, 1919). Additional documents, especially releases to the *Norddeutsche Allgemeine Zeitung,* appear in the contemporary tract by Hans, Count von Liebig, *Die Politik Bethmann Hollwegs: Eine Studie* (3 vols.; Munich, 1919).

Clemens von Delbrück, *Die wirtschaftliche Mobilmachung in Deutschland* (Munich, 1924), is by the first wartime Vice-Chancellor, but, unfortunately, it stays on its restricted subject. Karl Helfferich, *Der Weltkrieg* (3 vols.; Berlin, 1919), on the other hand, is like Churchill's *World Crisis;* it is a universal history centering on one man. It is a difficult book to use because much of it is based upon Helfferich's diary or private notes—it was said of him that he took notes on everything—yet these notes are not printed verbatim, nor is their use confessed, and one never knows whether Helfferich is to be taken at his word or not. Few other civilians in the imperial government left comparable records. Some reminiscent letters by the Foreign Minister, Gottlieb von Jagow, appear as appendices to J. H. von Bernstorff, *Erinnerungen und Briefe* (Zürich, 1936), which has been translated as *Memoirs of Count Bernstorff* (New York, 1936). Some immensely important letters and reminiscences by the Chief of the Civil Cabinet, especially on the period, 1916–1917, appear in Bernhard Schwertfeger (ed.), *Kaiser und Kabinettschef: Nach eigenen Aufzeichnungen und den Briefwechsel des Wirklichen Geheimen Rats Rudolf von Valentini* (Oldenburg, 1931). Otto Hammann, the Chancellor's press secretary, has some penetrating reflections and one or two important letters in his *Bilder aus der letzten Kaiserzeit* (Berlin, 1922). Illuminating on one particular question is the justificatory article by a onetime Secretary of State in the Chancellery, Arnold Wahnschaffe, "Der Reichskanzler von Bethmann Hollweg und die preussische Wahlreform," *Deutsche Revue,* XLVII (June, 1922), 193–203.

On the naval and military side there is a more extensive literature. Tirpitz published not only *Politische Dokumente* but also *Erinnerungen* (Leipzig, 1919), translated as *My Memoirs* (New York, 1919). The first wartime Chief of the Naval Staff left some important notes: Hugo von Pohl, *Aus Aufzeichnungen und Briefen während der Kriegszeit* (Berlin, 1920). Admiral Reinhold Scheer, Chief of the High Seas Fleet, wrote *Deutschlands Hochseeflotte im Weltkrieg* (Berlin, 1920) and *Vom Segelschiff zum U-Boot* (Leipzig, 1925), both translated, *Germany's High Seas Fleet in the World War* (London, 1920) and *From Sailing Ship to U-Boat* (London, 1925). Some other useful works by and about naval officers are: Paul Behncke, *Unsere Marine im Weltkriege und ihr Zusammenbruch* (Berlin, 1919), Ulrich von Hassell, *Tirpitz: sein Leben und Wirken mit Berücksichtigung seiner Beziehungen zu Adalbert von Stosch* (Stuttgart, 1920), Adolf von Trotha, *Grossadmiral von Tirpitz, Flottenbau und Reichsgedanke* (Breslau, 1933), and Albert Hopmann, *Kriegstagebuch eines deutschen Seeoffiziers* (Berlin, 1925).

From the army there is, first of all, Falkenhayn's *Die oberste Heeresleitung 1914–1916 in ihren wichtigsten Entschliessungen* (Berlin, 1920), translated as *The German General Staff and Its Decisions* (London, 1920). The best biography is Hans von Zwehl, *Erich von Falkenhayn* (Berlin, 1926). Hindenburg's *Aus meinem Leben* (Leipzig, 1920) contributes little. John W. Wheeler-Bennett, *Wooden Titan: Hindenburg in Twenty Years of German History, 1914–1934* (New York, 1936), is a superb biography and the best study not only of the Field Marshal but of Ludendorff as well. The First Quartermaster General's own *Meine Kriegserinnerungen, 1914–1918* (Berlin, 1919), translated as *Ludendorff's Own Story* (2 vols.; New York, 1920), is a revealing self-portrait, despite its dogged adherence to documents. One needs only to set it beside Hindenburg's *Aus meinem Leben* to see why Ludendorff was the dominant partner. Even more revealing is Ludendorff's later *Kriegführung und Politik* (Berlin, 1922). Colonel M. Bauer, *Der grosse Krieg in Feld und Heimat: Erinnerungen und Betrachtungen* (Tübingen, 1922), and Ernst von Wrisberg, *Erinnerungen an die Kriegsjahre im Königlich Preussischen Kriegsministerium* (3 vols.; Leipzig, 1921–1922), are by officers who served at Supreme Headquarters. Wilhelm Nicolai, *Nachrichtendienst, Presse, und Volkstimmung im Weltkrieg* (Berlin, 1920), is by Ludendorff's press chief. Other useful military writings are Helmuth von Moltke, *Erinnerungen, Briefe, Dokumente, 1877–1916* (Stuttgart, 1922), Karl Friedrich Nowak (ed.), *Die Aufzeichnungen des General-majors Max Hoffmann* (2 vols.; Berlin, 1929–1930), translated as *War Diaries and Other Papers* (2 vols.; London, 1929–1930), and Crown Prince Rupprecht von Bayern, *Mein Kriegstagebuch* (3 vols.; Berlin, 1928).

From diplomats there is relatively little. Of first importance for this study were, of course, Bernstorff's *Erinnerungen* and especially his *Deutschland und Amerika* (Berlin, 1920), translated as *My Three Years in America* (London, 1920). The latter volume is informative but, more important, it shows the mixed suaveness, capability, and gentility of the man. Other books relating to German diplomacy, propaganda, and intrigue in the United States have more bearing on American than on German history. Notable among these are Franz von Papen, *Die Wahrheit eine Gasse* (Munich, 1952), translated as *The Memoirs of Franz von Papen* (New York, 1953), Karl Boy Ed, *Verschwörer?: Die ersten 17 Kriegsmonate in den Vereinigten Staaten von Nordamerika* (Berlin, 1920), Bernhard Dernburg, *Von beiden Ufern* (Berlin, 1917), and Franz Rintelen von Kleist, *The Dark Invader* (London, 1933). Constantin Dumba, *Dreibund und Ententepolitik in den alten und neuen Welt*

(Vienna, 1930), translated as *Memoirs of a Diplomat* (Boston, 1932), is by the Austrian ambassador in Washington. Of rather more importance for German policy are the reminiscences of the German and Austrian representatives at one another's military headquarters: August von Cramon, *Unser österreich-ungarischer Bundesgenosse im Weltkriege: Erinnerungen aus meiner vierjährigen Tätigkeit als bevollmächtiger deutscher General beim k.u.k. Armeeoberkommando* (Berlin, 1922), and Josef, Count Stürgkh, *Im deutschen grossen Hauptquartier* (Leipzig, 1921). Equally important are the writings of Austrian statesmen themselves, especially Count Julius Andrassy, *Diplomatie und Weltkrieg* (Berlin, 1920), Count Stefan Burian, *Drei Jahre aus der Zeit meiner Amstführung im Kriege* (Berlin, 1923), and Otto, Count Czernin, *Im Weltkrieg* (Berlin, 1919). The Burian and Czernin volumes have been translated: *Austria in Dissolution* (London, 1925), and *In the World War* (New York, 1920).

Still another group of books is by or about men who had unofficial entree to imperial circles. Bernhard Huldermann, *Albert Ballin* (Berlin, 1922), reproduces some wartime letters from the head of the Hamburg-America line, but it is less important for the war years than for the period before 1914. Victor Naumann, *Dokumente und Argumente* (Berlin, 1928), contains some extremely perceptive notes and comments by Count Hertling's adviser and roving envoy. Theodor Wolff, *Der Marsch durch zwei Jahrzehnte* (Amsterdam, 1936), is by the editor of the *Berliner Tageblatt,* a frequenter of the Chancellery. Bernhard Guttmann, *Bethmann–Tirpitz–Ludendorff: Regierung und Nebenregierung* (Frankfurt am Main, 1919) and *Schattenriss einer Generation, 1888–1919* (Stuttgart, 1950), are by a *Frankfurter Zeitung* editor who served with Hammann during the war. Hugo, Baron von Reischach, *Unter drei Kaisern* (Berlin, 1922), and Adolf Wermuth, *Ein Beamtenleben* (Berlin, 1922), deal almost exclusively with prewar years but contain sidelights on Bethmann's personality and relations with the court and the bureaucracy. Some interesting material from the papers of the Austrian journalist, Heinrich Kanner, is included in Ralph H. Lutz (ed.), *The Fall of the German Empire* (2 vols.; Palo Alto, Calif., 1932).

By and about party leaders in the Reichstag, there is, first of all, Westarp's *Konservative Politik,* which contains many notes on conferences among right-wing leaders and, despite its massive chaos, supplies a remarkable insight into the Conservative mind. There is some information about the National Liberal leader in the family biography,

Karola Bassermann, *Ernst Bassermann: Das Lebensbild eines Parlamentariers aus Deutschlands glücklicher Zeit* (Mannheim, 1919). The indispensable work on Bassermann is Theodor Eschenburg's sympathetic *Das Kaiserreich am Scheideweg: Bassermann, Bülow und der Block: Nach unveröffentlichen Papieren aus dem Nachlass Ernst Bassermanns* (Berlin, 1929), but unfortunately it deals only with the Bülow period. Gustav Stresemann, *Reden und Schriften, 1897–1926* (2 vols.; Dresden, 1926), from Bassermann's deputy and successor, contains relatively little, and most biographies of Stresemann tend to slight the early war years. The one exception is Rochus, Baron von Rheinbaben, *Stresemann: Der Mensch und der Staatsmann* (Dresden, 1928), which includes extracts from wartime speeches and an apologetic section on Stresemann's role in the U-boat agitation. Ludwig Männer, *Prinz Heinrich zu Schoenaich-Carolath: Ein parlamentarisches Leben der wilhelminischen Zeit, 1852–1920* (Stuttgart, 1931), is about an anti-Bassermann National Liberal. Matthias Erzberger, *Erlebnisse im Weltkrieg* (Berlin, 1920), by the Centrist leader, is almost silent on the U-boat issue, probably because Erzberger found it difficult to remember his changes of front. His wartime career is fully described, however, in Klaus Epstein's forthcoming biography, itself a major contribution to the history of German politics. Theodor Heuss, *Friedrich Naumann: Der Mann, das Werk, die Zeit* (Stuttgart, 1937), is a disjointed but extremely useful work on the leading Christian socialist. Conrad Haussmann, *Schlaglichter, Reichstagsbriefe, und Aufzeichnungen* (Frankfurt am Main, 1924), Friedrich von Payer, *Von Bethmann Hollweg bis Ebert: Erinnerungen und Bilder* (Frankfurt am Main, 1924), and Ernst Müller-Meiningen, *Parlamentarismus: Betrachtungen, Lehren, und Erinnerungen aus deutschen Parlamenten* (Berlin, 1926), are by Progressive members of the budget committee; the first two were friends and supporters of Bethmann. The most important book from the socialist side is Philipp Scheidemann, *Der Zusammenbruch* (Berlin, 1921), based upon a wartime diary. Much of its content and some additional information is incorporated in Scheidemann's later *Memoiren eines Sozialdemokraten* (2 vols.; Dresden, 1928), of which there is a translation, *The Making of a New Germany: The Memoirs of Philipp Scheidemann* (2 vols.; New York, 1929). Additional literature is listed in the splendid bibliographical essay appended to Carl E. Schorske, *German Social Democracy, 1905–1917: The Development of the Great Schism* (Cambridge, Mass., 1955). From the Danish member of the budget committee there is Hans Peter Hanssen, *Fra Krigstiden: Dagsbogs optegnelser* (Copenhagen, 1925), of which there is a full not not complete translation, *The Diary of a Dying Empire* (Bloomington, Ind., 1955).

Newspapers

Owing to the extremes and varieties of partisanship among German newspapers, it is necessary to use several for a full picture of domestic politics. The *Norddeutsche Allgemeine Zeitung* was a government organ in all but name, and so during the war were most of the great independent newspapers. The *Kölnische Zeitung* was notoriously such and had been for a generation. The *Frankfurter Zeitung* and the *Berliner Tageblatt* were more disguisedly official. The *Vossische Zeitung*, by the war years, had lined up with the right wing of the Progressive party. The chief Conservative organs were the *Neue Preussische Zeitung* (known universally and cited here as the *Kreuzzeitung*) and the *Deutsche Tageszeitung*. The editor and chief foreign affairs columnist for the former were respectively Roesicke and Westarp, both Conservative members of the budget committee; Reventlow, the naval affairs columnist for the latter, had the closest connections with Tirpitz and the Navy Ministry. The Berlin *Post* represented the Free Conservatives. Although the National Liberals had many journals, few were distinguished. The *Magdeburgische Zeitung* was reputed to be Bassermann's personal organ. The two leading *Zentrum* papers were the *Kölnische Volkzeitung*, speaking for the rightist Rhineland group, and *Germania*, the more leftist Berlin organ. For the right Progressives, the *Vossische Zeitung* serves, and the left Progressives were so closely tied to the government that their journals are indistinguishable from the semiofficial. *Vorwärts*, the leading socialist organ, actually spoke for the later Independents, while lesser journals, especially the *Leipziger Volkszeitung*, represented the majority.

Files of most of these journals exist in more or less complete form in the Library of Congress, the New York Public Library, the Harvard University Libraries, or the Hoover Institution for the Study of War and Peace at Stanford University. The principal exceptions are *Germania* and the *Magdeburgische Zeitung* of which, so far as I can discover, there are no files in the United States.

The task of searching the German press is greatly lightened by the existence of various guides. Otto Groth, *Die Zeitung* (4 vols.; Mannheim, 1928–1930), contains everything that is known about ownership and orientation among the partisan press. Historical background can be obtained in Hale's *Publicity and Diplomacy,* cited in the English section above, and in E. Malcolm Carroll, *Germany and the Great Powers, 1866-1914: A Study in Public Opinion and Foreign Policy* (New York, 1938). Extracts from newspapers and supplementary comment appear in the invaluable *Schulthess' europäischer Geschichtskalendar* (Munich, 1861 *et seq.*) and in various Tagebücher, notably Richard Dehmel, *Zwischen Volk und Menschheit: Kriegstagebuch* (Berlin, 1919), Eduard Engel, *Ein Tagebuch* (3 vols.; Berlin, 1916-1918), and A. H. Fried, *Mein Kriegstagebuch* (Zürich, 1918).

Most important of all are the periodic Allied surveys of the German press. Redaction des 'Documents sur la guerre,' *Résumé de la presse allemande,* usually appeared monthly, with special supplements as, for example, on the Bavarian press or on books and pamphlets devoted to a special topic. The British War Office published *Daily Extracts from the Foreign Press* from September, 1915, to March, 1916. This then became the *Daily Review of the Foreign Press.* In July, 1916, there was added a *Weekly Supplement,* giving additional material from the German and Austrian press. In November, 1916, this was replaced by a weekly *Enemy Press Supplement.* So far as I can detect, the reporting in both digests is fair and comprehensive. In addition, the French and British editors summarize and quote from newspapers whose files are now unobtainable or inaccessible.

Studies

GENERAL. Just as the available sources for German wartime history are more abundant, so naturally are studies of it. Two first-rate general histories extend through the war years: Johannes Ziekursch, *Politische Geschichte des neuen deutschen Kaiserreiches* (3 vols.; Stuttgart and Frankfurt am Main, 1926-1930), and Fritz Hartung, *Deutsche Geschichte von Frankfurter Frieden bis zum Vertrag von Versailles, 1871-1919* (Bonn, 1929). R. M. Veit Valentin, *Deutschlands Aussenpolitik von Bismarcks Abgang bis zum Ende des Weltkrieges* (Berlin, 1921), though largely outdated, retains some value because of the author's wartime position in the Foreign Ministry and also because of his distinction as a historian. The most important interpretive work on the period is Arthur Rosenberg, *Die Entstehung der deutschen Republik, 1871-1918* (Berlin, 1928), translated as *The Birth of the German Republic* (London, 1931). No student of the period can escape its influence.

SUBMARINE WARFARE. A recent work, Walther Hubatsch, *Die Ära Tirpitz: Studien zur deutschen Marinepolitik, 1890-1918* (Göttingen,

1955), is mostly about the prewar years, but it is almost as valuable in setting the scene as is Woodward's volume on the British side. On submarine operations, besides Spindler's official volumes, there are several more or less technical studies: Albert Gayer, *Die deutschen U-Boote in ihrer Kriegführung, 1914–1918* (Berlin, 1920) and "Summary of German Submarine Operations in the Various Theaters of War from 1914 to 1918," *Proceedings of the United States Naval Institute,* LI (1926), 621–659, Adolphe Laurens, *Histoire de la guerre sous-marine allemande* (Paris, 1930), Andreas Michelsen, *Der U-Bootskrieg* (Leipzig, 1925), and Maurice Prendergast and R. H. Gibson, *The German Submarine War, 1914–1918* (New York, 1931). On the *Lusitania* sinking, the relevant documents are collected in Thomas A. Bailey, "German Documents relating to the *Lusitania,*" *Journal of Modern History,* VIII (1936), 320–337, and analyzed in the same writer's "The Sinking of the *Lusitania,*" *American Historical Review,* XLI (1935–1936), 54–73.

DIPLOMACY AND DOMESTIC POLITICS. On war aims and mediation there is an extensive literature. The best single book is Hans W. Gatzke, *Germany's Drive to the West: A Study of Germany's Western War Aims during the First World War* (Baltimore, 1950), but there is still value in E. O. Volkmann, *Die Anexionsfrage des Weltkrieges,* which is volume XII, part 1, of *Die Ursachen des Deutschen Zusammenbruches im Jahre 1918,* cited above, and in Dahlin's *French and German Public Opinion on Declared War Aims,* and Forster's *Failures of Peace.* Alfred Kruck, *Geschichte des Alldeutschen Verbandes* (Wiesbaden, 1954), is the most recent study of the Pan-German League and is fuller on the war years than is Lothar Werner's penetrating *Der Alldeutsche Verband, 1890–1918: Ein Beitrag zur Geschichte der öffentlichen Meinung in Deutschland* (Berlin, 1935). Two useful monographs on party attitudes are Hermann Ostfeld, *Die Haltung der Reichstagsfraktion der Fortschrittliche Volkspartei zu den Anexions- und Friedensfrage in den Jahren 1914–1918* (Kallmünz, 1934), and Frida Wacker, *Die Haltung der Deutschen Zentrumspartei zur Frage der Kriegsziele im Weltkrieg, 1914–1918* (Lohr am Main, 1937). Of real importance are two articles by John L. Snell, "Socialist Unions and Socialist Patriotism in Germany, 1914–1918," *American Historical Review,* LIX (1953), 66–76, and "German Socialism and the Peace Crisis of 1916," *Journal of Central European Affairs,* XII (1953), 368–381, and Henry Cord Meyer's penetrating *Mitteleuropa in German Thought and Action, 1815–1945* (The Hague, 1955).

On the diplomatic aspects of the peace question, the outstanding work is still Richard Fester, *Die Politik Kaiser Karls und der Wendepunkt des Weltkrieges* (Munich, 1925), partially supplemented by the same author's *Die politischen Kämpfe um den Frieden (1916–1918) und das Deutschtum* (Munich, 1938). Fester had access to the archive files opened for the Reichstag inquiries. Esther C. Brunauer, "The Peace Proposals of December 1916–January 1917," *Journal of Modern History,* IV (1932), 544–571, is a résumé from the printed documents.

On party politics during the war, an excellent study has recently appeared in the U.S.S.R.: E. K. Eggert, *Bor'ba Klassov i Partii v Germanii, 1914–1917* (Moscow, 1957). I am heartened that Mr. Eggert and I independently reached many of the same conclusions, differing chiefly where he (or I) met doctrinal impedimenta. Among older works, Viktor Bredt, *Der deutsche Reichstag im Weltkrieg,* which is volume VIII of *Die Ursachen des Deutschen Zusammenbruches im Jahre 1918,* still stands out. Ernst Deuerlein, *Der Bundesratsausschuss für die auswärtigen Angelegenheiten, 1870–1918* (Regensburg, 1955), is a special study of the utmost importance, reproducing as appendices the protocols of committee meetings and utilizing much new material from the Bavarian state archives. Ludwig Bergsträsser, *Die preussische Wahlrechtsfrage im Kriege und die Entstehung der Osterbotschaft 1917* (Tübingen, 1929), and Willy Bongard, *Die Zentrumsresolution von 7. Oktober 1916* (Cologne, 1937), are important monographs.

On political parties themselves, most studies concentrate on the socialists. Eugen Präger, *Geschichte der U.S.P.D.: Entstehung und Entwicklung der Unabhängigen Sozialdemokratischen Partei Deutschlands* (Berlin, 1921), is still the basic chronicle and compilation of documents. A. Joseph Berlau, *The German Social Democratic Party, 1914–1921* (New York, 1949), is the fullest study. Though Schorske's *German Social Democracy, 1905–1917* deals only briefly with the war years, it is absolutely indispensable; it is one of the half-dozen most important works on Wilhelmine Germany. Karl Bachem, *Vorgeschichte, Geschichte, und Politik der Deutschen Zentrumspartei* (8 vols.; Cologne, 1927–1931), is loosely organized but full of information, especially on party politics within the various German states. Eschenburg's *Das Kaiserreich am Scheideweg* and Walter Koch, *Volk und Staatführung vor dem Weltkriege* (Stuttgart, 1935), though dealing with other periods, are indispensable for understanding the National Liberals. Hans Booms, *Die deutschkonservative Partei: Preussischer Charakter, Reichsauffas-*

sung, Nationalbegriff (Düsseldorf, 1954), is a brisk but thoughtful general history. Klemens von Klemperer, *Germany's New Conservatism: Its History and Dilemma in the Twentieth Century* (Princeton, 1957), deals with a later period, but bracketed with Eckart Kehr's classic *Schlachtflottenbau und Parteipolitik, 1894–1901* (Berlin, 1930), sheds much light on the wartime Conservative party.

There are three brief studies that touch on the interaction among domestic politics, foreign policy, and strategy. Erwin Direnberger, *Oberste Heeresleitung und Reichsleitung, 1914–1918* (Berlin, 1936), is a Nazi tract of little consequence. Horst Bülter, "Zur Geschichte Deutschlands im ersten Weltkrieg (1914–1915)," *Zeitschrift für Geschichtswissenschaft*, III (1955), 835–855, is a Marxist analysis centering on the SPD left. Paul R. Sweet, "Leaders and Policies: Germany in the Winter of 1914–1915," *Journal of Central European Affairs*, XVI (1956), 229–252, is a careful study of east vs. west strategic debates, utilizing material from the Foreign Ministry archives.

UNITED STATES

Archives and Documents

The National Archives in Washington, D.C., contain practically all records of the war years and are open without restriction. The State Department, however, has published practically all the important European correspondence in *Foreign Relations of the United States, Supplement: The World War* (7 vols.; Washington, D.C., 1928–1932). Certain additional material, particularly affidavits in the submarine cases, appears in the *European War* series entitled *Diplomatic Correspondence with Belligerent Governments relating to Neutral Rights and Duties,* and some intragovernmental correspondence is printed, along with a selection of diplomatic documents, in Carlton Savage (ed.), *Policy of the United States toward Maritime Commerce in War* (2 vols.; Washington, D.C., 1936). The fullest collection of letters exchanged between the Department of State and the White House and within the Department of State is *The Lansing Papers, 1914–1920* (2 vols.; Washington, D.C., 1939). Only a few important items are not included in one or the other of these collections, and most of those are in two special files: one of letters exchanged between Woodrow Wilson and William Jennings Bryan, the other of papers from the Joint State and Navy Neutrality

Board, both in the Foreign Affairs Division of the National Archives. I looked at the general correspondence files of the Secretary of War and the Secretary of the Navy, both in the National Archives, but found little of value. Material on war planning, which might be useful, is still under security classification.

Manuscripts, Collections, Memoirs, and Biographies

The most important sources are the private papers of American policymakers. The manuscripts of Woodrow Wilson in the Manuscripts Division of the Library of Congress form a vast collection, of which the extracts printed in Ray Stannard Baker, *Woodrow Wilson: Life and Letters* (8 vols.; New York, 1927–1939), are only a sample. Baker's collection of manuscripts relating to Wilson, including additional correspondence and records of interviews with the President's associates, is also deposited in the Library of Congress. The more important speeches and public documents have been printed in Ray Stannard Baker and William E. Dodd (eds.), *The Public Papers of Woodrow Wilson* (6 vols.; New York, 1925–1927). The papers of E. M. House at the Yale University Library include not only all the colonel's correspondence but also his manuscript diary, all of which may now be read by scholars. Needless to say, only fragments of the House Papers appear in Charles Seymour, *The Intimate Papers of Colonel House* (4 vols.; Boston, 1926–1928). The Wilson, Ray Stannard Baker, and House collections form the backbone for any study of American policy during the period.

The papers of Robert Lansing are disappointing. As *The Lansing Papers* indicates, he left most of his files with the State Department, and his private papers, deposited at the Library of Congress, contain mostly incoming letters from friends and acquaintances. A desk diary, mainly a calendar of appointments, is included and is sometimes useful. A private diary, also included, is really a collection of occasional memoranda jotted down by Lansing, apparently to clear his own mind. Some but not all of these memoranda were printed by him in his *War Memoirs* (Indianapolis, 1935). The papers of his predecessor, William Jennings Bryan, are in the Library of Congress, but they are even more disappointing than Lansing's. Old neighbors in Lincoln, Nebraska, say that before Bryan transferred his residence to Florida he burned manuscripts by the wheelbarrow-load. The items he kept were mostly mementoes. Not all of them are unimportant, but most of those that are not have been published either in *The Lansing Papers* or in William Jennings Bryan and Mary Baird Bryan, *The Memoirs of William Jennings Bryan* (Philadelphia, 1925).

Some useful manuscript collections are those of Josephus Daniels, Wilson's Secretary of the Navy, Frank L. Polk, who succeeded Lansing as Counselor for the Department of State, Chandler P. Anderson, an occasional legal adviser to the Department, Walter H. Page, the ambassador in London, and various opposition leaders and observant citizens like Theodore Roosevelt, William Howard Taft, Henry White, and Oswald Garrison Villard. The Daniels papers in the Library of Congress include an irregular diary, especially illuminating for the prewar period and for the critical cabinet meetings of 1917. Polk's papers, part of the E. M. House collection at Yale, also include a diary, especially useful for late 1916. Anderson's diary, in the Library of Congress, has some very important entries, but it was also kept irregularly. The cream of Page's diary and correspondence, kept in the Houghton Library at Harvard University, has already been published in Burton J. Hendrick, *The Life and Letters of Walter Hines Page* (3 vols.; New York, 1925–1926). All of Theodore Roosevelt's important letters appear in Elting E. Morison *et al.* (eds.), *The Letters of Theodore Roosevelt* (8 vols.; Cambridge, Mass., 1951–1954). The Taft and White papers are in the Library of Congress. The Villard papers are in the Houghton Library.

In addition to the printed works mentioned above, there are several others that contain important material. David F. Houston, *Eight Years with Wilson's Cabinet, 1913–1920* (2 vols.; New York, 1926), reproduces diary notes by the Secretary of Agriculture. Anne W. Lane and Lewis H. Wall, *The Letters of Franklin K. Lane* (Boston, 1922), contains some illuminating correspondence from the files of the Secretary of the Interior. The memoir of Wilson's private secretary, Joseph P. Tumulty, *Woodrow Wilson as I Know Him* (New York, 1921), is supplemented by John M. Blum, *Joe Tumulty and the Wilson Era* (Boston, 1951), which contains judicious extracts from the Tumulty papers. There is less in the autobiography of Wilson's Secretary of the Treasury, William G. McAdoo, *Crowded Years* (Boston, 1931), still less in those of the Secretary of the Navy, Josephus Daniels, *The Wilson Era* (2 vols.; Chapel Hill, N.C., 1944), and the Secretary of Commerce, William C. Redfield, *With Congress and Cabinet* (New York, 1924), and practically nothing at all in that of the Vice-President, *Recollections of Thomas R. Marshall* (Indianapolis, 1925). William Phillips, *Ventures in Diplo-*

macy (Boston, 1953), is the lighthearted autobiography of one of Wilson's Assistant Secretaries of State.

Among biographies of government leaders, the outstanding one is Baker's *Wilson*. It is more valuable, however, for its extracts from the manuscripts than for the critical judgments of the writer. Arthur S. Link's monumental biography has, at this writing, reached only the outbreak of the war, but nowhere can one see more deeply into the heart and mind of the President than in the two volumes which Link has completed: *Wilson: The Road to the White House* (Princeton, 1947) and *Wilson: The New Freedom* (Princeton, 1956). Arthur G. Walworth, *Woodrow Wilson: A Biography* (2 vols.; New York, 1958), is a sympathetic portrait, more penetrating than Baker's, but certain to be superseded by Link's successive volumes. Of shorter sketches the best are H. C. F. Bell, *Woodrow Wilson and the People* (New York, 1945), John M. Blum, *Woodrow Wilson and the Politics of Morality* (Boston, 1956), and John A. Garraty, *Woodrow Wilson* (New York, 1956).

A work in a special category is Alexander L. and Juliette L. George, *Woodrow Wilson and Colonel House: A Personality Study* (New York, 1956), a psychoanalytic study of the two men, full of shrewd but uncertain insights. George Sylvester Viereck, *The Strangest Friendship in History: Woodrow Wilson and Colonel House* (New York, 1932), is a much more orthodox portrayal, only mildly revisionist despite the author's wartime work as a German propagandist. Arthur D. Howden-Smith, *Mr. House of Texas* (New York, 1940), is a singularly unilluminating biography by a onetime secretary to the colonel. By far the best portrait of House is still Charles Seymour's running commentary in *The Intimate Papers of Colonel House,* supplemented by the same author's reflective essay, "The Role of Colonel House in Wilson's Diplomacy," in Edward H. Buehrig (ed.), *Wilson's Foreign Policy in Perspective* (Bloomington, Ind., 1957).

On other figures in the government biographical literature is scarce, and much of it is valueless. Julius W. Pratt has a sketch of Lansing in Samuel F. Bemis (ed.), *American Secretaries of State and Their Diplomacy* (10 vols.; New York, 1927–1929), X, 47–175, but it was written before the most important Lansing materials came to light. An important reappraisal of Lansing appears in Edward H. Buehrig, *Woodrow Wilson and the Balance of Power* (Bloomington, Ind., 1955). Daniel M. Smith, "Robert Lansing and the Formulation of American Neutrality Policies, 1914–1915," *Mississippi Valley Historical Review,* XLIII

(1956), 59–81, details Lansing's activities during the early part of the war. On Bryan the only really competent work is Merle E. Curti, *Bryan and World Peace* (Northampton, Mass., 1931). It is probably true that in the modern climate of opinion no man who can genuinely under-stand Bryan will be capable of writing his biography. Those that have been printed are either malicious, like Paxton Hibben and C. Hartley Grattan, *The Peerless Leader* (New York, 1929), and M. R. Werner, *Bryan* (New York, 1929), or reverential, like John C. Long, *Bryan, the Great Commoner* (New York, 1928), and Wayne C. Williams, *William Jennings Bryan* (New York, 1936). The sketch of Bryan in Bemis' *Secretaries of State* is by Joseph V. Fuller. Mary Synon, *McAdoo* (Indianapolis, 1924), is thin. Frederick Palmer, *Newton D. Baker: America at War* (2 vols.; New York, 1931), is useful only for the last months of the neutrality years. Blum's *Tumulty and the Wilson Era* is, of course, a first-rate book, but it is necessarily cursory on the 1914–1917 period. Frank Freidel, *Franklin D. Roosevelt: The Apprenticeship* (Boston, 1952), sheds light on the whole period, even though Roosevelt's official position was a minor one.

On figures outside the administration there is an important though restricted literature. By and about influential members of the Senate, there are: Claude G. Bowers, *Beveridge and the Progressive Era* (New York, 1932), Belle Case LaFollette and Fola LaFollette, *Robert M. LaFollette, June 14, 1855–June 18, 1925* (2 vols.; New York, 1953), Philip C. Jessup, *Elihu Root* (2 vols.; New York, 1938), Francis B. Simkins, *Pitchfork Ben Tillman* (Baton Rouge, La., 1944), and George C. Osborn, *John Sharp Williams* (Baton Rouge, La., 1943). By and about influential members of the House, there are: Champ Clark, *My Quarter Century of American Politics* (2 vols.; New York, 1920), Rixey Smith and Norman Beasley, *Carter Glass: A Biography* (New York, 1939), John A. Garraty, *Henry Cabot Lodge* (New York, 1953), Alex M. Arnett, *Claude Kitchin and the Wilson War Policies* (Boston, 1937), and George W. Norris, *Fighting Liberal* (New York, 1945).

Some useful reminiscences by journalists are Oswald Garrison Villard, *Fighting Years: Memoirs of a Liberal Editor* (New York, 1939), and *The Autobiography of William Allen White* (New York, 1946), to which should be added three outstanding biographies: John L. Heaton, *Cobb of the World* (New York, 1924), Willis F. Johnson, *George Harvey, "A Passionate Patriot"* (Boston, 1929), and Walter Johnson, *William Allen White's America* (New York, 1946).

Nearly all diplomats serving in the United States or representing the United States abroad have set down their recollections or have been written about. The letters of Sir Cecil Spring-Rice, Arthur Willert's extracts from the Wiseman papers, and the memorial volume on Macchi di Cellere have been mentioned in the literature on Britain; the writings of Bernstorff, Papen, Boy Ed, Dernburg, and Dumba have been listed among works on Germany. Two additional works by diplomats serving in the United States are Jean Jules Jusserand, *Le sentiment américain pendant la guerre* (Paris, 1931), an essay by the French ambassador, and Horst P. Falcke, *Vor dem Eintritt Amerikas in den Weltkrieg* (Dresden, 1928), a confession, in effect, by a former German Consul General in New York.

Of writings by and about American diplomats, the most important single work is Hendrick's *Page.* On the French mission there are T. Bentley Mott, *Myron T. Herrick: Friend of France* (New York, 1930), and *The War Memoirs of William Graves Sharp* (London, 1931). James W. Gerard has written three books: *My Four Years in Germany* (New York, 1917), *Face to Face with Kaiserism* (New York, 1918), and *My First Eighty Three Years in America* (New York, 1951). Some of his First Secretary's diary is presented in Joseph C. Grew, *Turbulent Era: A Diplomatic Record of Forty Years, 1904–1945* (2 vols.; Boston, 1952). There are also useful writings by men who served in Belgium, Sweden, Italy, and Turkey: Allan Nevins (ed.), *The Letters and Journals of Brand Whitlock* (2 vols.; New York, 1936), Hugh Gibson, *A Journal from Our Legation in Belgium* (New York, 1917), Ira Nelson Morris, *From an American Legation* (New York, 1936), Thomas Nelson Page, *Italy and the World War* (New York, 1920), and Henry Morgenthau, *Ambassador Morgenthau's Story* (New York, 1918).

Newspapers

Although the American press has been used extensively by historians, it does not have the same value for political studies as the more partisan press of Europe. In most cases, one can assume nothing more about an American newspaper than that it spoke for its editorial board. The New York *Times* is the most useful daily chronicle, and it occasionally surveyed press comment throughout the country. The New York *World* has special value because it was regarded as a spokesman for the administration, and, whether it was or not, it tried to act the part. The Providence *Journal* is occasionally valuable for chauvinist opinion, the

New York *Evening Post* for liberal neutralism, and the Chicago *Tribune* for neutralist opinion in a German and Irish stronghold. The Washington *Post* has double utility, both for local notes and for a strongly neutralist editorial policy.

The Literary Digest, weekly, and *Current Opinion,* monthly, printed generous extracts from á wide sampling of American newspapers. Of unusual value are the extracts from the British *American Press Résumés,* printed in H. C. Peterson, *Propaganda for War: The Campaign against American Neutrality, 1914-1917* (Norman, Okla., 1939), and the commentaries on local press opinion in John C. Crighton, *Missouri and the World War, 1914-1917* (Columbia, Mo., 1947), and Cedric C. Cummins, *Indiana Public Opinion and the World War, 1914-1917* (Indianapolis, 1945). Edwin C. Costrell, *How Maine Viewed the War, 1914-1917* (Orono, Me., 1940), is also useful, but much less comprehensive. Different cross-sections are analyzed in Harold C. Syrett, "The Business Press and American Neutrality, 1914-1917," *Mississippi Valley Historical Review,* XXXII (1945), 215-230, and Ray H. Abrams, *Preachers Present Arms: A Study of Wartime Attitudes and Activities of the Churches and Clergy in the United States, 1914-1918* (Philadelphia, 1933), a careful study of the religious press.

Studies

GENERAL. The extensive literature on America in the Wilson years is described or discussed in a number of bibliographies. Samuel F. Bemis and Grace Gardner Griffin, *Guide to the Diplomatic History of the United States, 1775-1921* (Washington, D.C., 1935), is exhaustive. Oscar Handlin *et al., Harvard Guide to American History* (Cambridge, Mass., 1954), is very full. A notable special bibliography is Bibliographische Vierteljahreshefte der Weltkriegsbücherei, volumes XX-XXII: *Bibliographie zur Geschichte der Vereinigten Staaten im Weltkrieg* (Stuttgart, 1939), a list of holdings in the once great World War library in Stuttgart. Arthur S. Link has an extensive bibliographical essay in *Woodrow Wilson and the Progressive Era, 1910-1917* (New York, 1954). Two others are Richard W. Leopold, "The Problem of American Intervention, 1917: An Historical Retrospect," *World Politics,* II (1950), 405-425, and Richard L. Watson, Jr., "Woodrow Wilson and His Interpreters, 1947-1957," *Mississippi Valley Historical Review,* XLIV (1957), 207-236. The abundance and accessibility of such aids make it unnecessary to be more than highly selective here.

The best survey of the period is Link's *Woodrow Wilson and the Progressive Era.* Frederic L. Paxson, *American Democracy and the World War* (3 vols.; Boston and Berkeley, Calif., 1936–1948), is panoramic rather than interpretive.

NEUTRALITY. Of the many studies that deal with Wilson's diplomacy as pathologically aberrant, the bulkiest is Charles Callan Tansill, *America Goes to War* (Boston, 1938); the best written is Walter Millis, *Road to War: America, 1914–1917* (Boston, 1935). Harley Notter, *The Origins of the Foreign Policy of Woodrow Wilson* (Baltimore, 1937), is more solid and more sympathetic. By far the best early study, and the only one that views events on the other side of the ocean as anything but ripples from American tides, is Charles Seymour, *American Diplomacy during the World War* (Baltimore, 1934), supplemented by the same writer's *American Neutrality, 1914–1917* (New Haven, 1935). Of more recent date are two provocative analyses, both concerned rather with the efficiency than with the morality of Wilson's policies: Robert E. Osgood, *Ideals and Self-Interest in America's Foreign Relations* (Chicago, 1953), and Buehrig's *Woodrow Wilson and the Balance of Power.* Arthur Link has given a reflective forecast of the interpretations that will appear in later volumes of the biography in *Wilson the Diplomatist* (Baltimore, 1957).The sagest commentary is in two essays by William L. Langer in Langer, Link, and Eric Goldman, *Woodrow Wilson and the World Today* (Bryn Mawr, Pa., 1957).

Legal questions are dealt with in Alice M. Morrissey, *The American Defense of Neutral Rights, 1914–1917* (Cambridge, Mass., 1939), polemically in Edwin M. Borchard and William P. Lage, *Neutrality for the United States* (New Haven, 1937), more temperately in James W. Garner, *International Law and the World War* (2 vols.; New York, 1920), Malbone W. Graham, *The Controversy between the United States and the Allied Governments Respecting Neutral Rights and Commerce during the Period of American Neutrality, 1914–1917* (Austin, Texas, 1923), and Edgar Turlington, *Neutrality, Its History, Economics and Law: The World War Period* (New York, 1936).

Among monographs and articles only a few stand out. Richard W. Van Alstyne, "The Policy of the United States regarding the Declaration of London at the Outbreak of the Great War," *Journal of Modern History,* VII (1935), 434–447, describes the legal controversy. Charles A. Beard, "New Light on Bryan and War Policies," *New Republic* (June 17, 1936), 177–178, analyzes data turned up in the Nye committee hearings. Joseph V. Fuller, "The Genesis of the Munitions Traffic," *Journal of Modern History,* VI (1934), 280–293, offers the thesis that Wilson's failure to restrict arms shipments was the root cause of American involvement in the war. J. C. Crighton, "The *Wilhelmina:* An Adventure in the Assertion and Exercise of American Trading Rights during the World War," *American Journal of International Law,* XXXIV (1940), 74–88, provides a full analysis. Arthur S. Link, "The Cotton Crisis, The South, and Anglo-American Diplomacy, 1914–1915," in J. C. Sitterson (ed.), *Studies in Southern History in Memory of Albert Ray Newsome, 1894–1951* (Chapel Hill, N.C., 1957), is extremely useful. Thomas A. Bailey, "The United States and the Blacklist during the Great War," *Journal of Modern History,* VI (1934), 14–35, deals fully with the hottest Anglo-American issue of 1916. Johannes Kühn, *Die Friedensbemühung der Präsident Wilson im Weltkrieg* (Berlin, 1928), is a useful if pedestrian survey. Samuel R. Spencer, Jr., *Decision for War, 1917* (Rindge, N.H., 1953), describes the provocations of January–March, 1917.

PUBLIC OPINION. In addition to the writings of Peterson, Crighton, Cummins, Costrell, Syrett, and Abrams cited above, there are several works on important ethnic groups. On the German-Americans the two standard works are Carl Wittke, *German-Americans and the World War* (Columbus, Ohio, 1936), and Clifton J. Child, *The German-Americans in Politics, 1914–1917* (Madison, Wis., 1939). On the Irish allies of the German-Americans there is a useful summary in Carl Wittke, *The Irish in America* (Baton Rouge, La., 1956), while Charles Callan Tansill, *America and the Fight for Irish Freedom* (Chicago, 1957), displays with partisan zeal the cleavages among Irish-American groups, G. M. Stephenson, "The Attitude of Swedish-Americans toward the World War," *Proceedings of the Mississippi Valley Historical Association,* X, part 1 (1918–1919), 79–84, suggests that there were also divisions among these putative allies of the German-Americans. There is a regrettable shortage of information on possible pro-Ally groups like English, French, south Slav, and Russian-Americans, though a beginning is made in Suzanne Tassier, *La Belgique et l'entrée en guerre des États-Unis, 1914–1917* (Brussels, 1951).

In the 1920's and 1930's, propaganda seemed a dark and potent force to many scholars. Peterson in his *Propaganda for War* seems to argue that Sir Gilbert Parker and a small staff operating from Wellington House were the engineers of American intervention. James D. Squires, *British Propaganda at Home and in the United States from 1914 to 1917* (Cambridge, Mass., 1935), is a more sedate analysis. The market for revelations was satisfied chiefly by confessions from the German side, of which the outstanding are George Sylvester Viereck, *Spreading Germs of Hate* (New York, 1930), and Rintelen's *The Dark Invader*. In the large literature on German activities in the United States, the best single work is Henry Landau, *The Enemy Within: The Inside Story of German Sabotage in America* (New York, 1937), which is based in part on materials sequestered by the United States Secret Service.

The role of economic interest groups in fostering war sentiment was fully explored by the Nye committee: 74 Congress, 2 session, Senate Document Number 944, "Report of the Special Senate Committee on the Investigation of the Munitions Industry." The forty parts of this report and the accompanying hearings display beyond a shadow of doubt the absurdity of the munitions-makers conspiracy theory.

On the background of American attitudes toward the various belligerents, the major works are H. C. Allen, *Great Britain and the United States,* two detailed and complementary diplomatic studies: Lionel Gelber, *The Rise of Anglo-American Friendship: A Study in World Politics, 1896–1906* (Toronto, 1938), and Charles S. Campbell, *Anglo-American Understanding, 1898–1903* (Baltimore, 1957), Elizabeth B. White, *American Opinion of France: From Lafayette to Poincaré* (New York, 1927), Clara E. Schieber, *The Transformation of American Sentiment toward Germany, 1870–1914* (Boston, 1923), Ilse Kunz-Lack, *Die deutsch-amerikanischen Beziehungen, 1890–1914* (Stuttgart, 1935), and Alfred Vagts' monumental *Deutschland und die Vereinigten Staaten in der Weltpolitik* (2 vols.; London, 1935).

Index

QUADRANGLE PAPERBACKS

History

Frederick Lewis Allen. *The Lords of Creation.* QP35
William Sheridan Allen. *The Nazi Seizure of Power.* QP302
Lewis Atherton. *Main Street on the Middle Border.* QP36
Thomas A. Bailey. *Woodrow Wilson and the Lost Peace.* QP1
Thomas A. Bailey. *Woodrow Wilson and the Great Betrayal.* QP2
Charles A. Beard. *The Idea of National Interest.* QP27
Carl L. Becker. *Everyman His Own Historian.* QP33
Ray A. Billington. *The Protestant Crusade.* QP12
Kenneth E. Boulding. *The Organizational Revolution.* QP43
John Chamberlain. *Farewell to Reform.* QP19
Alice Hamilton Cromie. *A Tour Guide to the Civil War.*
Robert D. Cross. *The Emergence of Liberal Catholicism in America.* QP44
Chester McArthur Destler. *American Radicalism, 1865-1901.* QP30
Robert A. Divine. *The Illusion of Neutrality.* QP45
Elisha P. Douglass. *Rebels and Democrats.* QP26
Herman Finer. *Road to Reaction.* QP5
Felix Frankfurter. *The Commerce Clause.* QP16
Lloyd C. Gardner. *A Different Frontier.* QP32
Edwin Scott Gaustad. *The Great Awakening in New England.* QP46
Ray Ginger. *Altgeld's America.* QP21
W. O. Henderson. *The Industrial Revolution in Europe.* QP303
William B. Hesseltine. *Lincoln's Plan of Reconstruction.* QP41
Raul Hilberg. *The Destruction of the European Jews.* QP301
Frederic C. Howe. *The Confessions of a Reformer.* QP39
Louis Joughin and Edmund M. Morgan. *The Legacy of Sacco and Vanzetti.* QP7
Edward Chase Kirkland. *Dream and Thought in the Business Community, 1860-1900.* QP11
Edward Chase Kirkland. *Industry Comes of Age.* QP42
Adrienne Koch. *The Philosophy of Thomas Jefferson.* QP17
Gabriel Kolko. *The Triumph of Conservatism.* QP40
Walter LaFeber. *John Quincy Adams and American Continental Empire.* QP23
David E. Lilienthal. *TVA: Democracy on the March.* QP28
Arthur S. Link. *Wilson the Diplomatist.* QP18
Huey P. Long. *Every Man a King.* QP8
Gene M. Lyons. *America: Purpose and Power.* QP24
Jackson Turner Main. *The Antifederalists.* QP14
Ernest R. May. *The World War and American Isolation, 1914-1917.* QP29
Henry F. May. *The End of American Innocence.* QP9
George E. Mowry. *The California Progressives.* QP6
Frank L. Owsley. *Plain Folk of the Old South.* QP22
David Graham Phillips. *The Treason of the Senate.* QP20
Julius W. Pratt. *Expansionists of 1898.* QP15
John P. Roche. *The Quest for the Dream.* QP47
David A. Shannon. *The Socialist Party of America.* QP38
Richard W. Van Alstyne. *The Rising American Empire.* QP25
Willard M. Wallace. *Appeal to Arms.* QP10
Norman Ware. *The Industrial Worker, 1840-1860.* QP13
Albert K. Weinberg. *Manifest Destiny.* QP3
Bernard A. Weisberger. *They Gathered at the River.* QP37
Bell I. Wiley. *The Plain People of the Confederacy.* QP4
William Appleman Williams. *The Contours of American History.* QP34
William Appleman Williams. *The Great Evasion.* QP48
Esmond Wright. *Causes and Consequences of the American Revolution.* QP31

Philosophy

James M. Edie. *An Invitation to Phenomenology.* QP103
James M. Edie. *Phenomenology in America.* QP105
Manfred S. Frings. *Heidegger and the Quest for Truth.* QP107
Moltke S. Gram. *Kant: Disputed Questions.* QP104
George L. Kline. *European Philosophy Today.* QP102
Lionel Rubinoff. *Faith and Reason.* QP106
Pierre Thévenaz. *What Is Phenomenology?* QP101

Social Science

George and Eunice Grier. *Equality and Beyond.* QP204
William Loren Katz. *Teachers' Guide to American Negro History.* QP210
Charles O. Lerche, Jr. *Last Chance in Europe.* QP207
David Mitrany. *A Working Peace System.* QP205
Martin Oppenheimer and George Lakey. *A Manual for Direct Action.* QP202
Fred Powledge. *To Change a Child.* QP209
Lee Rainwater. *And the Poor Get Children.* QP208
Clarence Senior. *The Puerto Ricans.* QP201